Access Data Analysis Cookbook

DATE DUE

Ken Bluttman and Wayne S. Freeze

O'REILLY®

Beijing · Cambridge · Farnham · Köln · Paris · Sebastopol · Taipei · Tokyo

Access Data Analysis Cookbook
by Ken Bluttman and Wayne S. Freeze

Published by O'Reilly Media, Inc., 1005 Gravenstein Highway North, Sebastopol, CA 95472.

O'Reilly books may be purchased for educational, business, or sales promotional use. Online editions are also available for most titles (*safari.oreilly.com*). For more information, contact our corporate/institutional sales department: (800) 998-9938 or *corporate@oreilly.com*.

Editor: Simon St.Laurent

Production Editor: Sumita Mukherji

Copyeditor: Rachel Head

Proofreader: Sumita Mukherji

Indexer: Julie Hawks

Cover Designer: Karen Montgomery

Interior Designer: David Futato

Illustrators: Robert Romano and Jessamyn Read

Printing History:

May 2007:   First Edition.

 This book uses RepKover,™ a durable and flexible lay-flat binding.

ISBN-10: 0-596-10122-8
ISBN-13: 978-0-596-10122-0
[M]

*I dedicate this book to Chestnut
(September 29, 1995–April 16, 2007),
my ever-faithful cocker spaniel who followed me
around like the puppy dog he was, even in his old
age. I always watched over him, and now he is
watching over us. We miss you.*

—Ken Bluttman

*To my father, Jay B. Freeze, who taught me how
to survive when things get rough. I miss you.*

—Wayne S. Freeze

Table of Contents

Preface

Business users are often surprised at Access' power and flexibility. People frequently say to me things like "Access won't work for this—we have 13,000 records!" I just have to laugh when I hear such statements. As I (and, I imagine, many of you reading this book) know, Access can easily handle that much data, and then some.

So, just how powerful is Access? Access has the goods under the hood to do a lot of things that may not be obvious. How can you find out about them? Well, you've come to the right place. This book showcases many mini-solutions in Access that have likely befuddled some and had others wondering what other types of data Access can be coerced into providing.

Access Data Analysis Cookbook is about solutions to real-world problems. This is not a book about designing forms, learning about primary keys, or discussing the use of built-in wizards to make easy queries or reports. This book is about applying Access to the business grindstone.

Within the dozens of recipes contained in this book, you will learn new ways to query data, how to move data in and out of Access in several different ways, how to calculate answers to financial and investment questions, and much, much more.

 As of this writing, Access 2007 has just become available. The recipe solutions in this book apply to all version of Access, and the figures are from both Access 2007 and Access 2003. The bells and whistles and new interface of the new release are not factors here; across versions, SQL, VBA, DAO, and ADO have remained constant.

Who Should Read This Book

I would not suggest this book for brand-new Access users, but anyone with some Access experience should do well with it. As long as you understand how to get around the Access user interface, basic table structures and relations among them, and how to construct simple queries, you should be able to follow along. Even seasoned developers will pick up new tips and techniques. Considering that many recipes center around business issues rather than technical issues, everyone should be able to gain some smarts about analysis and reporting—the world that users inhabit.

What's in This Book

Access Data Analysis Cookbook focuses on data. The recipes provide example queries, programming tips, and a smattering of math, all with a view to getting answers from your data. Here is a summary of the chapters' contents:

Chapter 1, *Query Construction*
> Explores ways of developing basic and sophisticated queries. In this chapter, a variety of query issues are addressed, including the use of the AND, OR, IN, and NOT operators; creating union queries; and understanding join types.

Chapter 2, *Calculating with Queries*
> Illustrates further ways of using queries to find answers to real problems. It demonstrates how to apply aggregate functions, custom functions, regular expressions, and crosstabs.

Chapter 3, *Action Queries*
> Shows how to apply queries to perform nonpassive activities such as inserting, updating, and deleting data.

Chapter 4, *Managing Tables, Fields, Indexes, and Queries*
> Introduces programmatically creating and manipulating tables and queries.

Chapter 5, *Working with String Data*
> Delivers a plateful of recipes to manage text-based data. This chapter introduces methods to isolate parts of a string, methods to remove spaces at the ends of and in the middle of strings, and how to work with numbers that are stored as text.

Chapter 6, *Using Programming to Manipulate Data*
> Discusses several ways to use arrays, how to read from and write to the Windows Registry, how to encrypt data, and how to use transaction processing. Recipes here also cover search methods, charts, manipulating data relationships, and more.

Chapter 7, *Importing and Exporting Data*
> Covers the various methods of moving data into and out of Access: import/export specifications, using the FileSystemObject, XML with XSLT, and communicating with SQL Server. Exchanging data with other applications in the Office suite is also covered. Ever wondered how to create an RSS feed? You can read all about that in this chapter, too.

Chapter 8, *Date and Time Calculations*

Shows the various ways to get answers from time-based data. This chapter shows how to add time, count elapsed time, work with leap years, and manage time zones in your calculations.

Chapter 9, *Business and Finance Problems*

Covers a variety of real-life business issues. Methods for calculating depreciation, loan paybacks, and return on investment (ROI) are introduced, and investment concerns such as moving averages, Head and Shoulders patterns, Bollinger Bands, and trend calculations are explored. One recipe explains how latitude and longitude are used to determine distances between geographical areas. This is the basis for the service many web sites offer of helping you find doctors, stores, or other services within a given mileage.

Chapter 10, *Statistics*

Is a great chapter for math enthusiasts (myself included). Many statistical techniques are explored in this chapter, including frequency, variance, kurtosis, linear regression, combinations, and permutations. All the recipes here have value in data analysis. And after all, Access is all about data and what to do with it!

Conventions Used in This Book

The following typographical conventions are used in this book:

Plain text

Used for table and field names, menu options, dialog box options, queries, and keyboard shortcuts

Italic

Used for new terms and URLs, commands, file extensions, filenames, directory or folder names, and UNC pathnames

`Constant width`

Used for command-line elements, SQL keywords, VBA functions, variables, properties, objects, methods, and parameters, as well as computer output and code examples

`Constant width italic`

Indicates a placeholder (for which you substitute an actual name) in an example or registry key

 Indicates a tip, suggestion, or general note

 Indicates a warning or caution

Using Code Examples

This book is here to help you get your job done. In general, you may use the code in this book in your programs and documentation. You do not need to contact us for permission unless you're reproducing a significant portion of the code. For example, writing a program that uses several chunks of code from this book does not require permission. Selling or distributing a CD-ROM of examples from O'Reilly books does require permission. Answering a question by citing this book and quoting example code does not require permission. Incorporating a significant amount of example code from this book into your product's documentation does require permission.

We appreciate, but do not require, attribution. An attribution usually includes the title, author, publisher, and ISBN. For example: "*Access Data Analysis Cookbook* by Ken Bluttman and Wayne S. Freeze. Copyright 2007 O'Reilly Media, Inc., 978-0-596-10122-0."

If you feel your use of code examples falls outside fair use or the permission given above, feel free to contact us at *permissions@oreilly.com*.

We'd Like Your Feedback!

The information in this book has been tested and verified to the best of our ability, but mistakes and oversights do occur. Please let us know about any errors you find, as well as your suggestions for future editions, by writing to:

> O'Reilly Media, Inc.
> 1005 Gravenstein Highway North
> Sebastopol, CA 95472
> 800-998-9938 (in the U.S. or Canada)
> 707-829-0515 (international or local)
> 707-829-0104 (fax)

You can also send us messages using email. To be put on our mailing list, or to request a catalog, send email to:

> *info@oreilly.com*

To ask technical questions or comment on the book, send email to:

> *bookquestions@oreilly.com*

For corrections and amplifications to this book, check out O'Reilly Media's online catalog page at:

> *http://www.oreilly.com/catalog/9780596101220*

Acknowledgments

From Ken Bluttman

My many thanks to the extreme patience of Simon St.Laurent. Simon has been great in working with me around my crazed schedule and endless personal interruptions. While I was writing this book, my car got smashed by a tree, I broke my shoulder, my wife conquered her battle with cancer, and my dad passed away. Life really is a roller coaster!

Much gratitude to Wayne S. Freeze, who came to our aid at a point where I had to take a break. Wayne picked up where I left off and wrote a substantial portion of the second half of the book. Kudos to Wayne!

Special thanks to all the support staff at O'Reilly. A lot of players behind the scenes have their hands in any book project. It's a big stretch from my typing and testing to the finished product in your hands.

Special thanks to Doug Klippert and Michael Schmalz for their technical reviews. I have worked with both of these gentlemen on a number of books and am deeply grateful to them for their knowledge and insight.

This book is in honor of my father, Herbert Bluttman, with whom I battled much over many issues, and to whom the winds of fortune blew in such a way that while I had several books published, he could not get his one and only work out to the world. I used to dread your phone calls, but as soon as they no longer came, I realized how much I missed hearing from you. Displeasure is temporary, but love is forever.

From Wayne S. Freeze

To Ken (aka Mr. Access Analyst)—I enjoyed working with you on this book, and I'm happy your world is getting back to normal. To Simon (aka the Tireless Editor)— thank you for your patience when things got challenging. One of these days, I hope to write another, less stressful book with you. To Sumita (aka Ms. Eagle Eye)—thank you for transforming my raw words into something that sounds great. To all the staff members at O'Reilly that left their mark on this book (aka the Quality Team)—y'all did an incredible job, and I'm proud to be associated with you.

To Christopher and Samantha (aka My Wonderful Children)—remember to chase your dreams, for without dreams, life isn't worth living. To Jill (aka the Best Writer in the Family and My Bestest Friend)—like any great artist, you're never truly satisfied with your work, even when someone manages to pry it out of your hands. I know that someday soon, you'll search for new dreams to replace the ones that have come true. And always remember, I love you.

CHAPTER 1

Query Construction

Select queries are an essential part of any database system. These queries, which passively gather data (without changing the source data), are what we rely on to answer our questions about our data. In its most basic form, a select query merely returns records from a table verbatim. That's not of much interest, since viewing the table itself would provide the same information. It's when you add criteria, joins, and useful SQL functions and methods that select queries become valuable.

This chapter provides several tips for getting select queries to go the extra mile. Recipes in this chapter explain how to prompt for criteria at runtime, how to use logic operators to get the criteria just the way you need them, and how to handle duplicate records.

To make queries easier to read and work with, you'll also find a recipe on using aliases, which provides a neat method to give nicknames to your tables. Another recipe explains how to use union queries to work around the problem of how to combine data from different tables so it can be treated as one source.

1.1 Finding Unmatched Records

Problem

I have a table that lists expenses incurred by employees. Some of these records do not match any records in the Employees table. How can I easily get a list of these unmatched expense records without having to examine every record in the table?

Solution

A special type of join called a *left join* (see Recipe 1.13) is used to identify records in one table that do not have matches within another table. The match, of course, has to be tested on a common field between tables—usually the unique key field of the parent table. The technique depends on having the criterion call for the matching field to be Null in the parent table. In other words, the query should return records from the child table in which no record (a Null) is found in the parent table.

Confused? Luckily, you can spare yourself the challenge of creating that query by using the Find Unmatched Query Wizard. The wizard will create the underlying SQL and run the query for you.

Figure 1-1 shows two tables: one lists employees, and the other lists expenses for which employees need to be reimbursed.

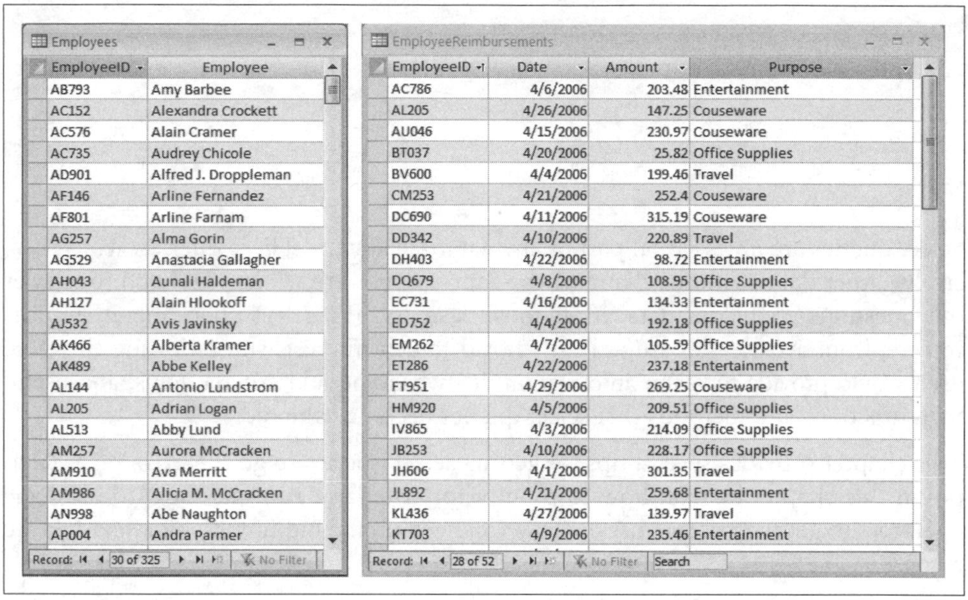

Employees

EmployeeID	Employee
AB793	Amy Barbee
AC152	Alexandra Crockett
AC576	Alain Cramer
AC735	Audrey Chicole
AD901	Alfred J. Droppleman
AF146	Arline Fernandez
AF801	Arline Farnam
AG257	Alma Gorin
AG529	Anastacia Gallagher
AH043	Aunali Haldeman
AH127	Alain Hlookoff
AJ532	Avis Javinsky
AK466	Alberta Kramer
AK489	Abbe Kelley
AL144	Antonio Lundstrom
AL205	Adrian Logan
AL513	Abby Lund
AM257	Aurora McCracken
AM910	Ava Merritt
AM986	Alicia M. McCracken
AN998	Abe Naughton
AP004	Andra Parmer

Record: 30 of 325 No Filter

EmployeeReimbursements

EmployeeID	Date	Amount	Purpose
AC786	4/6/2006	203.48	Entertainment
AL205	4/26/2006	147.25	Couseware
AU046	4/15/2006	230.97	Couseware
BT037	4/20/2006	25.82	Office Supplies
BV600	4/4/2006	199.46	Travel
CM253	4/21/2006	252.4	Couseware
DC690	4/11/2006	315.19	Couseware
DD342	4/10/2006	220.89	Travel
DH403	4/22/2006	98.72	Entertainment
DQ679	4/8/2006	108.95	Office Supplies
EC731	4/16/2006	134.33	Entertainment
ED752	4/4/2006	192.18	Office Supplies
EM262	4/7/2006	105.59	Office Supplies
ET286	4/22/2006	237.18	Entertainment
FT951	4/29/2006	269.25	Couseware
HM920	4/5/2006	209.51	Office Supplies
IV865	4/3/2006	214.09	Office Supplies
JB253	4/10/2006	228.17	Office Supplies
JH606	4/1/2006	301.35	Travel
JL892	4/21/2006	259.68	Entertainment
KL436	4/27/2006	139.97	Travel
KT703	4/9/2006	235.46	Entertainment

Record: 28 of 52 No Filter Search

Figure 1-1. Employees and EmployeeReimbursements tables

A number of records in the EmployeeReimbursements table are "orphan" records—that is, they do not match any employee records in the table on the left (the parent table). The Find Unmatched Query Wizard will identify these records for you. From the Query tab in the Access database window, click the New button, or use the Insert → Query menu option to display the New Query dialog box shown in Figure 1-2. Select Find Unmatched Query Wizard, and click the OK button.

The wizard runs through a few screens. You'll need to:

1. Select the table or query that contains the records you want to identify. In this example, the EmployeeReimbursements table contains the records of interest (that is, the records that have no matches to the employee records themselves).
2. Select the table that contains the records to match against.
3. From each table, select the field to match on. Often this is the key field in one table and a foreign key in the other table.
4. Select which fields from the table or query chosen in the first step should be included in the returned records.

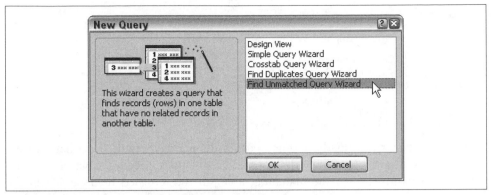

Figure 1-2. Selecting the Find Unmatched Query Wizard

Figure 1-3 shows the returned records from the EmployeeReimbursements table that do not have matches in the Employees table, based on the EmployeeID field.

EmployeeID	Date	Amount	Purpose
RX332	4/13/2006	210.28	Travel
FT951	4/29/2006	269.25	Couseware
PZ114	4/16/2006	141.61	Travel
EC731	4/16/2006	134.33	Entertainment
DQ679	4/8/2006	108.95	Office Supplies
LA179	4/5/2006	230.38	Travel
AC786	4/6/2006	203.48	Entertainment
TF246	4/12/2006	17.44	Travel
IV865	4/3/2006	214.09	Office Supplies
BT037	4/20/2006	25.82	Office Supplies
AU046	4/15/2006	230.97	Couseware
QX653	4/15/2006	223.69	Travel
PJ656	4/6/2006	112.87	Entertainment
SM185	4/23/2006	258.96	Entertainment
EM262	4/7/2006	105.59	Office Supplies

EmployeeReimbursements Without Matching Employees

Record: 1 of 15   No Filter   Search

Figure 1-3. Unmatched records have been identified

Discussion

The wizard assembled this SQL statement:

```
SELECT EmployeeReimbursements.*
FROM EmployeeReimbursements LEFT JOIN
Employees ON
EmployeeReimbursements.EmployeeID =
Employees.EmployeeID
WHERE (((Employees.EmployeeID) Is Null));
```

The SQL looks for records that do not exist in the matching table (i.e., that return a Null). It is not possible to include any fields from the matching table because no records are returned from the matching table; all the returned fields are from the table in which unmatched records are expected.

See Also

- Recipe 1.13

1.2 Making AND and OR Do What You Expect

Problem

Logic operators are not conceptually difficult to follow, but combining and nesting them does add complexity. If you don't construct complex SQL statements very carefully, they may return incorrect or incomplete results, sometimes without reporting any errors.

Solution

Logic operators provide the flexibility to construct criteria in any way that suits your requirements. The AND operator returns true when *all* conditions are met; the OR operator returns true as long as *one* condition is met. In terms of how this applies to SQL construction, OR is used to set criteria for which one condition must be met, while AND is used to set criteria for which all the conditions must be met. Some examples are presented in Table 1-1.

Table 1-1. Examples of using logic operators

SQL statement	Description

`SELECT DISTINCT State, City,`
`Count(LastName) AS Customers`
`FROM tblCustomers`
`GROUP BY State, City`
`HAVING State="NY" AND City="Yonkers"`
	This gives a count of customers located in Yonkers, NY. Only customer records in which both the state is New York *and* the city is Yonkers are counted.

Table 1-1. Examples of using logic operators (continued)

SQL statement	Description
SELECT DISTINCT State, City, Count(LastName) AS Customers FROM tblCustomers GROUP BY State, City HAVING State="NY" AND City="Yonkers" OR City="Albany"	This gives a count of customer records for which the state is New York and the city is either Yonkers or Albany. This produces an unintended result. The OR statement does not properly apply to both Yonkers and Albany. Any Yonkers customers must be in New York, but the way this SQL statement is constructed, Albany customers do not have to be in New York. Consequently, as Figure 1-4 shows, customers in Albany, GA will also be returned.
SELECT DISTINCT State, City, Count(LastName) AS Customers FROM tblCustomers GROUP BY State, City HAVING State="NY" AND (City="Yonkers" OR City="Albany")	This correctly returns customer records for customers located only in Yonkers, NY and Albany, NY. Enclosing the cities and the OR operator in parentheses ensures that both cities must also match the state of New York on a record-by-record basis.

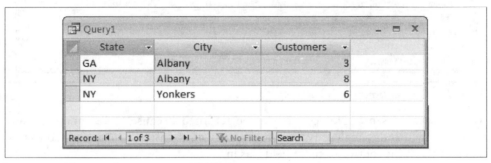

Figure 1-4. The second query returns all Albany customers

Discussion

OR is applied amongst records; AND is applied across fields. What does this mean? Figure 1-5 shows the tblCustomers table that is used as the example in this recipe. The OR operation involves evaluating the value in a particular field *in each record*. A single record cannot contain both Albany and Yonkers in its City field; it can contain at most one of those values. So, searching for customers in Albany *or* Yonkers requires looking for these values in the City field of each record (or, in our example, at least those records in which the state is New York). Thought of another way, when using OR, you can apply the statement multiple times to the same field. For example:

```
City="Albany" OR City="Syracuse" Or City="Yonkers"
```

The AND operator, however, is not used on the same field. A SQL condition like this:

```
City="Albany" AND City="Yonkers"
```

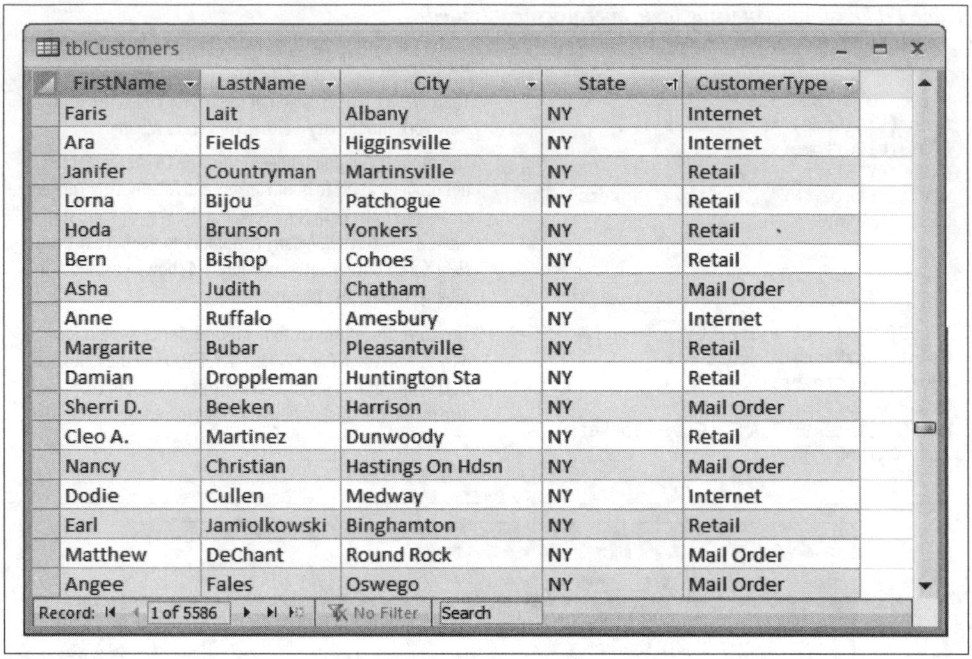
tblCustomers

FirstName	LastName	City	State	CustomerType
Faris	Lait	Albany	NY	Internet
Ara	Fields	Higginsville	NY	Internet
Janifer	Countryman	Martinsville	NY	Retail
Lorna	Bijou	Patchogue	NY	Retail
Hoda	Brunson	Yonkers	NY	Retail
Bern	Bishop	Cohoes	NY	Retail
Asha	Judith	Chatham	NY	Mail Order
Anne	Ruffalo	Amesbury	NY	Internet
Margarite	Bubar	Pleasantville	NY	Retail
Damian	Droppleman	Huntington Sta	NY	Retail
Sherri D.	Beeken	Harrison	NY	Mail Order
Cleo A.	Martinez	Dunwoody	NY	Retail
Nancy	Christian	Hastings On Hdsn	NY	Mail Order
Dodie	Cullen	Medway	NY	Internet
Earl	Jamiolkowski	Binghamton	NY	Retail
Matthew	DeChant	Round Rock	NY	Mail Order
Angee	Fales	Oswego	NY	Mail Order

Record: 1 of 5586 No Filter Search

Figure 1-5. Each customer is in a single city

would make no sense. No records can be returned because there cannot be any records in which the single City field holds two values. Instead, AND is applied to pull together the values of two or more fields, as in:

```
State="New York" AND City="Yonkers"
```

The query grid in Access is flexible enough to handle any combination of OR and AND operators. Figure 1-6 shows how the grid is used to return customer records from New York where the customer type is Retail or Wholesale, as well as customer records from Florida where the customer type is Internet or Mail Order. Internet and Mail Order customers from New York will not be returned, nor will Retail or Wholesale customers from Florida.

Along a single Criteria row, all of the conditions set in the different fields must be met (i.e., this is an AND operation). The SQL statement Access generates bears this out:

```
SELECT [FirstName] & " " & [LastName] AS Customer,
City, State, CustomerType
FROM tblCustomers
WHERE
(((State)="NY") AND
((CustomerType)="Retail" Or (CustomerType)="Wholesale"))
OR
(((State)="FL") AND
((CustomerType)="Mail Order" Or (CustomerType)="Internet"))
ORDER BY tblCustomers.CustomerType;
```

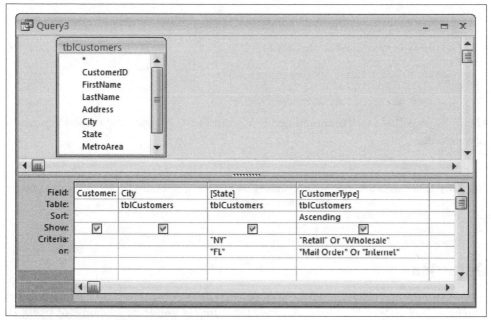

Figure 1-6. Applying AND and OR in the query grid

As you can see, the SQL condition for NY is followed by AND to get Retail and Wholesale customers from that state.

1.3   Working with Criteria Using the IN Operator

Problem

Using multiple OR operators in the query grid makes for an unmanageable experience. If too many values and ORs are placed in a grid column, the column may expand to be bigger than the viewable area.

Solution

A way to save space in the query grid is to use the IN operator. IN is used in conjunction with a list of values from which any value can be returned. This essentially means that the IN operator works in the same fashion as the OR operator. It is not required that all conditions be met; meeting one of the conditions suffices.

Here is a SQL statement that returns records for students that took at least one of the listed courses:

```
SELECT Students.Student, Student_Grades.Course,
Student_Grades.Instructor
FROM Students INNER JOIN Student_Grades ON
Students.StudentID = Student_Grades.StudentID
```

```
WHERE
(((Student_Grades.Course)="Beginner Access"))
OR
(((Student_Grades.Course)="Beginner Excel"))
OR
(((Student_Grades.Course)="Advanced Access"))
OR
(((Student_Grades.Course)="Advanced Excel"));
```

Using IN provides a more streamlined SQL statement. Notice how the WHERE section
has shrunk:

```
SELECT Students.Student, Student_Grades.Course,
Student_Grades.Instructor
FROM Students INNER JOIN Student_Grades ON
Students.StudentID = Student_Grades.StudentID
WHERE Student_Grades.Course In
("Beginner Access","Beginner Excel",
"Advanced Access","Advanced Excel");
```

Discussion

The IN operator provides a syntax convenience. It makes it easier to eyeball a set of
criteria values to which OR logic is applied. Figure 1-7 shows an example of using IN
to return records where the instructor is either Brown or Maxwell.

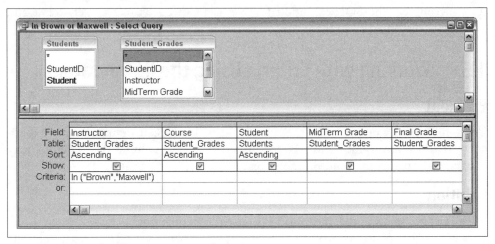

Figure 1-7. Using the IN operator to specify the instructor

That's simple enough to follow: when the instructor is either Brown or Maxwell, the
record is returned. Figure 1-8 shows an example of using IN in two fields.

The example shown in Figure 1-8 returns records in which either Brown or Maxwell
taught Beginner Access, Advanced Access, or Intro to VBA. In other words, all combinations of these instructors and courses are returned.

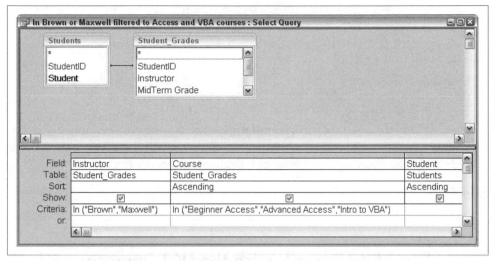

Figure 1-8. Using the IN operator for both the Instructor and Course fields

Adding criteria to other fields will further cut down the number of returned records. The next example adds new criteria to the row. The Instructor and Course fields still have IN operators, but now only records that have a MidTerm Grade and a Final Grade of 85 or better are returned. Here is the SQL statement for this query:

```
SELECT Student_Grades.Instructor, Student_Grades.Course,
Students.Student, Student_Grades.[MidTerm Grade],
Student_Grades.[Final Grade]
FROM Students INNER JOIN Student_Grades ON
Students.StudentID = Student_Grades.StudentID
WHERE (((Student_Grades.Instructor) In
("Brown","Maxwell")) AND ((Student_Grades.Course) In
("Beginner Access","Advanced Access","Intro to VBA")) AND
((Student Grades.[MidTerm Grade])>=85) AND
((Student_Grades.[Final Grade])>=85))
ORDER BY Student_Grades.Course, Students.Student;
```

The IN operator is handy when using subqueries. A *subquery* returns a set of records to which the rest of a query can apply further criteria. The following SQL statement returns information for those students who got a 90 or better in either Advanced Access or Advanced Excel *and* took either Beginner Access or Beginner Excel last year:

```
SELECT Student_Grades.Instructor, Student_Grades.Course,
Students.Student, Student_Grades.[MidTerm Grade],
Student_Grades.[Final Grade]
FROM Students INNER JOIN Student_Grades ON
Students.StudentID = Student_Grades.StudentID
WHERE (((Student_Grades.Course) In
("Advanced Access","Advanced Excel")) AND
((Student_Grades.[Final Grade])>=90) AND
((Students.StudentID) In
(Select Stud_ID From LastYear Where
```

```
(Course="Beginner Access") Or (Course="Beginner Excel"))))
ORDER BY Student_Grades.Course, Students.Student;
```

The IN operator is applied to the LastYear table through a subquery. Here is the portion of the SQL that does this:

```
((Students.StudentID) In
(Select Stud_ID From LastYear Where
(Course="Beginner Access") Or (Course="Beginner Excel"))))
```

The Select statement within the larger SQL statement is where the subquery starts. The subquery returns StudentIDs that have matches in the LastYear table (on the Stud_ID field) for those students who took Beginner Access or Beginner Excel.

See Also

- Recipe 1.9

1.4   Excluding Records with the NOT Operator

Problem

I have a large number of client names in my data. I need to return a list of clients that are not on the Hold list. Most clients are OK, so most will be returned in the query. How do I keep out the few clients who are on hold?

Solution

The method here is to exclude records from being returned, rather than the typical approach of identifying records that are to be returned. Figure 1-9 shows two database tables. The table on the left is a list of client orders. The table on the right is a list of clients (by ClientID) who are "on hold"—that is, clients whose accounts are in arrears and whose orders should not be shipped. Running a query that causes the clients identified in the OnHold table to be excluded from the Clients table is the key to this recipe.

A subquery works well here to gather the records from the second table into the query result. Using the NOT operator provides the twist to make the records excluded instead of included.

The NOT operator is placed in front of the subquery to reverse the logic. If NOT were left out, the query would return records that match in both tables. When NOT is applied, only those records from the Clients table that do not have matching records in the OnHold table are returned. Here is the SQL statement:

```
SELECT Clients.ClientID, Clients.Client,
Clients.OrderDate, Clients.OrderAmount
FROM Clients
WHERE (((Clients.ClientID)
NOT In (Select ClientID from OnHold)));
```

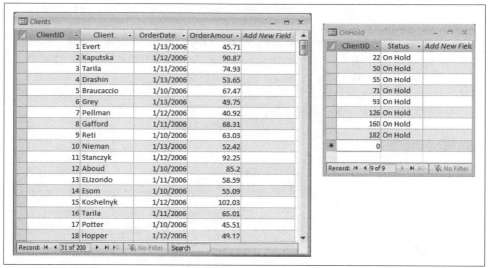

Figure 1-9. A table of clients and a table of clients on hold

Discussion

NOT is a logic operator that reverses a Boolean state, so NOT true equals false, and NOT false equals true. When a query calls for matching criteria, preceding the criteria construct with NOT flips this around and calls for records that specifically do *not* match the criteria.

Our sample Clients table has 200 records, and the OnHold table has 8 records. The result is that the query returns 192 records—that is, all orders for clients who are not on hold.

See Also

- Recipe 1.9

1.5   Parameterizing a Query

Problem

I need to construct a query that takes a criterion, but the criterion's value will not be known until the query is run. When it's time to run the query, the user needs a way to supply the criterion without going into the design of the query.

Solution

A query can be designed to accept parameters at the time it is run. Typically, an input box will appear in which the user enters the value for the criterion. A query can have any number of criteria entered in this fashion. A set of brackets defines the question asked in the input box. The brackets and the prompt to the user are placed in the Criteria row of the query grid for the given field. For example, using "[Enter an age]" as the criterion for a field instructs Access to present this prompt in a dialog box, as shown in Figure 1-10.

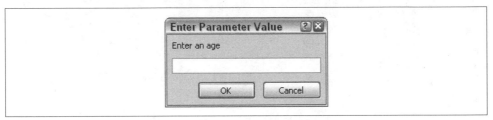

Figure 1-10. Prompting the user to enter a parameter into a query

Discussion

When a query is run, a traditional form is often displayed to enable users to enter parameter values or make selections from a list. But the ability to place parameters directly in the structure of a query provides a great alternative to having to build a form that gathers input. When the criteria are simple, just using brackets in the query design will suffice.

Figure 1-11 shows the query design that prompts the user to enter an age. When the query is run, the dialog shown in Figure 1-10 will appear, and the returned records will be filtered to those that match the entered value.

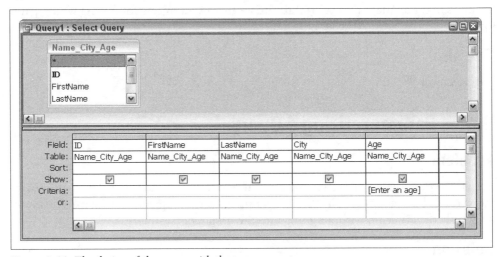

Figure 1-11. The design of the query with the age parameter

Here is the actual SQL statement that is built using the query grid:

```
SELECT Name_City_Age.ID, Name_City_Age.FirstName,
Name_City_Age.LastName, Name_City_Age.City,
Name_City_Age.Age
FROM Name_City_Age
WHERE (((Name_City_Age.Age)=[Enter an age]));
```

Note that in the `WHERE` clause the phrase "Enter an age" appears enclosed in brackets.

Although the phrase "Enter an age" is used here to define the criterion for a field named Age, there is no strict requirement to use the word "age" in the bracketed phrase. We could just as well have used "Enter a number"; it wouldn't matter because the text in the brackets does not have to contain the name of the field for which it is used.

A query can have multiple parameters, and these parameters fit in with the structure of the SQL `WHERE` clause. A common criterion structure is to use a range of values to determine which records to return. In the current example, a query might need to return all records that fit within a range of ages. The `Between/And` SQL construct is used for this purpose. Figure 1-12 shows the modification in the query design.

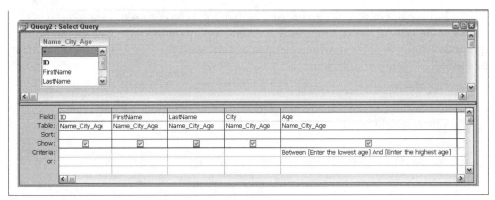

Figure 1-12. A query that uses two parameters to filter a single field

Here's the updated SQL:

```
SELECT Name_City_Age.ID, Name_City_Age.FirstName,
Name_City_Age.LastName, Name_City_Age.City,
Name_City_Age.Age
FROM Name_City_Age
WHERE (((Name_City_Age.Age) Between
[Enter the lowest age] And
[Enter the highest age]));
```

When this query is run, two prompts will appear: one asks for the lowest age, and the other asks for the highest age. Figure 1-13 shows a sample of returned records when the range was defined as between the ages of 20 and 40.

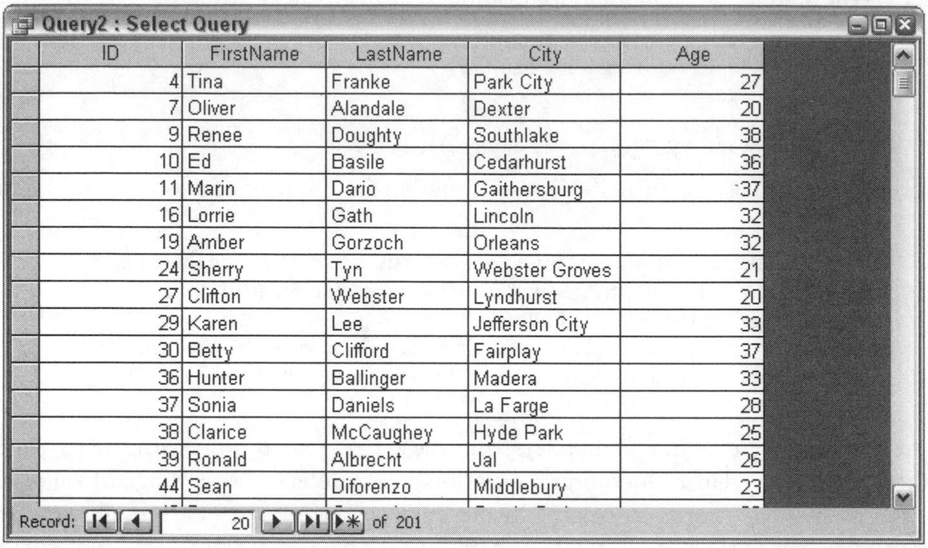

Query2 : Select Query

ID	FirstName	LastName	City	Age
4	Tina	Franke	Park City	27
7	Oliver	Alandale	Dexter	20
9	Renee	Doughty	Southlake	38
10	Ed	Basile	Cedarhurst	36
11	Marin	Dario	Gaithersburg	37
16	Lorrie	Gath	Lincoln	32
19	Amber	Gorzoch	Orleans	32
24	Sherry	Tyn	Webster Groves	21
27	Clifton	Webster	Lyndhurst	20
29	Karen	Lee	Jefferson City	33
30	Betty	Clifford	Fairplay	37
36	Hunter	Ballinger	Madera	33
37	Sonia	Daniels	La Farge	28
38	Clarice	McCaughey	Hyde Park	25
39	Ronald	Albrecht	Jal	26
44	Sean	Diforenzo	Middlebury	23

Record: 20 of 201

Figure 1-13. Returned records for the age range 20–40

The SQL `Like` operator can also be used with a bracketed prompt. `Like` is used with a wildcard to return records in which the criterion fits a pattern. For example, in a query that returns all those whose last names start with the letter D, the `WHERE` portion of the SQL statement looks like this:

```
WHERE (((LastName) Like "D*"));
```

Using the `Like` operator with a parameter prompt requires the brackets, of course, and careful placement of the wildcard character (*) and the quotation marks, as follows:

```
WHERE (((LastName) Like
[Enter the first letter of the last name: ] & "*"));
```

Figure 1-14 shows how this is entered in the query grid.

To return a smaller set of results, you can match on a more complex pattern; for example, the user can enter "De" to have names such as Deere returned, but not names such as Dole. In this case, you'll need to adjust the phrasing of the prompt accordingly. Phrasing prompts correctly is as much art as it is SQL.

The example here uses an asterisk wildcard. Any number of characters can be returned in place of that wildcard, but the character(s) entered as the parameter are what fine-tunes the record filtering.

Specifying a data type for the parameter

In certain situations, you must indicate the data type of the parameter. You do this when:

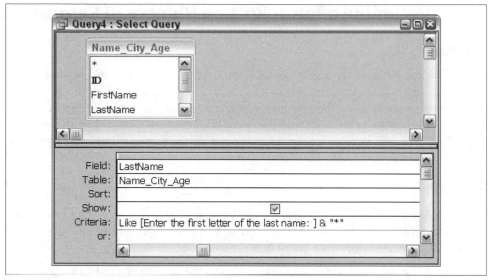

Figure 1-14. Using the Like operator

- Using a crosstab query
- Using a query as the source for a chart
- Prompting for Boolean (true/false) values
- Prompting for fields from a table in an external database

Parameter data types are entered in the Query Parameters dialog (see Figure 1-15).

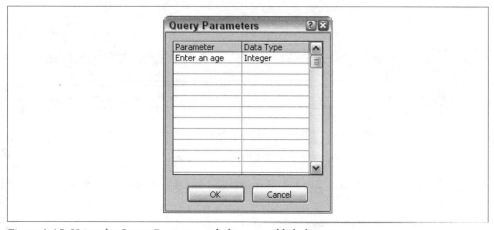

Figure 1-15. Using the Query Parameters dialog to establish data types

To display the dialog, select the Query → Parameters menu option. In the left side of the dialog, enter the prompts that you've established in the design grid. Then select the data types in the right side of the dialog.

1.6   Returning a Top or Bottom Number of Records

Problem

I have a large table of data that contains thousands of records and several dozen fields. I create models based on various fields and/or ranges of values in the fields. I use queries to set up the sums using SQL aggregates and expressions. This is exactly what I need, but the problem is that the number of records slows down the processing. When I'm testing calculations, I don't need *all* the records. How can I pull out just a handful of them to use for testing?

Solution

The SQL TOP predicate is just what is called for here. It lets you specify how many records to return, either as an exact number or as a percentage of the total number of records in the underlying table or query.

Let's say you have a standard select query such as the one shown in Figure 1-16. The SQL statement is:

```
SELECT SampleNum, Identifier, Fact1, Fact2,
Fact3, Fact4, Fact5, Fact6, Fact7, Fact8
FROM ConsumerTrendData;
```

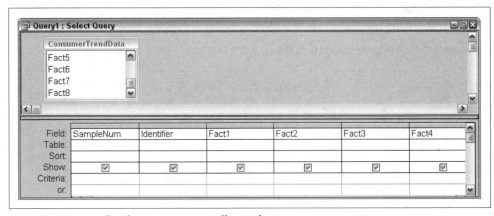

Figure 1-16. A simple select query returns all records

To specify a subset of records to search through to test the query—say, 40—use the TOP predicate, as follows:

```
SELECT TOP 40 SampleNum, Identifier, Fact1,
Fact2, Fact3, Fact4, Fact5, Fact6,
Fact7, Fact8
FROM ConsumerTrendData;
```

TOP comes directly after the SELECT keyword, and is followed by the number of records to return. Instead of reducing the number of returned records based on criteria, TOP reduces the number of returned records without any bias.

When working with the Access query grid, you can opt to use TOP by going into the query properties. To do this, use the View → Properties menu option while designing the query. The properties sheet that opens may display the properties for a field. If this is the case, click on the top pane of the query designer (above the grid) but not on any tables—in other words, click on the empty area. This will ensure that the properties sheet displays the query properties (see Figure 1-17).

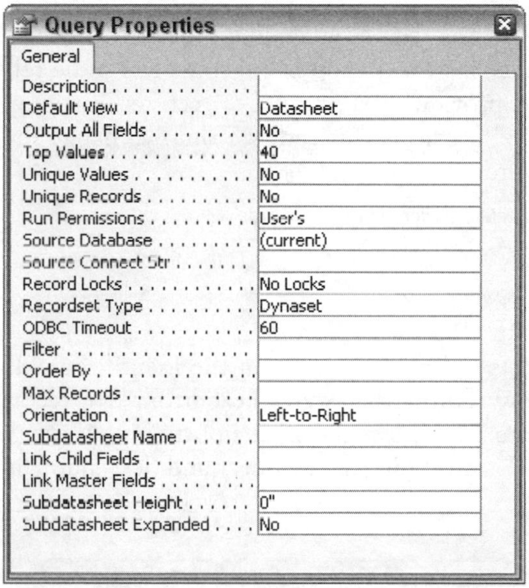

Figure 1-17. The Query Properties sheet

One of the properties is Top Values. In Figure 1-17, you can see that the value of 40 is already entered.

Discussion

To return a percentage of the records, you can place a percent sign (%) after the entered number in the Top Values property on the properties sheet, or you can enter the word PERCENT directly in the SQL statement. Here, for example, is the SQL to return the top 20 percent of the records:

```
SELECT TOP 20 PERCENT SampleNum, Identifier,
Fact1, Fact2, Fact3, Fact4, Fact5,
Fact6, Fact7, Fact8
FROM ConsumerTrendData;
```

Using TOP to return the "top" X number of records begs the question of what makes the hierarchy of records in a table. Only the application of an index or sort provides any structure to the records. We often use AutoNumber fields, which order the records. But what happens when we sort on another field? The "top" records change.

Using the TOP predicate requires that the use of a sort, or lack thereof, always be considered. Here is an example of returning the top five records of a sorted table:

```
SELECT TOP 5 SampleNum, Identifier, Fact1,
Fact2, Fact3, Fact4, Fact5, Fact6,
Fact7, Fact8
FROM ConsumerTrendData
ORDER BY Identifier;
```

Now that we've sorted the data in ascending order (the default sort direction) with the ORDER BY clause, asking for the top five records has some relevance. Turning this upside down would provide the bottom five records. But how could we do that? There is no "bottom" predicate. Instead, we simply change the sort to descending using the DESC keyword:

```
SELECT TOP 5 SampleNum, Identifier, Fact1,
Fact2, Fact3, Fact4, Fact5, Fact6,
Fact7, Fact8
FROM ConsumerTrendData
ORDER BY Identifier DESC;
```

This example requests a descending sort on the Identifier field. Requesting the top five records will now return what were the bottom five records when we did an ascending sort. Figure 1-18 shows the results of running these two queries. The sort on the Identifier field is ascending in one query and descending in the other.

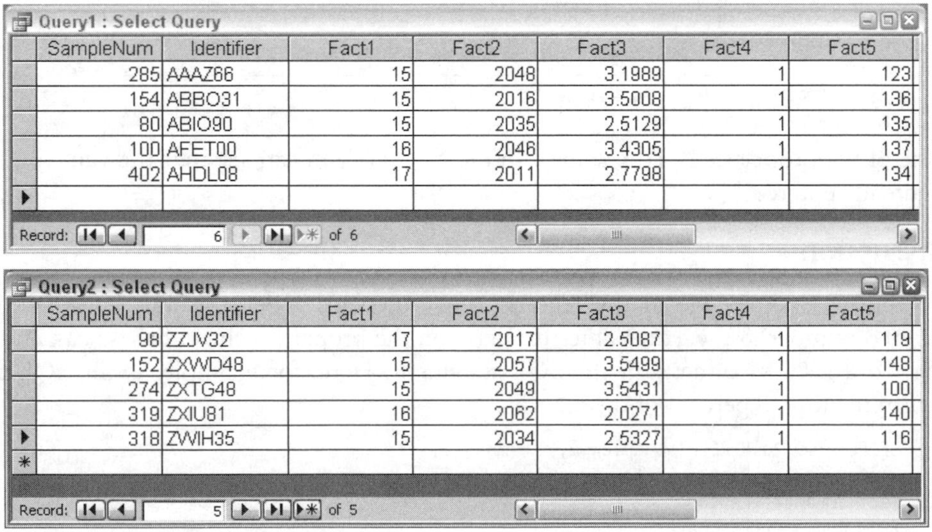
Query1 : Select Query

SampleNum	Identifier	Fact1	Fact2	Fact3	Fact4	Fact5
285	AAAZ66	15	2048	3.1989	1	123
154	ABBO31	15	2016	3.5008	1	136
80	ABIO90	15	2035	2.5129	1	135
100	AFET00	16	2046	3.4305	1	137
402	AHDL08	17	2011	2.7798	1	134

Record: 6 of 6

Query2 : Select Query

SampleNum	Identifier	Fact1	Fact2	Fact3	Fact4	Fact5
98	ZZJV32	17	2017	2.5087	1	119
152	ZXWD48	15	2057	3.5499	1	148
274	ZXTG48	15	2049	3.5431	1	100
319	ZXIU81	16	2062	2.0271	1	140
318	ZWIH35	15	2034	2.5327	1	116

Record: 5 of 5

Figure 1-18. Ascending and descending sorts

1.7 Returning Distinct Records

Problem

When running select queries, you may need to control whether duplicate records are returned in the query result. However, there could be disagreement about what constitutes uniqueness and duplication. Often, a few fields may contain duplicate information among records, and it's the additional fields that bring unique values to the records. How can queries be managed with regard to controlling how duplicate information is handled?

Solution

Figure 1-19 shows a table in which there are records that are near duplicates. None are exact duplicates since the CustomerID field ensures uniqueness. However, the two records for Vickie Storm could be seen as duplicates, as all fields except the CustomerID field hold duplicate information. The records for Ebony Pickett also contain some duplicate information, although two different cities are listed.

CustomerID	FirstName	LastName	City	State
6	Genny	Carr	Dallas	TX
7	Frederick	Davis	Scranton	PA
2	Maria	Dealton	North Bend	IL
9	Andy	Martinez	Croton On Hudson	NY
3	Elaine	Pawlak	Binghamton	NY
8	Ebony	Pickett	Atlantic City	NJ
4	Ebony	Pickett	Princeton	NJ
5	Vickie	Storm	Providence	RI
1	Vickie	Storm	Providence	RI

Record: I◀ ◀ 10 of 10 ▶ ▶I ▶ 🍸 No Filter Search

Figure 1-19. A table with duplicates

SQL provides ways of handling how records such as these are returned or excluded when select queries are run. Access makes use of the SQL predicates Distinct and DistinctRow:

Distinct
> Bearing in mind that not all fields need to be included in a select query, Distinct will exclude duplicates when the duplication occurs within just the selected fields, regardless of whether the complete set of record fields would prove the records to be unique.

DistinctRow

> DistinctRow is used to manage duplicates in a query that joins tables. Assuming unique records in the parent table, DistinctRow lets you avoid having duplicates returned from the child table.

You can incorporate these predicates by using the query designer or writing them directly into the SQL statement. With a query in design mode, use the View → Properties menu option to display the Query Properties dialog box, shown in Figure 1-20. Two properties are of interest here: Unique Values and Unique Records. These can both be set to No, but only one at a time can be set to Yes.

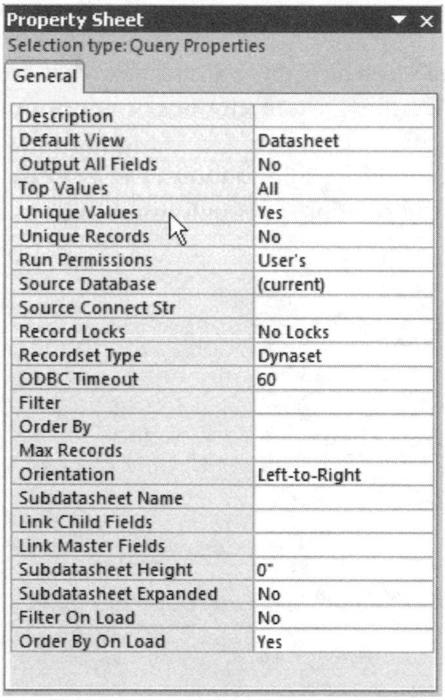

Property Sheet	▼ ✕
Selection type: Query Properties	
General	
Description	
Default View	Datasheet
Output All Fields	No
Top Values	All
Unique Values	Yes
Unique Records	No
Run Permissions	User's
Source Database	(current)
Source Connect Str	
Record Locks	No Locks
Recordset Type	Dynaset
ODBC Timeout	60
Filter	
Order By	
Max Records	
Orientation	Left-to-Right
Subdatasheet Name	
Link Child Fields	
Link Master Fields	
Subdatasheet Height	0"
Subdatasheet Expanded	No
Filter On Load	No
Order By On Load	Yes

Figure 1-20. Setting the Unique Values and Unique Records properties

Setting Unique Values to Yes places the DISTINCT predicate in the SQL statement. For example:

```
SELECT DISTINCT Customers.FirstName,
Customers.LastName, Customers.Address,
Customers.City, Customers.State
FROM Customers;
```

Similarly, setting the Unique Records property to Yes places the DISTINCTROW predicate just after the SELECT keyword.

Discussion

For our sample table, a simple select query of the Customers table on just the First-Name and LastName fields would return nine records, without regard to the fact that the returned results would show two records for Ebony Pickett and two records for Vickie Storm. Using `Distinct` in the SQL statement will change the returned count to seven records. In particular, this SQL statement:

```
Select Distinct FirstName, LastName From Customers
Order By LastName
```

produces the result shown in Figure 1-21.

Figure 1-21. Distinct records are returned

When the City and State fields are added to the SQL statement, like this:

```
Select Distinct FirstName, LastName, City, State
From Customers
Order By LastName
```

eight records are returned (see Figure 1-22). The additional record appears because Ebony Pickett is listed in two unique cities. As far as the query goes, there are now two unique Ebony Pickett records, and they are both returned. Vickie Storm still has just one record returned, however, because the source data for her city and state are identical in both of her records.

Using DistinctRow

Now, let's take a closer look at using `DistinctRow`, which manages duplicates in multi-table joins. Figure 1-23 shows two tables: a Customers table (this table does not contain any duplicates) and a table of purchases related back to the customers.

Figure 1-22. Distinct records are returned based on additional fields

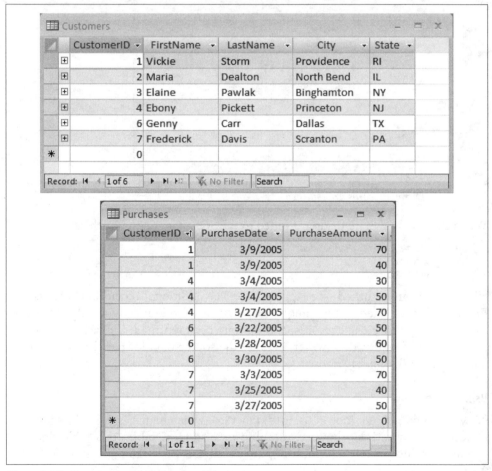

Figure 1-23. Customers and Purchases tables

Say you want to find out which customers have placed orders. A SQL statement that joins the tables but does not use DistinctRow will return a row count equivalent to the number of records in the child (Purchases) table. Here is a simple SQL statement that returns the names of the customers who placed each of the orders:

```
SELECT Customers.CustomerID, Customers.FirstName,
Customers.LastName
FROM Customers INNER JOIN Purchases ON
Customers.CustomerID = Purchases.CustomerID;
```

The result of running this query is shown in Figure 1-24. No fields from the Purchases table have been included, but the effect of the multiple child records is seen in the output—a customer name is listed for each purchase.

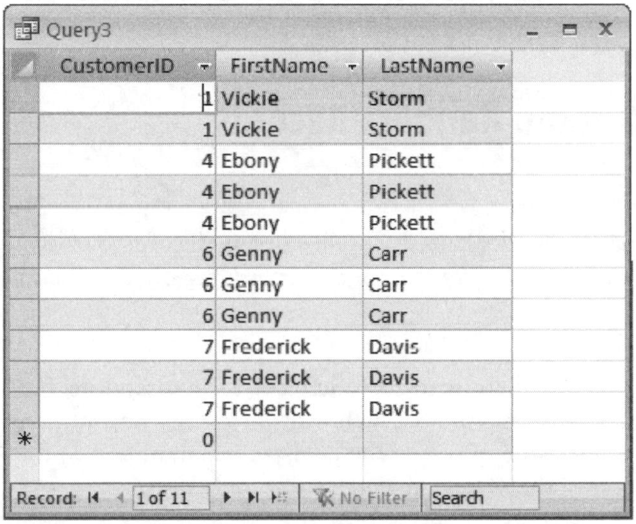

Figure 1-24. The simple query returns duplicate master records

Adding the DistinctRow predicate ensures that the returned master records are free of duplicates:

```
SELECT DistinctRow Customers.CustomerID,
Customers.FirstName, Customers.LastName
FROM Customers INNER JOIN Purchases ON
Customers.CustomerID = Purchases.CustomerID;
```

The result is shown in Figure 1-25.

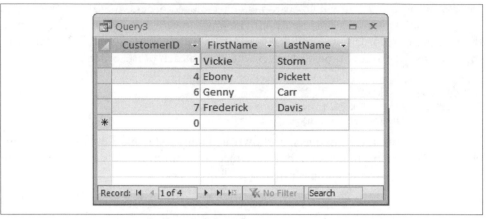

Figure 1-25. Using DistinctRow avoids duplicate records

1.8   Returning Random Records

Problem

For efficient analysis work, I need to pull random records out of my source table. Each time I run a query, I'd like to have the records returned in an unknown order.

Solution

The technique to apply here is to sort the records on a random value using the Rnd function. Figure 1-26 shows a table with three fields. To return the records in a random order, pass the name of one of the fields as the argument to the Rnd function in the ORDER BY clause of the SQL statement.

For example, using the Temperature field, the SQL statement necessary to return the records in random order is:

```
SELECT Samples.Location, Samples.Temperature, Samples.Date
FROM Samples
ORDER BY Rnd(Samples.Temperature);
```

Figure 1-27 shows the result of running the query. Bear in mind that each time the query is run, the records will be returned in a different order.

Discussion

Using the Rnd function on one field while performing an ascending or descending sort on another field provides an interesting, sometimes useful result. For example, this SQL statement performs sorts on two fields (one ascending and one random):

```
SELECT Samples.Location, Samples.Temperature,
Samples.Date
FROM Samples
ORDER BY Samples.Location, Rnd(Samples.Temperature);
```

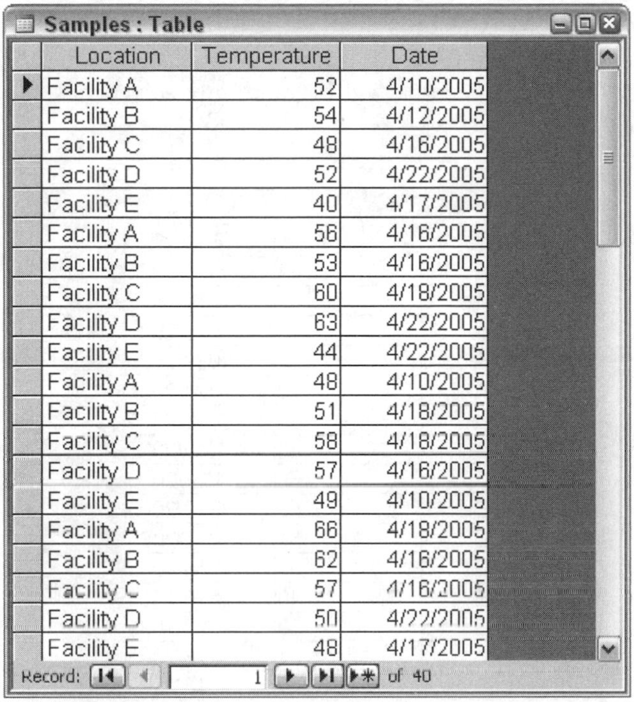

Samples : Table

Location	Temperature	Date
Facility A	52	4/10/2005
Facility B	54	4/12/2005
Facility C	48	4/16/2005
Facility D	52	4/22/2005
Facility E	40	4/17/2005
Facility A	56	4/16/2005
Facility B	53	4/16/2005
Facility C	60	4/18/2005
Facility D	63	4/22/2005
Facility E	44	4/22/2005
Facility A	48	4/10/2005
Facility B	51	4/18/2005
Facility C	58	4/18/2005
Facility D	57	4/16/2005
Facility E	49	4/10/2005
Facility A	66	4/18/2005
Facility B	62	4/16/2005
Facility C	57	4/16/2005
Facility D	50	4/22/2005
Facility E	48	4/17/2005

Record: 1 of 40

Figure 1-26. A table from which random records are required

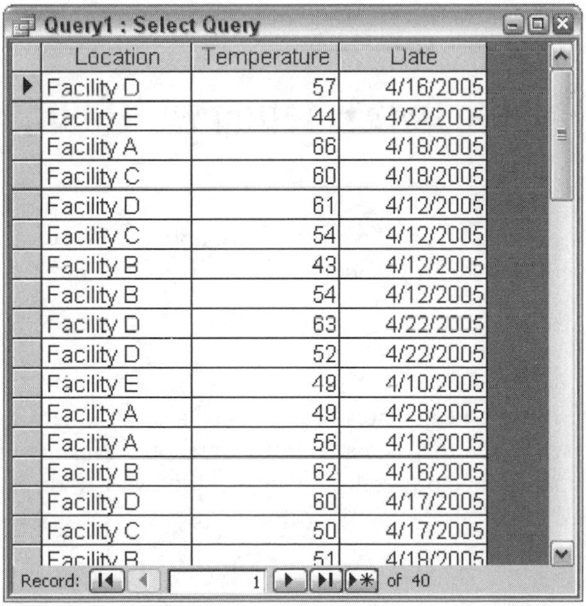

Query1 : Select Query

Location	Temperature	Date
Facility D	57	4/16/2005
Facility E	44	4/22/2005
Facility A	66	4/18/2005
Facility C	60	4/18/2005
Facility D	61	4/12/2005
Facility C	54	4/12/2005
Facility B	43	4/12/2005
Facility B	54	4/12/2005
Facility D	63	4/22/2005
Facility D	52	4/22/2005
Facility E	48	4/10/2005
Facility A	49	4/28/2005
Facility A	56	4/16/2005
Facility B	62	4/16/2005
Facility D	60	4/17/2005
Facility C	50	4/17/2005
Facility B	51	4/18/2005

Record: 1 of 40

Figure 1-27. Queried records are returned in a random order

Figure 1-28 shows the result of running this query. An ascending sort is done on the Location field, so Facility A records float to the top. However, the temperatures are sorted randomly. Thus, each time this query is run, all the Facility A records will be on top, but the Facility A records will be randomly sorted based on the way the Temperature field is handled.

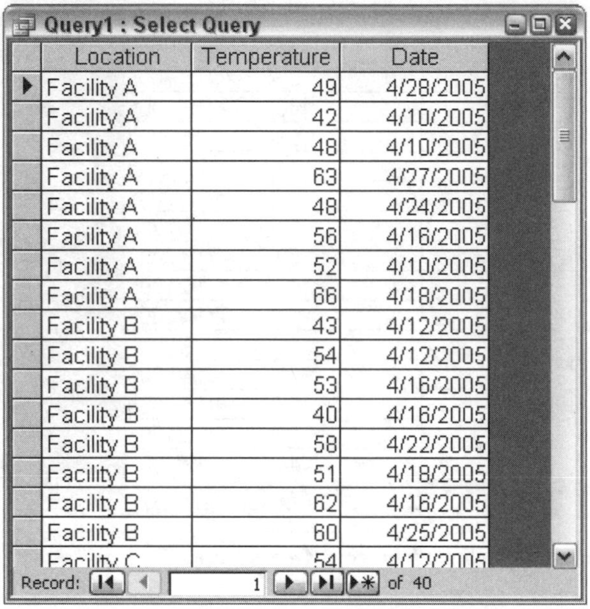

Query1 : Select Query

Location	Temperature	Date
Facility A	49	4/28/2005
Facility A	42	4/10/2005
Facility A	48	4/10/2005
Facility A	63	4/27/2005
Facility A	48	4/24/2005
Facility A	56	4/16/2005
Facility A	52	4/10/2005
Facility A	66	4/18/2005
Facility B	43	4/12/2005
Facility B	54	4/12/2005
Facility B	53	4/16/2005
Facility B	40	4/16/2005
Facility B	58	4/22/2005
Facility B	51	4/18/2005
Facility B	62	4/16/2005
Facility B	60	4/25/2005
Facility C	54	4/12/2005

Record: [◄◄] [◄] 1 [►] [►►] [►*] of 40

Figure 1-28. One field is sorted in ascending order and another is randomly sorted

1.9   Fine-Tuning Data Filtering with Subqueries

Problem

I need to determine which records in a table have above-average values for a particular quantitative field. How can I calculate the average and filter the records in one query?

Solution

The AVG aggregate function calculates the average value of a field across the records included in a query. While that is a straightforward operation, comparing the value in each record to the average presents a challenge. One way to do this is to use a *subquery*. A subquery is literally a query within a query, typically located within the WHERE section of the main query.

Figure 1-29 shows a table of teams and their scores for the season. The task is to identify which teams have a season score that is greater than the average of all the scores.

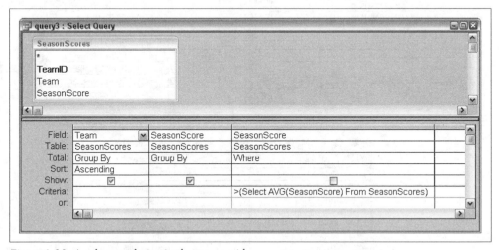

Figure 1-29. A table of teams and scores

A little finesse with SQL is required to identify the teams that beat the average. The AVG aggregate function (see Recipe 2.1) is needed, but it is not applied in the typical way in the query grid. Figure 1-30 shows how the query is entered into the query grid. Select View → Totals while designing the query to display the Total row in the grid. Then, create an additional column in the grid based on the SeasonScore field. Don't select AVG in the Total row; instead, select Where from the drop-down list, and enter the subquery in the Criteria row.

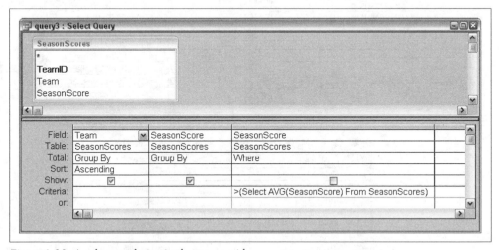

Figure 1-30. A subquery design in the query grid

In this example, the greater-than sign (>) precedes the subquery, since we are look-ing for scores that are greater than the average. The AVG function appears in the subquery itself, which has the following syntax:

```
Select AVG(SeasonScore) From SeasonScores
```

Here's the full SQL statement:

```
SELECT Team, SeasonScore
FROM SeasonScores
WHERE (((SeasonScore)>
(Select AVG(SeasonScore) From SeasonScores)))
GROUP BY Team, SeasonScore
ORDER BY Team;
```

Discussion

In the preceding example, the subquery resides in the WHERE section of the outer query. An alternative is to have the subquery act as one of the fields in the outer query's SELECT section. Figure 1-31 shows two tables and a query. On the left is the SeasonScores table presented earlier. On the right is a related child table that lists game dates and locations for each team in the first table. The query, whose result is shown underneath the tables, has returned the date of the last game played by each team.

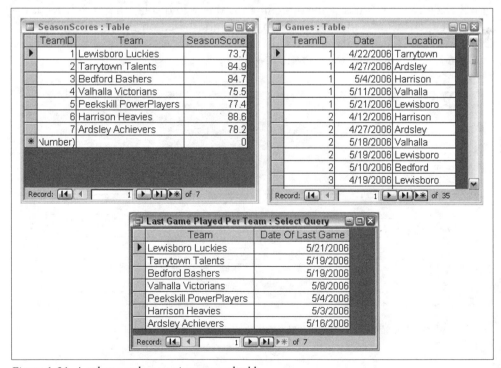

Figure 1-31. A subquery that queries a second table

Here is the SQL statement of the Last Game Played Per Team query in Figure 1-31:

```
SELECT SeasonScores.Team,
(Select Max(Date) From Games Where
Games.TeamID = SeasonScores.TeamID)
AS [Date Of Last Game]
FROM SeasonScores;
```

The subquery is placed where a field would typically go. It is encased in parentheses and is given an alias for the field name (Date Of Last Game) outside of the subquery. Within the subquery is the join between the two tables.

 There are other ways to return the same information, using different query constructs—for example, the tables could be joined and a Max of Date could be used. Working it in as a subquery serves here to illustrate a new method.

Removing excessive queries

One of the advantages of using subqueries is the avoidance of nested queries. Let's look at an example. Say you have two tables: tblCustomers, which contains customer names; and tblCustomerReachOut, which contains the dates at which customers were contacted. The CustomerID field is present in both tables, as shown in Figure 1-32. Now, consider the task of gathering a list of customers who have not been contacted in more than 60 days.

CustomerID	CustomerFirstName	CustomerLastName	CustomerAddr1
310	Lennie	Leishman	4 Pear Drive
311	Daniel	Schames	302 Limekiln W:
312	Karen	Dixon	170 Lake Drive
313	Connie	Erdman	361 Madelyne D
314	Lyndon	Drayton	155 Lindale Blvd
315	Lajuane	Joyce	131 Mcniel Blvd
316	Bruce	Pitsch	144 Peartree Dr
317	Ernestine	Naughton	345 Riggins Str(
318	Ebony	Brady	309 Highview Dı
319	Abraham	Halpern	9 Mariposa Stre
320	Nancy A.	Balkin	4 Beaverson Dr
321	Mary Lou	Ankenbaur	5 Maxwelton Blv
322	Victor	Brightman	3 Castro Blvd
323	Jovett	Rivera	383 Morrill Drive
324	Dawna	Sayer	357 Vallette Ave
325	Ernice	Cohen	397 Haywood S:
326	LouAnne	Dwyer	381 Globe Way
327	Ruben	Cronin	347 Autumn Str

Record: 2 of 200

tblCustomerReachOut : Table

CustomerID	ContactDate
353	3/15/2005
353	5/25/2005
353	5/30/2005
353	6/7/2005
360	8/2/2004
360	10/7/2004
360	2/16/2005
360	2/20/2005
368	4/14/2005
368	5/1/2005
368	5/3/2005
368	6/1/2005
371	1/19/2005
371	2/1/2005
371	3/3/2005

Record: 12 of 48

Figure 1-32. A table of customers and a table of contact dates

Let's look at a common approach to extracting the desired information. First, a query is constructed that returns—from the table of contact dates—records in which the last contact date is more than 60 days from the present date, as shown in Figure 1-33.

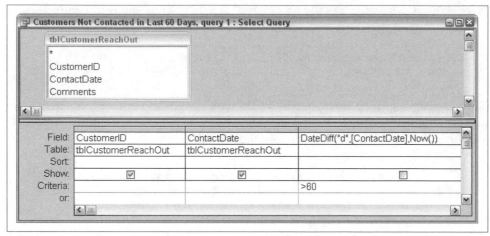

Figure 1-33. A query that returns records based on elapsed time

The query in Figure 1-33 is then queried from another query. This next query effectively takes the records from the first query and matches them with customer names from the tblCustomers table. This second query is shown in Figure 1-34.

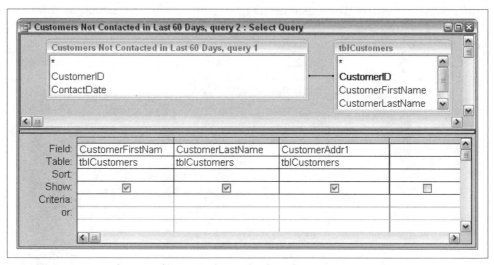

Figure 1-34. A query that uses the returned records of another query

To summarize, two queries have been constructed, though one would do the trick. When this inefficient design is perpetuated repeatedly in a database, the database can become laden with dozens of queries that seem isolated on the surface. When viewing a list of all the queries in a database (on the Queries tab), there is no immediate method to know which queries are called by others. Nested queries do work, but they're often unnecessary.

In contrast to the approach just described, here is the SQL of a query/subquery construction that returns the same records:

```
SELECT DISTINCT tblCustomers.CustomerFirstName,
tblCustomers.CustomerLastName, tblCustomers.CustomerAddr1
FROM tblCustomers
WHERE (((tblCustomers.CustomerID)
In (Select tblCustomerReachOut.CustomerID FROM tblCustomerReachOut
WHERE DateDiff("d",[ContactDate],Now()))>60)));
```

This SQL statement uses a subquery to return the CustomerIDs from the tblCustomerReachOut table for customers who were last contacted more than 60 days earlier (the DateDiff function is used to calculate the elapsed time). The returned CustomerIDs are matched with related records in the tblCustomers table, thereby returning the customer names. Note that the SQL statement uses the DISTINCT predicate (discussed in Recipe 1.7), as the returned records from the tblCustomerReachOut table can include duplicate CustomerIDs. This makes sense because customers are likely to be contacted more than once. Using the DISTINCT predicate ensures that the final returned list of names will not contain duplicates.

1.10   Combining Data with Union Queries

Problem

I need to combine sets of data so I can run analyses on them. The sets of data are identical but sit in different tables. There's no way to combine the data in the query grid. I could use append queries to copy data from the various tables to a master table, but this is inefficient. The data in the smaller tables changes from time to time, and having to rerun the appends is a nuisance. Isn't there a way to simply combine the data at any time as needed, so the latest data in the smaller tables is always present?

Solution

A union query is the perfect vehicle for combining identically structured data. To create a union query, place Union SQL clauses between the Select statements that query the tables.

Figure 1-35 shows three tables with an identical structure. Let's take a look at how to combine the data from these three tables.

Union queries must be written in the SQL pane of the query designer. It is not possible to represent them in the query grid. Here's a SQL statement written in the SQL pane of the query designer:

```
SELECT * From SeasonScores_Putnam
Union
SELECT * From SeasonScores_Rockland
Union
SELECT * From SeasonScores_Westchester;
```

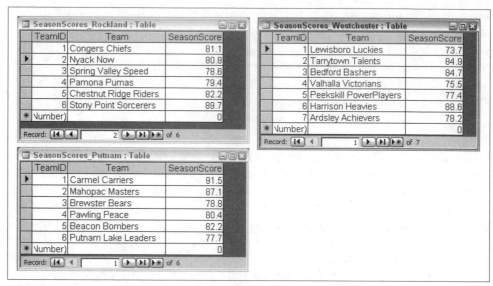

Figure 1-35. Three tables with identically structured data

Running the query returns a single set of data, shown in Figure 1-36.

TeamID	Team	SeasonScore
1	Carmel Carriers	91.5
1	Congers Chiefs	81.1
1	Lewisboro Luckies	73.7
2	Mahopac Masters	87.1
2	Nyack Now	80.8
2	Tarrytown Talents	84.9
3	Bedford Bashers	84.7
3	Brewster Bears	78.8
3	Spring Valley Speed	78.6
4	Pamona Pumas	79.4
4	Pawling Peace	80.4
4	Valhalla Victorians	75.5
5	Beacon Bombers	82.2
5	Chestnut Ridge Rider:	82.2
5	Peekskill PowerPlayer	77.4
6	Harrison Heavies	88.6
6	Putnam Lake Leaders	77.7
6	Stony Point Sorcerers	89.7
7	Ardsley Achievers	78.2

Figure 1-36. The result of running a union query

All the records from the three tables are now together in one place. This query can be saved and then used as the source for other queries and further analysis. For example, this saved query can be used in a query that calculates an average or some other summarization. If and when any data changes back in the source tables, the new data will flow through to the output of this union query, as each time it is rerun, it uses the latest data from the source tables.

Discussion

A hard-and-fast rule is that all the selects feeding into a union query must have the same number of fields. In the previous example, this was a given because the three source tables were identical in structure. However, imagine assembling a list of names from various data tables, such as a Contacts table, a Prospects table, and a HolidayList table.

Figure 1-37 shows the design of these three tables. Each table has a field for a first name and a last name, although the fields are not named exactly the same. Also note that the number of fields is not consistent among all the tables. To avoid this being an issue, you must specify actual field names in the Select statements and ensure that you specify the same number of fields from each table.

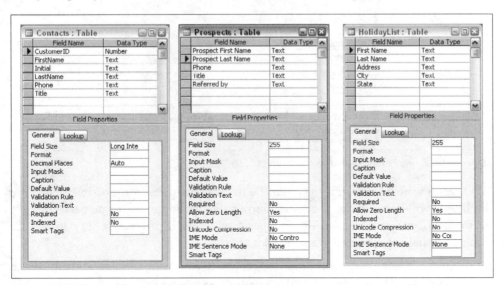

Figure 1-37. Three tables with similar information

A union SQL statement that will combine the first and last names from these tables can be written like this:

```
SELECT FirstName, LastName From Contacts;
Union
Select [First Name], [Last Name] From HolidayList
Union
```

```
Select [Prospect First Name], [Prospect Last Name]
From Prospects
Order By LastName, FirstName
```

 Brackets ([]) must be placed around field and table names that contain spaces.

The result of the query is shown in Figure 1-38. The field names presented in the query (FirstName and LastName) are taken from the first Select statement.

FirstName	LastName
Russell	Abrams
Andrea	Abumra
Lanica	Abumra
Lois	Aceto
Colleen	Aguilera
Solomon	Ahern
William	Aiona
Bill	Albrecht
Temujin	Aleni
Willetta	Allsmith
Bennie	Alvard
Susanne	Alvard
Dawn	Ames
Travis	Antoon
Cleo	Armstrong

Record: 1 of 287

Figure 1-38. A union query based on three tables

While each source table on its own may be free of duplicates, it is possible that some duplicates will occur in the combined output. For example, the same person might be in the Contacts table and the Prospects table. SQL provides a way to handle duplicates that appear when union queries are run.

By default, a union query will drop duplicates. If you want to include them in the result, you'll need to use the Union All construct, as shown here:

```
SELECT FirstName, LastName From Contacts;
Union All
Select [First Name], [Last Name] From HolidayList
Union All
Select [Prospect First Name], [Prospect Last Name]
From Prospects
Order By LastName, FirstName
```

Including the All keyword forces duplicates to be preserved in the query result.

1.11   Inserting On-the-Fly Fields in Select Queries

Problem

I need to include additional information in a query's output. The information is sometimes based on the fields in the query, but at other times, it just needs to be inserted as a fixed message. How can I do this?

Solution

In the Field row of the Access query design grid, you can enter a name that will appear in the output as a field name, as any standard field name would. Follow this with a colon (:) and the value that will go into the new field, and you have created a new output field that exists only during the run of the query. This field is not saved back into any source tables. The value that goes into the new field can be dependent on other fields in the query, or it can be completely independent.

Figure 1-39 shows a table of clients and balances due.

	FirstName	LastName	Address	City	State	Balance
▶	Abe	Elberfeld	144 Memorial	Keller	TX	225
	Rose	Iaconi	108 Moniteau	Eliot	ME	125
	Till	Towers	167 Powhatto	Newton	IL	75
	Courtney	Hape	Excelsior Aver	Rancho Cuca	CA	80
	Lenay	Weber	185 Fieldcrest	Leverett	MA	75
	Morin	Knight	Mariposa Way	Old Saybrook	CT	420
	Clay	Flakoll	6 Mendota Wa	Webster Grov	MO	0
	Sandi	Paschetto	7 Kurre Way	Ottawa	IL	0
	Katherine	Coleman	186 Milton Roa	Tiffin	OH	75
	Lorrie	Sater	178 Picardy S	Veradale	WA	75
	Natasha	Bevens	Pearlman Stre	Neenah	WI	100
	Deseree A.	Owsley	Annabelle Driv	Briarcliff Mano	NY	0
	Radcliff	Light	10 Court Blvd	Tavernier	FL	125
	Fred	Scannell	133 Rose Wa	Riverhead	NY	225
	Zeina	Ivie	170 Orchard F	Webb City	MO	75
	Bob	Epstein	146 Harbor W	Lake Bluff	IL	225
	Wilfred	Martino	Ocean Avenue	Chesapeake	VA	100
	Rob	Haiek	Yellowood Blv	Beaman	IA	0
	J.B.	Dykestra	100 F Drive	Austin	TX	125
	Sarae	Frost	182 Newflow [	Stewartville	MN	75

Record: [◀◀] [◀]   1   [▶] [▶▶] [▶*] of 100

Figure 1-39. A table of clients and balances due

Figure 1-40 shows a query based on the table. In the query are two created fields that do not actually exist in the table. The first is named Client. The value for the Client field comes from a concatenation of the FirstName and LastName table fields.

Another new field—Message—provides a fixed string when the query is run. The Message field is populated with an expression that has nothing to do with any table fields.

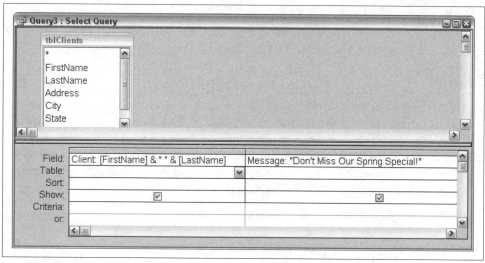

Figure 1-40. A query with expression-based fields

As shown in Figure 1-41, the query result contains two fields that list the clients' full names and the fixed message.

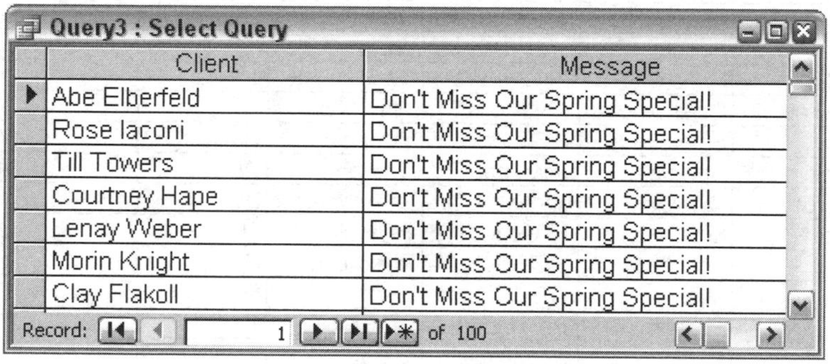

Figure 1-41. The result of running the query

Discussion

Using expression-based fields in queries provides ways to treat records with some intelligence. A useful example involves using an expression to return a message for certain records based on the value of a table field. Figure 1-42 shows how the IIf function is incorporated into our derived Message field. Now, the message about the Spring Special will appear only in records that have a balance of 100 or less.

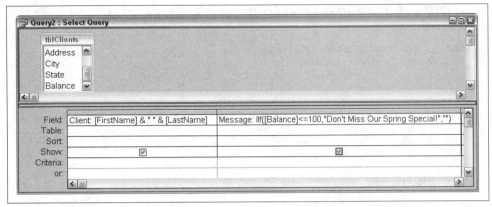

Figure 1-42. Using a condition in a field expression

Here is the SQL statement for the query in Figure 1-42:

```
SELECT [FirstName] & " " & [LastName] AS Client,
IIf([Balance]<=100,"Don't Miss Our Spring Special!","")
AS Message
FROM tblClients;
```

When you run this query, you'll find that clients with balances over 100 do not have the message written into their records. What is the point of this? This technique may be useful in a mail merge, for example. When creating letters or statements to clients, you may wish to advertise the Spring Special to just those customers with a low balance or a balance of zero.

1.12   Using Aliases to Simplify Your SQL Statements

Problem

Table names precede field names in SQL statements, so queries that use multiple fields and tables wind up being very long. Is there a way to use shortcut identifiers instead for the table names?

Solution

Yes, there is! In a SQL statement, any table name can be given an alias. The place to do this is after the FROM keyword, where the table name is entered. Follow the table name with an alias of your choosing (make sure it is not a reserved word, an existing field name, etc.). Then, use the alias instead of the table name in the other areas of the SQL statement. Let's look at an example.

Using the Access query grid to assemble the query results in this SQL statement that addresses a single table:

```
SELECT tblCustomers.CustomerCompanyName,
tblCustomers.CustomerFirstName,
tblCustomers.CustomerLastName,
tblCustomers.CustomerAddr1,
tblCustomers.CustomerAddr2,
tblCustomers.CustomerCity,
tblCustomers.CustomerState,
tblCustomers.CustomerZip,
tblCustomers.CustomerHomePhone,
tblCustomers.CustomerWorkPhone
FROM tblCustomers;
```

Here is the same query, this time using the alias C for tblCustomers. The alias is placed just after the table name in the FROM section, and all references to the table name in the rest of the query just use the alias:

```
SELECT C.CustomerCompanyName,
C.CustomerFirstName, C.CustomerLastName,
C.CustomerAddr1, C.CustomerAddr2, C.CustomerCity,
C.CustomerState, C.CustomerZip, C.CustomerHomePhone,
C.CustomerWorkPhone
FROM tblCustomers C;
```

This SQL statement is much shorter and easier to follow.

Discussion

Aliases are also useful—perhaps even more so—with queries that address multiple tables. Here is the SQL statement of a query that addresses three tables (tblCustomers, tblInvoices, and tblInvoicePayments). Inner joins connect the tables on key fields:

```
SELECT tblCustomers.CustomerCompanyName,
tblCustomers.CustomerFirstName,
tblCustomers.CustomerLastName,
tblCustomers.CustomerAddr1,
tblCustomers.CustomerAddr2,
tblCustomers.CustomerCity,
tblCustomers.CustomerState,
tblCustomers.CustomerZip,
tblInvoices.InvoiceNumber,
tblInvoices.InvoiceDate,
tblInvoices.Status,
tblInvoices.Hours, tblInvoices.Rate,
tblInvoicePayments.PaymentAmount,
tblInvoicePayments.PaymentDate,
tblInvoicePayments.PaymentType
FROM (tblCustomers INNER JOIN tblInvoices ON
tblCustomers.CustomerID = tblInvoices.CustomerID)
INNER JOIN tblInvoicePayments ON
tblInvoices.InvoiceID = tblInvoicePayments.InvoiceID;
```

Now, here is the same SQL statement, but with aliases of C for tblCustomers, I for tblInvoices, and P for tblInvoicePayments:

```
SELECT C.CustomerCompanyName, C.CustomerFirstName,
C.CustomerLastName, C.CustomerAddr1,
C.CustomerAddr2, C.CustomerCity, C.CustomerState,
C.CustomerZip, I.InvoiceNumber, I.InvoiceDate,
I.Status, I.Hours, I.Rate, P.PaymentAmount,
P.PaymentDate, P.PaymentType
FROM (tblCustomers C INNER JOIN tblinvoices I ON
C.CustomerID=I.CustomerID) INNER JOIN
tblInvoicePayments P ON I.InvoiceID=P.InvoiceID;
```

Clearly, the SQL statement with aliases is shorter. Again, each table is assigned its alias just after its name appears in the FROM and INNER JOIN sections.

1.13   Creating a Left Join

Problem

I have a table of students and a table of courses they have taken. Not every student has taken a course. I want a listing of all the students and any courses they have taken, including students who have not yet taken a course. However, when I run the query normally, I only get back records of students who have taken at least one course.

Solution

Figure 1-43 shows the standard query you would use to query from two tables. This query will return all records from Students who have related records in Courses Taken. If, for a given student, there is more than one record in Courses Taken, the number of related records in Courses Taken is the number of records that will be returned for that given student. But students with no matched courses are left out of the returned records altogether.

Figure 1-43 shows an *inner join*. To ensure that all records from the master table (Students) appear in the results, the query must be changed to a *left join*. This is easy to do when the query is in design mode: either use the View → Join Properties menu option, or double-click on the line that connects the table to display the Join Properties dialog box, shown in Figure 1-44.

In the Join Properties dialog box are three numbered options. The first one is the standard inner join. The second one creates a left join. The third option creates a right join (see Recipe 1.14). Select the second option and click OK. Now, when the query is run, all records from the Students table will appear, as shown in Figure 1-45.

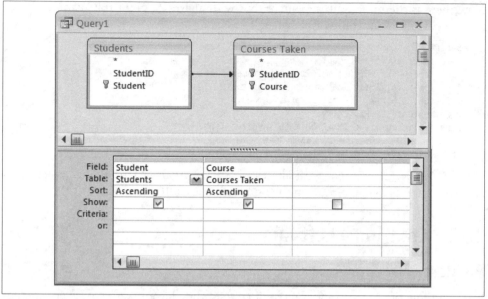

Figure 1-43. An inner join query returns only matched records

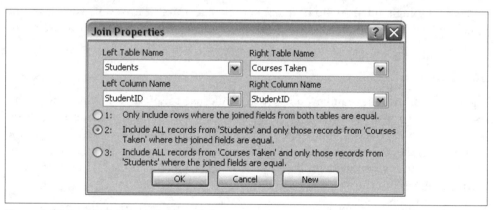

Figure 1-44. Setting the properties for a left join

Discussion

A left join returns all records from the master table, and probably all records from the child table (here, Courses Taken). This last fact depends on whether referential integrity exists between the tables. In other words, if referential integrity is enforced, each record in the Courses Taken table must match to a record in the Students table. Then, even though there are student records with no matching courses, all course records must belong to students and hence are returned in the query.

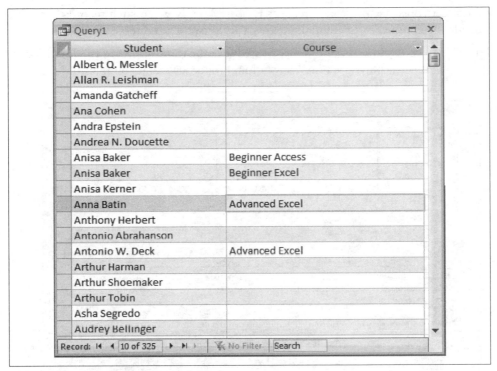

Figure 1-45. The result of running a left join query

If referential integrity is not applied, any records in Courses Taken that do not relate to records in the Students table will not be included in the query's returned records.

1.14 Creating a Right Join

Problem

I have a parent table and a child table. The parent table contains customers, and the child table contains purchases, but some records in the Purchases table do not belong to any customer. I need to run a query that returns all the records from the Purchases table, even if there is no matching customer. At the very least, this will help me identify purchases that are not being billed to anyone.

Solution

The request here is for a *right join*. In a right join, all records are returned from the child table, including those that have no match in the parent table. For any such records to exist in the child table, referential integrity must not exist between the tables. The presence of orphan records is possible only when such records can exist outside the confines of referential integrity with the parent table.

Figure 1-46 shows how a right join is created: use the third option in the Join Properties dialog box (displayed via the View → Join Properties menu command).

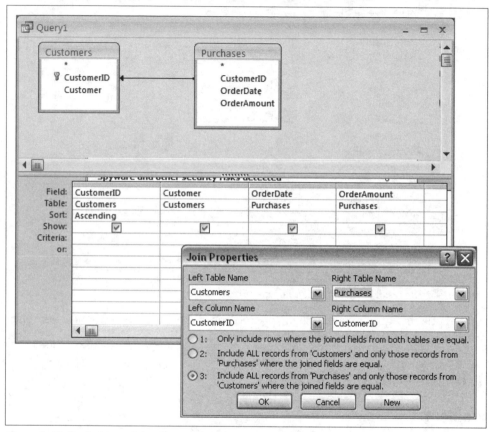

Figure 1-46. Setting up a right join in a query

Discussion

When a right join query is run, the number of returned records matches the number of records in the child table (assuming no criteria were used). For fields from the parent table, there will be blank data for the records in which there is no match between tables. Figure 1-47 shows the result of running the right join query.

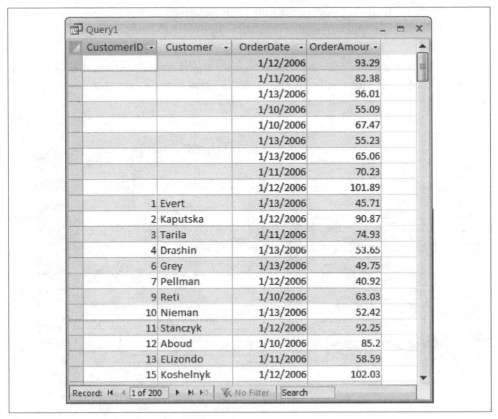

CustomerID ▾	Customer ▾	OrderDate ▾	OrderAmour ▾
		1/12/2006	93.29
		1/11/2006	82.38
		1/13/2006	96.01
		1/10/2006	55.09
		1/10/2006	67.47
		1/13/2006	55.23
		1/13/2006	65.06
		1/11/2006	70.23
		1/12/2006	101.89
1	Evert	1/13/2006	45.71
2	Kaputska	1/12/2006	90.87
3	Tarila	1/11/2006	74.93
4	Drashin	1/13/2006	53.65
6	Grey	1/13/2006	49.75
7	Pellman	1/12/2006	40.92
9	Reti	1/10/2006	63.03
10	Nieman	1/13/2006	52.42
11	Stanczyk	1/12/2006	92.25
12	Aboud	1/10/2006	85.2
13	ELizondo	1/11/2006	58.59
15	Koshelnyk	1/12/2006	102.03

Record: I◄ ◄ 1 of 200 ► ►I ►☆   ☆ No Filter | Search

Figure 1-47. The result of running a right join query

1.15   Creating an Outer Join

Problem

I wish to combine the output of both a left join and a right join into a single query, but I can't get Access to do this type of "outer join."

Solution

A left join will return all the records from the table on the right side (the parent) and any related records from the table on the left side (the child). A right join will return all the records from the table on the left side and any related records from the table on the right side. An outer join combines these two outputs into one.

Access doesn't directly support outer joins, but because it is reasonable to create left and right joins, these two constructs can be brought together with a union query (see Recipe 1.10).

Figure 1-48 shows two database tables. Not all the teams in the Teams table have matching records in the Games table, and the Games table contains some records that have no relation to the teams in the Teams table.

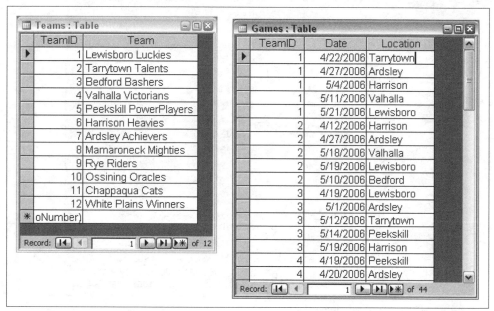

Figure 1-48. Two tables with some related and some orphan records

To create an outer query, you must be in the SQL pane of the query designer. The following is the SQL that would simulate an outer query for these tables by combining the output of a left join with a right join:

```
SELECT Teams.Team, Games.Date, Games.Location
FROM Games LEFT JOIN Teams ON
Games.TeamID=Teams.TeamID
UNION
SELECT Teams.Team, Games.Date, Games.Location
FROM Games RIGHT JOIN Teams ON
Games.TeamID = Teams.TeamID
ORDER BY Team, Date;
```

Discussion

When the query is run (see Figure 1-49), there are, as expected, some blanks in the fields from the Teams table and the Games table (from Figure 1-48). The majority of records are matched. Running a standard inner join query on these tables returns 35 records—the count of records that match. This outer join result returns 49 records. There are 14 records that have blanks for the source from one table or the other.

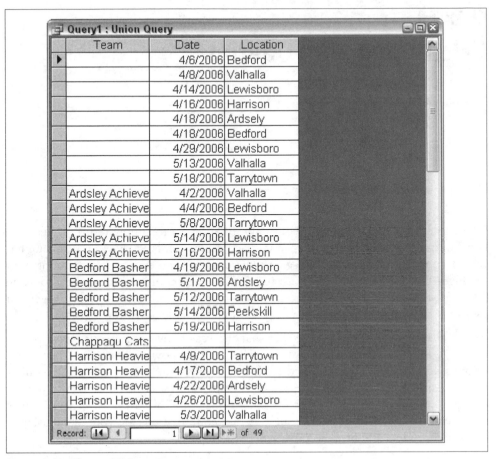

Figure 1-49. The result of running an outer join

See Also

- Recipe 1.13
- Recipe 1.14
- Recipe 1.10

CHAPTER 2

Calculating with Queries

Queries can tell you a lot about your data. In addition to simply returning records, you can use aggregate functions that are part of the SQL language to return summaries of your data. There are aggregate functions that can sum, average, count, find the highest or lowest value, or return the standard deviation in the data, just to name a few. Not all are covered in the recipes in this chapter, but once you have a general idea of how aggregate functions work, you should be able to use any of them.

In this chapter, you'll also find recipes that showcase how to use your own custom, non-SQL functions from within a query. This is a very powerful technique because it enables you to design functions that deliver values that meet your exact requirements. And that's not all! There is also a recipe that describes how to use regular expressions, which provide powerful pattern-matching abilities, as well as recipes that demonstrate how to return all possible combinations of your data using a Cartesian product and how to construct crosstab queries.

2.1   Finding the Sum or Average in a Set of Data

Problem

Sometimes I need to summarize numerical data in a table. I know how to do this in a report—by using a calculation in a text box, in the report's footer. But how can I get a sum or average without having to create a report (or pull out a calculator)?

Solution

SQL provides aggregate functions that provide summaries of data. Two popular aggregate functions are Sum and Avg (for calculating the average). You can easily incorporate these into your query's design right within the query grid.

To use an aggregate function, select the View → Totals menu option while in the query grid (or, in Access 2007, click the Sigma (Σ) button in the Ribbon). This makes the Total row display in the grid. The Total row provides the assorted aggregate functions in a drop-down list.

Say you have a tblSales table containing a Customer_ID field, a PurchaseDate field, and an Amount field. There are records spanning dates from 2002 through 2005. To get a fast grand total of all the amounts in the table, just apply the Sum function to the Amount field. Figure 2-1 shows the design of the query, with the Sum function selected from the drop-down list in the Total row for the Amount field.

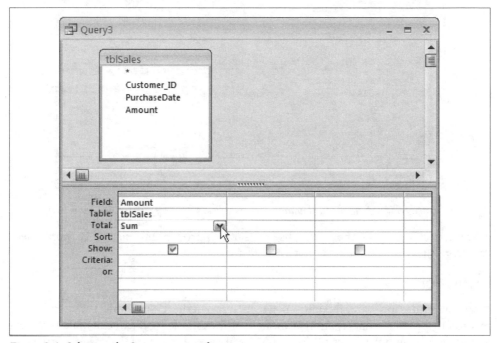

Figure 2-1. Selecting the Sum aggregate function

Figure 2-2 shows the result of running the query.

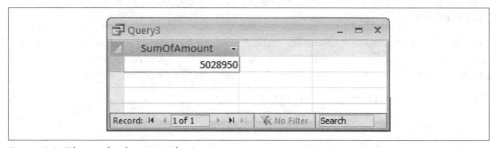

Figure 2-2. The result of running the Sum query

Note that a derived field name, SumOfAmount, has been used in the result. If you want, you can change this name in the SQL or by using an expression in the Field row of the query grid. Figure 2-3 shows how you can change the returned field name to Grand Total by using that name in the Field row, along with a colon (:) and the real field name.

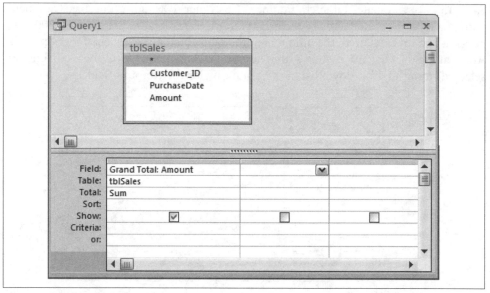

Figure 2-3. Specifying a dynamic field name

To return an average of the values, use the same approach, but instead of Sum, select Avg from the drop-down list in the Total row.

Discussion

Aggregate functions are flexible. You can apply criteria to limit the number of records to which the aggregation is applied—for example, you can calculate the average amount from purchases in just 2005. Figure 2-4 shows how to design a query to do so. Note that the criterion to limit the Amount field is placed in the second column, not in the same column that contains the Avg function. Also, the Show box is unchecked in the column with the criterion, so only the average in the first column is displayed when the query is run.

Figure 2-5 shows another example: a query design to calculate an average amount from amounts that are greater than or equal to 200. The average returned by this query will be higher than that returned by a query based on all the records.

The SQL generated from this design is:

```
SELECT Avg(tblSales.Amount) AS AvgOfAmount
FROM tblSales
WHERE (((tblSales.Amount)>=200));
```

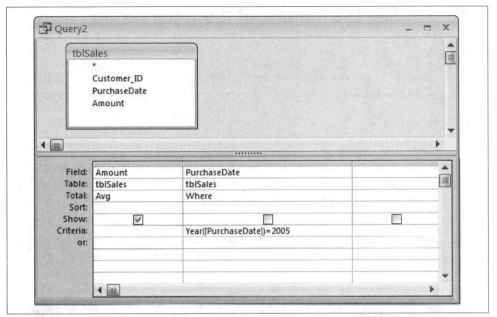

Figure 2-4. Calculating the average of purchases in 2005

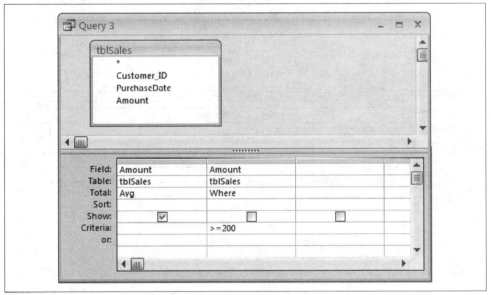

Figure 2-5. Calculating an average of purchases above a threshold

2.2   Finding the Number of Items per Group

Problem

I have a table of data containing customer address information. One of the fields is State. How do I create a query to return the number of customers in each state?

Solution

When a query uses aggregate functions, the Group By clause is a keystone. This SQL clause provides a grouping segregation, which then allows aggregation summaries to be applied per grouping. In this example, the Group By clause is applied to the State field. Then, the Count aggregate function is used to return the count of customers per group (i.e., per state).

Figure 2-6 shows the design of the query. The first column groups the State field. In the second column, the Count function is selected from the drop-down list in the Total row.

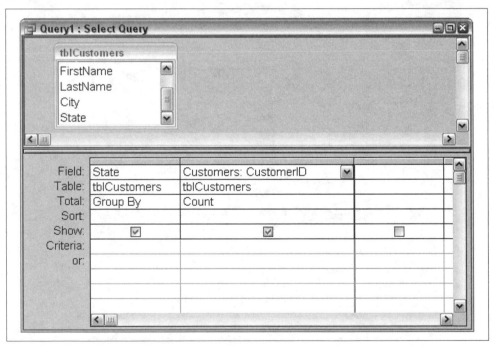

Figure 2-6. Using Count with Group By

Figure 2-7 shows the result of running the query. The number of customers in each state is returned.

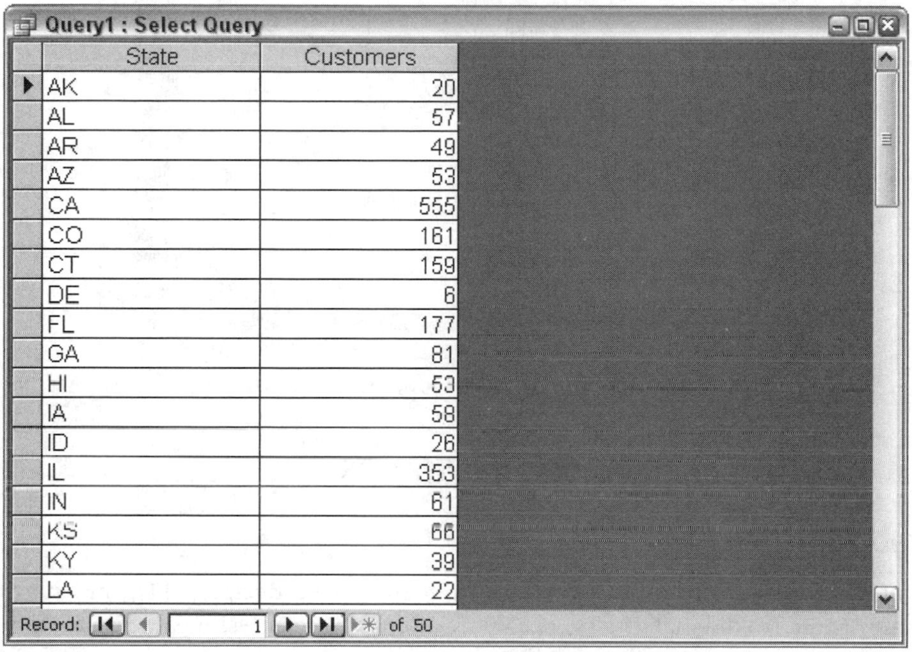
Query1 : Select Query

State	Customers
AK	20
AL	57
AR	49
AZ	53
CA	555
CO	161
CT	159
DE	6
FL	177
GA	81
HI	53
IA	58
ID	26
IL	353
IN	61
KS	66
KY	39
LA	22

Record: 1 of 50

Figure 2-7. Returned counts per state

Discussion

The `Group By` clause can be applied to more than one field. In such a case, in sequence, each field that uses `Group By` further defines the narrowness of the count at the end.

Let's refine our count so we can see how many customers are in each city within each state. Figure 2-8 shows the breakdown of customers in Alaska by city. In the query result shown in Figure 2-7, Alaska has a count of 20 customers. In the query result shown in Figure 2-8, there are still 20 customers listed in Alaska, but now you can see the counts per city.

The SQL statement for the query in Figure 2-8 is this:

```
SELECT tblCustomers.State, tblCustomers.City,
Count(tblCustomers.CustomerID) AS Customers
FROM tblCustomers
GROUP BY tblCustomers.State, tblCustomers.City;
```

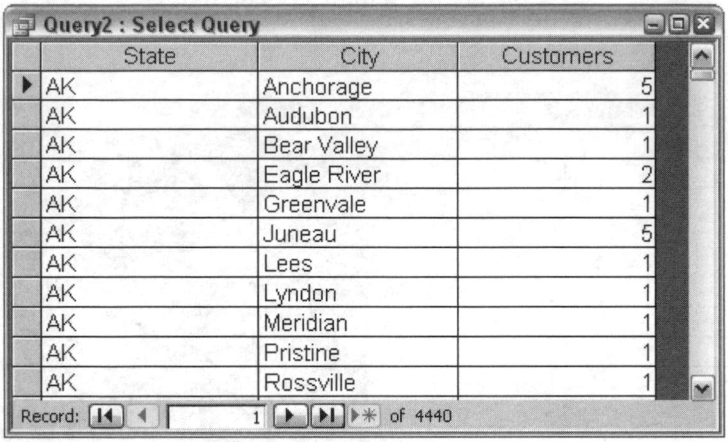

Query2 : Select Query

State	City	Customers
AK	Anchorage	5
AK	Audubon	1
AK	Bear Valley	1
AK	Eagle River	2
AK	Greenvale	1
AK	Juneau	5
AK	Lees	1
AK	Lyndon	1
AK	Meridian	1
AK	Pristine	1
AK	Rossville	1

Record: 1 of 4440

Figure 2-8. Count of customers grouped by state and city

2.3 Using Expressions in Queries

Problem

I know how to create on-the-fly fields in a query (see Recipe 1.11), and how to include some conditional intelligence. How, though, do I access a value that is not in an underlying table or query, but instead comes from another table altogether? How can I develop comprehensive expressions in a query?

Solution

Expressions are a powerful feature in Access. Expressions are used in a number of ways, such as for referencing forms and controls (whether from a macro, from a query, or from VBA). For this example, we'll use an expression within a query that accesses data from tables not included in the query's `Select` statement.

Figure 2-9 shows a query based on two tables: tblClients and tblPets. The key between these tables is ClientID. A field called PetID is the unique key for pets in the tblPets table. Two external tables, tblServiceDates and tblServiceDates_New, contain records of visits made by each pet. The first service date table, tblServiceDates, contains records for pets with PetIDs of up to 299. Higher PetIDs have service date records in the tblServiceDates_New table.

In the query in Figure 2-9 is a field based on a built-up expression, shown here:

```
Last Service Date: IIf([PetID]<300,
DLookUp("Max(DateOfService)",
"tblServiceDates","[Pet_ID]=" & [PetID]),
DLookUp("Max(DateOfService)",
"tblServiceDates_New",
"[Pet_ID]=" & [PetID]))
```

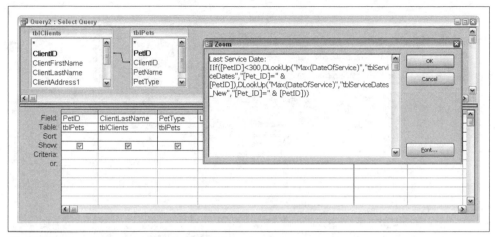

Figure 2-9. A query with an expression

This expression combines functions (IIf, DLookup, and Max) to find the last service date for each pet from the respective service date tables.

The full SQL statement that is generated from this design is:

```
SELECT tblPets.PetID, tblClients.ClientLastName,
tblPets.PetType, IIf([PetID]<300,
DLookUp("Max(DateOfService)",
"tblServiceDates","[Pet_ID]=" & [PetID]),
DLookUp("Max(DateOfService)","tblServiceDates_New",
"[Pet_ID]=" & [PetID])) AS [Last Service Date]
FROM tblClients INNER JOIN tblPets ON
tblClients.ClientID = tblPets.ClientID;
```

In summary, within a query, it is possible to build up a sophisticated expression that uses functions to address data and calculate results that stand outside of the standard SQL syntax.

Discussion

Entering complex expressions into a single row in the query grid can be difficult, given the limited width of a computer monitor. One workaround is to use the Zoom box, as demonstrated in Figure 2-9. To display the Zoom box, right-click on the query grid where you want the entry to go, and select Zoom from the pop-up menu. Pressing Shift-F2 also displays the Zoom box.

Another choice on the pop-up menu is Build. Selecting this displays the Expression Builder dialog box, seen in Figure 2-10. This utility makes it easy to assemble complex expressions, as it makes all the database objects, functions, and more available for you to use with just a few mouse clicks.

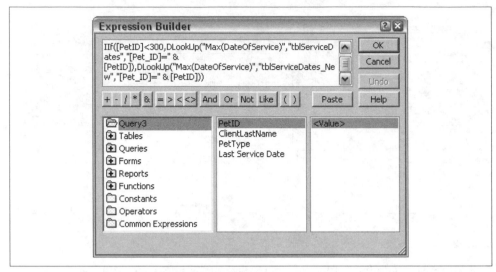

Figure 2-10. The ever-popular Expression Builder

2.4   Using Custom Functions in Queries

Problem

I often write long code routines to read through a table and process its data. It would be great if I could reduce the amount of code required by not creating and reading through a recordset. A select query addresses the table just as well. Is there a way to just apply the processing portion of the code direct from a query?

Solution

Calling a function from a query is relatively easy. Just use an extra column in the query grid to create a derived field. In that field, place an expression that calls the function; the returned value from the function is what will appear in the query result.

Figure 2-11 shows a table with records of activities performed for different clients. The records list the client name, the date when the work was done, the number of hours it took, and the type of work that was performed. The task is to calculate how much to charge for the work, per record.

First, let's develop a function that we can call from a query. It's important that this is a function and not just a sub. We need a returned value to appear in the query results, and while functions return values, subs do not. Here is the bill_amount function:

```
Function bill_amount(the_date As Date, the_hours As Integer, _
    the_client As String, WorkType As String) As Single
bill_amount = 0 'in case of unexpected input
Select Case WorkType
```

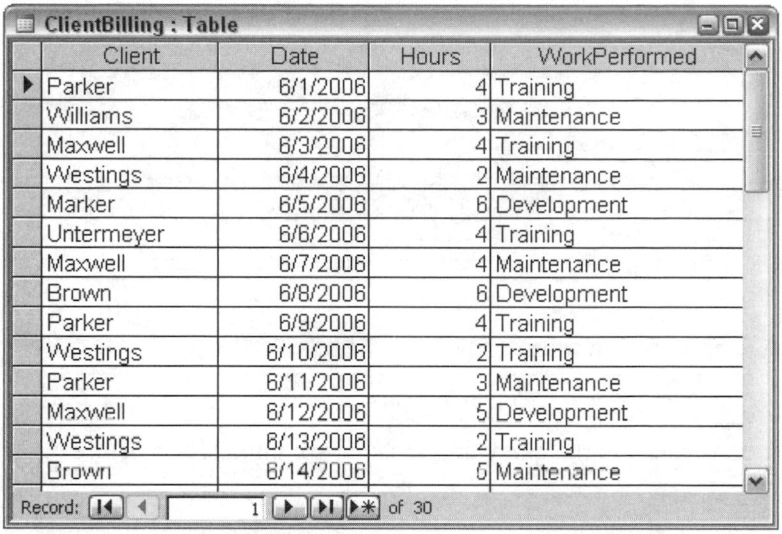

ClientBilling : Table

Client	Date	Hours	WorkPerformed
Parker	6/1/2006	4	Training
Williams	6/2/2006	3	Maintenance
Maxwell	6/3/2006	4	Training
Westings	6/4/2006	2	Maintenance
Marker	6/5/2006	6	Development
Untermeyer	6/6/2006	4	Training
Maxwell	6/7/2006	4	Maintenance
Brown	6/8/2006	6	Development
Parker	6/9/2006	4	Training
Westings	6/10/2006	2	Training
Parker	6/11/2006	3	Maintenance
Maxwell	6/12/2006	5	Development
Westings	6/13/2006	2	Training
Brown	6/14/2006	5	Maintenance

Record: 1 of 30

Figure 2-11. A table containing records of work performed for clients

```
    Case "Training"
      bill_amount = the_hours * 80
    Case "Development"
      bill_amount = the_hours * 120
    Case "Maintenance"
      'Parker gets reduced rate regardless of day of week
      'Other clients have separate weekday and weekend rates
      If the_client <> "Parker" Then
        If Weekday(the_date) = 1 Or Weekday(the_date = 7) Then
          bill_amount = the_hours * 95
        Else
          bill_amount = the_hours * 75
        End If
      Else
        bill_amount = the_hours * 60
      End If
  End Select
  End Function
```

The function takes four arguments—one each for the four fields in the table—and calculates the amount to bill based on different facets of the data. The type of work performed, the client for whom it was performed, and whether it was done on the weekend (determined with the `Weekday` function) all determine which hourly rate to use. The hourly rate and the number of hours are then multiplied to determine the billing amount.

Figure 2-12 shows the query design. Note that you don't have to place the table fields in the grid unless you want them to appear with the values returned from the function.

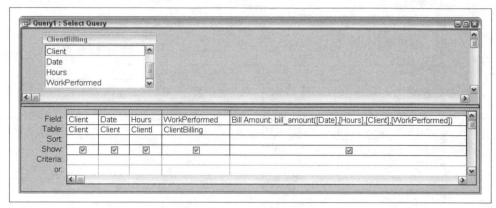

Figure 2-12. A custom function is called from a query

The function is called in the query in a separate column. The structure of the expression is:

```
Bill Amount: bill_amount([Date],[Hours],[Client],[WorkPerformed])
```

Bill Amount is the name of the temporary field. bill_amount is the name of the function, and the four fields are included as arguments. The fields are each encased in brackets, consistent with the standard Access field-handling protocol.

When the query is run, the fifth column contains the billable amount, as shown in Figure 2-13.

Client	Date	Hours	WorkPerformed	Bill Amount
Parker	6/1/2006	4	Training	320
Williams	6/2/2006	3	Maintenance	285
Maxwell	6/3/2006	4	Training	320
Westings	6/4/2006	2	Maintenance	190
Marker	6/5/2006	6	Development	720
Untermeyer	6/6/2006	4	Training	320
Maxwell	6/7/2006	4	Maintenance	380
Brown	6/8/2006	6	Development	720
Parker	6/9/2006	4	Training	320
Westings	6/10/2006	2	Training	160
Parker	6/11/2006	3	Maintenance	180
Maxwell	6/12/2006	5	Development	600
Westings	6/13/2006	2	Training	160
Brown	6/14/2006	5	Maintenance	475

Record: 1 of 30

Figure 2-13. The billable amounts are returned

Discussion

Calling functions from queries opens up many ways of working with your data. The function used in this example is short and processes an easy calculation. But do note that this function actually calls another function, Weekday. The point is that you can develop sophisticated functions that perform all types of processing.

Both custom functions and built-in functions can be called from a query. Further, the query does not have to be a select query; you can call functions from action queries (discussed in Chapter 3) as well. Figure 2-14 shows an example of using two built-in functions, IIf and Weekday, to update the value in a field. If the date falls on the weekend, -Weekend is appended to the client name.

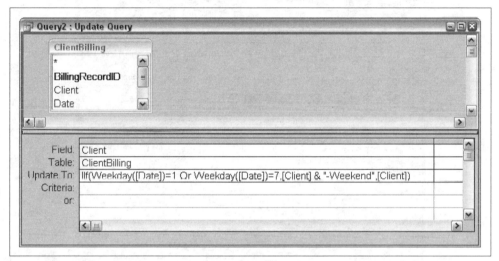

Figure 2-14. Built-in functions used in an update query

Take a closer look at the expression used in the Update To row:

```
IIf(Weekday([Date])=1 Or Weekday([Date])=7,[Client] & "-Weekend",[Client])
```

If the weekday is a 1 or a 7 (a Sunday or a Saturday), -Weekend is appended to the client name; otherwise, the client name is used for the update as is. In other words, every row is updated, but most rows are updated to the existing value.

2.5   Using Regular Expressions in Queries

Problem

Regular expressions provide the ability to set up sophisticated string patterns for matching records. Can a regular expression be used as the criterion in a query?

Solution

Regular expressions, popularized by Perl and other Unix-based languages, provide powerful string-matching capabilities. For Access and other Windows-based applications, adding a reference to the VBScript Regular Expressions library makes using regular expressions possible. You can set up the reference in the Visual Basic Editor (VBE). To display the VBE from Access, just press Alt-F11. While in the VBE, use the Tools → References menu option to display the References dialog. Then set a reference to Microsoft VBScript Regular Expressions 5.5 (your version number may be different), as shown in Figure 2-15.

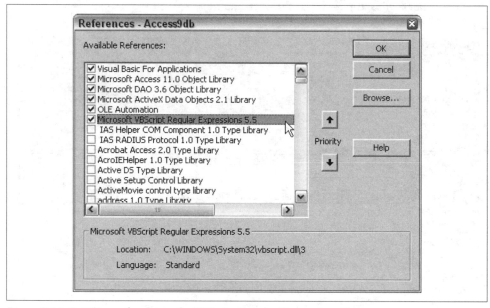

Figure 2-15. Setting a reference to the VBScript Regular Expressions library

Figure 2-16 shows a table with hypothetical transaction records.

The values in the TransactionRecord field are concatenations of separate codes and values that follow this pattern:

- The first character is a letter that signifies a type of transaction. For example, an A could mean an adjustment, and a D could mean a deposit.
- The next two characters are numbers that represent a transaction type.
- The next two characters are a department code. For example, LE is Legal, SA is Sales, HR is Human Resources, WA is Warehouse, and so on.
- The last three numbers are an amount.

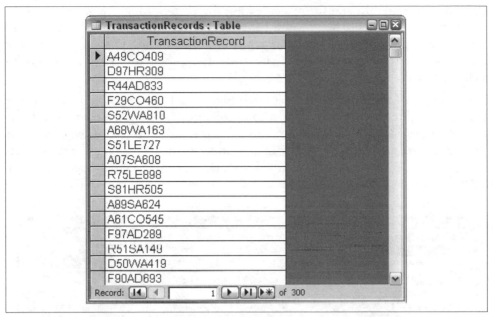

Figure 2-16. A table with transaction records

Given this pattern, let's construct a query that will identify transactions that are either adjustments or deposits, are for the Sales department, and are for amounts of 500 or greater. Put another way, our task will be to identify transaction records consisting of an A or a D, followed by any two numbers, followed by SA, followed by a number that is 5 or greater, and any two other numbers.

To make use of pattern matching, we'll use a custom function to create a regular expression (regexp) object. In a separate code module, enter this function:

```
Function validate_transaction(transaction_record As String, _
    match_string As String) As String
  validate_transaction = "Invalid Record"
  Dim regexp As regexp
  Set regexp = New regexp
  With regexp
    .Global = True
    .IgnoreCase = True
    .Pattern = match_string
    If .Test(transaction_record) = True Then
      validate_transaction = "Valid Record"
    End If
  End With
  Set regexp = Nothing
End Function
```

The transaction record and the regular expression pattern to match are given to the function as arguments. The function code initially sets the return value to Invalid Record. A regexp object is set, and the transaction record is tested against the pattern. If the transaction record matches the pattern, the return value is changed to Valid Record.

Now, we'll call this function from a query. Figure 2-17 shows a select query that places the call to the function in the second column. Note that the column with the function to call is set to a descending sort. This is so all valid records will appear at the top. Unlike a typical select query that returns just the records that match the criteria, in this case all records are returned, so it makes sense to group together all the valid records.

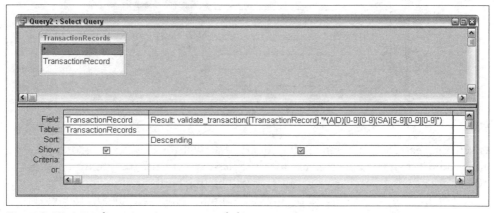

Figure 2-17. A regular expression pattern coded into a query

Figure 2-18 shows the result of running the query. The valid records are at the top.

Discussion

The pattern used for matching the transaction records look like this:

```
^(A|D)[0-9][0-9](SA)[5-9][0-9][0-9]
```

A detailed explanation of regular expression syntax is beyond the scope of this recipe, but in a nutshell, here is what the pattern calls for:

- (A|D) indicates to match an A or a D.
- [0-9] indicates to match any single numerical digit between 0 and 9 (effectively, any number).
- (SA) indicates to match SA.
- [5-9] indicates to match any numerical digit between 5 and 9. Since this is followed in the pattern by two more occurrences of [0-9] (i.e., any number), taken together, a value of 500 or greater is sought.

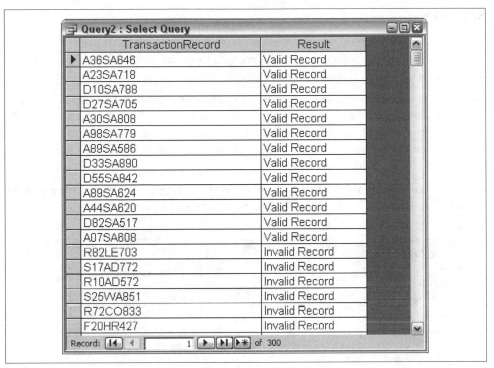

Figure 2-18. Records are validated using a regular expression

Test is just one method of the regexp object. There also are Execute and Replace methods. Execute creates a collection of matches. This is useful in code-centric applications, where further processing would take place in a routine. The Replace method replaces a match with a new string.

See Also

- Recipe 2.4
- *Mastering Regular Expressions* by Jeffrey E. F. Friedl (O'Reilly)
- *Regular Expression Pocket Reference* by Tony Stubblebine (O'Reilly)

2.6 Using a Cartesian Product to Return All Combinations of Data

Problem

I have a list of teams and a list of locations with ballparks. I wish to create a master list of all the combinations possible between these two lists.

Solution

We typically use queries to limit the amount of returned records, and at the very least, we expect the number of returned records to be no greater than the number of records in the largest table or query being addressed.

However, there is a special type of join, called a *Cartesian join*, that returns the multiplicative result of the fields in the query (otherwise known as the *Cartesian product*). A Cartesian join is the antithesis of standard joins—it works as if there is no join. Whereas the other join types link tables together on common fields, no field linking is required to return a Cartesian product.

Figure 2-19 shows a table of teams and a table of locations. Simply put, we are looking for all the combinations that can exist between these two tables.

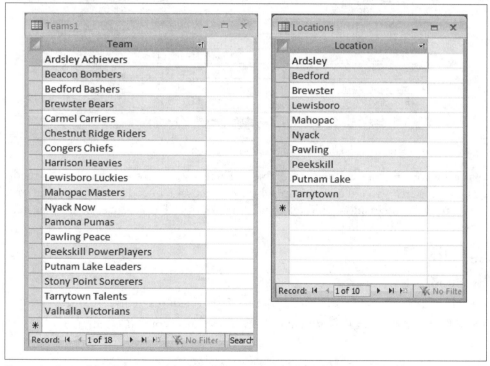

Figure 2-19. A table of teams and a table of locations

Figure 2-20 shows the design of a query that essentially has no join. There is no line connecting the tables. In fact, the single fields in each table really don't relate to each other.

The SQL generated by the design in Figure 2-20 looks like this:

```
SELECT Teams1.Team, Locations.Location
FROM Teams1, Locations;
```

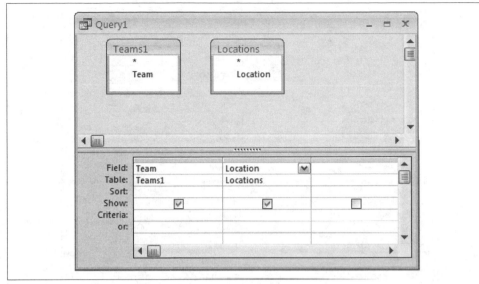

Figure 2-20. Design of a Cartesian join

Note that even in the SQL, no join is stated.

When the query is run, all possible combinations are returned. The Teams1 table has 18 records, and the Locations table has 10 records. Figure 2-21 shows the query result, which returns 180 records.

Discussion

What if, for example, you needed a master list of all possible team versus team combinations? This task is a little different, as it involves creating a Cartesian product of a single field. If you design a query with one table and just pull the field into two columns, you will not gain any new records or combinations. You need a duplicate teams table to make this work.

Copy the Teams1 table and name the copy Teams2. You now have two tables that are identical, apart from their names. When making a Cartesian query that's based on two identical fields, your aim will typically be to get all possible combinations except for an entity combined with itself. For example, there is no point in matching a team with itself—the Carmel Carriers will never play against the Carmel Carriers!

Figure 2-22 shows a design that will return all possible match combinations, except those where the teams are the same. The SQL statement for this query is:

```
SELECT Teams1.Team, Teams2.Team
FROM Teams1, Teams2
WHERE (((Teams1.Team)<>[Teams2].[Team]))
GROUP BY Teams1.Team, Teams2.Team;
```

Figure 2-21. The number of returned records equals the product of the numbers of records in the source tables

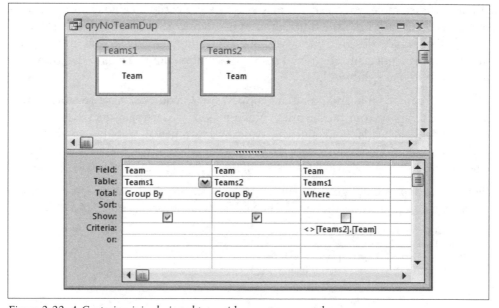

Figure 2-22. A Cartesian join designed to avoid same-name matches

Figure 2-23 shows the result of running the query. Notice that there is no record in which the Ardsley Achievers appear in both columns—this type of duplication has been avoided. To confirm this, you can check the number of returned records. There are 18 teams, and 18 multiplied by 18 is 324, yet only 306 records were returned. The 18 records that would have shown the same team name in both columns did not make it into the result.

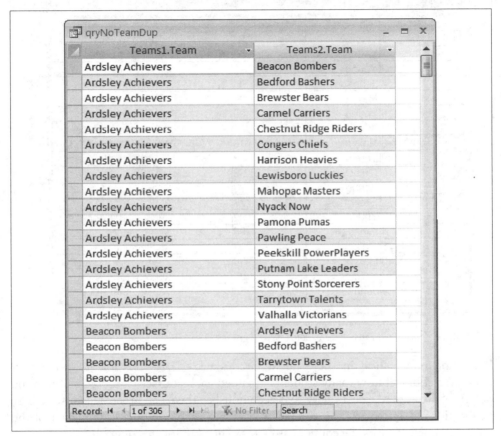

Figure 2-23. A Cartesian product without same-name matches

2.7 Creating a Crosstab Query to View Complex Information

Problem

How can I view my relational data in a hierarchical manner? I know I can use Group By clauses in a query, but with an abundance of data points, this becomes cumbersome and creates many records. Is there another way to see summaries of data based on groupings?

Solution

A crosstab query is a great alternative to a standard select that groups on a number of fields. Figure 2-24 shows the Student_Grades table, which has five fields: StudentID, Instructor, MidTerm Grade, Final Grade, and Course.

StudentID	Instructor	MidTerm Grad	Final Grade	Course
1	Quincy	94	97	Intro to VBA
2	Young	81	74	Intro to VBA
3	Young	92	78	Advanced Excel
4	Johnson	93	74	Beginner Excel
5	Maxwell	93	95	Beginner Excel
6	Young	80	91	Beginner Excel
7	Young	91	92	Advanced Excel
8	Maxwell	78	78	Beginner Access
9	Young	83	73	Advanced Access
10	Quincy	88	94	Advanced Access
11	Young	83	82	Beginner Access
12	Brown	77	95	Intro to VBA
13	Young	82	89	Beginner Access
14	Johnson	80	82	Advanced Access
15	Quincy	92	86	Beginner Excel
16	Maxwell	86	72	Advanced Excel
17	Quincy	90	96	Intro to VBA
18	Johnson	80	73	Beginner Access

Record: 1 of 300

Figure 2-24. A table with instructors, courses, and grades

Using the information in the Student_Grades table, it is possible to get a per-instructor count of how many students attended each course. Figure 2-25 shows the design of a standard select query that accomplishes this. The Group By clauses create delineations of Instructor and Course, and within each combination, a Count of the StudentID field returns the count of students. The SQL for this query is:

```
SELECT Student_Grades.Instructor,
Student_Grades.Course,
Count(Student_Grades.StudentID) AS CountOfStudentID
FROM Student_Grades
GROUP BY Student_Grades.Instructor, Student_Grades.Course;
```

Running the query in Figure 2-25 produces a result with 25 records, shown in Figure 2-26.

Now for the alternative. A crosstab query will return the same student counts, per instructor, per course; however, the layout will be smaller. The design of the crosstab query is shown in Figure 2-27. Crosstabs require a minimum of one Row Heading field, one Column Heading field, and one Value field in which the reporting is done.

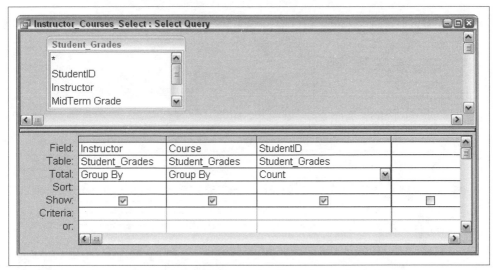

Figure 2-25. *A select query that returns the count of students per instructor, per class*

Instructor	Course	CountOfStudentID
Brown	Advanced Access	11
Brown	Advanced Excel	10
Brown	Beginner Access	6
Brown	Beginner Excel	15
Brown	Intro to VBA	13
Johnson	Advanced Access	17
Johnson	Advanced Excel	6
Johnson	Beginner Access	11
Johnson	Beginner Excel	11
Johnson	Intro to VBA	14
Maxwell	Advanced Access	9
Maxwell	Advanced Excel	17
Maxwell	Beginner Access	13
Maxwell	Beginner Excel	13
Maxwell	Intro to VBA	5
Quincy	Advanced Access	14
Quincy	Advanced Excel	10

Record: |◄| ◄ | 1 | ► | ►| | ►* of 25

Figure 2-26. *Returned student counts from a select query*

In this case, the Value field is the StudentID field, and Count is the selected aggregate function (as it was in the equivalent select query). The Instructor field is designated as a Row Heading, and the Course field is designated as the Column Heading.

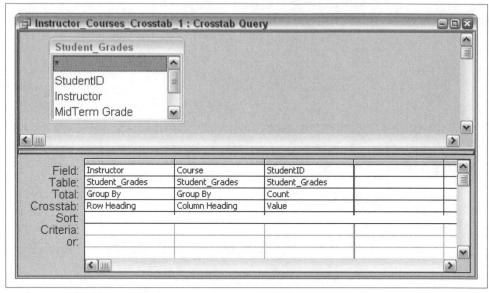

Figure 2-27. The design of the crosstab query to count student records

The SQL behind the crosstab query reads like this:

```
TRANSFORM Count(Student_Grades.StudentID) AS CountOfStudentID
SELECT Student_Grades.Instructor
FROM Student_Grades
GROUP BY Student_Grades.Instructor
PIVOT Student_Grades.Course;
```

Note the `TRANSFORM` and `PIVOT` statements. These are unique to creating a crosstab and are explained in the Discussion section. Figure 2-28 shows the result of running the query. Just five rows are returned—one for each instructor—and there is a column for each course.

Instructor	Advanced Access	Advanced Excel	Beginner Access	Beginner Excel	Intro to VBA
Brown	11	10	6	15	13
Johnson	17	6	11	11	14
Maxwell	9	17	13	13	5
Quincy	14	10	12	9	15
Young	11	15	18	15	10

Record: 1 of 5

Figure 2-28. The result of running the crosstab query

Discussion

To recap, a crosstab query requires:

- One or more Row Heading fields
- One Column Heading field
- One Value field

To create a crosstab query, select the Query → Crosstab Query menu option while in the query designer. This will cause the Crosstab row to display in the query grid. Alternatively, you can use the Crosstab Query Wizard. To launch the wizard, click the New button while the Queries tab is on top in the database window. Then, select Crosstab Query Wizard in the New Query dialog box.

 In Access 2007, click the Create tab in the Ribbon, and then click the Query Wizard.

In the SQL syntax, a TRANSFORM statement is what designates the query as a crosstab. Following directly after the TRANSFORM keyword are the aggregate function and the Value field to be used. The one or more fields following the SELECT statement are the Row Headings. The field following the PIVOT keyword is the field from which the column headings will be drawn.

The previous query produced results in which the row headings were the instructor names and the column headings were the course names (Figure 2-28). Swapping the fields in the SELECT and PIVOT sections reverses the structure of the output. In other words, using this SQL:

```
TRANSFORM Count(Student_Grades.StudentID) AS CountOfStudentID
SELECT Student_Grades.Course
FROM Student_Grades
GROUP BY Student_Grades.Course
PIVOT Student_Grades.Instructor;
```

creates the output shown in Figure 2-29. Now, the courses are listed as rows and the column headings are the instructor names. Regardless of the layout, the counts are consistent.

Sophisticated crosstabs

In the examples we've looked at so far in this recipe, after the TRANSFORM keyword, we've applied an aggregate function to a single field. A limitation of crosstab queries is that only one Value field can be evaluated; attempting to include a second aggregation would result in an error. But what if you need to process information from more than one field?

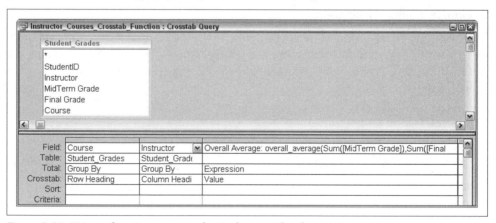

Figure 2-29. The crosstab with a different layout

While only one value can be returned for each row and column intersection, there are options for how that value is calculated. Let's say we need to find the overall average for each course—that is, the combined average of the MidTerm Grade and Final Grade fields. This will provide an overall average per course, per instructor. The catch here is that two fields contain values that need to be considered: MidTerm Grade and Final Grade.

To accomplish this task, we'll place a function call where the Value field is usually specified, and we'll select Expression in the Total row. Figure 2-30 shows the query design.

Figure 2-30. Using a function to return the single crosstab value

The full expression reads like this:

```
Overall Average: overall_average(Sum([MidTerm Grade]),
Sum([Final Grade]),Count([StudentID]))
```

The SQL statement looks like this:

```
TRANSFORM overall_average(Sum([MidTerm Grade]),
Sum([Final Grade]),Count([StudentID])) AS [Overall Average]
SELECT Student_Grades.Course
FROM Student_Grades
GROUP BY Student_Grades.Course
PIVOT Student_Grades.Instructor;
```

As the query runs, the overall_average function is called. The arguments it receives are the midterm grade, the final grade, and the count of students. Bear in mind that, one at a time, these three arguments are providing information based on a combination of instructor and course.

The overall_average function calculates the overall average by adding together the sum of each grade type (which creates a total grade), and then dividing the total by twice the student count—each student has two grades in the total, so to get the correct average, the divisor must be twice the student count. Here is the function:

```
Function overall_average(midterm_sum As Long, _
    final_sum As Long, student_count As Integer) As Single
  overall_average = (midterm_sum + final_sum) / (student_count * 2)
End Function
```

Figure 2-31 shows the result of running this crosstab. The returned values are the overall averages of the combined grades.

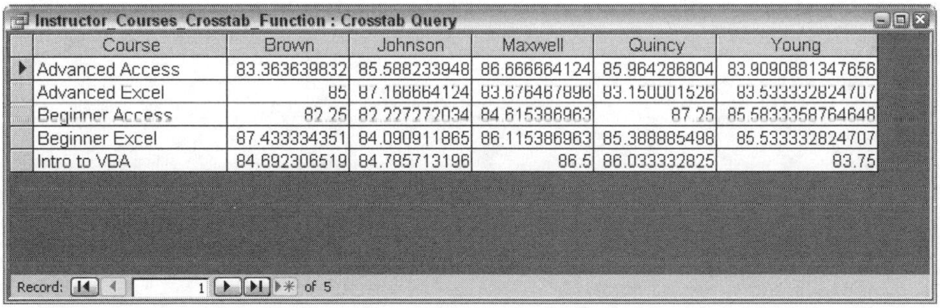

Course	Brown	Johnson	Maxwell	Quincy	Young
Advanced Access	83.363639832	85.588233948	86.666664124	85.964286804	83.9090881347656
Advanced Excel	85	87.166664124	83.6764678966	83.150001526	83.5333328247070
Beginner Access	82.25	82.227272034	84.615386963	87.25	85.5833358764648
Beginner Excel	87.433334351	84.090911865	86.115386963	85.388885498	85.533332824707
Intro to VBA	84.692306519	84.785713196	86.5	86.033332825	83.75

Instructor_Courses_Crosstab_Function : Crosstab Query

Record: 1 of 5

Figure 2-31. Result of the crosstab with a calculated value field

The returned values in Figure 2-31 are drawn out to several decimal places. Using the Round function helps pare them down. Here is the updated function, with the rounded values shown in Figure 2-32:

```
Function overall_average(midterm_sum As Long, _
    final_sum As Long, student_count As Integer) As Single
  overall_average = Round((midterm_sum + final_sum) / (student_count * 2))
End Function
```

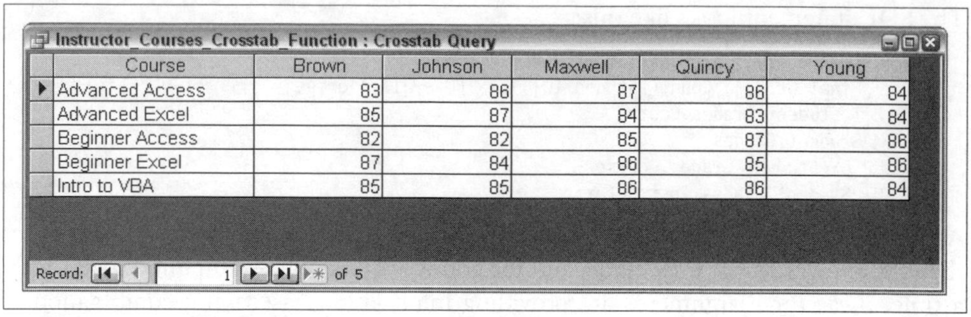

Course	Brown	Johnson	Maxwell	Quincy	Young
Advanced Access	83	86	87	86	84
Advanced Excel	85	87	84	83	84
Beginner Access	82	82	85	87	86
Beginner Excel	87	84	86	85	86
Intro to VBA	85	85	86	86	84

Figure 2-32. Rounded crosstab values

While you can only display a single value in the result, you have many options for calculating that value. The approach presented here—using a function to calculate a value it's not possible to determine with the singular aggregate functions—is a useful and flexible one.

CHAPTER 3

Action Queries

There are passive queries and there are action queries. A *passive query*, such as the standard select, pulls data into a result set, but does not alter any data (either in the source, or by virtue of persisting the returned data past the time the query has been run and left active).

Action queries, on the other hand, can alter source records and persist the returned records indefinitely. A delete query, for example, removes records from source tables—a completely destructive procedure. If the data hasn't been backed up, it's gone for good. Update queries also affect source data by changing the existing data. Again, unless the original data is backed up before the operation is carried out, it's irrecoverable.

Append and make-table queries are types of action queries that do not alter source data but do persist the returned records into permanent results. An append query places returned records into an existing table, and a make-table query places returned records into a new table. We'll explore all of these types of queries in this chapter.

3.1   Running an Update Query

Problem

I need to edit the data in my table. The State field contains two-character acronyms, but I need to change these to the full state names. How can I do this?

Solution

Update Query is one of the types you can select when designing a query. Use the Query → Update Query menu option to prepare the grid.

In Access 2007, create a blank grid using the Ribbon, and select the Update query type in the query design view of the Ribbon.

When you create an update query, an *Update To* row appears in the query grid; you'll also find that the Sort and Show rows from the standard select query are no longer present.

Figure 3-1 shows the design of an update query that will replace all occurrences of NY in the State field with New York.

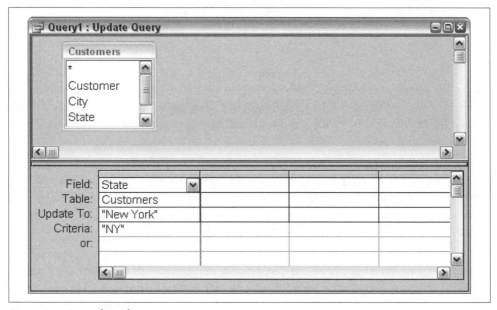

Figure 3-1. A simple update query

Note that the Criteria row holds the NY value—this is the value that already exists in the data and needs to be replaced. The value in the Update To row—New York—is the new replacement value. Using criteria here is vital, because you only want to update the records that have NY in the State field.

There is no requirement that an update query have a Where clause (which filters the records to be updated to those that match the criteria). An update query can simply update all records. At times that will be what you need, but in this example, updating all of the records would be catastrophic (remember, unless you have a backup, you can't undo the changes made by an update query).

When you run the query, a warning message like the one in Figure 3-2 will prompt you to confirm the operation. Click Yes to proceed.

This method completes an update for one state value. This is a workable solution, but running the update 50 times (once for each state) would be rather time-consuming. Fortunately, there are more efficient methods.

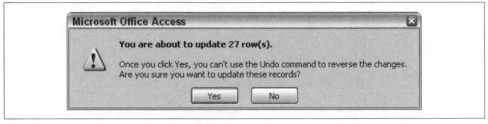

Figure 3-2. Confirmation to complete the update

One approach is to use a custom function in the query. A function that takes two-character state acronyms and returns the full state names is what's needed. Here is just such a function:

```
Function new_state_name(current_state_name As String) As String
   new_state_name = current_state_name
      If current_state_name = "NY" Then new_state_name = "New York"
      If current_state_name = "CT" Then new_state_name = "Connecticut"
      If current_state_name = "MA" Then new_state_name = "Massachusetts"
      If current_state_name = "CA" Then new_state_name = "California"
End Function
```

I've coded only a few states into this function for simplicity's sake, but you could code all 50, or just the states you need changed. Coding all 50 states this way would be tedious, but at least you would end up with a reusable function.

The function first assigns its return value to the incoming value (the current state acronym). This assures that if no match is found in the function, the original value is returned as if nothing happened. When the incoming value does match an If statement, the function's return value becomes the full state name.

Figure 3-3 shows how this query is set up in the query grid. Note that there are no criteria. All records are processed, so no criteria are set. The function call is in the Update To row, and the State field itself is sent as the function argument.

The result of running the query is shown in Figure 3-4. For states that have existing If statements in the function, the full state names are returned; for all other states, the original acronyms are left intact.

Yet another way to handle converting the acronyms to full state names is to use the built-in DLookup function. In this scenario, a table of state names is used. In the table are two fields: StateAcronym and StateName. Figure 3-5 shows the table.

The query setup is shown in Figure 3-6.

The call to the DLookup function in the Update To row reads like this:

```
DLookUp("[StateName]","States","[StateAcronym]='" & [State] & "'")
```

StateName and StateAcronym are the two fields in the States table, and State is the field in the Customers table. The States table has a record for each of the 50 states. Therefore, barring any misspellings, all the state acronyms in the Customers table will be updated to full state names when the query is run.

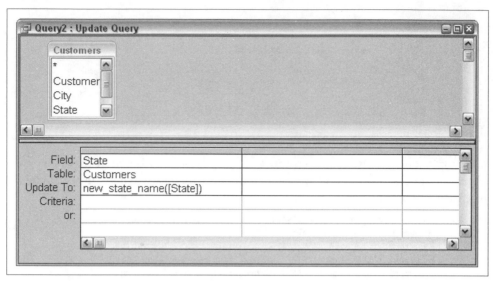

Figure 3-3. Using a custom function in an update query

Customer	City	State
Cabasos Aguilera	East Greenbush	New York
Roslyn Connolly	Santa Monica	California
Tinea Rost	Falmouth	ME
Garland Zavala	Wasilla	AK
Matt Kelley	Sandy	OR
Connie S. Brantuk	Milton	Massachusetts
Arthur Goodlock	Soquel	California
Lyndon Griffith	Port Charlotte	FL
Shawndra Braam	Folsom	California
Marie A. Antonoff	Mt Pocono	PA
Cheri S. Rubin	West Hempstead	New York
Sam Hlookoff	Cannon Falls	MN
Nicole B. Hudson	Riverdale	GA
Melissa Crossman	Arlington Hts	IL
Donald M. S. Gove	Orleans	Massachusetts
Michael A. Teitelbaum	Cresskill	NJ
Almond U. Gisewhite	Topeka	KS
Mariann Uteeson	Long Island City	New York

Record: |◄| ◄| 1 |►|►I|►*| of 300

Figure 3-4. Records are updated

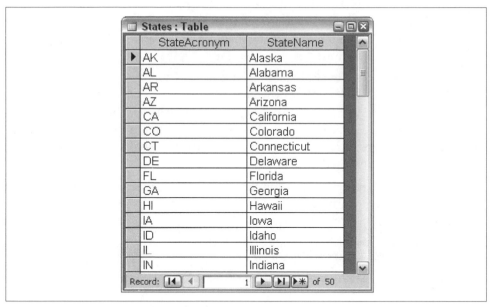

Figure 3-5. A table of state acronyms and names

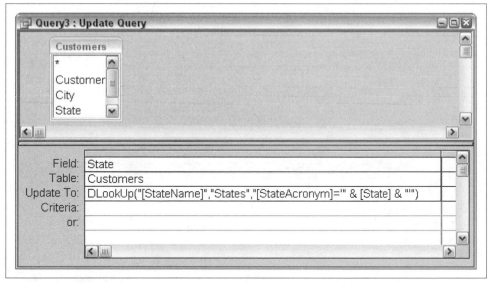

Figure 3-6. An update query uses the DLookup function

Discussion

The update queries presented so far have all addressed a single field. The SQL statement for the query in Figure 3-1 is short. Here it is:

```
UPDATE Customers SET Customers.State = "New York"
WHERE (((Customers.State)="NY"));
```

Update queries start with the UPDATE SQL keyword, followed by the name of the table and a SET clause indicating the field to be updated (more than one field can be updated, as explained below). Any criteria used to limit which records receive an update are specified in the WHERE clause.

The criteria do not have to be based on the field receiving the update. The preceding example does use criteria based on the same field, but compare that with this SQL statement:

```
UPDATE Customers SET Customers.State = "New York"
WHERE (((Customers.City)="New York City"));
```

In this example, the State field is updated to New York when the value in the City field is New York City.

Any number of fields can be updated at once, although they will all share any criteria applied in the query. Figure 3-7 shows a query design in which three fields are updated to None when a fourth field's value equals Discontinued.

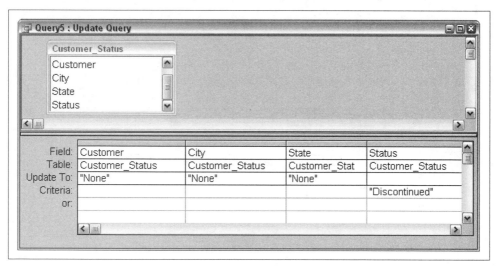

Figure 3-7. An update on multiple fields

Here's the SQL statement for the query in Figure 3-7:

```
UPDATE Customer_Status SET
Customer_Status.Customer = "None",
Customer_Status.City = "None",
Customer_Status.State = "None"
WHERE (((Customer_Status.Status)="Discontinued"));
```

In accordance with SQL syntax, the query begins with the UPDATE keyword, followed by the table name, followed by the SET clause. Then, all the fields that are being updated are listed, with each of these fields being assigned a new value. Finally, if criteria are used, the WHERE statement specifies them.

3.2 Appending Data

Problem

When I run a query that selects certain records from my data table, I need to have the returned records added to a different table.

Solution

You'll often need to archive older data, completed transactions, and the like. This is commonly done by moving the identified records into another table. This second table is typically structurally the same as the first one, so the records transfer neatly from one table to the next. However, this is not a strict requirement—the archive table may have additional fields listing information such as the date the record was written into the archive, who authorized the archive, and so on.

One of the action queries—the *append query*—is the workhorse for getting this done. An append query tacks records onto an existing table. Often, these records are drawn from a different table, but they could come from a process, or as calculated fields, or even from the same table.

 When appending records to the same table from which they are drawn, take care to avoid any key violations.

Figure 3-8 shows a table of transaction records for various clients. The records are for various dates and various amounts, and the transactions have differing statuses.

A likely task is to clear the transaction table of older, completed records. Say you have an archive table (Transactions_Archive) in which you store such records. You can easily arrange a query in the query grid that will filter out the completed records from the transaction table so that you can move them into your archive table. Figure 3-9 shows the design of an append query with criteria that look for records dated earlier than 4/1/2006 that have a status of "Paid in Full." Running this query will place the identified records into the Transactions_Archive table (this is not readily apparent in Figure 3-9, but as part of the query design, the target table was selected in the Append dialog box).

Assuming that the fields in the Transactions_Archive table are identical to those in the Transactions table, the field names in the Append To row will appear automatically, without you needing to identify them. If you're appending to a table that has different field names, you will need to match the source and destination fields.

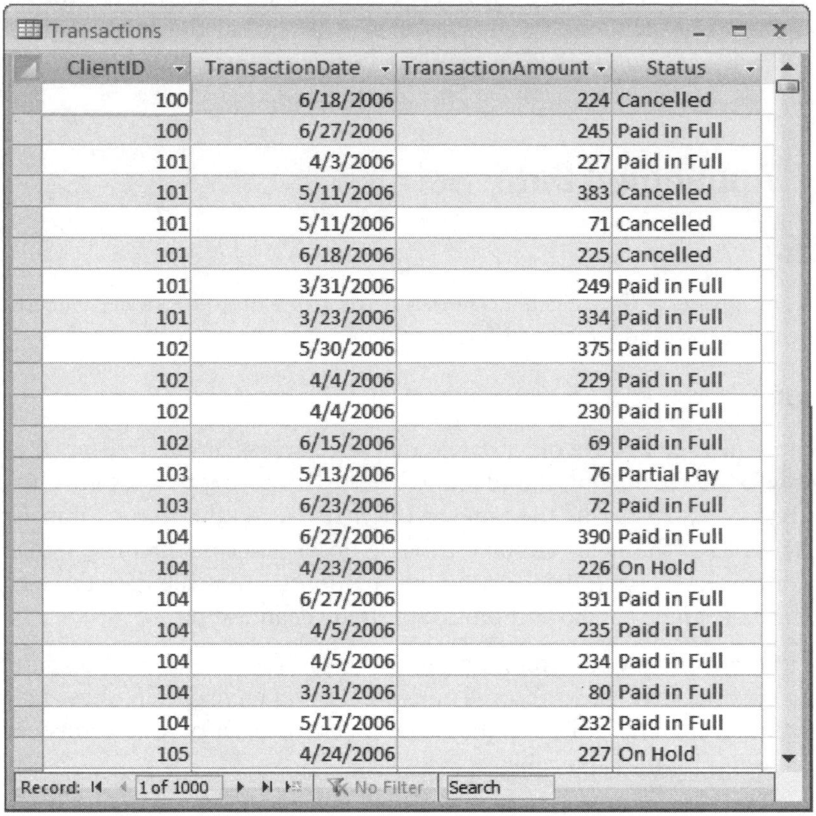

Transactions

ClientID	TransactionDate	TransactionAmount	Status
100	6/18/2006	224	Cancelled
100	6/27/2006	245	Paid in Full
101	4/3/2006	227	Paid in Full
101	5/11/2006	383	Cancelled
101	5/11/2006	71	Cancelled
101	6/18/2006	225	Cancelled
101	3/31/2006	249	Paid in Full
101	3/23/2006	334	Paid in Full
102	5/30/2006	375	Paid in Full
102	4/4/2006	229	Paid in Full
102	4/4/2006	230	Paid in Full
102	6/15/2006	69	Paid in Full
103	5/13/2006	76	Partial Pay
103	6/23/2006	72	Paid in Full
104	6/27/2006	390	Paid in Full
104	4/23/2006	226	On Hold
104	6/27/2006	391	Paid in Full
104	4/5/2006	235	Paid in Full
104	4/5/2006	234	Paid in Full
104	3/31/2006	80	Paid in Full
104	5/17/2006	232	Paid in Full
105	4/24/2006	227	On Hold

Record: 1 of 1000 No Filter Search

Figure 3-8. A table of transaction records

The SQL statement of the query in Figure 3-9 looks like this:

```
INSERT INTO Transactions_Archive
( ClientID, TransactionDate, TransactionAmount, Status )
SELECT Transactions.ClientID,
Transactions.TransactionDate, Transactions.TransactionAmount,
Transactions.Status
FROM Transactions
WHERE (((Transactions.TransactionDate)<#4/1/2006#)
AND ((Transactions.Status)="Paid in Full"));
```

Append queries begin with the unique Insert Into SQL lingo, followed by the destination table name and the field names from the destination table, in parentheses. Then a SELECT statement gets the records from the source table (here, Transactions), filtered according to the criteria. Note that the number of fields designated in the source must match the number of fields designated in the target. However, not all the fields from the source table have to be used.

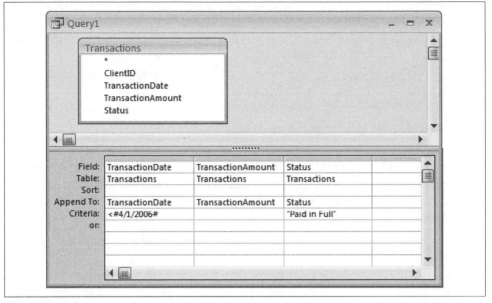

Figure 3-9. An append query

When this query is run, the records are added to the Transactions_Archive table. But that's just half the story—the records have been copied into the archive table, but they still exist in the source table. A separate delete query must be used to delete them. Delete queries are discussed in Recipe 3.3.

Discussion

The solution just described illustrates how append queries are typically put to use: a subquery gathers records, filtered or not, from the source table, and these records are placed in the destination table.

Now, let's look at another insertion method. You can insert actual values instead of using fields as the source of values. The following SQL statement again targets the Transactions_Archive table, but this time actual hardcoded values are inserted. The Values clause contains those values, within a set of parentheses:

```
Insert Into Transactions_Archive
Values (2000, #4/10/2006#, 35.25, 'Paid in Full')
```

There are a couple of key points to mention here:

- `Insert Into <table name>` is the correct way to begin the SQL statement.
- The `Values` keyword contains hardcoded values. Each value must be treated in a specific way, according to the data type of the field into which it is being inserted. Numeric values need no qualifiers; they can just be entered as integers, real numbers, etc. (e.g., 2000 or 35.25). Dates must be enclosed in pound signs (#), and text must be enclosed in quotation marks (single or double will work).

The four source values in the previous example match the order and data types of the four fields in the destination table, so it was not necessary to list the table fields. However, doing so would not cause any errors, and, because it's clearer, might even be preferable. Here is the SQL for this case:

```
Insert Into Transactions_Archive
(ClientID, TransactionDate, TransactionAmount, Status)
Values (2000, #4/10/2006#, 35.25, 'Paid in Full')
```

This works exactly the same as the last SQL statement.

Indicating the field names of the destination table is required when the values are not in the correct order, or when some fields are skipped. For example, a new record to be inserted may only have values in the ClientID and TransactionAmount fields; the other fields' values may not yet be known, so they are skipped. The SQL in this situation might look like this:

```
Insert Into Transactions_Archive(ClientID, TransactionAmount)
Values (2000, 35.25)
```

In this case, only two destination fields receive values. This is perfectly valid, and provided the fields that are not filled in can accept null or zero-length values, the insert will complete.

Appending from a recordset

The Insert Into statement is often used as part of VBA/ADO processing. As a recordset is looped through, a table is populated. This code illustrates:

```
Sub append_routine()
  Dim conn As ADODB.Connection
  Set conn = CurrentProject.Connection
  Dim rs_transactions As New ADODB.Recordset
  Dim ssql As String
  'get all records from Transactions
  ssql = "Select * From Transactions"
  rs_transactions.Open ssql, conn, adOpenKeyset, adLockOptimistic
  Do Until rs_transactions.EOF
    'If the transaction date is April 1, then
    'insert into archive table with 0 amount
    If rs_transactions.Fields("TransactionDate") = #4/1/2006# Then
      ssql = "Insert Into Transactions_Archive Values ("
      ssql = ssql & rs_transactions.Fields("ClientID") & ", "
      ssql = ssql & "#" & _
          rs_transactions.Fields("TransactionDate") & "#, "
      ssql = ssql & 0 & ", "
      ssql = ssql & "'April''s Fools Day Free Giveaway')"
      conn.Execute ssql
    End If
  rs_transactions.MoveNext
  Loop
  'delete from transactions all 4/1/2006 records
  ssql = "Delete * From Transactions Where "
```

```
    ssql = ssql & " Transactions.TransactionDate=#4/1/2006#"
    conn.Execute ssql
    rs_transactions.Close
    Set rs_transactions = Nothing
    conn.Close
    MsgBox "done"
End Sub
```

In this code example, a recordset (rs_transactions) contains all the records from the Transactions table. As the recordset is looped through, the TransactionDate field is tested to see if its value is 4/1/2006. If it is, an Insert Into SQL statement is assembled. For example:

```
Insert Into Transactions_Archive Values
(106, #4/1/2006#, 0, 'April''s Fools Day Free Giveaway')
```

 A few sharp eyes, I'm sure, will have noticed the two sequential single quotation marks in April''s. This prevents the error that would otherwise occur when you attempt to insert a text value containing an apostrophe.

This statement copies all April 1 records to the archive table, and, in the process, gives each of them a zero transaction amount. After the recordset is finished looping, a delete query is run to delete all the April 1, 2006 records from the Transactions table. Here is the snippet of code that handles the delete:

```
'delete from transactions all 4/1/2006 records
ssql = "Delete * From Transactions Where "
ssql = ssql & " Transactions.TransactionDate=#4/1/2006#"
conn.Execute ssql
```

Using VBA code to run through a set of data and make decisions on how to append the data to another table is great when the conditions become complex. For example, what if the rules were to reduce the balance to 0, but only for certain clients, for transactions made on specific dates, and, further, only if the client's overall balance is less than 100, and the last order was placed sometime in the past 30 days?

That type of filtering gets tricky with just the query grid, so knowing how to assemble SQL weaved within lines of conditional testing done with VBA is an excellent skill to have in your proverbial programmer's toolbox.

3.3   Deleting Data

Problem

I have to delete some data from a table. The records that need to be deleted should match my specified criteria, and the other records must be left intact. What is a safe way to do this?

Solution

A *delete query* will delete from a table records that match the specified criteria. If no criteria are used, certainly precaution should prevail. A delete query with no filtering will completely empty out a table.

 A delete query deletes data, but leaves the table intact. The table itself is not deleted.

To delete just some data from a table, design a delete query that filters to records that should be deleted. Figure 3-10 shows a delete query that will delete records in which the state is CA (California). This means only those records that have CA in the State field will be deleted; other records will be left intact. Bear in mind that even though only a single field is placed in the query grid in Figure 3-10, running the query won't just delete any matching values found in that field—any matching records will be deleted completely. It is not necessary to place all the fields in the query grid; just place the ones in which criteria will be applied. When using a query to delete all records (no criteria), you can drag the table asterisk to the grid. The asterisk means all fields.

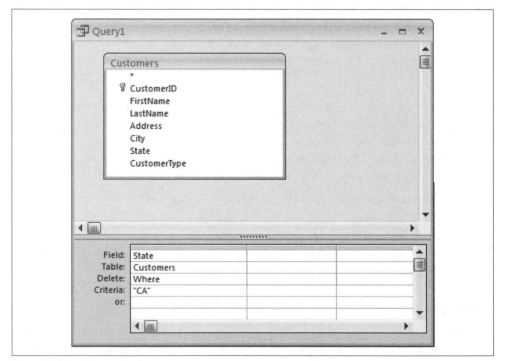

Figure 3-10. A delete query with criteria

When designing a query, use the Query → Delete Query menu option to have the query act as a delete query. In Access 2007, use the appropriate buttons on the Ribbon. The SQL for the query in Figure 3-10 is this:

```
DELETE Customers.State
FROM Customers
WHERE (((Customers.State)="CA"));
```

This is a fairly straightforward SQL. It's quite similar to that of a select query, other than the fact this query begins with the DELETE keyword. An interesting twist, though, is that the message implied in the above SQL is not quite accurate. As explained earlier, the action deletes entire records, not just values in the State field. A better structure of the syntax would be:

```
DELETE Customers.*
FROM Customers
WHERE (((Customers.State)-"CA"));
```

The difference is using an asterisk to indicate all fields instead of using the entered name of a single field. Sometimes the way Access writes out SQL that is defined in the grid is not the best representation of the intended action. It works, but it can be confusing.

Discussion

When deleting records from a table that participates in a relationship, further consideration and steps come into play. Because a parent and child table are related (a one-to-many relationship), it would be a violation of referential integrity to delete records in the parent table that would leave "orphans" in the child table.

Access provides a facility to take care of this dilemma for you, but it's important to understand the issue. Let's consider an example. Figure 3-11 shows an established relationship between a Customers table and a Transactions table. Note that the Enforce Referential Integrity option is checked in the Edit Relationships dialog (displayed by double-clicking on the line connecting the tables, or selecting the Tools → Edit Relationships menu option). This means records in the Transactions table must match records in the Customers table. Specifically, each record in the Transactions table must contain in its CustomerID field a value that matches the value in the CustomerID field of a record in the Customers table.

Each record in the Customers table must have a unique value in the CustomerID field. Therefore, the number of records in the Customers table is the same as the number of unique CustomerIDs. This is how the Customers table plays the role of the "one" or parent table in the relationship.

In contrast, the CustomerID field in the Transactions table does not have to contain unique values. You will likely find that many of the customers (records in the Customers table) will have several matching child records (records in the Transactions table)—a successful business is sure to have loyal customers that are repeat buyers.

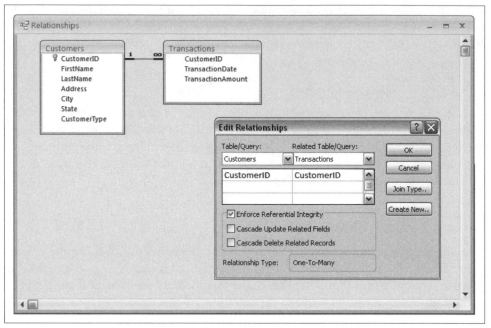

Figure 3-11. Reviewing the relationship between two tables

Again, the only requirement for records in the Transactions table is that the value in the CustomerID field must match a value in the same field in the Customers table.

Now, suppose you want to delete a customer from the Customers table. Because referential integrity is on, but cascading deletes are not enabled (see Figure 3-11), if the customer record has any matching transaction records, Access will prevent you from simply deleting the customer. Referential integrity will not allow an action to create orphan records. Customers are not required to have transaction records, so the deletion of a customer with no related transaction records is allowed, but if there are any related transaction records, the customer cannot be deleted.

If the customer has related transactions, you must first delete those transaction records before you can delete the customer record. There is no restriction on deleting transaction records because you cannot create an orphan customer. Orphan records can exist only in the child or "many" table.

So, how do you delete all of a customer's transactions? The delete query in Figure 3-12 will delete records in the Transactions table for the customer named April Kramer. April Kramer has a CustomerID, which the query uses to identify the correct records to delete. Note that the first two columns have Where in the Delete row—these are the criteria. The third column identifies the table from which the records will be deleted (Transactions); it has From in the Delete row.

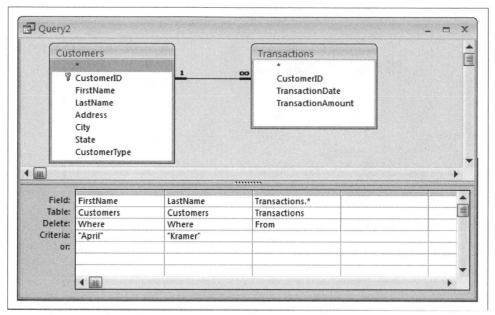

Figure 3-12. Deleting records from one table based on criteria in another table

The Access-generated SQL for the query in Figure 3-12 is as follows:

```
DELETE Customers.FirstName, Customers.LastName, Transactions.*
FROM Customers INNER JOIN Transactions ON
Customers.CustomerID = Transactions.CustomerID
WHERE (((Customers.FirstName)="April") AND
((Customers.LastName)="Kramer"));
```

This is confusing because the field names from the Customers table (FirstName and LastName) appear after the DELETE keyword. Based on this, one might conclude that the record from the Customers table will be deleted. However, that is not the case. The child transaction records are deleted, but the customer record remains. The customer record is then deleted in a second query, as shown in Figure 3-13.

 Deleting the April Kramer customer record in this manner is problematic, because there could be more than one April Kramer. The use of the name serves the point of the recipe, but in practice, CustomerID is the only field in which a guarantee exists that you'll delete the intended target customer.

You only have to take the step of deleting the child records first if cascading deletes are not enabled (i.e., if the Cascade Delete Related Records option is not checked in the Edit Relationships dialog). When this option is selected, deleting records from a parent table automatically deletes related records in child tables. In this case, simply deleting April Kramer from the Customers table will cause her transaction records to be removed as well without any further effort.

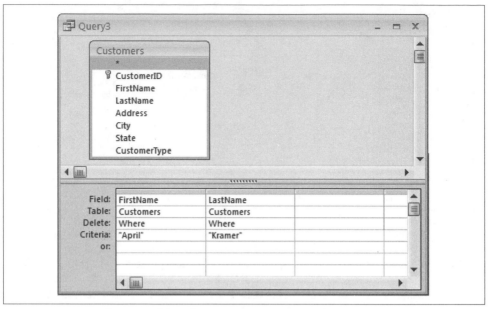

Figure 3-13. A second query to delete the customer

This is a real time-saver, but it comes with a price. Cascading deletes make it easy to delete a lot of valuable data. If you're going to enable this option, be sure to archive your old data frequently. Deletes are final, and unless you've copied your records to archive tables, you'll have no way to undo these operations. Without some backup facility in place, the dangers of using cascading deletes may outweigh any time-savings. Be sure to consider this option carefully before using it.

3.4   Creating Tables with Make-Table Queries

Problem

How do you create a new table to hold the records returned from a select query?

Solution

When you query records from an existing table or tables, you may want to place the returned records into a new table. This is accomplished with a *make-table query*.

If data already exists in tables, why bother making new tables holding the same data? Here are a couple of reasons:

- To combine related, nonhierarchical data into a single table.
- To segregate a larger table of data into a number of smaller tables. The segregation is typically based on values in one or more key fields.

To illustrate the first example, Figure 3-14 shows two tables that are essentially related—they share a common EmployeeID field. However, there is no one-to-many relationship. Each table contains a single record per employee. Keeping the employee names in one table, and the hire date/department information in another table, might have some business relevance, but it serves no particular design purpose. Combining this data into a single table has merit. The combined table will have one EmployeeID field and three data fields.

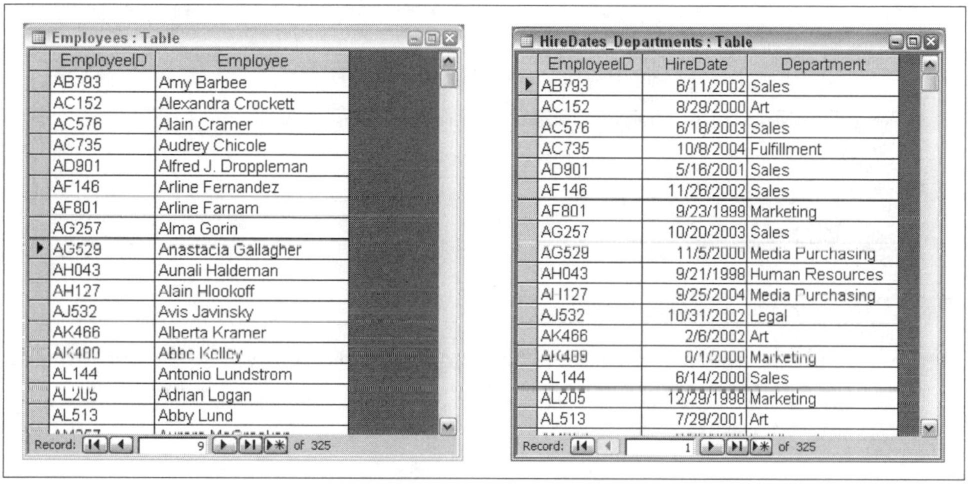

Figure 3-14. Two tables with one-to-one data

To produce the combined table, place the two existing tables into an Access query design, and place all the fields in the grid (including only one instance of the EmployeeID field). Designate the query as a make-table query by using the Query → Make-Table Query menu option. (In Access 2007, use the buttons on the Ribbon.) When you specify this type of query, the Make Table dialog box appears. In this dialog, you can either enter the name of a new table, or select an existing one from the drop-down list.

Figure 3-15 shows a query that returns records from the two tables and combines them into a new table named EmployeeFullHireData.

The SQL statement looks like this:

```
SELECT Employees.EmployeeID, Employees.Employee,
HireDates_Departments.HireDate,
HireDates_Departments.Department INTO EmployeeFullHireData
FROM Employees INNER JOIN HireDates_Departments ON
Employees.EmployeeID = HireDates_Departments.EmployeeID;
```

Note that the key part of the SQL when a table is created is SELECT *fields* INTO *newTableName*, followed by the FROM clause, and any joins and/or criteria.

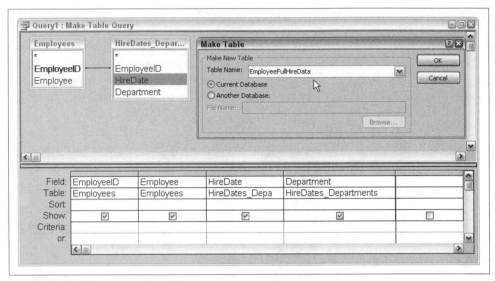

Figure 3-15. Designing a make-table query

Figure 3-16 shows the result of running the make-table query. All the information now sits together in one table. No data relationships are lost; each employee's name, hire date, and department are listed.

EmployeeID	Employee	HireDate	Department
AB793	Amy Barbee	6/11/2002	Sales
AC152	Alexandra Crockett	8/29/2000	Art
AC576	Alain Cramer	6/18/2003	Sales
AC735	Audrey Chicole	10/8/2004	Fulfillment
AD901	Alfred J. Dropplemar	5/16/2001	Sales
AF146	Arline Fernandez	11/26/2002	Sales
AF801	Arline Farnam	9/23/1999	Marketing
AG257	Alma Gorin	10/20/2003	Sales
AG529	Anastacia Gallagher	11/5/2000	Media Purchasing
AH043	Aunali Haldeman	9/21/1998	Human Resources
AH127	Alain Hlookoff	9/25/2004	Media Purchasing
AJ532	Avis Javinsky	10/31/2002	Legal
AK466	Alberta Kramer	2/6/2002	Art
AK489	Abbe Kelley	6/1/2000	Marketing
AL144	Antonio Lundstrom	6/14/2000	Sales
AL205	Adrian Logan	12/29/1998	Marketing
AL513	Abby Lund	7/29/2001	Art

Record: 1 of 325

Figure 3-16. A combined table created with a make-table query

As stated earlier, another use for a make-table query is to segregate a large table of data into smaller sets of data. An example of this would be to separate out the records from the table in Figure 3-16 by department. For example, from this table, you could create a table of just Sales employees; here is the SQL statement:

```
SELECT EmployeeFullHireData.EmployeeID,
EmployeeFullHireData.Employee,
EmployeeFullHireData.HireDate,
EmployeeFullHireData.Department
INTO SalesDepartmentStaff
FROM EmployeeFullHireData
WHERE (((EmployeeFullHireData.Department)="Sales"));
```

Keep in mind that creating the new table containing the Sales department employee records does not delete these records from the original table. A separate delete query would take care of that.

Discussion

You can use a make-table query to overwrite an existing table. When an existing table name is placed after the INTO keyword, the structure of the existing table and its data are completely overwritten by whatever field structure is provided by the make-table query. The table name remains the same, but the before and after states of the table are not required to be similar in any way.

Another way to use a make-table query is to use temporary fields in the SQL syntax. This creates a new table with a single record. The fields and the data are specified in the SQL. Here is an example:

```
Select 123 as myValue, 'Ken' as myName into myNewTable
```

Running this simple SQL statement creates a new myNewTable table with a single record. It has two fields: the myValue field contains the value 123, and the myName field contains Ken. Notice there are no From or Where sections in the SQL, since no source table is addressed.

Managing Tables, Fields, Indexes, and Queries

We use tables to store data, indexes to organize and order data, and queries to work with data. In a perfect world, when a database goes into production, our development effort is finished.

Alas, this is not a typical scenario. New requirements come along. Table structures have to be changed. New indexes are needed. New queries are called for to match the new schema. The recipes in this chapter address how to manage these things programmatically. If you have done much work with Access, you know how tedious it can be to manually create tables. Often, you have no choice but to manually create database objects, but when you're faced with having to create a number of tables or queries that are similar, having a way to automate their creation is a boon. Knowing how to programmatically add and delete fields—and create and use indexes—can also save you a lot of time.

4.1 Creating Tables Programmatically

Problem

Creating tables manually on the Tables tab of the database window is a tedious process, especially when you're designing several tables. What are the programmatic alternatives?

Solution

There are four good programmatic methods for creating tables: DAO, ADOX, SQL, and XML/XSD. Other methods do exist, such as getting a table definition from a web service, but the four options just mentioned are the most common.

This recipe will demonstrate how to use each of these methods to create a table with the following properties and fields:

- The table name is Sales.
- There is a SalesID field, which is an AutoNumber field, and serves as the primary key.
- There is a SalesPerson field, which is a Text data type.
- There is a SalesDate field, which is a Date data type.
- There is a SalesAmount field, which is a Single data type (numeric with a decimal portion).

Using DAO to create a table

Data Access Objects (DAO) is a mature standard that has been around through many previous versions of Access. In Access 2003, DAO is still alive and kicking and enjoys a dedicated reference, i.e., you don't have to go out of your way to reference the library.

 If you are not using Access 2003, you may have to set the DAO reference. To learn how to do so, read the next section, which explains how to set the reference for ADOX. The instructions are the same for DAO, except that you'll need to check the box for Microsoft DAO 3.6 Object Library in the reference list (your version number may be different, but that's fine).

The following code uses DAO to create the Sales table:

```
Sub make_DAO_table( )
  Dim tbl As DAO.TableDef
  Dim fld As DAO.Field
  Dim ndx As DAO.Index
  Set tbl = New TableDef
  With tbl
    .Name = "Sales"
    Set fld = .CreateField("SalesID", dbLong)
    fld.Attributes = dbAutoIncrField
    .Fields.Append fld
    .Fields.Append .CreateField("SalesPerson", dbText)
    .Fields.Append .CreateField("SalesDate", dbDate)
    .Fields.Append .CreateField("SalesAmount", dbSingle)
    Set ndx = .CreateIndex("PrimaryKey")
    With ndx
      .Fields.Append .CreateField("SalesID")
      .Primary = True
    End With
    .Indexes.Append ndx
  End With
  CurrentDb.TableDefs.Append tbl
  MsgBox "done"
End Sub
```

Using ADOX to create a table

ADOX is an extension of ActiveX Data Objects (ADO). You'll need to add a reference to ADOX manually if you want to use this method of creating tables. In a code module, use the Tools → References menu option to display the References dialog box, shown in Figure 4-1. Scroll through the list and find "Microsoft ADO Ext. 2.7 for DDL and Security." (Your version number may be different; that's fine.) Check the reference, and click the OK button.

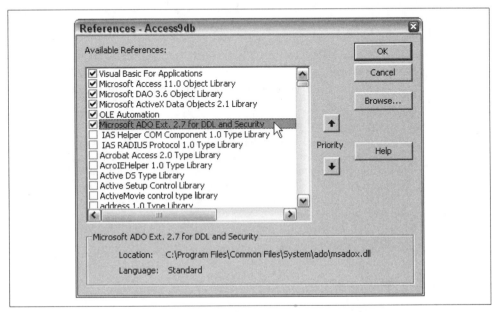

Figure 4-1. Setting a reference to ADOX

The following code uses ADOX to create the Sales table:

```
Sub make_ADOX_table( )
  'must set reference to
  'Microsoft ADO Ext. 2.7 for DDL and Security
  Dim cat As New ADOX.Catalog
  Dim tbl As New ADOX.Table
  Dim col As New ADOX.Column
  cat.ActiveConnection = CurrentProject.Connection
  With col
    Set .ParentCatalog = cat
    .Name = "SalesID"
    .Type = adInteger
    .Properties("Autoincrement") = True
  End With
  With tbl
    .Name = "Sales"
    .Columns.Append col
    .Columns.Append "SalesPerson", adVarWChar, 100
```

```
      .Columns.Append "SalesDate", adDate
      .Columns.Append "SalesAmount", adSingle
      .Keys.Append "PrimaryKey", adKeyPrimary, "SalesID"
   End With
   cat.Tables.Append tbl
   Set cat = Nothing
   Set col = Nothing
   MsgBox "done"
End Sub
```

Using SQL to create a table

Structured Query Language (SQL) contains a subset of statements collectively known as Data Definition Language (DDL).

Don't confuse DDL with DLL (Dynamic Link Library). DDL manages database objects. A DLL is a compiled procedure library.

SQL is the standard for querying and manipulating data. However, the DDL statements are used to manipulate database structures. The following SQL does just that, using the Create Table construct:

```
Sub make_SQL_table()
   Dim conn As ADODB.Connection
   Set conn = CurrentProject.Connection
   Dim ssql As String
   ssql - "Create Table Sales (" & _
   "[SalesID] AutoIncrement PRIMARY KEY, " & _
   "[SalesPerson] Text (50), " & _
   "[SalesDate] DateTime, " & _
   "[SalesAmount] Real)"
   conn.Execute ssql
   MsgBox "done"
End Sub
```

Note that ADO is used to execute the SQL statement. This has no bearing on the previous ADOX example. You may need to set a reference to the ADO library; to do this, follow the instructions in the preceding section for referencing ADOX. The ADO library is named Microsoft ActiveX Data Objects 2.1 Library (your version number may be different).

Using an XSD schema definition to create a table

An eXtensible Markup Language (XML) schema holds the definition of a data structure. Schema files have the .xsd (XML Schema Definition) file extension.

The following code deviates a bit from the previous examples. The small subroutine calls the built-in ImportXML Access method, which imports an external schema file:

```
Sub make_schema_table()
   Application.ImportXML _
```

```
        Application.CurrentProject.Path & "\sales.xsd", acStructureOnly
    MsgBox "done"
    End Sub
```

Access creates the Sales tables based on the instructions in the schema file, presented in Example 4-1.

Example 4-1. A schema file containing the definition for a table

```
<?xml version="1.0" encoding="UTF-8"?>
<xsd:schema xmlns:xsd="http://www.w3.org/2001/XMLSchema"
  xmlns:od="urn:schemas-microsoft-com:officedata">
<xsd:element name="dataroot">
<xsd:complexType>
<xsd:sequence>
<xsd:element ref="Sales" minOccurs="0" maxOccurs="unbounded"/>
</xsd:sequence>
<xsd:attribute name="generated" type="xsd:dateTime"/>
</xsd:complexType>
</xsd:element>
<xsd:element name="Sales">
<xsd:annotation>
<xsd:appinfo>
<od:index index-name="PrimaryKey" index-key="SalesID "
  primary="yes" unique="yes" clustered="no"/>
</xsd:appinfo>
</xsd:annotation>
<xsd:complexType>
<xsd:sequence>
<xsd:element name="SalesID" minOccurs="1" od:jetType="autonumber"
  od:sqlSType="int" od:autoUnique="yes" od:nonNullable="yes" type="xsd:int"/>
<xsd:element name="SalesPerson" minOccurs="0"
  od:jetType="text" od:sqlSType="nvarchar">
<xsd:simpleType>
<xsd:restriction base="xsd:string">
<xsd:maxLength value="255"/>
</xsd:restriction>
</xsd:simpleType>
</xsd:element>
<xsd:element name="SalesDate" minOccurs="0"
  od:jetType="datetime" od:sqlSType="datetime" type="xsd:dateTime"/>
<xsd:element name="SalesAmount" minOccurs="0"
  od:jetType="single" od:sqlSType="real" type="xsd:float"/>
</xsd:sequence>
</xsd:complexType>
</xsd:element>
</xsd:schema>
```

To create this schema file, create the Sales table using one of the previously described methods (or manually, for that matter), and export the table as XML. When doing so, select the option to export the schema, as shown in Figure 4-2.

Figure 4-2. Selecting to export the table design as a schema

Discussion

The methods just discussed illustrate four different approaches to creating the Sales table with the four required fields. The first field, SalesID, is created as an AutoNumber field, and is the primary key. One of the key differences between the DAO, ADOX, and SQL approaches is how this is handled. The DAO method creates SalesID as a Long data type, and then, to make it an AutoNumber field, sets the field's attribute to autoincrement:

```
.Name = "Sales"
Set fld = .CreateField("SalesID", dbLong)
fld.Attributes = dbAutoIncrField
.Fields.Append fld
```

AutoNumber fields are always Long, but with the functionality to increment the value as each new record is placed in the table.

Later in the DAO code example, an index is created and applied to the SalesID field, and the `Primary` property is set to `True`:

```
Set ndx = .CreateIndex("PrimaryKey")
With ndx
  .Fields.Append .CreateField("SalesID")
  .Primary = True
End With
.Indexes.Append ndx
```

In the ADOX example, the data type for SalesID is set to Integer. In ADO, the Integer type is the same as the Long type in Access. (The ADO SmallInt type is the equivalent of the Integer type in Access.) The `Autoincrement` property is then set to True. The result is the creation of an AutoNumber type for the SalesID field:

```
With col
  Set .ParentCatalog = cat
  .Name = "SalesID"
  .Type = adInteger
  .Properties("Autoincrement") = True
End With
```

The SalesID field is then set to be the primary key by using the Keys.Append method, and specifying the the name of the index, the type of key, and the name of the field. The type of key can be adKeyPrimary for a primary key, adKeyUnique for a unique key, and adKeyForeign for foreign keys. Note that when appending a foreign key, you will also have to specify the name of the table and column:

```
.Keys.Append "PrimaryKey", adKeyPrimary, "SalesID"
```

The SQL example is simpler. The single line that specifies the SalesID field includes the parameters that make it both the primary key and an AutoNumber field:

```
[SalesID] AutoIncrement PRIMARY KEY
```

Testing for the table's existence

It's a good idea to check whether a table exists before you try to create it. An efficient way of doing this is to wrap the table-creation routine inside a call to a function that tests all the existing tables to see if one has the name you are going to use for the new table. Here is a revision of the routine that uses SQL to create a table. The routine now includes a call to the DoesTableExist function, which is listed under the SQL routine in Example 4-2. The table name (Sales) is passed to the function. If the function does not find a Sales table, the table is created; otherwise, a message appears indicating that the table already exists.

Example 4-2. Testing to see whether a table exists before creating it

```
Sub make_SQL_table()
  If DoesTableExist("Sales") = False Then
    Dim conn As ADODB.Connection
    Set conn = CurrentProject.Connection
    Dim ssql As String
    ssql = "Create Table Sales (" & _
    "[SalesID] AutoIncrement PRIMARY KEY, " & _
    "[SalesPerson] Text (50), " & _
    "[SalesDate] DateTime, " & _
    "[SalesAmount] Real)"
    conn.Execute ssql
    MsgBox "done"
  Else
    MsgBox "Sales table already exists"
  End If
End Sub

Function DoesTableExist(table_name As String) As Boolean
  Dim db As Database
  Dim tbl As TableDef
  Set db = CurrentDb()
  DoesTableExist = False
  For Each tbl In db.TableDefs
    If tbl.Name = table_name Then DoesTableExist = True
  Next tbl
End Function
```

Which method should you use?

There is no definitive answer. If you're already comfortable with one of the methods, stick to it. Your application may call for table creation, but chances are you won't have to make a huge number of tables that often. Performance (speed) is therefore not likely to be a big issue, and all of these methods will leave manual table creation in the dust. On the other hand, if you don't need to create multiple tables, there isn't much sense in automating table creation.

Let's put automated multiple table creation to the test. Example 4-3 contains two routines: the make_a_bunch_of_tables routine repeatedly calls the make_a_table routine, each time passing a table name and a set of field names. This quickly makes a number of tables.

Example 4-3. Automated multiple table creation

```
Sub make_a_bunch_of_tables()
  make_a_table "Cars", "CarID", "CarType", "PurchaseDate", "Amount"
  make_a_table "Tools", "ToolID", "ToolType", "PurchaseDate", "Amount"
  make_a_table "Hats", "HatID", "HatType", "PurchaseDate", "Amount"
  MsgBox "All Tables Made"
End Sub

Sub make_a_table(Table As String, F1 As String, _
    F2 As String, F3 As String, F4 As String)
  Dim conn As ADODB.Connection
  Set conn = CurrentProject.Connection
  Dim ssql As String
  ssql = "Create Table " & Table & "(" & _
  "[" & F1 & "] AutoIncrement PRIMARY KEY, " & _
  "[" & F2 & "] Text (50), " &
  "[" & F3 & "] DateTime, " & _
  "[" & F4 & "] Real)"
  conn.Execute ssql
  conn.Close
End Sub
```

The routines in Example 4-3 create three tables in an instant. The tables (Cars, Tools, and Hats) are structured the same, so only the table name and field names are passed to the make_a_table routine. However, if desired, you can add more arguments (for example, to accept data types and other properties). This gives you a lot of control over the automated table-creation process.

4.2   Altering the Structure of a Table

Problem

How can I programmatically change the structure of an existing table? How do I add fields, drop fields, or just change the data types for existing fields?

Solution

You can carry out all of these tasks manually, in the design of a table, or program-matically, using DAO, ADOX, or SQL. Either way, each of these actions comes with some considerations:

Adding new fields

> The only restriction is that you cannot add an AutoNumber field to a table that already has such a field. Only one AutoNumber field is allowed per table.

> If you add an AutoNumber field to a table that does not already have one, the existing records will be filled in with the sequential numbering scheme in the new field. This is helpful.

Deleting fields

> Aside from any issues involved in deleting data from a table that participates in a relationship, the obvious caution to heed is that you will permanently lose the data in the deleted fields.

Changing a field type

> The success of this action depends on the actual data types in question. For example, an alphanumeric value that contains letters will not convert to a num-ber type. You can convert a Text type to a numeric type, but you will lose your data in the process.

> Also, you can't change a field to an AutoNumber type if there are any records in the table. The only way to get an AutoNumber field into a table with existing records is to add it as a new field. Then, if it makes sense, you can delete the field it was meant to replace.

Programmatically adding and deleting a field

Example 4-4 shows how to add and delete a field using DAO, ADOX, and SQL. There is a separate routine for each method that adds a Comments field to the Sales table and then deletes it. The Comments field is a Text data type, and is set at a size of 100 characters.

Example 4-4. Three methods to add and delete fields

```
Sub field_DAO( )
  Dim db As DAO.Database
  Dim tbl As DAO.TableDef
  Dim fld As DAO.Field
  Set db = CurrentDb
  Set tbl = db.TableDefs("Sales")
  With tbl
    'add new field
    .Fields.Append .CreateField("Comments", dbText, 100)
    'delete field
    .Fields.Delete ("Comments")
  End With
```

Example 4-4. Three methods to add and delete fields (continued)

```
  MsgBox "done"
End Sub

Sub field_ADOX()
  'must set reference to
  'Microsoft ADO Ext. 2.7 for DDL and Security
  Dim cat As New ADOX.Catalog
  cat.ActiveConnection = CurrentProject.Connection
  With cat.Tables("Sales")
     'add field
     .Columns.Append "Comments", adVarWChar, 100
     'drop field
     .Columns.Delete ("Comments")
  End With
  Set cat = Nothing
  MsgBox "done"
End Sub

Sub field_SQL()
  Dim conn As ADODB.Connection
  Set conn = CurrentProject.Connection
  Dim ssql As String
  ssql - "Alter Table Sales " & _
      "ADD COLUMN Comments TEXT(100)"
  conn.Execute ssql
  ssql = "Alter Table Sales " & _
      "Drop COLUMN Comments"
  conn.Execute ssql
  MsgBox "done"
End Sub
```

Refer to Recipe 4.1 for instructions on how to create the Sales table, then use one of the approaches listed here to add and delete the Comments field. There's one caveat: because the field is added and then immediately deleted, you will not see it when viewing the Sales table. To work around this, comment out the code line that deletes the field. For example, in the field_ADOX example, put an apostrophe in front of the line that deletes the field. The line will then look like this:

```
     '.Columns.Delete ("Comments")
```

Changing a field's data type

SQL provides an Alter Column construct that's useful for changing a field's data type. The following code shows how the Alter statement is used to change the existing Comments field to the Integer type (in Access, this appears as the Long data type):

```
  Sub alter_field_SQL()
     Dim conn As ADODB.Connection
     Set conn = CurrentProject.Connection
     Dim ssql As String
     'alter field to be Integer (Long)
```

```
        ssql = "Alter Table Sales " & _
        "Alter COLUMN Comments Integer"
        conn.Execute ssql
        conn.Close
        MsgBox "done"
    End Sub
```

Discussion

Typically, you will be changing data types to accommodate larger data. For example, increasing the size of a text field from 50 to 100 characters makes sense, as does changing a data type from Long to Double to allow for large numbers with decimals.

Changing to a smaller data type can cause data loss. Make sure you have a justifiable need to alter a field to a smaller type or another type that will cause data loss, such as going from Text to a numeric type. Practical sense shows that being able to accommodate occasional larger pieces of data is better than trying to gain small optimizations by squeezing fields.

For example, you might expect a phone number field to need to accommodate only up to 14 characters for U.S./Canadian-style phone numbers in the format (111)-111-1111. Most of the time, that will be sufficient. But what happens if you need to enter a phone number that has an extension? The insert will bomb, or the data will be truncated. A lost phone number could cause more of a problem for a company than a tiny bit of extra required memory. With that in mind, it might make more sense to set the phone number field to a larger size—say, 30 characters—capable of accommodating occasional nonstandard phone numbers.

4.3   Creating and Using an Index

Problem

Tables usually have a primary key. How can other table indexes be created and used?

Solution

While in the design view of a table, use the View → Indexes menu option to display the Indexes dialog box. (In Access 2007, use the Table Tools → Design view of the Ribbon.) Figure 4-3 shows the dialog sitting over the table for which it is displaying index information.

A table can have up to 32 indexes, and each index can contain up to 10 fields. In this case, there is a single index named PrimaryKey, which is based on the ClientID field. Values in the ClientID field must be unique because the Unique property is set to Yes.

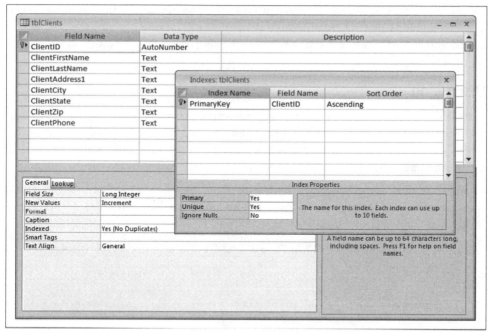

Figure 4-3. A table index

What if the tblClients table didn't have this unique ClientID field? You could use a combination of other fields to ensure uniqueness among records. For example, combining the fields that contain the first name, last name, and address should ensure unique records. Providing a name and selecting these fields in the Indexes dialog box, as shown in Figure 4-4, creates the new index.

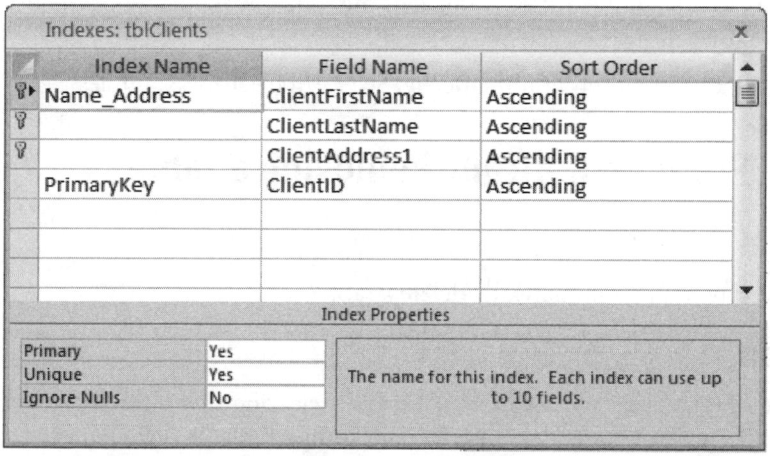

Figure 4-4. A new index is created

As shown in Figure 4-4, the Primary property for the Name_Address index is set to Yes. This means that when this table is opened in Datasheet view, the sort established in the Name_Address index will sort the records. Only one index at a time can be the Primary index.

Discussion

A table can have multiple indexes. It's good practice to provide indexes on fields that are often sorted on, but this is not a requirement, and it's not generally necessary for tables that contain a small or moderate number of records. Still, knowing how to create and apply an index is handy when performance issues do pop up.

Indexes are also useful when working with DAO or ADO recordsets. In this situation, applying a predesigned index provides an immediate ordering of the table. Indexes are applied only to table-type recordsets.

Here is an example of opening a table-type recordset and applying an index:

```
Sub apply_index()
  Dim db As DAO.Database
  Set db = CurrentDb
  Dim recset As DAO.Recordset
  Set recset = db.OpenRecordset("tblClients")
  recset.Index = "Name_Address"
  ''
  'perform processing here
  ''
  recset.Close
  db.Close
  Set recset = Nothing
  Set db = Nothing
End Sub
```

Once the table-based recordset is opened, the index is applied, and the order of the records follows the sorting scheme of the index.

Indexes can be created programmatically. See Recipe 4.1 for examples.

4.4   Programmatically Removing a Table

Problem

Is there a way to programmatically delete a table?

Solution

First, let's make clear the distinction between clearing out a table and removing a table. One action involves deleting the data from a table. A delete query (see Recipe 3.3) is the best bet for that. The other action involves removing the table entirely.

There are two useful approaches for this. One option is to use the `DoCmd` object with the `DeleteObject` method:

```
DoCmd.DeleteObject acTable, "tblTransactions"
```

When using the `DeleteObject` method, you specify the object type, and then the name of the object to delete.

The other method uses SQL and the `Drop` statement:

```
Sub drop_table()
    Dim conn As ADODB.Connection
    Set conn = CurrentProject.Connection
    Dim ssql As String
    ssql = "Drop Table tblServices"
    conn.Execute ssql
    conn.Close
End Sub
```

The SQL syntax is similar to that for the `DeleteObject` method: the `Drop` statement is followed by the object type, and then the name of the object to delete.

Discussion

Regardless of which method you use, it is wise to ask for confirmation first. Deleting a table accidentally can be catastrophic. Here is a routine that prompts for confirmation before deleting a table:

```
Sub delete_table()
    Dim proceed As Integer
    proceed = MsgBox("Do you wish to delete the table?", _
        vbYesNo, "Confirm Table Delete")
    If proceed = vbYes Then
        DoCmd.DeleteObject acTable, "tblTransactions"
        MsgBox "Table deleted"
    Else
        MsgBox "Delete canceled"
    End If
End Sub
```

When the routine is run, the message shown in Figure 4-5 is displayed. Only a Yes answer will run the table delete.

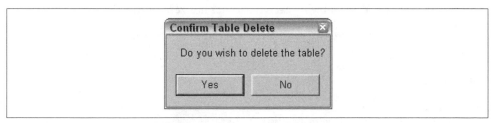

Figure 4-5. Confirming a table delete

4.5 Programmatically Creating a Query

Problem

It's one thing to assemble SQL statements in code and run them. But how do you create permanent queries with programming code that will then appear on the Queries tab?

Solution

You can easily create stored queries programmatically with either DAO or SQL. Figure 4-6 shows a query that was manually assembled and saved. It is a permanent object in the Access database, and appears under Queries in the database window.

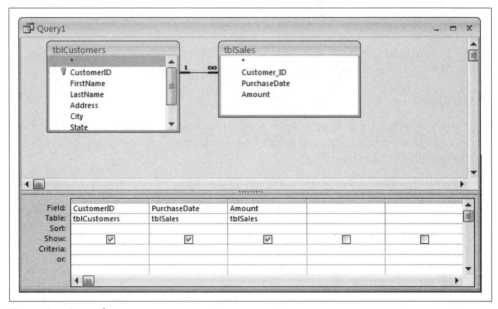

Figure 4-6. A saved query

The query contains three fields: the CustomerID field from the tblCustomers table, and the PurchaseDate and Amount fields from the tblSales table. There is a one-to-many relationship between these tables—each customer has zero or more sales records.

Here is DAO code that will create this query programmatically:

```
Sub create_querydef()
  Dim db As DAO.Database
  Set db = CurrentDb
  Dim qd As DAO.QueryDef
  Dim ssql As String
  ssql = "SELECT tblCustomers.CustomerID, "
  ssql = ssql & "tblSales.PurchaseDate, tblSales.Amount "
  ssql = ssql & "FROM tblCustomers INNER JOIN tblSales ON "
  ssql = ssql & "tblCustomers.CustomerID = tblSales.Customer_ID;"
```

```
    Set qd = db.createquerydef("DAO_Query", ssql)
    db.Close
    Set db = Nothing
    MsgBox "done"
End Sub
```

In DAO, the QueryDef object can either represent a saved query (of the QueryDefs collection) or be used with the createquerydef method of the DAO Database object. In the preceding example, the SQL statement is assembled and used with the createquerydef method. The name for the query to be saved as—DAO_Query, in this example—is also supplied.

Alternatively, you can use SQL to create and store a query. The SQL term for a query is a *view*, and the Create View construct is used:

```
Sub createview( )
    Dim conn As ADODB.Connection
    Set conn = CurrentProject.Connection
    Dim ssql As String
    ssql = "Create View qryCustomerSales (CustID, PurchDate, Amt) As "
    ssql = ssql & "SELECT tblCustomers.CustomerID, "
    ssql = ssql & "tblSales.PurchaseDate, tblSales.Amount "
    ssql = ssql & "FROM tblCustomers INNER JOIN tblSales ON "
    ssql = ssql & "tblCustomers.CustomerID = tblSales.Customer_ID;"
    conn.Execute ssql
    conn.Close
    MsgBox "done"
End Sub
```

The SQL statement, beginning with Create View, is assembled, and the Execute method of the ADO Connection object applies the SQL statement and creates the query.

Discussion

Let's explore how the Create View SQL statement works. After the Create View keywords, a list of field names is supplied. These names serve as aliases for the fields listed in the subsequent Select statement. In other words, the aliases CustID, PurchDate, and Amt are provided for the CustomerID, PurchaseDate, and Amount fields. The SQL statement that is stored looks like this:

```
SELECT tblCustomers.CustomerID AS CustID,
tblSales.PurchaseDate AS PurchDate, tblSales.Amount AS Amt
FROM tblCustomers INNER JOIN tblSales ON
tblCustomers.CustomerID = tblSales.Customer_ID;
```

Creating action queries

The preceding examples created select queries. To create permanent action queries (e.g., update, append, or delete queries), use the DAO model. The SQL approach requires an inner Select statement, which limits the query to being one that selects data. The DAO approach, on the other hand, simply stores whatever SQL statement it is handed.

Here is an example of creating a delete query:

```
Sub create_querydef_Delete( )
  Dim db As DAO.Database
  Set db = CurrentDb
  Dim qd As DAO.QueryDef
  Dim ssql As String
  ssql = "Delete * From tblSales"
  Set qd = db.createquerydef("Delete_Sales", ssql)
  db.Close
  Set db = Nothing
  MsgBox "done"
End Sub
```

In this code, the simple `Delete * From tblSales` is stored as a delete query.

The following code uses DAO to create a make-table query (in this case, the query creates a table of sales records for customers from Texas):

```
Sub create_querydef_MakeTable( )
  Dim db As DAO.Database
  Set db = CurrentDb
  Dim qd As DAO.QueryDef
  Dim ssql As String
  ssql = "Select tblCustomers.CustomerID,tblSales.PurchaseDate, "
  ssql = ssql & " tblSales.Amount Into tblTexasCustomerSales "
  ssql = ssql & "FROM tblCustomers INNER JOIN tblSales ON "
  ssql = ssql & "tblCustomers.CustomerID = tblSales.Customer_ID "
  ssql = ssql & "Where tblCustomers.State='TX'"
  Set qd = db.createquerydef("Create_Texas_Sales", ssql)
  db.Close
  Set db = Nothing
  MsgBox "done"
End Sub
```

To be clear, running this routine simply creates the query and saves it within the Access database; it does not run the query. When the query is run, a table named tblTexasCustomerSales, populated with sales information for Texas customers, will be created.

Working with String Data

Text-based data can contain more than just the letters of the alphabet. Numbers can be treated as text, and there are many characters that are neither letters nor numbers, but are vital to text-based work. Consider tabs, carriage returns, spaces, backspaces, and many of the symbols used in everyday work (hyphens, currency symbols, etc.). These all need to be as accessible and pliable as the letters and numbers.

In this chapter, you'll find recipes illustrating how to find text strings within other text strings, how to replace text strings with others, and how to remove unwanted spaces from text strings. There's also a recipe that discusses different methods for combining text strings, and one that reveals how to sort numbers that are stored as text.

5.1 Returning Characters from the Left or Right Side of a String

Problem

How can I isolate a certain number of characters at the beginning or end of a text string? Going a step further, is there a way to return the left and right portions of a text string based on a character found in the string itself?

Solution

The `Left` and `Right` functions return characters from the beginning and end of a text string, respectively. Both functions take two arguments: the string being addressed, and the number of characters to return. For example:

- `Left("cat", 1)` returns "c"
- `Left("cat", 2)` returns "ca"
- `Right("Apple Pie", 3)` returns "Pie"
- `Right("Apple Pie", 15)` returns just "Apple Pie," even though 15 characters were requested—there are only nine characters, so nine characters are returned

Discussion

Since `Left` and `Right` are functions, they are usually structured to return the result to a variable. For example:

```
Sub test_left_function( )
   Const phrase = "The cow jumped over the moon"
   Dim phrase_part As String
   phrase_part = Left(phrase, 7)
   'further processing
End Sub
```

In this example, `phrase_part` is assigned the seven leftmost characters of the constant `phrase`; `phrase_part` therefore receives the value "The cow" (don't forget the space counts as a character).

Sometimes you know how many characters you need to retrieve from the start or end of a string. At other times, though, the number of characters to return depends on the data itself. The classic example of this is parsing full names into first and last names. The key to how many characters to grab from the start or end depends on the position of the space between the first and last names. In each of these full names, for example, the space between the first and last names occurs in a different position:

- George Washington
- Mark Twain
- Isaac Newton

Therefore, simply assigning a set number of characters to return from the beginning or end of each of these strings won't work as a way to isolate the first and last names of these three historical figures.

In this case, finding the position of the space is key to knowing how many characters to return with both the `Left` and `Right` functions. Here, the `InStr` and `Len` functions work in tandem with the `Left` and `Right` functions to successfully parse the names:

```
Sub parse_name(full_name)
   Dim first_name As String
   Dim last_name As String
   first_name = _
       Left(full_name, InStr(full_name, " ") - 1)
   last_name = _
       Right(full_name, Len(full_name) - InStr(full_name, " "))
   'further processing
End Sub
```

The routine is structured to take a full name as an argument. `InStr` returns the position of the space. The first name occupies all characters to the left of the space. The last name occupies the characters to the right of the space.

5.2   Returning Characters from the Middle of a String When the Start Position and Length Are Known

Problem

In the data I work with, a key part of the data is embedded in a string. It's six charac-ters long, and starts in the third position. Is there any easy way to extract these characters?

Solution

The easy fix for this recipe is to use the Mid function. Mid takes three arguments: the string, the starting position within the string, and the number of characters to return. Here are some examples:

- Mid("banana", 3, 3) returns "nan"
- Mid("banana split", 6, 7) returns "a split"
- Mid("abcdefghijklm", 3, 6) returns "cdefgh"

Discussion

As a function, Mid is usually structured to return the result to a variable:

```
Sub mid_test()
  Const phrase = "A stitch in time saves nine"
  Dim phrase_part As String
  phrase_part = Mid(phrase, 3, 6)
  'further processing
End Sub
```

In this example, phrase_part is assigned the value "stitch."

As stated earlier, in addition to the string itself, the Mid function accepts the start position within the string and the length of the substring to return. What if the length is not known, but is dependent on the position of a certain character? That is, say you wish to return a substring that is identified by starting at a certain position and ending with a certain letter. Here is a way to combine the Mid and InStr functions to get this to work:

```
Sub mid_test_2()
  Const phrase = "A stitch in time saves nine"
  Dim phrase_part As String
  phrase_part = Mid(phrase, 3, InStr(1, phrase, "e") - 2)
  'further processing
End Sub
```

Here, the substring to be returned starts at the third position; InStr determines that first occurrence of the letter "e" is at the sixteenth position. One less than the value of the starting position is subtracted from the result of the InStr function to determine the length of the substring to return. This formula neatly returns "stitch in time."

5.3 Returning the Start Position of a Substring When the Characters Are Known

Problem

My data contains a sequence of characters embedded in a larger text string. The sequence of characters is always the same, but the starting position of the characters differs between records. What is an easy way to determine the starting position in each record?

Solution

The InStr function is useful in this situation. It determines the starting position of a string within a larger string. Since the string being sought is already known, determining its length is not an issue.

Figure 5-1 shows a table with records. Within each record is the substring 7XR3G. The positioning of this substring is not consistent across records.

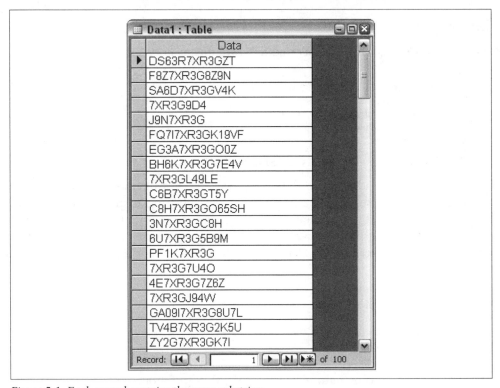

Figure 5-1. Each record contains the same substring

You can use a query to determine the substring's start position in each record. You'll need to build a temporary field as an expression with the InStr function, as shown in Figure 5-2.

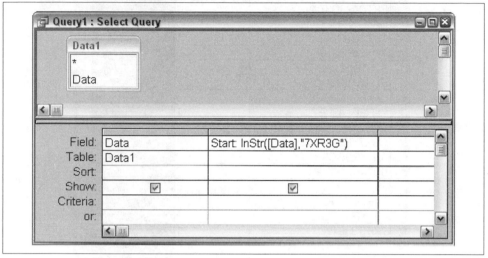

Figure 5-2. Using InStr in a query

Figure 5-3 shows the result of running the query.

Discussion

InStr returns the starting position for a given substring. But what if the substring occurs more than once in the larger string? You may need to be able to determine where each occurrence begins, not just the first occurrence.

A little VBA code helps out in this situation. InStr returns 0 when the substring is not found, so the trick is to keep testing until it returns that value. Until that point, each time the substring is found, the next starting position to test from is the position where it was just found, plus one. Here is a routine that searches for all occurrences of the substring ABC in the Data field of each record in the sample recordset:

```
Sub multiple_InStr( )
  Dim conn As ADODB.Connection
  Set conn = CurrentProject.Connection
  Dim rs As New ADODB.Recordset
  Dim ssql As String
  Dim found_pos As Integer
  ssql = "Select * From Data2"
  rs.Open ssql, conn, adOpenKeyset, adLockOptimistic
  Do Until rs.EOF
    found_pos = 0
    found_pos = InStr(1, rs.Fields("Data"), "ABC")
```

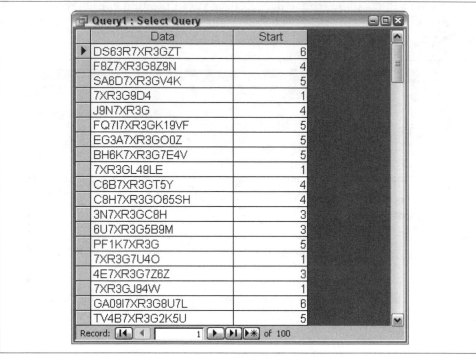

Figure 5-3. The start position in each record is returned

```
    If found_pos > 0 Then
      Do Until found_pos = 0
        Debug.Print rs.Fields("Data") & " " & found_pos
        found_pos = InStr(found_pos + 1, _
            rs.Fields("Data"), "ABC")
      Loop
    End If
  rs.MoveNext
  Loop
  rs.Close
  Set rs = Nothing
  Set conn = Nothing
End Sub
```

If the initial test returns a value greater than zero, a Do Until loop is used to keep testing until zero is returned. The found_pos variable holds the starting position for the next search in the current record.

This example is structured to write the complete string followed by the position at which the substring is found to the immediate window. The results are shown in Figure 5-4. Strings containing more than one occurrence of the substring ABC are listed more than once, with the numbers to the right indicating the start positions of each occurrence.

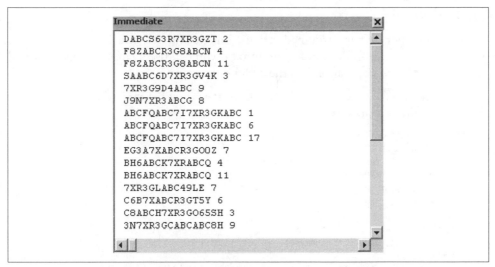

```
Immediate                                                 ✕
    DABCS63R7XR3GZT  2
    F8ZABCR3G8ABCN  4
    F8ZABCR3G8ABCN  11
    SAABC6D7XR3GV4K  3
    7XR3G9D4ABC  9
    J9N7XR3ABCG  8
    ABCFQABC7I7XR3GKABC  1
    ABCFQABC7I7XR3GKABC  6
    ABCFQABC7I7XR3GKABC  17
    EG3A7XABCR3GOOZ  7
    BH6ABCK7XRABCQ  4
    BH6ABCK7XRABCQ  11
    7XR3GLABC49LE  7
    C6B7XABCR3GT5Y  6
    C8ABCH7XR3GO65SH  3
    3N7XR3GCABCABC8H  9
◀                                                       ▶
```

Figure 5-4. Finding the starting positions of all occurrences of a substring

5.4   Stripping Spaces from the Ends of a String

Problem

We have data that is imported from an external system. Often, the data is padded with spaces at one or both ends. What is the best way to remove these spaces? Do we need a routine that counts spaces until a valid character is found?

Solution

The Trim, LTrim, and RTrim functions all serve to remove spaces: Trim removes spaces at both ends of a string, while LTrim and RTrim remove spaces from the left or right side of a string, respectively.

Here are some examples:

- Trim(" apple ") returns "apple"
- LTrim(" apple ") returns "apple "
- RTrim(" apple ") returns " apple"

Neither Trim, LTrim, nor RTrim removes spaces from the inside of a string. The functions remove only leading and trailing spaces. If you need to remove internal spaces, check out Recipe 5.5.

Discussion

The Trim functions return trimmed strings, but do not tell you how many spaces were removed. If this information is important, you can use a small routine that will handle both the trim operation and the count of removed spaces.

All that is required is to compare the length of the string before and after the trim. A short code routine works well here:

```
Sub trim_and_count( )
  Dim conn As ADODB.Connection
  Set conn = CurrentProject.Connection
  Dim rs As New ADODB.Recordset
  Dim ssql As String
  Dim original_length As Integer
  Dim trimmed_name As String
  ssql = "Select * From Data3"
  rs.Open ssql, conn, adOpenKeyset, adLockOptimistic
  Do Until rs.EOF
    original_length = Len(rs.Fields("Name_Before_Trim"))
    rs.Fields("Name_After_Trim") = _
      Trim(rs.Fields("Name_Before_Trim"))
    rs.Fields("Number_Of_Spaces_Removed") = _
      original_length - Len(rs.Fields("Name_After_Trim"))
    rs.MoveNext
  Loop
  rs.Close
  Set rs = Nothing
  Set conn = Nothing
End Sub
```

This routine allows you to compare the original and trimmed strings, and see at a glance how many spaces were removed. The result is shown in Figure 5-5. The original names, some of which have leading and/or trailing spaces, appear in the first field; the second field is populated with the names (with spaces removed), and the third field displays the number of spaces removed from each name.

During the processing, the length of the "before" name is stored in the original_length variable; the "after" length is then subtracted from this value, providing the number of removed spaces.

5.5   Stripping Spaces from the Middle of a String

Problem

Data comes into our system with embedded spaces. These need to be removed. What is the best way to do this?

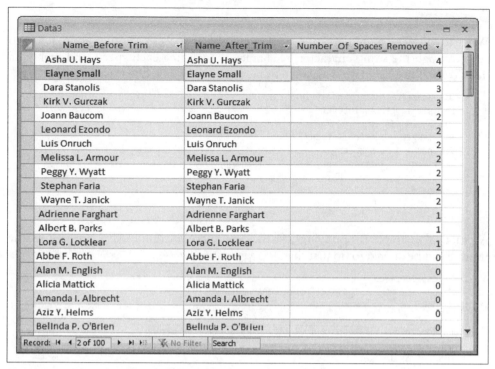

Name_Before_Trim	Name_After_Trim	Number_Of_Spaces_Removed
Asha U. Hays	Asha U. Hays	4
Elayne Small	Elayne Small	4
Dara Stanolis	Dara Stanolis	3
Kirk V. Gurczak	Kirk V. Gurczak	3
Joann Baucom	Joann Baucom	2
Leonard Ezondo	Leonard Ezondo	2
Luis Onruch	Luis Onruch	2
Melissa L. Armour	Melissa L. Armour	2
Peggy Y. Wyatt	Peggy Y. Wyatt	2
Stephan Faria	Stephan Faria	2
Wayne T. Janick	Wayne T. Janick	2
Adrienne Farghart	Adrienne Farghart	1
Albert B. Parks	Albert B. Parks	1
Lora G. Locklear	Lora G. Locklear	1
Abbe F. Roth	Abbe F. Roth	0
Alan M. English	Alan M. English	0
Alicia Mattick	Alicia Mattick	0
Amanda I. Albrecht	Amanda I. Albrecht	0
Aziz Y. Helms	Aziz Y. Helms	0
Belinda P. O'Brien	Belinda P. O'Brien	0

Record: 2 of 100   No Filter   Search

Figure 5-5. Names treated with the Trim function

Solution

Removing spaces from the inner part of a string involves two operations: identifying the spaces, and concatenating the remaining parts of the string once the spaces have been removed.

To remove all the spaces from a string in one easy step, use the Replace function. Replace works on a string by replacing one substring with another. In this case, you want to replace each space with a zero-length string. For example:

```
Replace("Good Morning Have A Nice Day"," ","")
```

returns:

```
GoodMorningHaveANiceDay
```

Here, the Replace function takes as arguments a string, a substring to search for (a space, signified as " "), and a second substring to replace the first one (a zero-length string, signified as two quotation marks with no space in between).

Additional uses for the Replace function are discussed in Recipe 5.6.

Discussion

What if you need more control over the removal of spaces? Another approach is to read through the string character by character, analyzing each space, and making a decision about what to do with it—a framework might look like this:

```
Sub spaces(full_string As String)
  Dim str_length As Integer
  Dim pos As Integer
  str_length = Len(full_string)
  For pos = 1 To str_length
    If Mid(full_string, pos, 1) = " " Then
      'processing goes here
    End If
  Next pos
End Sub
```

A practical example is removing just the first space encountered. Here is how the routine can be altered to do just that:

```
Sub test_function()
  MsgBox remove_first_space("apple banana orange")
End Sub

Function remove_first_space(full_string As String) As String
  Dim str_length As Integer
  Dim pos As Integer
  str_length = Len(full_string)
  For pos = 1 To str_length
    If Mid(full_string, pos, 1) = " " Then
      remove_first_space = Left(full_string, pos - 1) & _
        Right(full_string, Len(full_string) - pos)
      Exit For
    End If
  Next pos
End Function
```

In this example, the test_function sub sends the "apple banana orange" argument to the remove_first_space function, which loops through each character of the argument looking for spaces. When a space is encountered, the function's return value is set to the part of the string argument to the left of the space, concatenated with the portion of the string to the right of the space. Then, the Exit For statement breaks out of the loop and the function completes. In other words, when "apple banana orange" is sent to the function, it returns "applebanana orange"—the first space is removed.

5.6   Replacing One String with Another String

Problem

I need to replace one subset of characters in my data with another set. There's a catch, though—if the subset of characters exists more than once in the larger text string, the requirement is to replace the last subset only. How can I do this?

Solution

Replace is the best function to easily change one substring for another within a larger string. Replace has three required arguments and three optional ones:

- The string to search (required)
- The substring to search for (required)
- The replacement substring (required)
- The position from which to start searching (if omitted, the default is 1)
- The number of replacements to make (if omitted, all occurrences of the search string will be replaced)
- The Compare format (optional; we can ignore this for this recipe)

Even with these options, it would be impossible to isolate and replace just the last occurrence of the search string using Replace. Instead, use the InStr function to find the start position of the last occurrence of the search string, and then use InStr's return value as the position from which the Replace function should begin searching:

```
Sub find_last_occur()
  Dim original_string
  Dim search_string As String
  Dim replace_string
  Dim new_string As String
  Dim found_pos As Integer
  Dim last_found_pos As Integer

  original_string = "abcdefgabcd"
  search_string = "abc"
  replace_string = "xyz"

  found_pos = InStr(1, original_string, search_string)
  'if one occurence exists then keep checking
  'and store each successive found position in last_found_pos
  If found_pos > 0 Then
    last_found_pos = found_pos
    Do Until found_pos = 0
      found_pos = InStr(found_pos + 1, _
          original_string, search_string)
```

```
    If found_pos > 0 Then last_found_pos = found_pos
  Loop
  'now use Replace, knowing where last occurence starts
  new_string = Left(original_string, last_found_pos - 1) & _
      Replace(original_string, search_string, replace_string, last_found_pos)
  End If
End Sub
```

In summary, this routine uses the InStr function to locate the last occurrence of the search string, then the Replace function to replace it with the desired value. The result is that the portion of the original string that appeared to the left of the last occurrence of the search string is concatenated with the portion that appeared to the right, with the replacement in place.

This method works, but it's a little difficult to follow. Is there an easier way?

Discussion

Of course there is! The problem was that we couldn't easily tell where the last occurrence of the search string was within the larger string. But what if we reverse the original string? Now, the last occurrence of the search string appears first. It's also reversed, but that's no matter. Using the StrReverse function on all the pertinent strings keeps them all in sync.

Here is a routine that produces the same result as the previous one, but with less code:

```
Sub reverse_and_find( )
  Dim original_string
  Dim search_string As String
  Dim replace_string
  Dim new_string As String
  original_string = "abcdefgabcd"
  search_string = "abc"
  replace_string = "xyz"
  new_string = Replace(StrReverse(original_string), _
      StrReverse(search_string), _
      StrReverse(replace_string), 1, 1)
  new_string = StrReverse(new_string)
End Sub
```

This smaller routine simply reverses all the involved strings, then does a replacement on the first occurrence of the reversed search string (which was the last occurrence before the original string was reversed). There is no guesswork involved in finding the first occurrence—simply supplying the value of 1 to the Replace function takes care of everything. At the end of the routine, the new_string variable itself is reversed back to the original order.

Both routines return "abcdefgxyzd" as the value of new_string.

5.7   Concatenating Data

Problem

How can I combine text strings together?

Solution

The ampersand character (&) is the concatenation character. Here are some examples:

- "Hello" & "Goodbye" returns "HelloGoodbye"
- "Hello " & "Goodbye" returns "Hello Goodbye"
- "Hello" & " " & "Goodbye" returns "Hello Goodbye"

Notice that in both the second and third examples, there's a space between Hello and Goodbye. The second example provides the space because there is a space after the Hello within the quotation marks, and the third example provides the space as an independent string that is concatenated with the two others.

 The + operator can also be used for string concatenation.

Discussion

You often need to consider spaces when concatenating text. Simply combining two values may not produce the desired result—for example, concatenating George and Washington produces GeorgeWashington, which is probably not what you need. Therefore, concatenating a space between other words is a common requirement.

Usually, manually adding a space to the end of each of the first strings (for example, changing George to George) is infeasible. When processing a large number of records, this method would take an impractical amount of time, and would also be error-prone.

Continuing with this example, say you need to combine all of the first and last names in your records into single full-name values. The technique, as previously mentioned, is to concatenate a space between the first and last names. But what about any stray spaces that may already be included before or after the names in your records? Including the Trim function as well will remove any such spaces before the single desired space is added with the concatenation.

Figure 5-6 shows a query based on a table with a FirstName field and a LastName field. Two expression-based fields have been added to the query design. Both concatenate the values in these fields into a single full name with a space in between; however, the second expression field first applies Trim on the FirstName and LastName fields.

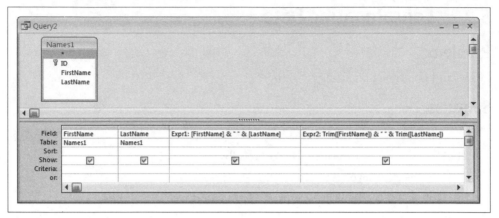

Figure 5-6. Concatenating first names and last names

Figure 5-7 shows the results returned by the two expression fields. Note that several extra spaces appear in the source fields (FirstName and LastName). These could be from the external source that created the data (assuming the data was imported), or just from sloppy user entry.

FirstName	LastName	Expr1	Expr2
Dawn	Baucom	Dawn Baucom	Dawn Baucom
Danny	Strapseer	Danny Strapseer	Danny Strapseer
Alexandra	Donegan	Alexandra Donegan	Alexandra Donegan
Clifford	Schroeder	Clifford Schroeder	Clifford Schroeder
Marie	Owsley	Marie Owsley	Marie Owsley
Debi	Schaeper	Debi Schaeper	Debi Schaeper
Sandy	Schutz	Sandy Schutz	Sandy Schutz
Jesse	Flagg	Jesse Flagg	Jesse Flagg
Ronn	Reinhardt	Ronn Reinhardt	Ronn Reinhardt
R.H.	Bonanno	R.H. Bonanno	R.H. Bonanno
Chuck	Fenter	Chuck Fenter	Chuck Fenter
Patrick	Erskine	Patrick Erskine	Patrick Erskine
Yuny	Featherstone	Yuny Featherstone	Yuny Featherstone
Abbe	Domanski	Abbe Domanski	Abbe Domanski

Record: I◄ ◄ 17 of 100 ► ►I ►* | No Filter | Search

Figure 5-7. Running the query with the concatenation

Both expression fields correctly add a space between the first and last names. However, the second expression field cleanses the data first via the `Trim` function. The result is a clean concatenation of first name, space, and last name.

Using the Join function

The Join function provides an alternative method for concatenating strings. Join takes any number of strings, presented as an array, and concatenates them together, using an optional delimiter (a character or characters) to place in between each string. Here is an example:

```
Sub join_example()
    Dim myArray(5) As String
    myArray(0) = "up"
    myArray(1) = "down"
    myArray(2) = "here"
    myArray(3) = "there"
    myArray(4) = "beyond"
    Dim joined As String
    joined = Join(myArray, ",")
    Debug.Print joined
End Sub
```

Running this code results in:

```
up,down,here,there,beyond,
```

Notice that the delimiter is a comma (,), and notice that it is placed after each array element—even the last one! The comma after beyond is not likely desirable, so here is an update of the routine that removes it:

```
Sub join_example()
    Dim myArray(5) As String
    myArray(0) = "up"
    myArray(1) = "down"
    myArray(2) = "here"
    myArray(3) = "there"
    myArray(4) = "beyond"
    Dim joined As String
    joined = Join(myArray, ",")
    joined = Left(joined, Len(joined) - 1)
    Debug.Print joined
End Sub
```

Including the line that uses the Left and Len functions removes the trailing single-character delimiter.

To concatenate the array elements without any intervening characters or spaces, use an empty string for the delimiter:

```
joined = Join(myArray, "")
```

The result is:

```
updownheretherebeyond
```

Using the delimiter is optional, but when it is left out, a space is assumed. And yes, there will be an extra space at the end of the concatenation!

5.8   Sorting Numbers That Are Stored as Text

Problem

Our system stores certain numeric data as text. When it comes to sorting the data, it sorts alphanumerically, which is not appropriate for the reporting we need. How can the text-based numbers be coerced to sort as real numbers?

Solution

Figure 5-8 shows how apparently numeric data sorts when it is saved as the Text data type. All the ones come first, so numbers such as 1, 10, 100, 101, and so on will all appear before the number 2 in the list.

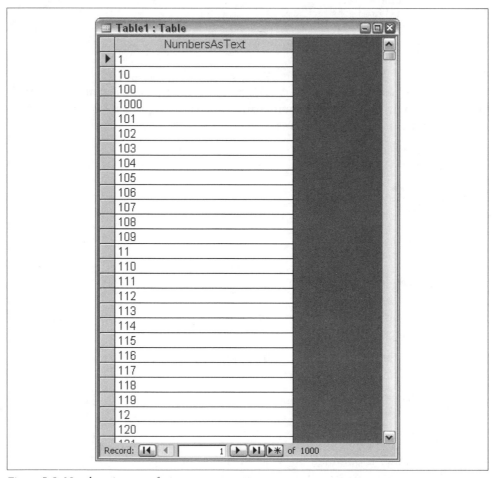

Figure 5-8. Numbers in a text format sort as text

To sort this data in the expected numerical way, you must add an extra field that, for each record, holds a converted value of the text-based number. The converted value becomes the real numeric data point. Then, the sort is placed on the new field.

Figure 5-9 shows a query design that includes an expression field that converts the text numbers to integers (with the CInt function). The sort is placed on this new field.

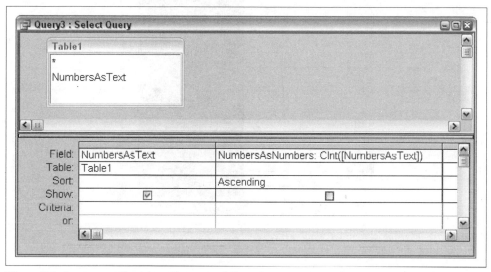

Figure 5-9. Sorting text-based numbers as valid numbers

Note that it is not necessary to have the expression field appear in the output. Figure 5-10 shows the result of running the query.

Discussion

An alternative method is to pad the text-based numbers with leading spaces or zeroes. The technique is to find the largest number and determine its length (i.e., how many characters long it is). You can then use this as a guide to determine how many spaces or zeroes to put in front of the other numbers in the data set.

In this example, the largest number is 1,000, which is four characters long. Therefore, values from 100 to 999 will be preceded with a single zero, values from 10 to 99 will be preceded with two zeroes, and values from 1 to 9 will be preceded with three leading zeroes.

Assuming the text-based numbers are in the Table2 table, here is a routine that will attend to these various padding requirements:

```
Sub pad_zeroes( )
    Dim conn As ADODB.Connection
    Set conn = CurrentProject.Connection
```

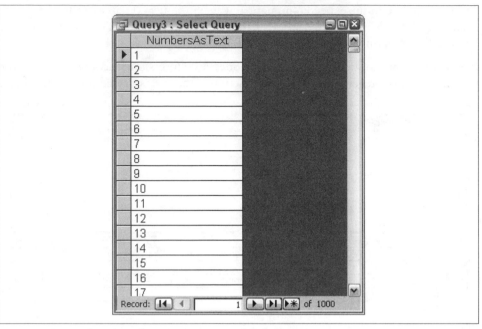

Figure 5-10. Text-based numbers now sort correctly

```
Dim rs As New ADODB.Recordset
rs.Open "Select * From Table2", conn, adOpenKeyset, adLockOptimistic
Do Until rs.EOF
  Select Case Len(rs.Fields(0))
    Case 1
      rs.Fields(0) = "000" & rs.Fields(0)
    Case 2
      rs.Fields(0) = "00" & rs.Fields(0)
    Case 3
      rs.Fields(0) = "0" & rs.Fields(0)
  End Select
rs.MoveNext
Loop
rs.Close
Set rs = Nothing
Set conn = Nothing
End Sub
```

Rather than checking the values themselves, the code checks the length of each value. So, for example, when the length is 2 (indicating any number from 10 to 99), two zeroes are placed in front of the value, and the concatenated value is saved back into the table.

Figure 5-11 shows the result of running the routine. The values, still text-based, have been padded with zeroes. When a sort is now applied, the numbers line up and appear in the correct sorted order.

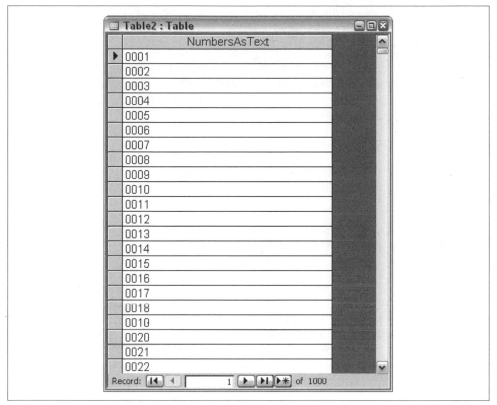

Figure 5-11. Padded text-based numbers now sort correctly

5.9   Categorizing Characters with ASCII Codes

Problem

We receive continuous data streams, and we need to categorize each character as a number, a lowercase letter, a capital letter, or "other" (tabs, carriage returns, etc.). We have set up an elaborate matching system that takes each character as it is read in and tests it against all the possible characters so we can identify and classify it. This approach is very inefficient. Is there an easier way to categorize a character as simply being an upper- or lowercase letter, a number, and so on?

Solution

The Asc function returns an integer that represents the character code of the first character in a string. If the string contains more than one character, just the first character is addressed.

Alphanumeric and other characters belong to a character set, such as that designed by the American National Standards Institute (ANSI). ASCII (American Standard Code for Information Interchange) is the standard used for the character codes.

Each character has a numeric equivalent. Within a given range, all uppercase letters follow each other, all lowercase letters follow each other, and so on. Specific character codes are also defined for commonly used nonalphanumeric characters. Table 5-1 displays a few of the character codes.

Table 5-1. Common character codes

Character(s)	Character code(s)
Tab	9
Carriage return	13
Space	32
Numbers (0–9)	48–57
Uppercase letters (A–Z)	65–90
Lowercase letters (a–z)	97–122

As individual characters are processed, they can be categorically identified by their numeric values. For example, the number 9 has a code of 57, the uppercase letter A has a code of 65, and the lowercase letter "z" has a code of 122. Here is a routine that takes a string of random characters, tests the character code of each one in turn, and adds to a count of uppercase, lowercase, numeric, or other type characters:

```
Sub what_am_i( )
Dim data As String
Dim data_length As Integer
Dim char_loop As Integer
Dim number_count As Integer
Dim upper_case_count As Integer
Dim lower_case_count As Integer
Dim other_count As Integer

data = "Hu46TTjsPR2e!#Y8"
data_length = Len(data)

number_count = 0
upper_case_count = 0
lower_case_count = 0
other_count = 0

For char_loop = 1 To data_length
  Select Case Asc(Mid(data, char_loop, 1))
    Case 48 To 57
```

```
        number_count = number_count + 1
      Case 65 To 90
        upper_case_count = upper_case_count + 1
      Case 97 To 122
        lower_case_count = lower_case_count + 1
      Case Else
        other_count = other_count + 1
    End Select
  Next char_loop
  Debug.Print number_count & " numbers found"
  Debug.Print upper_case_count & " upper case letters found"
  Debug.Print lower_case_count & " lower case letters found"
  Debug.Print other_count & " other characters found"
  End Sub
```

In the routine itself, the data string variable is set to a series of random characters. When adopting this routine, you can populate the data string with data from a table or an external system.

A loop is used to test each character and add to the appropriate count based on a range of character code values.

Discussion

The Asc function takes a character and returns its numeric character code. The complementary function is Chr, which takes a numeric value and returns the actual character. For example:

- Asc("A") returns "65"
- Chr(65) returns "A"

For more information, go into the Access Help system and look up character codes, ASCII codes, or the Asc and Chr functions. Navigating through some of the help topics will reveal the tables listing the actual character codes.

Many useful characters do not have related keys on a standard U.S. keyboard, but do have dedicated character codes. For example:

- For the copyright symbol (©), the character code is 0169.
- For the registered symbol (®), the character code is 0174.
- For the trademark symbol (™), the character code is 0153.
- For the cents symbol (¢), the character code is 0162.
- For the British pound symbol (£), the character code is 0163.
- For the Japanese yen symbol (¥), the character code is 0165.

To enter these characters in an Access table field or on a form, hold down the Alt key while entering their character codes. Be sure to include the leading 0, and note that you must enter the character code using your keyboard's numeric keypad only. Figure 5-12 shows these symbols entered into an Access table.

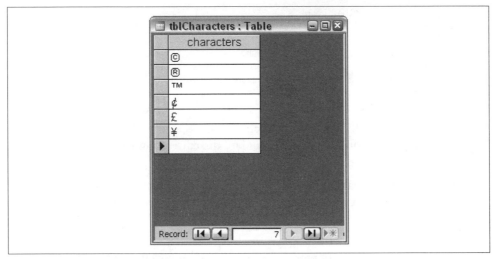

Figure 5-12. Nonkeyboard characters entered in an Access table

Using Programming to Manipulate Data

The ability to work with data and database functionality is greatly enhanced when programmed routines can be put to the task. Using VBA and other programming disciplines, developers can create sophisticated applications that reach beyond the capabilities of plain select and action queries.

This chapter offers a number of examples that show how code routines can be used to improve and enhance applications. Arrays are showcased, with discussions focusing on working with multiple dimensions and sorting. One recipe shows how to tap into Excel's extensive function library from Access, while others introduce simple and sophisticated methods of encrypting data and illustrate transaction processing. Working with charts, getting to the HTML source of web pages, and running Word mail merges directly from Access are also covered. There is even a recipe that illustrates how to build a user-friendly query construction form that lets users point and click their way through selecting criteria and running a query.

6.1   Using Excel Functions from Access

Problem

My work involves financial and statistical number crunching. The business data is stored in Access, but I use many of the functions available in Excel to get my work done. Is there a way to use the Excel functions directly from Access, rather than copying and pasting my data from Access into Excel?

Solution

Thanks to the availability of an object model paradigm for coding, it's relatively easy to hook into Excel and make use of Excel functions from within Access. An example will illustrate this clearly.

Figure 6-1 shows an Access table named tblLoans with parameters about different possible loans. For each record, the loan amount (the Principal, or Pv), the annual interest rate, the total number of monthly payments, and the period of interest are specified. The interest payment for the particular specified period needs to be calculated. The InterestPaid field can be populated using Excel's ISPMT function.

LoanID	Principal	AnnualInterestRate	TotalNumberOfPayments	PeriodNumber	InterestPaid
1	15000	0.065	24	12	
2	15000	0.065	36	16	
3	18000	0.0625	24	8	
4	18000	0.0625	36	32	
5	20000	0.06	36	32	
6	20000	0.06	48	1	
* (New)	0	0	0	0	

Record: I◄ ◄ 1 of 6 ► ►I ►I ⋉ No Filter | Search

Figure 6-1. A table filled with loan details

Here is the code routine that accomplishes this task:

```
Sub use_excel_1()
  Dim rs As New ADODB.Recordset
  Dim xcl As Object
  Set xcl = CreateObject("Excel.Application")
  rs.Open "Select * from tblLoans", CurrentProject.Connection, _
    adOpenKeyset, adLockOptimistic
  Do Until rs.EOF
    rs.Fields("InterestPaid") = _
      xcl.WorksheetFunction.ISPMT(rs.Fields("AnnualInterestRate") / 12, _
      rs.Fields("PeriodNumber") _
      rs.Fields("TotalNumberOfPayments"), _
      rs.Fields("Principal"))
    rs.MoveNext
  Loop
  rs.Close
  Set rs = Nothing
  Set xcl = Nothing
  MsgBox "done"
End Sub
```

 To use this routine, you will first need to add a reference to the Excel Object Library to your application. Choose Tools → References from the Visual Basic Editor's main menu to display the References dialog box. Scroll though the list of libraries until you find Microsoft Excel 11.0 Object Library (your version number may differ; don't worry). Place a checkmark next to it and press OK.

These two lines create a reference to Excel:

```
Dim xcl As Object
Set xcl = CreateObject("Excel.Application")
```

Next, a recordset is opened based on the tblLoans table. As each record is addressed, the values in the four table fields are sent to the ISPMT function. The key to making this happen is WorksheetFunction. This property belongs to the created Excel object (xcl); the Excel function we want to use is placed after the property name. Leaving out the function arguments for the moment, the syntax looks like this:

```
xcl.WorksheetFunction.ISPMT( )
```

Each Excel function requires a particular number of arguments. The best way to learn about a specific Excel function is to start up Excel itself and research the function. Figure 6-2 shows a screen from the Insert Function Wizard in Excel. This screen shows the arguments for the actual ISPMT (Payment) function:

Rate

   The interest rate per payment period of the loan

Per

   The particular period for which the interest rate is calculated

Nper

   The number of payments over the life of the loan

Pv

   The present value (this is the same as the principal of the loan)

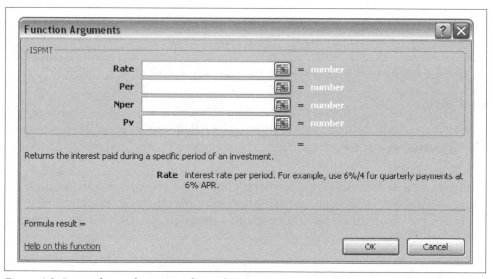

Figure 6-2. Researching a function with Excel's Insert Function Wizard

The four required arguments are passed to the Excel function as each Access record is processed. The function returns the periodic interest payment amount, which is placed in the InterestPaid field:

```
rs.Fields("InterestPaid") = _
    xcl.WorksheetFunction.ISPMT(rs.Fields("AnnualInterestRate") / 12, _
    rs.Fields("PeriodNumber") _
    rs.Fields("TotalNumberOfPayments"), _
    rs.Fields("Principal"))
```

Note that the order of the fields is dictated not by the order in which they appear in the Access table, but by the order in which the ISPMT function expects them. Also, note that the value for the annual interest field is divided by 12 because the purpose is to calculate the monthly payment. Therefore, the interest rate value that should be passed to the function therefore is one-twelfth of the annual interest rate.

Figure 6-3 shows the result of running the routine. The InterestPaid field is filled in for all records. Note that the values are negative numbers. This is normal, since Excel considers a payment a "cash flow out," and represents it as a negative.

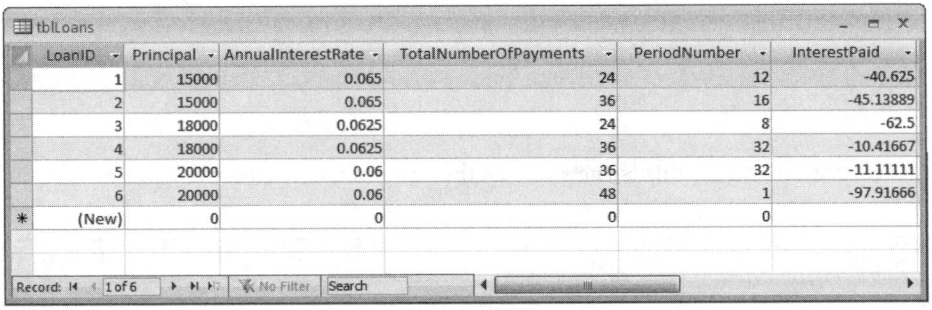

LoanID	Principal	AnnualInterestRate	TotalNumberOfPayments	PeriodNumber	InterestPaid
1	15000	0.065	24	12	-40.625
2	15000	0.065	36	16	-45.13889
3	18000	0.0625	24	8	-62.5
4	18000	0.0625	36	32	-10.41667
5	20000	0.06	36	32	-11.11111
6	20000	0.06	48	1	-97.91666
(New)	0	0	0	0	

Figure 6-3. Interest payments for particular periods have been calculated

Discussion

Excel has dozens of useful functions that can be called from Access. The best way to learn about them is to try out the different functions in Excel. They are categorized in the Insert Function dialog box, shown in Figure 6-4.

An Excel function might take a single argument, no arguments, dozens of arguments, or even arrays as arguments. This next example places values from the Access tblData table into two arrays and sends the arrays to Excel's Correl (correlation coefficient) function:

```
Sub use_excel_2( )
    Dim rs As New ADODB.Recordset
    Dim xcl As Object
    Dim observ1( ) As Integer
    Dim observ2( ) As Integer
```

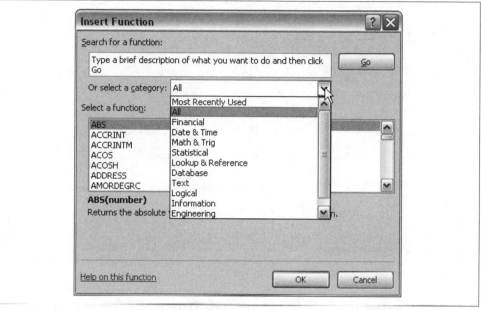

Figure 6-4. Excel's Insert Function dialog box

```
      Dim fill_array As Integer
      Dim answr
      Dim ssql As String
      ssql = "Select Observation1, Observation2 From tblData"
      rs.Open ssql, CurrentProject.Connection, adOpenKeyset, adLockOptimistic
      ReDim observ1(rs.RecordCount - 1)
      ReDim observ2(rs.RecordCount - 1)
      For fill_array = 0 To rs.RecordCount - 1
        observ1(fill_array) = rs.Fields("Observation1")
        observ2(fill_array) = rs.Fields("Observation2")
        rs.MoveNext
      Next fill_array
      Set xcl = CreateObject("Excel.Application")
      answr = xcl.WorksheetFunction.Correl(observ1, observ2)
      MsgBox answr
      rs.Close
      Set rs = Nothing
      Set xcl = Nothing
    End Sub
```

Two arrays, observ1 and observ2, are dimensioned and filled with values. The two arrays are then passed to Excel:

```
      answr = xcl.WorksheetFunction.Correl(observ1, observ2)
```

The answr variable holds the result of the calculation. Figure 6-5 shows the source data and the result returned from Excel's Correl function.

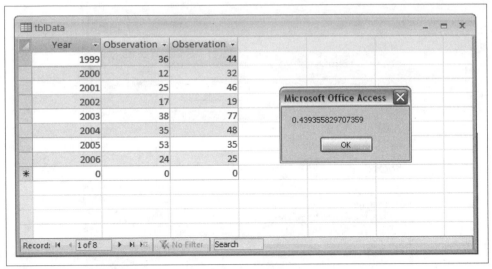

Figure 6-5. Access data and the result returned from Excel

6.2 Working with In-Memory Data

Problem

In my applications, I tend to create many variables. For example, I might have 12 variables, one for each month of the year. Is there a better way to manage my data during processing? Can I somehow cut down on the number of variables I use?

Solution

Arrays are a popular mechanism to store like values. Arrays work on a system of elements—that is, an array is a group of elements. While not required, arrays are typically used to group together common variables, such as the months of the year. Such an array would have 12 elements, and could itself be named after the year or with some other meaningful name.

Consider dimensioning these 12 unique variables:

```
Dim january As Single
Dim february As Single
Dim march As Single
Dim april As Single
Dim may As Single
Dim june As Single
Dim july As Single
Dim august As Single
Dim september As Single
Dim october As Single
Dim november As Single
Dim december As Single
```

That's 12 variables to keep track of in your code. Now, consider this dimensioning of an array with 12 elements:

```
Dim year_2006(12) As Single
```

Here, one line of code makes the memory space to hold 12 pieces of data.

When using an array, you address individual elements by their positions. By default, arrays are zero-based, which means the first element is referenced as 0, and the last element is referenced as (count of elements) minus 1. So, to fill a value for January, you would use syntax like this:

```
year_2006(0) = 27.75
```

And December would be addressed like this:

```
year_2006(11) = 38.25
```

Figure 6-6 shows a table in which each record contains a year's worth of data, broken out by month.

Year	January	February	March	April	May	June	July	August	September	October	November	December
1999	36	44	62	48	43	93	58	74	23	56	38	39
2000	12	72	46	79	68	45	38	14	86	52	45	15
2001	25	46	22	46	44	56	72	33	48	72	70	26
2002	17	19	43	64	27	35	75	48	26	80	67	38
2003	38	77	34	35	79	43	76	32	77	50	51	42
2004	35	48	63	85	90	23	32	75	86	23	48	55
2005	53	35	66	74	62	61	49	56	47	38	44	45
2006	24	26	75	48	36	60	66	22	48	62	37	40
0												

Record: 14 ◀ 1 ▶ ▶▮ ▶* of 8

Figure 6-6. A table of monthly data

The following routine fills the 12 individual month variables, without using an array:

```
Sub process_year_data_1( )
   Dim january As Single
   Dim february As Single
   Dim march As Single
   Dim april As Single
   Dim may As Single
   Dim june As Single
   Dim july As Single
   Dim august As Single
   Dim september As Single
   Dim october As Single
   Dim november As Single
   Dim december As Single
   Dim rs As New ADODB.Recordset
   rs.Open "Select * From tblYears Where Year=2006", _
      CurrentProject.Connection, adOpenKeyset, adLockOptimistic
   january = rs.Fields(1)
   february = rs.Fields(2)
```

```
    march = rs.Fields(3)
    april = rs.Fields(4)
    may = rs.Fields(5)
    june = rs.Fields(6)
    july = rs.Fields(7)
    august = rs.Fields(8)
    september = rs.Fields(9)
    october = rs.Fields(10)
    november = rs.Fields(11)
    december = rs.Fields(12)
    rs.Close
    Set rs = Nothing
    'further processing goes here
End Sub
```

By contrast, this shorter routine dimensions an array and fills it with the same 12 pieces of data:

```
Sub process_year_data_2()
    Dim year_2006(12) As Single
    Dim fill_array As Integer
    Dim rs As New ADODB.Recordset
    rs.Open "Select * From tblYears Where Year=2006", _
        CurrentProject.Connection, adOpenKeyset, adLockOptimistic
    For fill_array = 0 To 11
        year_2006(fill_array) = rs.Fields(fill_array + 1)
    Next fill_array
        rs.Close
    Set rs = Nothing
    'further processing goes here
End Sub
```

With either approach, the monthly data is available. However, using an array provides certain coding efficiencies. In the preceding routine, for example, the array was filled with a simple loop that matched each array element with a corresponding recordset field.

Discussion

As mentioned earlier, arrays are traditionally zero-based: the elements start at zero, and the last element is referenced by a number that is one less than the count of elements. As an alternative, you can instruct VBA to handle arrays as one-based. This is accomplished by including the Option Base 1 directive at the top of the module:

```
Option Compare Database
Option Base 1
Sub process_year_data_3()
    Dim year_2006(12) As Single
    Dim fill_array As Integer
    Dim rs As New ADODB.Recordset
    rs.Open "Select * From tblYears Where Year=2006", _
        CurrentProject.Connection, adOpenKeyset, adLockOptimistic
    For fill_array = 1 To 12
        year_2006(fill_array) = rs.Fields(fill_array)
```

```
    Next fill_array
      rs.Close
    Set rs = Nothing
    'further processing goes here
  End Sub
```

The `fill_array` loop now cycles from 1 to 12 instead of the previous range of 0 to 11. This is a personal choice; switching base is not required, but one-based arrays are easier for some developers to follow.

Using collections

An alternative to using an array for in-memory temporary storage is to use a custom *collection*. Like arrays, collections are often used to store like data. Here is the code to create a collection of 12 months and populate the collection with values from the sample table:

```
Sub make_collection( )
  Dim months As New Collection
  Dim rs As New ADODB.Recordset
  Dim monthname As String
  Dim monthvalue As Single
  rs.Open "Select * From tblYears Where Year=2006", _
    CurrentProject.Connection, adOpenKeyset, adLockOptimistic
  For fill_coll = 1 To 12
    monthvalue = rs.Fields(fill_coll)
    monthname = rs.Fields(fill_coll).Name
    months.Add monthvalue, monthname
  Next fill_coll
    rs.Close
  Set rs = Nothing
  'further processing goes here
  End Sub
```

In the first code line (after the Sub declaration), the variable `months` is dimensioned as a new collection. Further down, the names of the months and the values are read out of the recordset and into the two variables `monthname` and `monthvalue`. These, in turn, are used with the `Add` method of the collection.

The interim step of storing the month names and values from the recordset into the `monthname` and `monthvalue` variables is necessary. While this line of code will work to populate the collection:

```
    months.Add rs.Fields(fill_coll), rs.Fields(fill_coll).Name
```

if the recordset is subsequently closed, the collection will lose the values and become useless.

Working with a collection is easy. For example, to use the value for July, this type of syntax will do the trick:

```
    july_data = months.Item("July")
```

Collections have `Add`, `Item`, and `Remove` methods, and the single `Count` property. You can learn more about collections by looking them up in the Access Help system.

6.3 Working with Multidimensional Arrays

Problem

I know how to use arrays that are based on one dimension, but I have a new project in which I need to keep track of values in two dimensions. I have a number of departments, and now for each department I will have three years of total expenses to maintain in memory while processing. How can I use an array to hold this multi-faceted data?

Solution

One of the best ways to think about a multidimensional array is to use the example of an Excel worksheet. A single-dimensional array is like a set of values going down Column A. Adding a second dimension is like adding a set of values going down Column B. Figure 6-7 shows an Excel worksheet with two-dimensional data. There are three departments, and for each department there are three values. The departments are one dimension, and the numeric values are the second dimension.

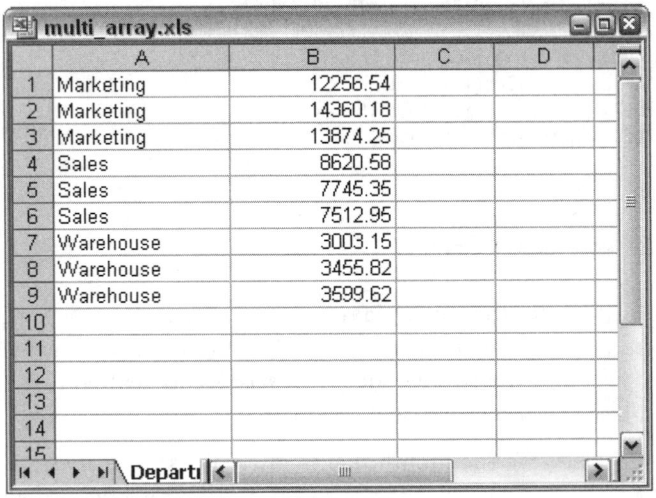

Figure 6-7. Two-dimensional data

In an Access code module, dimensioning an array with two dimensions listed in the Dim statement creates this type of structure. In this particular example, you have three departments and three years' worth of data. The following code shows you how to dimension and populate a two-dimensional array to hold this data. Note that the Option Base 1 statement is included so that the array elements are numbered starting with 1, not 0:

```
Option Base 1
Sub multi_array_1( )
```

```
      Dim myArray(3, 3) As Double
        myArray(1, 1) = 12256.54
        myArray(1, 2) = 14360.18
        myArray(1, 3) = 13874.25
        myArray(2, 1) = 8620.58
        myArray(2, 2) = 7745.35
        myArray(2, 3) = 7512.95
        myArray(3, 1) = 3003.15
        myArray(3, 2) = 3455.82
        myArray(3, 3) = 3599.62
      End Sub
```

Note how the Dim statement sets two dimensions for the array, each with three elements. This creates nine (three times three) distinct places to store values. Also, note that this array is set to the Double type to hold the decimal-based values.

When working with this data in code, you simply address the necessary array position to use the data. For example:

```
      sales_year_3 = myArray(2, 3)
```

Discussion

With multidimensional arrays, consideration should be given to how to enumerate each dimension. That is, the data itself should drive the order of the dimensions. For example, the following are two subroutines that work with the same data. The data contains the names of five cities, and the department that belongs to each city. An array to hold this data will have 10 distinct places to hold data because two pieces of information must be stored for each city (the name of the city, and the department name associated with that city). Here are the two subroutines:

```
      Sub multi_array_2()
        Dim myArray(5, 2) As String
          myArray(1, 1) = "Atlanta"
          myArray(2, 1) = "Chicago"
          myArray(3, 1) = "Cleveland"
          myArray(4, 1) = "Houston"
          myArray(5, 1) = "Portland"
          myArray(1, 2) = "Sales"
          myArray(2, 2) = "Headquarters"
          myArray(3, 2) = "Warehouse"
          myArray(4, 2) = "Customer Service"
          myArray(5, 2) = "International Sales"
      End Sub

      Sub multi_array_3()
        Dim myArray(2, 5) As String
          myArray(1, 1) = "Atlanta"
          myArray(1, 2) = "Chicago"
          myArray(1, 3) = "Cleveland"
          myArray(1, 4) = "Houston"
          myArray(1, 5) = "Portland"
```

```
        myArray(2, 1) = "Sales"
        myArray(2, 2) = "Headquarters"
        myArray(2, 3) = "Warehouse"
        myArray(2, 4) = "Customer Service"
        myArray(2, 5) = "International Sales"
    End Sub
```

In the first subroutine, the array is dimensioned as:

```
    Dim myArray(5, 2) As String
```

In the second subroutine, the array is dimensioned as:

```
    Dim myArray(2, 5) As String
```

To be clear, the order of (5, 2) or (2, 5) makes the difference here. Either arrangement stores the data, and a subjective decision drives the choice of arrangement. Figure 6-8 shows both arrangements of the data on an Excel worksheet. Visualizing the data and its layout in this fashion may help you think through organizing your multidimensional arrays.

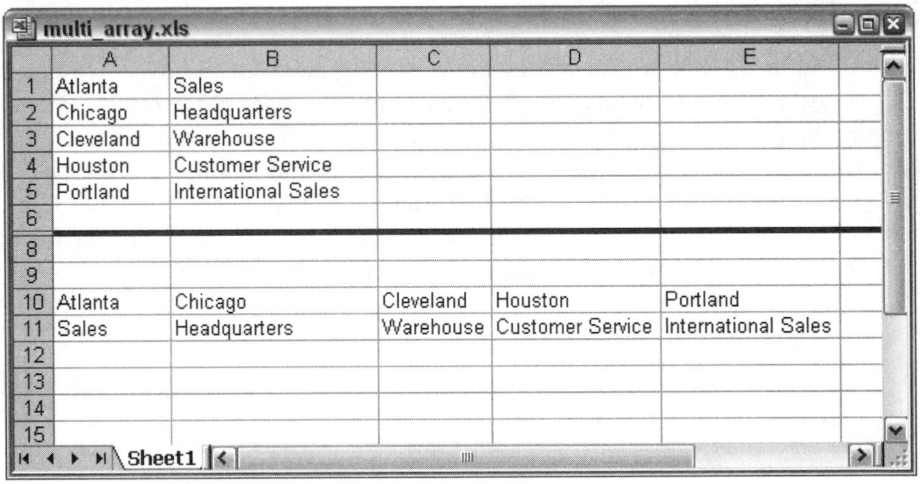

multi_array.xls

	A	B	C	D	E
1	Atlanta	Sales			
2	Chicago	Headquarters			
3	Cleveland	Warehouse			
4	Houston	Customer Service			
5	Portland	International Sales			
6					
8					
9					
10	Atlanta	Chicago	Cleveland	Houston	Portland
11	Sales	Headquarters	Warehouse	Customer Service	International Sales
12					
13					
14					
15					

Sheet1

Figure 6-8. Two arrangements of data

Working with three-dimensional data

Adding a third dimension to an array allows storage of even more complex data. Here is a code routine that dimensions and populates an array with three dimensions: (2, 3, 4). Multiplying the element numbers returns the number of distinct memory locations that are created for the array. In this case, there are 24:

```
    Sub multi_array_4()
        Dim myArray(2, 3, 4) As Integer
        myArray(1, 1, 1) = 1
        myArray(1, 1, 2) = 2
```

```
        myArray(1, 1, 3) = 3
        myArray(1, 1, 4) = 4
        myArray(1, 2, 1) = 5
        myArray(1, 2, 2) = 6
        myArray(1, 2, 3) = 7
        myArray(1, 2, 4) = 8
        myArray(1, 3, 1) = 9
        myArray(1, 3, 2) = 10
        myArray(1, 3, 3) = 11
        myArray(1, 3, 4) = 12
        myArray(2, 1, 1) = 13
        myArray(2, 1, 2) = 14
        myArray(2, 1, 3) = 15
        myArray(2, 1, 4) = 16
        myArray(2, 2, 1) = 17
        myArray(2, 2, 2) = 18
        myArray(2, 2, 3) = 19
        myArray(2, 2, 4) = 20
        myArray(2, 3, 1) = 21
        myArray(2, 3, 2) = 22
        myArray(2, 3, 3) = 23
        myArray(2, 3, 4) = 24
    End Sub
```

When Excel is used to model this data, the rows and columns of a worksheet are useful in showing only two of the dimensions. The trick is to add Excel's ability to present 3D data. This effect is accomplished by stacking worksheets.

Figure 6-9 shows how the data is placed in Excel. The figure displays two different worksheets. You can see this by looking at the worksheet tabs, named *1* and *2*. These names match the first dimension of the array, which is sized to two elements. The first 12 array assignments, in which the first element is numbered as 1, are displayed on the first worksheet. The second 12 are on the adjacent worksheet.

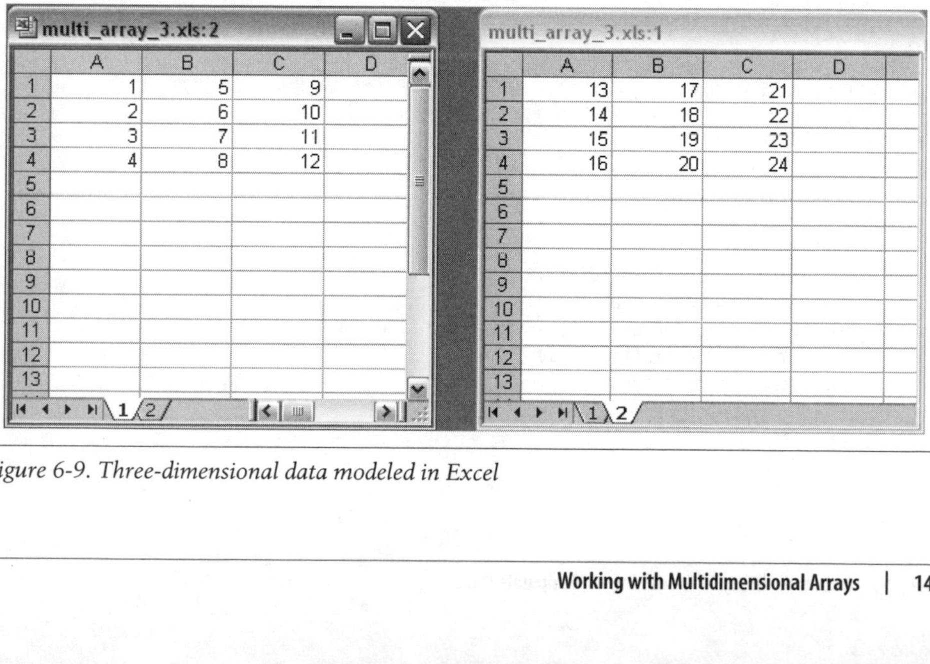

Figure 6-9. Three-dimensional data modeled in Excel

6.4   Sorting an Array

Problem

How can values in an array be sorted?

Solution

Several sorting algorithms are available. The *bubble sort* serves well to in sorting most arrays. This sort works by comparing two side-by-side elements in an array, and swapping them if they are in the wrong order of size. The array can be sorted in either ascending or descending order.

In an ascending sort, the bubble sort compares the values of the first two elements, and places the larger value in the higher (second) element. This testing is then continued for each successive pair of elements, such that the largest value floats to the top (like a bubble).

In the following example, a single-dimensional array is created and populated with values in a random order. Then the sort routine arranges the elements:

```
Sub bubble_sort( )
    Dim temp As Variant
    Dim elements As Integer
    Dim test As Integer
    Dim swap_elements_flag As Boolean
    Dim result As String

    'create array
    Dim arr(10)
    arr(0) = 4
    arr(1) = 3
    arr(2) = 7
    arr(3) = 8
    arr(4) = 1
    arr(5) = 44
    arr(6) = 25
    arr(7) = 9
    arr(8) = 15
    arr(9) = 12

    'sort array
    iteration_count = 0
    For elements = 0 To (UBound(arr) - 1)
      swap_elements_flag = False
      For test = 1 To (UBound(arr) - 1) - iteration_count
        If arr(test) < arr(test - 1) Then
            temp = arr(test)
```

```
            arr(test) = arr(test - 1)
            arr(test - 1) = temp
            swap_elements_flag = True
        End If
    Next test
    If swap_elements_flag = False Then Exit For
    iteration_count = iteration_count + 1
Next elements

'print result
result = ""
For elements = 0 To (UBound(arr) - 1)
    result = result & arr(elements) & " "
Next elements
Debug.Print result
End Sub
```

In a nutshell, the routine loops through the array, comparing successive pairs of elements. If their values need to be swapped, this is accomplished by using a temporary variable called temp. This variable holds the value of one of the elements while its position is overwritten with the element value next to it; the temp value then goes into that element.

This is repeated until no more element values are out of sync. The loop is then exited because the sorting is done. At the end of the routine, the array is written out to the immediate window. Figure 6-10 shows the result. Compare this with the order of the values when the array was created in the code routine (4 3 7 8 1 44 25 9 15 12).

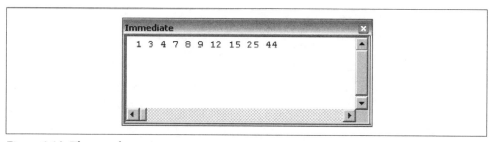

Figure 6-10. The sorted array

Discussion

An array can be sorted in ascending or descending order. In the preceding code, a simple change of operator (from less than to greater than) will swap the order. For a descending sort, change the appropriate line to:

```
    If arr(test) > arr(test - 1) Then
```

This produces the result seen in Figure 6-11.

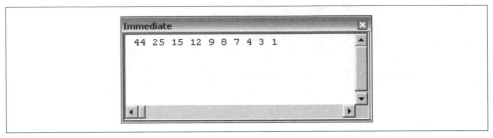

Figure 6-11. The array sorted in descending order

Sorting multidimensional arrays

Sorting multidimensional arrays is done in the same way as sorting single-dimensional arrays—you just have to select the dimension to sort. This next example is similar to the previous one, except the array has two dimensions, and a new variable, sort_element, controls which element to sort:

```
Sub bubble_sort_multi()
    Dim temp As Variant
    Dim elements As Integer
    Dim test As Integer
    Dim swap_elements_flag As Boolean
    Dim result As String

    Dim sort_element As Integer
    sort_element = 1

    'create two-dimensional array
    Dim arr(10, 2)
    arr(0, 0) = 4
    arr(1, 0) = 3
    arr(2, 0) = 7
    arr(3, 0) = 8
    arr(4, 0) = 1
    arr(5, 0) = 44
    arr(6, 0) = 25
    arr(7, 0) = 9
    arr(8, 0) = 15
    arr(9, 0) = 12

    arr(0, 1) = "zebra"
    arr(1, 1) = "eel"
    arr(2, 1) = "cat"
    arr(3, 1) = "dog"
    arr(4, 1) = "aardvark"
    arr(5, 1) = "lion"
    arr(6, 1) = "lamb"
    arr(7, 1) = "bear"
    arr(8, 1) = "goose"
    arr(9, 1) = "hamster"

    'sort array
    iteration_count = 0
```

```
    For elements = 0 To (UBound(arr) - 1)
      swap_elements_flag = False
      For test = 1 To (UBound(arr) - 1) - iteration_count
        If arr(test, sort_element) < arr(test - 1, sort_element) Then
          temp = arr(test, sort_element)
          arr(test, sort_element) = arr(test - 1, sort_element)
          arr(test - 1, sort_element) = temp
          swap_elements_flag = True
        End If
      Next test
      If swap_elements_flag = False Then Exit For
      iteration_count = iteration_count + 1
    Next elements

    'print result
    result = ""
    For elements = 0 To (UBound(arr) - 1)
      result = result & arr(elements, sort_element) & " "
    Next elements
    Debug.Print result
  End Sub
```

For this example, the sort_element variable can be assigned a value of 0 or 1. If the value is 0, the sort is applied to the numerical values that occupy the first set of positions of the second dimension. When sort_element has a value of 1, the sort is applied to the animal names, which occupy the second set of positions. Figure 6-12 shows the result of such a sort.

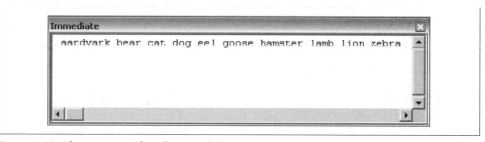

Figure 6-12. The array sorted on the second dimension

As with a single-dimensional array sort, the use of the greater-than or less-than sign drives whether the sort is done in ascending or descending order.

6.5   Flattening Data

Problem

How can relational data in a parent-child table relationship be combined to fit into one table? The data is meant for analysis in Excel, where the concept of one-to-many data is not well supported.

Solution

Whenever you run a select query based on parent and child tables, you'll usually see a higher degree of duplication in the data returned than you'll see when you run a query based on a single table. Of course, different factors are at play here, such as which fields (particularly those from the child table) are used. The use/avoidance of the Distinct and DistinctRow predicates (see Recipe 1.7) also affects the result.

Figure 6-13 shows the Access Relationships window. In this schema, for each client record from tblClients, there can be zero or more pet records in the tblPets table. Likewise, for each pet record from tblPets, there can be zero or more appointment records in the tblAppointments table.

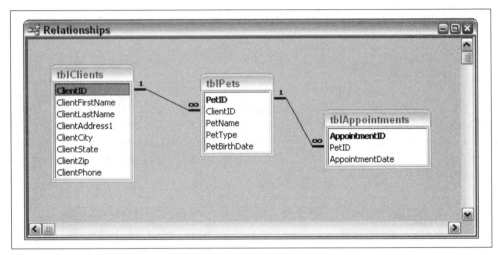

Figure 6-13. Related one-to-many data

Because many of the parent records will have multiple child records, when a select query includes fields from a child table, fields from the parent table are likely to be duplicated. Figure 6-14 shows a query design that returns records based on data from the parent and child tables.

When this query is run, each client will be listed once for each pet she owns: if a client has three pets, the client's name will appear three times. A run of this query is shown in Figure 6-15. Nancy A. Armstrong is listed twice; she owns a dog and a cat.

This query effectively combines the data from the two tables into a single table (a process known as *flattening*). You can now copy this flattened-down relational data into Excel for further analysis.

Flattened data has other uses as well—for example, it's commonly used as the source for a mail merge (see Recipe 6.15).

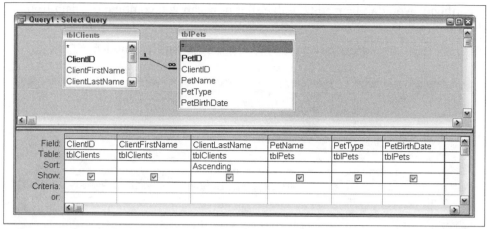

Figure 6-14. A query based on parent and child tables

ClientID	ClientFirstNam	ClientLastNam	PetName	PetType	PetBirthDate
388	Rubi	Aguilera	Max	Dog	4/19/2000
430	Shantell	Aiona	Zorro	Cat	11/10/1994
201	Norman	Aiona	Missy	Cat	5/26/1991
343	Faris	Alameda	Honey	Dog	1/14/1993
195	Line	Alandale	Bubbles	Cat	7/14/1991
128	Beatrice	Alandale	Lassie	Dog	1/8/1998
65	Joyce K.	Albrecht	Fido	Dog	8/27/1993
450	Ms.	Allen	Hunter	Cat	6/21/1997
412	Celine	Antonoff	Felix	Cat	11/16/1995
418	Lahring	Armas	Honey	Dog	11/4/1992
366	Nancy A.	Armstrong	Lassie	Dog	4/8/1994
366	Nancy A.	Armstrong	Leo	Cat	7/18/1995
84	Jessie	Arroyo	Fuzzy	Ferret	8/20/1991
346	Damian	Askvik	Climber	Cat	2/2/1996
275	Fran	Bachar	Lassie	Dog	5/24/1999
172	Nina	Backus	Paws	Cat	1/9/2001
107	Gintas	Baker	Tarka	Ferret	9/26/1990

Record: 1 of 438

Figure 6-15. The query returns flattened data

Discussion

Optimizing relational data to remove all redundant data points is a goal of good database design. However, sometimes it's necessary to give portability preference over efficiency.

Looking back at Figure 6-13, you'll see that the data model in this recipe has three levels of hierarchal data. Moving this data intact into Excel would be a chore, and even then it wouldn't be readily usable. But how can you combine the data from all three tables so that you can work with it in Excel?

Figure 6-16 shows a query based on all three tables of the data model.

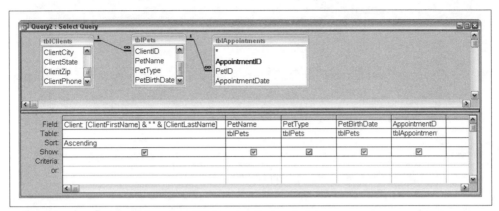

Figure 6-16. A select query based on three levels of hierarchal data

Figure 6-17 shows the result of running the query. It is easy to see the redundancy in the client names, and even in the pet names (which come from the middle table). Only the appointment dates stand as a unique factor in the records.

Client	PetName	PetType	PetBirthDate	AppointmentDate
Aaron Skibbe	Sniffer	Dog	5/8/1992	2/3/2002
Abby Lund	Royal	Dog	1/7/2001	5/9/2002
Abby Lund	Royal	Dog	1/7/2001	8/18/2003
Abe Naughton	Lassie	Dog	2/13/1991	5/6/2002
Abe Naughton	Lassie	Dog	2/13/1991	5/24/2002
Abe Naughton	Lassie	Dog	2/13/1991	2/8/2003
Alain Hlookoff	Nestie	Bird	2/21/1991	3/26/2003
Alan Davidson	Pretty Girl	Bird	7/24/1995	11/18/2002
Alan Davidson	Pretty Girl	Bird	7/24/1995	3/20/2003
Alberta Kramer	Honey	Dog	12/23/1997	9/15/2002
Alicia M. McCracken	Fido	Dog	7/11/1991	8/1/2002
Alma Gorin	Moon	Snake	3/5/1996	2/6/2003
Alma Gorin	Moon	Snake	3/5/1996	10/12/2003
Alma Pruett	Proud King	Horse	5/1/2001	5/22/2002
Alma Pruett	Proud King	Horse	5/1/2001	6/14/2003
Alma Pruett	Proud King	Horse	5/1/2001	11/17/2003

Record: 1 of 281

Figure 6-17. Three levels of data are flattened

6.6 Expanding Data

Problem

I have data that is redundant. In a single table, some fields have duplication. What is a good way to programmatically turn this table of data into a set of parent and child tables?

Solution

This problem is best illustrated with a real-life example. On a project I worked on recently, I built a data collection screen in which people could fill in their names and addresses, and make selections identifying their interests. This was an unbound form that was essentially capturing both the "one" and "many" sides of the data. The respondents' name and address information made up the data for the parent table. The interests each respondent selected became their associated child records. The form essentially was an entry vehicle for flat data that had to be promoted to fit the relational model. A simplified version of the form is shown in Figure 6-18.

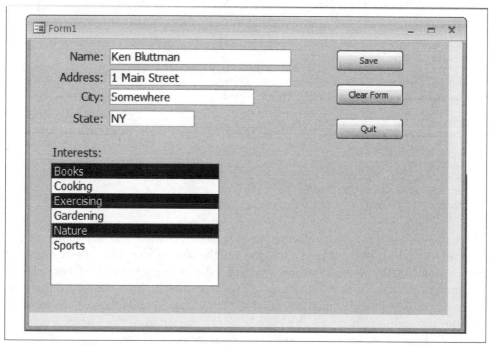

Figure 6-18. A data collection form

A click of the Save button ran this code:

```
Private Sub cmdSave_Click()
'assume name, address, city, and state are filled in and validated
'assume at least one interest has been selected

Dim conn As ADODB.Connection
Set conn = CurrentProject.Connection
Dim recset As New ADODB.Recordset
Dim ssql As String
Dim max_contact_id As Long
Dim itm As Variant

'insert contact information
ssql = "Insert Into tblContacts(Name, Address, City, State) "
ssql = ssql & " Values ("
ssql = ssql & "'" & Replace(Me.txtName, "'", "''") & "', "
ssql = ssql & "'" & Replace(Me.txtAddress, "'", "''") & "', "
ssql = ssql & "'" & Replace(Me.txtCity, "'", "''") & "', "
ssql = ssql & "'" & Replace(Me.txtState, "'", "''") & "')"
conn.Execute ssql

'get highest ContactID value
ssql = "Select Max(ContactID) as MaxContactID From tblContacts"
recset.Open ssql, conn, adOpenKeyset, adLockOptimistic
max_contact_id = recset.Fields("MaxContactID")
recset.Close

'store interests in tblInterests, using max_contact_id
For Each itm In Me.lstInterests.ItemsSelected
  ssql = "Insert Into tblInterests(ContactID, Interest)"
  ssql = ssql & " Values(" & max_contact_id & ", '" & _
      Me.lstInterests.ItemData(itm) & "')"
  conn.Execute ssql
Next
conn.Close
Set recset = Nothing
MsgBox "data saved"
End Sub
```

The code places the parent information (the contact name and address) into the tblContacts table. Then, a query is done on the key of the table, the ContactID AutoNumber field. Using the Max function, the highest value of ContactID is returned to the max_contact_id variable. This value must be from the record that was just written. Once the ContactID is known, the associated child records can be written into the tblInterests table. The ItemsSelected collection of the listbox is used to return each selected item, and a record is written for each selection.

Discussion

Expanding data, promoting data, normalizing data—whatever you wish to call it, it's a big subject in regard to database theory and practice. The overall goal is to remove redundancy in data. In the example in this recipe, the flat data entered via the form was manipulated into a relation. The full contact information was not written into the records along with the interests—only the ContactID was written, and it was used properly here as a foreign key.

Flat data that is already stored in a database table (or just in a text file or worksheet) can be promoted to a relational model in a similar fashion to that described here. You will need to decide which fields will go to the parent table, and which will go to the child table, but as long as the parent table that will become populated as you process the data has an AutoNumber field, you can always attain the max value from that field and use it as the foreign key in the child table.

6.7   Encrypting Data

Problem

How can I keep my data private? Is there a way to obscure the data so no one but me can make sense of it?

Solution

Encryption comes in many forms and levels of complexity. In many cases, a relatively easy encryption scheme is all that is needed. For example, the following code will encrypt the passed-in data by offsetting the character values in the data:

```
Function encrypt_decrypt_offset _
    (text As String, encrypt As Boolean) As String
Dim new_string As String
Dim loop1 As Integer
If text = "" Then
    encrypt_decrypt_offset = ""
    Exit Function
End If
new_string = ""
Select Case encrypt
  Case True
    For loop1 = 1 To Len(text)
      new_string = new_string & Chr(Asc(Mid(text, loop1, 1)) + 5)
    Next loop1
  Case False
    For loop1 = 1 To Len(text)
      new_string = new_string & Chr(Asc(Mid(text, loop1, 1)) - 5)
    Next loop1
End Select
encrypt_decrypt_offset = new_string
End Function

Sub test1( )
Dim altered_text As String
altered_text = encrypt_decrypt_offset("All good things in time", True)
```

```
MsgBox altered_text
altered_text = encrypt_decrypt_offset(altered_text, False)
MsgBox altered_text
End Sub
```

The encrypt_decrypt_offset function takes two arguments: a string of data, and a Boolean value to tell the function whether to encrypt or decrypt (actually, all the Boolean value does is control whether the function shifts character values up or down). The function works by converting the characters in the string to their numeric character codes (see Recipe 5.9), adjusting those values up or down, and then converting them back into letters, numbers, etc. An offset of 5 is hardcoded into the function, but any small number will do.

When the function runs, each character in the passed-in string is replaced with the character whose ASCII value is 5 greater or lower. For example, when the encrypt Boolean value is true, an "a" will be replaced with an "f"; when the encrypt Boolean value is false, an "f" will be replaced with an "a." These two operations are the reverse of each other.

In the preceding code, the test1 routine calls the function, passing it the hardcoded phrase "All good things in time." Figure 6-19 shows the returned encrypted message.

Figure 6-19. The encrypted message

The test1 routine then continues with another call to the function, this time reversing the encryption back to the plain text, as shown in Figure 6-20.

Figure 6-20. The decrypted message

For semivaluable information, and for a use with a nontechnical user community, this encryption scheme is probably adequate. Depending on how you code it, you can apply it to a table of data, or even just certain columns in a table.

Those with a keen eye, however, might see the weakness of this method. Each letter is encrypted with the same offset. Comparing the encrypted phrase in Figure 6-19 with the plain text in Figure 6-20, it's easy to see that all the spaces were changed to percent signs (%), that the two "l's" in All became two "q's," and so on. This encryption is easy to implement, but it wouldn't be too hard to crack either.

Discussion

You may require a stronger encryption method for your data. The following function takes a different approach, using a separate phrase (called a *key phrase*) to encrypt the data. One character at a time, the code loops through both the phrase to be encrypted and the key phrase (repeating this phrase as necessary). The XOR function is applied to each pair of characters to determine how to change the character in the plain text. This is known as XOR encryption.

XOR is a logic operator that works on the bits of the character to be converted (a single character, which is 1 byte long, has 8 bits; that is, 1 byte = 8 bits). Each character is converted to its binary value, which consists of 1s and 0s—for example, the lower-case letter "a" is converted to the binary 01100001. XOR then compares the bits in each position for the two characters. When the two bits are the same (e.g., 0 and 0), a 1 is returned for that bit position; when the bits are different (e.g., 0 and 1), a 0 is returned. The resulting binary number is then converted back into its ASCII equivalent.

This operation typically converts letters into nonalphabetic characters, which makes the encryption difficult to break. Using a lengthy key phrase further enhances the strength of the encryption. Let's look at an example:

```
Public Function encrypt_decrypt _
    (normal_text As String, encrypt_text As String)
Dim loop1 As Integer
Dim encrypt_char_pos As Integer
Dim encrypt_char_value As Integer
Dim normal_text_length As Integer
Dim encrypt_text_length As Integer
normal_text_length = Len(normal_text)
encrypt_text_length = Len(encrypt_text)
encrypt_char_pos = 0
For loop1 = 1 To normal_text_length
  encrypt_char_pos = encrypt_char_pos + 1
  If encrypt_char_pos > encrypt_text_length Then
    encrypt_char_pos = 1
```

```
                End If
                encrypt_char_value = Asc(Mid(encrypt_text, encrypt_char_pos, 1))
                Mid(normal_text, loop1, 1) = _
                    Chr(Asc(Mid(normal_text, loop1, 1)) Xor encrypt_char_value)
            Next loop1
            encrypt_decrypt = normal_text
            End Function

            Sub alter_text( )
            Dim altered_text As String
            altered_text = _
                encrypt_decrypt("This is the time to put new plans into action", _
                "apples and oranges are two fruits that come in a basket")
            MsgBox altered_text
            altered_text = _
                encrypt_decrypt(altered_text, _
                "apples and oranges are two fruits that come in a basket")
            MsgBox altered_text
            End Sub
```

The function is called from the alter_text routine. Within this example, two hard-coded phrases are passed. "This is the time to put new plans into action" is the phrase to be encrypted, and "apples and oranges are two fruits that come in a basket" is the key phrase used with XOR on a character-by-character basis. These two phrases are passed to the encrypt_decrypt function, and the altered_text variable receives the encrypted text (shown in Figure 6-21).

Figure 6-21. Encryption created with the XOR operator and a key phrase

The second part of the alter_text routine reverses the encryption by sending the encrypted text (as the altered_text variable) along with the same key phrase to the function. Applying XOR to the encrypted text simply reverses the text back to its plain state, which is shown in Figure 6-22.

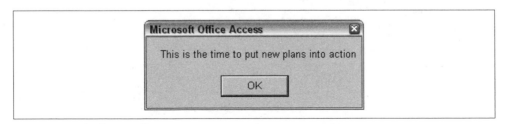

Figure 6-22. The decrypted text

6.8   Applying Proximate Matching

Problem

At times, it is necessary to look for data that is similar. This could mean words or names that are spelled just a bit differently, or that are the same length, or that start with the same character and are the same length even though the rest of the characters are different. How does one go about coding a routine to find such values?

Solution

Matching items that are similar is as much an art as it is a programming discipline. There are many rules that can be implemented, so it is best to determine your exact needs or expectations of how the data might be similar, and then code appropriately.

Figure 6-23 shows a table containing similar names. This recipe will discuss a few methods to compare each of these with the name Johnson (which just happens to be the first name anyway).

Figure 6-23. A table of similar names

Discussion

To demonstrate, we'll consider three matching approaches:

1. The first approach compares the lengths of the two strings and returns a percentage value indicating the closeness of the match. A result of 1 means the strings are exactly the same length; a lower result indicates that the record value is shorter, and a higher result indicates that it's longer.

2. The second approach returns a count of characters that match at the same position in each string, and the overall percentage of the match.

3. The third approach returns a 1 or a 0, respectively, to indicate whether the first character in the two strings matches.

The read_from_table routine opens the table shown in Figure 6-23 and loops through the records. The how_close routine is called, and it's sent three arguments: the value from the record, the name to match against (Johnson), and a flag to indicate which match type to use (1, 2, or 3). Here's the complete code:

```
Sub read_from_table()
Dim conn As ADODB.Connection
Set conn = CurrentProject.Connection
Dim rs As New ADODB.Recordset
Dim ssql As String
ssql = "Select * from Table1"
rs.Open ssql, conn, adOpenKeyset, adLockOptimistic
Do Until rs.EOF
    how_close rs.Fields(0), "Johnson", 1
rs.MoveNext
Loop
rs.Close
Set rs = Nothing
conn.Close
Set conn = Nothing
End Sub

Sub how_close(source_text As String, test_text As String, _
    match_type As Integer)
Dim source_length As Integer
Dim test_length As Integer
Dim match_strength As Single
Dim loop1 As Integer

source_length = Len(source_text)
test_length = Len(test_text)
match_strength = 0

'match_types are 1=comparison of length
'                2=same characters
'                3=same first character

Select Case match_type
  Case 1
    If source_length = test_length Then
      match_strength = match_strength + 1
    Else
      match_strength = source_length / test_length
    End If
    Debug.Print source_text & " " & test_text & " " & match_strength
  Case 2
    If source_length < test_length Then
       For loop1 = 1 To source_length
         If Mid(source_text, loop1, 1) = Mid(test_text, loop1, 1) Then _
```

```
                match_strength = match_strength + 1
         Next loop1
      Else
         For loop1 = 1 To source_length
            If Mid(source_text, loop1, 1) = Mid(test_text, loop1, 1) Then _
               match_strength = match_strength + 1
         Next loop1
      End If
      Debug.Print source_text & " " & test_text & " " & _
         match_strength & " of " & test_length & " " & _
         match_strength / test_length
   Case 3
      If Left(source_text, 1) = Left(test_text, 1) Then _
         match_strength = match_strength + 1
      Debug.Print source_text & " " & test_text & " " & match_strength
   End Select

   End Sub
```

Each match type (the third argument) writes its results—the record value, the hard-coded name, and an indication of the strength of the match—to the immediate window. Figure 6-24 shows the result when the first match type is sent as an argument, causing the match algorithm to test solely on length. Each record value is compared with Johnson, and a number is returned that indicates how close the lengths of the two strings are. A value of 1 indicates a perfect match.

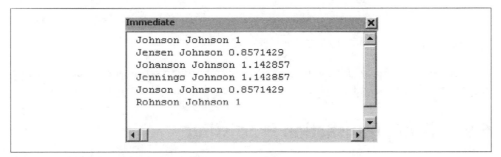

Figure 6-24. Matching on length

When the second match type is sent as an argument, the match algorithm tests the characters in each position in the record values with their counterparts in the other string. When the characters are the same, a 1 is added to the value of the match_ strength variable. As shown in Figure 6-25, the result in the immediate window indicates the number of matches out of the total number of characters in the hardcoded Johnson name, followed by the percentage of matches found. For example, comparing Jensen with Johnson resulted in just the first letter matching, producing only a 14.3 percent match.

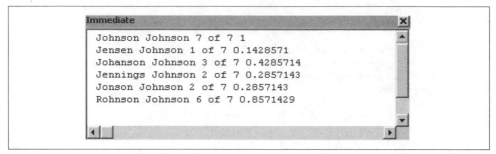

Figure 6-25. Matching on positional characters

The last match test is just on the first character. If the first character of both strings is the same, the match is made, regardless of the rest of the strings' compositions. As seen in Figure 6-26, only one match failed.

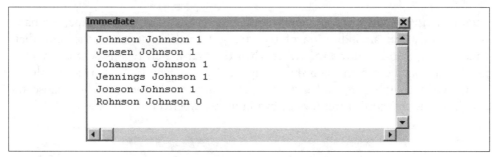

Figure 6-26. Matching on just the first character

This recipe should have given you some ideas about how to set up proximate matching algorithms. The exact rules to follow will be determined by your particular needs.

6.9 Using Transaction Processing

Problem

During a processing loop with a calculation, occasionally (because of incorrect data) the calculated value is not within the expected range. This can occur after dozens of good records have been processed. If/when a record with incorrect data is encountered, is there a way to reverse *all* of the processing that's taken place, back to the first record?

Solution

When processing is wrapped inside a transaction, it is easy to reverse the processing. Working with ADO, there are three methods of the connection object that are used with transaction processing:

`BeginTrans`

This statement is strategically placed at the position you want Access to reverse. All data writes are considered pending once `BeginTrans` is initiated.

`RollbackTrans`

This statement reverses the processing. It is optional, and is expected to be used only if an unexpected condition arises.

`CommitTrans`

This statement completes the transaction(s). The data updates to this point are considered pending. Issuing a `CommitTrans` is necessary to complete the pending updates.

Figure 6-27 shows a table with mileage per truck, client names, and start-and-end dates. The task is to calculate values that will populate the Expense column. Notice that the mileage value in the eighth record is –36. This is an unacceptable data point.

TruckPlate	Client	StartDate	EndDate	Mileage	Expense
BOR45	South	2/7/2005	2/7/2005	135	0
VRE92	Green	2/10/2005	2/13/2005	614	0
YPE99	Young	2/24/2005	2/25/2005	445	0
JYQ455	Nelson	3/2/2005	3/5/2005	790	0
NNE793	Park	3/4/2005	3/4/2005	54	0
JYQ455	Nelson	3/15/2005	3/20/2005	942	0
SDA782	Nelson	4/5/2005	4/6/2005	330	0
VRE92	Green	4/8/2005	4/8/2005	-36	0
BOR45	Green	4/12/2005	4/14/2005	300	0
VRE92	Park	4/24/2005	4/30/2005	2785	0
YPE99	Green	5/6/2005	5/7/2005	245	0
JYQ455	South	5/8/2005	5/9/2005	270	0
VRE92	Park	5/11/2002	5/11/2005	115	0

Record: 8 of 35

Figure 6-27. A table with mileage data

The following routine creates a recordset and loops through the records. Before the looping starts, the `BeginTrans` method is set on the connection object (conn). Multiplying the mileage values by 1.25 fills the Expense column. However, before the calculation is performed, the mileage is tested to see if the value is at least 1:

```
Sub rollback_all( )
    Dim conn As ADODB.Connection
    Set conn = CurrentProject.Connection
    Dim rs As New ADODB.Recordset
    Dim ssql As String
    ssql = "Select * from tblTrucksDates"
    rs.Open ssql, conn, adOpenKeyset, adLockOptimistic
    conn.BeginTrans 'starts before loop
    Do Until rs.EOF
      If rs.Fields("Mileage") < 1 Then
        conn.RollbackTrans 'rolls back all
```

```
        MsgBox "Processing rolled back"
        Exit Sub
    End If
    rs.Fields("Expense") = rs.Fields("Mileage") * 1.25
    rs.MoveNext
  Loop
  conn.CommitTrans 'commits once at the end
  rs.Close
  MsgBox "done"
End Sub
```

If the mileage value is less than 1, the RollbackTrans method is called, and the routine is exited. Because the BeginTrans method was placed before the loop, all the calculations are reversed, which leaves the table data in its original state. If all the data is valid (i.e., all the mileage values are 1 or higher), the CommitTrans method toward the end of the procedure commits the calculations.

Discussion

The placement of the transaction methods is key to how the commit or rollback operates. In the preceding example, the BeginTrans method was placed before the main processing loop, which kept all the calculations in a pending mode so that they could all be rolled back easily.

This illustrates the power of using transaction processing. If we hadn't used this approach, when the negative mileage value was found, we would have had to run an update query to initialize the Expense values in all the records back to 0. That might not sound like a big deal, but imagine the dilemma if the values to return to were all different. A simple update query would not help you roll back the changes. In such a case, using transaction processing ensures that you can roll back to initial values without a hitch.

6.10   Reading from and Writing to the Windows Registry

Problem

Through the years, I have used *.ini* files to store application data. But *.ini* files are vulnerable and can be moved around or deleted. This creates production issues. What is a safer way to store data that needs to be held outside of the application itself?

Solution

The Windows Registry is the ideal repository for data that is stored outside of Access. It is less vulnerable than independent *.ini* files, and because there are built-in programming commands for working with the Registry, using the Registry to store data is a breeze.

Data stored in the Registry has a hierarchical structure, similar to the way *.ini* files are arranged. Data is stored by application name, a section name within the application name, and then by key. A particular key holds a setting that can be saved or retrieved. There can be multiple key/setting pairs (also known as name/value pairs) within each section.

Discussion

You don't have to become intricately familiar with the Registry to use it—the VBA commands ease the burden. There are four VBA commands that make use of the Registry:

SaveSetting

This command is used to write data into the Registry. Four pieces of information are required: the application name, the section name, the key name, and the setting (the actual value being stored). Here is an example of creating two sections with varied key/setting pairs:

```
Sub write_registry( )
    SaveSetting "my_app", "User", "Name", "Ken"
    SaveSetting "my_app", "User", "Registration", "12345"
    SaveSetting "my_app", "User", "Level", "Manager"
    SaveSetting "my_app", "Preferences", "OpeningForm", "frmMain"
    SaveSetting "my_app", "Preferences", "DefaultPrinting", "Preview"
End Sub
```

GetSetting

This command returns data from the Registry. Three pieces of information are required: the application name, the section name, and the key name. The returned data point is a single value (the setting that matches the supplied key name). For example:

```
Sub read_registry( )
    Dim z As String
    z = GetSetting("my_app", "User", "Name")
    'process something with z
    z = GetSetting("my_app", "Preferences", "OpeningForm")
    'process something with z
End Sub
```

Typically, a variable is assigned the returned value, and further processing takes place. In the preceding example, the variable z is used to house the returned setting value.

GetAllSettings

This command also returns data from the Registry. Two pieces of information are required: the application name and the section name. Instead of returning a single value, GetAllSettings returns a two-dimensional array that contains all of the key/setting pairs within the designated section. You can use the returned data by working with the array. In this example, the variable `app_settings` is used as the array to hold the returned key/setting pairs from the User section:

```
Sub get_all_settings()
  Dim app_settings
  Dim array_loop As Integer
  app_settings = GetAllSettings("my_app", "User")
  For array_loop = LBound(app_settings, 1) To _
      UBound(app_settings, 1)
    Debug.Print app_settings(array_loop, 0), _
        app_settings(array_loop, 1)
  Next array_loop
End Sub
```

The first dimension of the array holds the key names, and the second dimension holds the setting values. The returned data is written to the immediate window. The data is the same as that written to the Registry with the `write_registry` routine presented earlier. Compare the returned data shown in Figure 6-28 with the values written to the Registry. They are the same values for the User section.

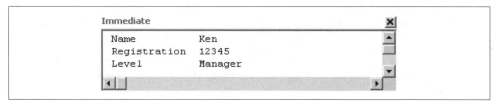

Figure 6-28. Returned key/setting pairs

DeleteSetting

This command deletes Registry entries. Two pieces of information are required: the application name and the section name. Optionally, a key name can also be included. When just the application name and the section name are provided, the entire section is removed, including all the key/setting pairs within it. The following code shows how to delete the entire Preferences section:

```
Sub delete_section_from_registry()
  DeleteSetting "my_app", "Preferences"
End Sub
```

You can include a key name to delete just one key/setting pair from within the specified section. For example, the following code deletes just the Level key (and its associated setting) from the User section:

```
Sub delete_key_from_registry()
  DeleteSetting "my_app", "User", "Level"
End Sub
```

Writing to and reading from the Registry is an easy way to share cross-database or cross-application information. Within a single database application, it is feasible to store such data within a database table. However, if you store the information outside of the database application, it's readily available to other applications. Even non-Access applications can use the information, because Registry data is available to any application that can read from the Registry. For example, an Excel workbook can read the values written by an Access application.

6.11   Creating Charts

Problem

I know how to place a simple chart on a form and have it display summary information. But what if I need more sophistication, such as showing information that is related, but not within the current bound record or table?

Solution

 This solution applies to Access 2003 and earlier versions. At the end of the recipe, you'll find comments about charts in Access 2007.

Let's start with the basics. Access has a basic chart control that is bound to a form via a parent and child key, in the same manner that a subform is in sync with the parent form on which it's placed. In Access 2003 and earlier versions, you add a chart to a form using the Insert → Chart menu command.

Figure 6-29 shows a form based on a table of customers. The Record Source of the form is the tblCustomers table. The chart is bound to the Customer records, but the Row Source of the chart is this SQL statement, based on the tblAnnualSales table:

```
SELECT tblAnnualSales.yr, tblAnnualSales.Amount FROM tblAnnualSales;
```

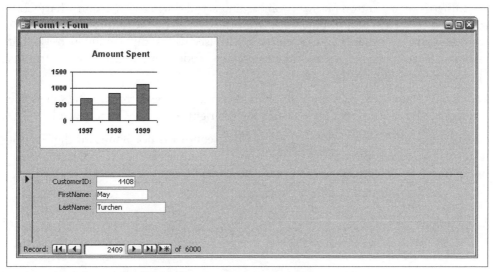

Figure 6-29. A form with a bound chart

Figure 6-30 shows the two tables. The tables relate in the CustomerID field. This field isn't included in the SQL statement; it isn't necessary because the chart and the form are CustomerID-related in the Link Child Fields and Link Master Fields properties.

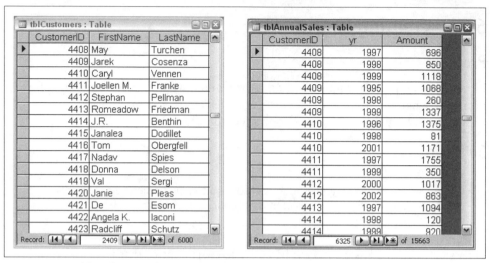

Figure 6-30. Tables of customers and annual sales

As the user browses records on the form, the chart updates to show the annual sales for the currently displayed customer. There is no need for coding past setting the properties mentioned earlier.

Discussion

An alternative chart control is the MS Chart. While in a form's design mode, click on the More Controls button on the Toolbox, and scroll down to Microsoft Chart Control 6.0 (your version may be different). Draw the control on the form. At first, it might seem unrelated to the data you are working with (see the example in Figure 6-31), but once you've set some properties and written some code to manipulate the control, its appearance will support the data.

Figure 6-32 shows the two types of chart controls on one form. On the left is the standard chart control from Figure 6-29. On the right is the MS Chart control.

Unlike a standard chart control, the MS Chart control is not bound to the data; it needs to be seeded with data to graph. This is accomplished in the On Current event of the form. As a record is made current, this code runs and updates the MS Chart:

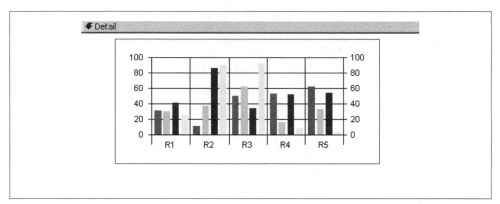

Figure 6-31. The plain MS Chart control

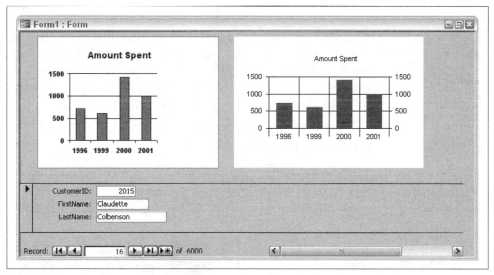

Figure 6-32. Two charts on one form

```
Private Sub Form_Current( )
Dim rec_count As Integer
Dim current_rec As Integer
Dim conn As ADODB.Connection
Set conn = CurrentProject.Connection
Dim ssql As String
Dim rs As New ADODB.Recordset
ssql = "SELECT tblAnnualSales.yr, tblAnnualSales.Amount "
ssql = ssql & "FROM tblAnnualSales Where tblAnnualSales.CustomerID=" & _
    Me.txtCustomerID
```

```
      rs.Open ssql, conn, adOpenKeyset, adLockOptimistic
      rec_count = rs.RecordCount
      current_rec = 1
      With Me.MSChart1
        .Plot.Axis(VtChAxisIdX, 1).AxisTitle.Visible = True
        .chartType = VtChChartType2dBar
        .ColumnCount = 1
        .RowCount = rec_count
        Do Until rs.EOF
          .Column = 1
          .Row = current_rec
          .RowLabel = rs.Fields("yr")
          .Data = rs.Fields("Amount")
          current_rec = current_rec + 1
        rs.MoveNext
        Loop
      End With
    End Sub
```

You have a great amount of programmatic control with an MS Chart. In a nutshell, you can code the chart type, factors about the axes, the series, and other appearance and data attributes. In this example, the data to be plotted is returned from a recordset based on the tblAnnualSales table, so the two charts display the same information. Now let's look at retooling the MS Chart control to display some other data.

Figure 6-33 shows the form with the chart on the right displaying the number of items purchased per year, instead of the amount spent.

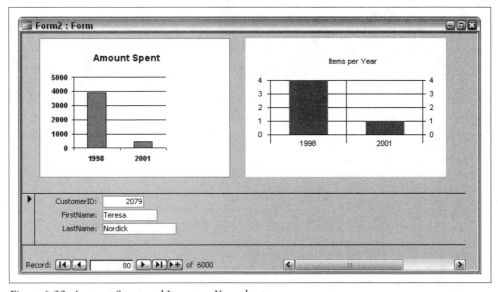

Figure 6-33. Amount Spent and Items per Year charts

In this example, a different SQL statement to different data drives what the chart on the right displays. Here is the updated code:

```
Private Sub Form_Current()
Dim rec_count As Integer
Dim current_rec As Integer
Dim conn As ADODB.Connection
Set conn = CurrentProject.Connection
Dim ssql As String
Dim rs As New ADODB.Recordset
ssql = "SELECT Year([PurchaseDate]) As Yr, Count(tblSales.Amount) "
ssql = ssql & "As CountofAmount FROM tblSales "
ssql = ssql & "GROUP BY tblSales.CustomerID, Year([PurchaseDate]) "
ssql = ssql & "HAVING tblSales.CustomerID=" & Me.txtCustomerID
rs.Open ssql, conn, adOpenKeyset, adLockOptimistic
rec_count = rs.RecordCount
current_rec - 1
With Me.MSChart1
  .Plot.Axis(VtChAxisIdX, 1).AxisTitle.Visible = True
  .chartType = VtChChartType2dBar
  .ColumnCount = 1
  .RowCount = rec_count
  Do Until rs.EOF
    .Column = 1
    .Row = current_rec
    .RowLabel = rs.Fields("yr")
    .Data = rs.Fields("CountOfAmount")
    current_rec = current_rec + 1
  rs.MoveNext
  Loop
End With
End Sub
```

The displayed data is queried from the tblSales table, which contains detailed records about purchases. The purchase count per year, per current customer, is queried and used to populate the chart.

Charts in Access 2007

In Access 2007, MS Graph is the tool used to create charts (you may be familiar with this tool from Word or PowerPoint). Additionally, there is a custom ActiveX chart control that can be placed on a form. Figure 6-34 shows a chart created with the custom control, along with a properties sheet showing the datasheet that provides the source of the data. This control can also display data from SQL Server and many other sources. Variations of the properties sheet let you control the many facets of the chart: series formatting, axes settings, and so on. In the upper-right corner of Figure 6-34, the mouse pointer shows where to find the control. It is not a standard tool; you must manually select it from the Controls drop-down list.

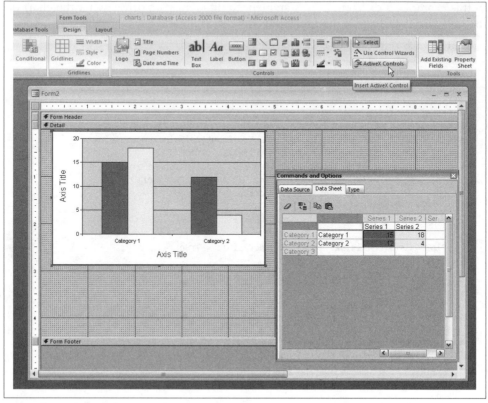

Figure 6-34. Using the ActiveX chart control

6.12   Scraping Web HTML

Problem

How can I access web sites' HTML code so I can collect data from varied sources to include in my database?

Solution

Setting a reference to the Microsoft Internet Controls provides a way, through code, to navigate to web sites and access their HTML source code. To set the reference, launch the Visual Basic Editor from Access by pressing Alt-F11, then use the Tools → References menu option to display the References dialog box. Check the box next to Microsoft Internet Controls, as shown in Figure 6-35, and click OK.

In a code module, you can use the `InternetExplorer` control to navigate to and access the HTML of a web page:

```
Sub get_html_1( )
Dim myExplorer As InternetExplorer
```

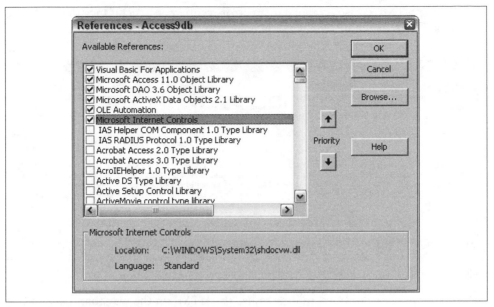

Figure 6-35. Setting a reference to Microsoft Internet Controls

```
Set myExplorer = New InternetExplorer
Dim page_source As String
On Error Resume Next

retry1:
myExplorer.Navigate URL:="http://www.bluttman.com"
If Err.Number <> 0 Then 'GoTo retry1
   Err.Clear
   GoTo retry1
End If

retry2:
page_source = myExplorer.Document.documentElement.innerhtml
If Len(page_source) > 0 Then
   Debug.Print page_source
Else
   GoTo retry2
End If
Set myExplorer = Nothing
Debug.Print "done"
End Sub
```

Since Internet connections can be intermittent, the code is structured such that the connection is tried over and over until it succeeds. In the section that starts with the retry1: label, the myExplorer object attempts to navigate to a site, using the Navigate method. If it fails, the error is caught, and the navigation is attempted again. This cycles until the navigation is successful.

Reading the HTML is also wrapped in an error-testing construct. Once the HTML is read, it is sent to the immediate window. Figure 6-36 shows an example.

```
Immediate                                                                    ✕
here
<HEAD><TITLE>Ken Bluttman</TITLE>
<META content="Bluttman, Ken Bluttman, Access, Excel, Word, PowerPoint, Office, VBA, VB, Vi
<META content="Ken Bluttman" name=description></HEAD>
<BODY text=#ffffff vLink=#ffff42 link=#ffe7c6 bgColor=#666666><FONT face="Arial, Helvetica"
<CENTER>
<TABLE width="95%">
<TBODY>
<TR>
<TD vAlign=top align=left width="30%"><IMG src="KenandMatt3.JPG"> <BR><FONT size=2><A href=
-TOP: 0px; MARGIN-LEFT: 0px; BORDER-LEFT: medium none; MARGIN-RIGHT: 0px; BORDER-BOTTOM: me
ARGIN-TOP: 0px; MARGIN-LEFT: 0px; BORDER-LEFT: medium none; MARGIN-RIGHT: 0px; BORDER-BOTTO
<TD vAlign=top align=middle width="40%"><FONT size=3><U>May 26, 2005</U><BR>I have a <A hre
  the night Wishy ate through the ethernet cable. Literally cut it into two pieces! Quite a
<TD vAlign=top width="3%">      </TD>
<TD vAlign=top><FONT size=2><BR><BR><A href="kb_writings.html">Full list of Ken's publicati
<CENTER>
```

Figure 6-36. HTML gathered through programming

You can adapt the get_html_1 routine to use the HTML in the way that makes sense for your needs.

Discussion

The preceding example showed how to navigate to a site and capture its HTML. The following example expands on this, showing how to search multiple sites for a phrase:

```
Sub search_site( )
  get_html_2 "http://www.6finestrings.com", "guitar"
  get_html_2 "http://www.logicstory.com", "VBA"
End Sub

Sub get_html_2(site As String, Optional key_phrase As String)
Dim myExplorer As InternetExplorer
Set myExplorer = New InternetExplorer
Dim page_source As String
Dim found_pos As Integer
On Error Resume Next

retry1:
myExplorer.Navigate URL:=site
If Err.Number <> 0 Then
    Err.Clear
    GoTo retry1
End If

retry2:
page_source = myExplorer.Document.documentElement.innerhtml
If Len(page_source) > 0 Then
    If Len(key_phrase) > 2 Then
```

```
                found_pos = 0
                found_pos = InStr(1, page_source, key_phrase)
                If found_pos > 0 Then
                    Do Until found_pos = 0
                        Debug.Print Mid(page_source, found_pos, 50)
                        found_pos = InStr(found_pos + 1, page_source, key_phrase)
                    Loop
                End If
            Else
                Debug.Print page_source
            End If
        Else
            GoTo retry2
        End If
        Set myExplorer = Nothing
        Debug.Print "done"
    End Sub
```

The get_html_2 routine takes as arguments a web site URL, and an optional phrase. If just the URL is supplied, the routine returns the full HTML for the page. If a phrase is supplied, the HTML of the site is searched for occurrences of the phrase. If the phrase is found, 50 characters beginning from the position of the start of the phrase are returned (this number, of course, can be changed).

The get_html_2 routine is called by the search_site routine, which passes the argument(s).

This recipe shows how to access the HTML of a web page. Once the HTML is available within code, you can do a lot with it. For example, you may want to examine the HTML for links, keywords, graphic file names, or other data.

6.13 Creating Custom Report Formatting

Problem

How can I control the appearance of items on a report? I want to be able to accentuate particular values when they pass a threshold I provide. The overall purpose is to highlight exceptional reportable values.

Solution

Since reports have code-behind modules, there are many ways to alter their formatting. Each control on a report can be addressed individually. The trick is to know what properties you can manipulate. All properties are accessed via the Properties collection, but you need to know how to specify the individual properties by name. For example, here is how to change the foreground color of a text box on a report:

```
    Me.txtQ1.Properties("ForeColor") = vbBlue
```

This routine, which can be placed in the report's Open event, cycles through the properties and lists their names and values in the immediate window:

```
Private Sub Report_Open(Cancel As Integer)
  On Error Resume Next
  For z = 0 To Me.txtAvgQ1.Properties.Count - 1
  Debug.Print Me.txtAvgQ1.Properties(z).Name & Chr(9) & _
      Me.txtAvgQ1.Properties(z).Value
  Next z
End Sub
```

The On Error Resume Next statement is included because not every property has a value. The result of running this code can be seen in Figure 6-37 (of course, there are more properties than just those shown in the figure). Bear in mind that this is a list of properties for a text box. Other controls, and the report sections, will have some properties that are unique to those particular objects.

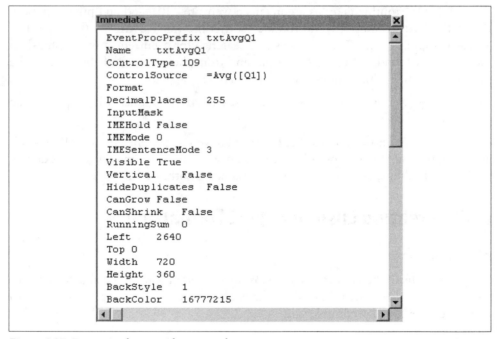

Figure 6-37. Properties for a text box control on a report

Discussion

Figure 6-38 shows a simple report design. In the Detail section are four text box controls, named txtQ1, txtQ2, txtQ3, and txtQ4. In the Report Footer section are four text box controls named txtAvgQ1, txtAvgQ2, txtAvgQ3, and txtAvgQ4. We'll specify some formatting to be applied to these text box controls when the report is run, if certain values are present in the data.

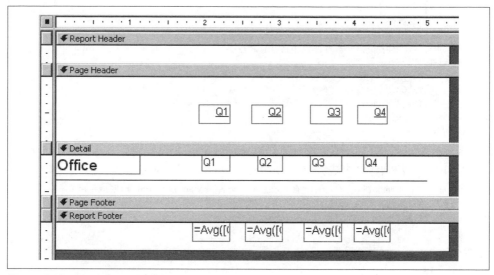

Figure 6-38. A simple report design

Code that tests values and formats the controls is found in two routines: the Format event of the detail section, and the Format event of the report footer. The first routine formats the controls in the detail section. The controls are first initialized to be black and not italic. This is necessary because the routine will be run multiple times (once for each record).

After the initialization, each of the data fields (Q1, Q2, etc.) is tested for its value. If the value is over the given threshold for that field, the control that houses that piece of data is changed to be blue and italic. Note how precisely you can control the formatting: if the values of Q1, Q2, or Q3 are >80, the formatting is applied; the value of Q4, however, must be greater than 85 for the formatting to be applied. Here's the complete routine:

```
Private Sub Detail_Format(Cancel As Integer, FormatCount As Integer)
   Me.txtQ1.Properties("ForeColor") = vbBlack
   Me.txtQ2.Properties("ForeColor") = vbBlack
   Me.txtQ3.Properties("ForeColor") = vbBlack
   Me.txtQ4.Properties("ForeColor") = vbBlack
   Me.txtQ1.Properties("FontItalic") = False
   Me.txtQ2.Properties("FontItalic") = False
   Me.txtQ3.Properties("FontItalic") = False
   Me.txtQ4.Properties("FontItalic") = False

   If Me.Q1 > 80 Then
      Me.txtQ1.Properties("ForeColor") = vbBlue
      Me.txtQ1.Properties("FontItalic") = True
   End If
   If Me.Q2 > 80 Then
      Me.txtQ2.Properties("ForeColor") = vbBlue
      Me.txtQ2.Properties("FontItalic") = True
```

```
      End If
    If Me.Q3 > 80 Then
        Me.txtQ3.Properties("ForeColor") = vbBlue
        Me.txtQ3.Properties("FontItalic") = True
    End If
    If Me.Q4 > 85 Then
        Me.txtQ4.Properties("ForeColor") = vbBlue
        Me.txtQ4.Properties("FontItalic") = True
    End If
End Sub
```

The second routine tests which of the four averages in the report footer is highest. The control holding the highest average is given a blue border:

```
Private Sub ReportFooter_Format(Cancel As Integer, FormatCount As Integer)
    If Me.txtAvgQ1 > Me.txtAvgQ2 Then
        If Me.txtAvgQ1 > Me.txtAvgQ3 Then
            If Me.txtAvgQ1 > Me.txtAvgQ4 Then
                Me.txtAvgQ1.Properties("BorderStyle") = 1
                Me.txtAvgQ1.Properties("BorderColor") = vbBlue
            Else
                Me.txtAvgQ4.Properties("BorderStyle") = 1
                Me.txtAvgQ4.Properties("BorderColor") = vbBlue
            End If
        Else
            If Me.txtAvgQ3 > Me.txtAvgQ4 Then
                Me.txtAvgQ3.Properties("BorderStyle") = 1
                Me.txtAvgQ3.Properties("BorderColor") = vbBlue
            Else
                Me.txtAvgQ4.Properties("BorderStyle") = 1
                Me.txtAvgQ4.Properties("BorderColor") = vbBlue
            End If
        End If
    Else
        If Me.txtAvgQ2 > Me.txtAvgQ3 Then
            If Me.txtAvgQ2 > Me.txtAvgQ4 Then
                Me.txtAvgQ2.Properties("BorderStyle") = 1
                Me.txtAvgQ2.Properties("BorderColor") = vbBlue
            Else
                Me.txtAvgQ4.Properties("BorderStyle") = 1
                Me.txtAvgQ4.Properties("BorderColor") = vbBlue
            End If
        Else
            If Me.txtAvgQ3 > Me.txtAvgQ4 Then
                Me.txtAvgQ3.Properties("BorderStyle") = 1
                Me.txtAvgQ3.Properties("BorderColor") = vbBlue
            Else
                Me.txtAvgQ4.Properties("BorderStyle") = 1
                Me.txtAvgQ4.Properties("BorderColor") = vbBlue
            End If
        End If
    End If
End Sub
```

Figure 6-39 shows the report after it is run. As expected, for Q1, Q2, and Q3, any value over 80 is italicized and appears in blue; for Q4, the value is italicized and printed in blue only if it is over 85. Also, the highest average on the bottom has a blue border around it.

	Q1	Q2	Q3	Q4
Denver	96	70	88	85
Tuscon	78	77	76	74
Spokane	80	74	84	87
	84.67	73.67	82.67	82

Figure 6-39. The report with custom formatting

Working at the level of controls, within the report events, opens the door for many formatting possibilities. This recipe touched on the basics, but some experimentation on your part will reveal numerous ways to enhance your reports.

6.14 Rounding Values

Problem

What are some ways I can control rounding of Single or Double number types? How does the Round function work, and are there alternatives?

Solution

The Round function takes a decimal value and rounds it to the number of decimal points supplied to the function. It accepts two arguments: the number being treated, and the number of decimal places to round to. Here are some examples:

- Round(45.8645618, 0) returns 46
- Round(45.8645618, 1) returns 45.9
- Round(45.8645618, 2) returns 45.86
- Round(45.8645618, 3) returns 45.865
- Round(45.8645618, 4) returns 45.8646
- Round(45.8645618, 5) returns 45.86456
- Round(45.8645618, 6) returns 45.864562

Using the Round function in a routine is straightforward. Here is an example of applying Round to a set of table records:

```
Sub access_round( )
  Dim conn As ADODB.Connection
  Set conn = CurrentProject.Connection
  Dim rs As New ADODB.Recordset
  Dim z As Integer
  Dim ssql As String
  ssql = "Select * from data"
  rs.Open ssql, conn, adOpenKeyset, adLockOptimistic
  For z = 1 To 3
    Debug.Print rs.Fields(1)
    Debug.Print Round(rs.Fields(1), 0)
    Debug.Print Round(rs.Fields(1), 1)
    Debug.Print Round(rs.Fields(1), 2)
    Debug.Print Round(rs.Fields(1), 3)
    Debug.Print Round(rs.Fields(1), 4)
    Debug.Print Round(rs.Fields(1), 5)
    Debug.Print Round(rs.Fields(1), 6)
    rs.MoveNext
  Next z
End Sub
```

Discussion

The Access Round function is not as strong as its Excel cousin, so this is a good place to use Excel for some extra muscle. (For an introduction to using Excel functions from within Access, see Recipe 6.1.)

There are three ways that Excel can run circles around Access' rounding. First, if you pass a negative number to Access' Round function as the second argument (the number of places to round to), an error will be generated. Not so with the Excel Round function. Here is a routine that calls the Round function in Excel to manipulate the Access values:

```
Sub excel_round( )
  Dim xcl As Object
  Set xcl = CreateObject("Excel.Application")
  Dim conn As ADODB.Connection
  Set conn = CurrentProject.Connection
  Dim rs As New ADODB.Recordset
  Dim z As Integer
  Dim ssql As String
  ssql = "Select * from data"
  rs.Open ssql, conn, adOpenKeyset, adLockOptimistic
  For z = 1 To 3
    Debug.Print rs.Fields(1)
    Debug.Print xcl.WorksheetFunction.Round(rs.Fields(1), 6)
    Debug.Print xcl.WorksheetFunction.Round(rs.Fields(1), 5)
    Debug.Print xcl.WorksheetFunction.Round(rs.Fields(1), 4)
    Debug.Print xcl.WorksheetFunction.Round(rs.Fields(1), 3)
    Debug.Print xcl.WorksheetFunction.Round(rs.Fields(1), 2)
    Debug.Print xcl.WorksheetFunction.Round(rs.Fields(1), 1)
```

```
        Debug.Print xcl.WorksheetFunction.Round(rs.Fields(1), 0)
        Debug.Print xcl.WorksheetFunction.Round(rs.Fields(1), -1)
        Debug.Print xcl.WorksheetFunction.Round(rs.Fields(1), -2)
        rs.MoveNext
    Next z
End Sub
```

Note that the last two `Debug.Print` lines send -1 and -2, respectively, as the number of decimal places to round to. Figure 6-40 shows the values written to the immediate window. The plain value 46 is returned with 0 as the decimal argument. In other words, the value is rounded to the ones position. When the decimal argument is -1, the value 50 is returned. In this case, the number is rounded a further position point to the left; i.e., to the tens position. When the decimal argument is -2, the value is rounded to the nearest hundred. The initial value of 45.8645618 is on the low side of 100, so the returned value is 0.

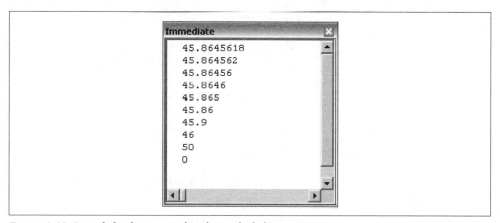

Figure 6-40. Rounded values created with Excel's help

Excel provides two additional functions that offer control on rounding: `RoundUp` and `RoundDown`. As their names imply, these functions can be used to force the rounding effect to all up or all down. Here is a variation of the preceding routine in which all occurrences of the Round function have been changed to `RoundDown`:

```
Sub excel_rounddown( )
    Dim xcl As Object
    Set xcl = CreateObject("Excel.Application")
    Dim conn As ADODB.Connection
    Set conn = CurrentProject.Connection
    Dim rs As New ADODB.Recordset
    Dim z As Integer
    Dim ssql As String
    ssql = "Select * from data"
    rs.Open ssql, conn, adOpenKeyset, adLockOptimistic
    For z = 1 To 3
        Debug.Print rs.Fields(1)
        Debug.Print xcl.WorksheetFunction.RoundDown(rs.Fields(1), 6)
        Debug.Print xcl.WorksheetFunction.RoundDown(rs.Fields(1), 5)
```

```
    Debug.Print xcl.WorksheetFunction.RoundDown(rs.Fields(1), 4)
    Debug.Print xcl.WorksheetFunction.RoundDown(rs.Fields(1), 3)
    Debug.Print xcl.WorksheetFunction.RoundDown(rs.Fields(1), 2)
    Debug.Print xcl.WorksheetFunction.RoundDown(rs.Fields(1), 1)
    Debug.Print xcl.WorksheetFunction.RoundDown(rs.Fields(1), 0)
    Debug.Print xcl.WorksheetFunction.RoundDown(rs.Fields(1), -1)
    Debug.Print xcl.WorksheetFunction.RoundDown(rs.Fields(1), -2)
    rs.MoveNext
  Next z
End Sub
```

As you might imagine, the results (shown in Figure 6-41) are different.

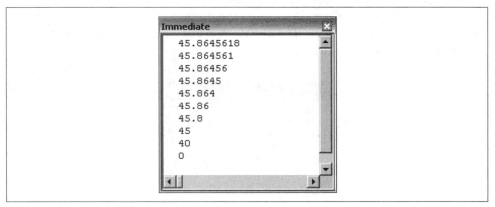

Figure 6-41. Values returned with Excel's RoundDown function

Of course, the RoundUp function returns another variation of results. For example, using RoundUp, the value 100 is returned from this line:

```
    Debug.Print xcl.WorksheetFunction.RoundUp(rs.Fields(1), -2)
```

6.15   Running Word Mail Merges

Problem

How can I run a dynamic Word mail merge from Access? The goal is to have the source of the merge be based on a query of data from the database itself, and to have the database start the merge operation and use the selected set of records.

Solution

With programmatic control over Word, it is easy to run a mail merge from Access. This example assumes that you've already created a Word mail merge document—and that the merge fields are in place within the document—and have been associated with database fields. The remaining task is to select which records (based on criteria) should be included in the merge.

Figure 6-42 shows the design of a sample merge document.

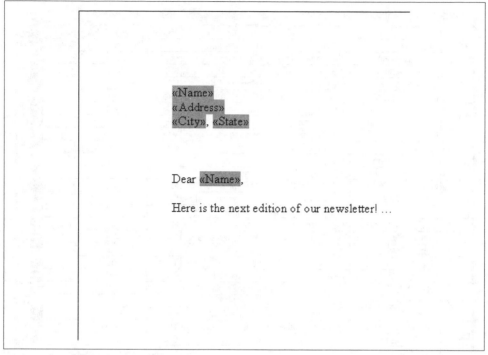

«Name»
«Address»
«City», «State»

Dear «Name»,

Here is the next edition of our newsletter! …

Figure 6-42. A simple mail merge document

The fields shown in the Word document match fields from the source Access table, shown in Figure 6-43. Note that not all of the fields in the table are placed in the Word document. The extra fields can be used for filtering the records that will be used as the mail merge source, if desired. This Access routine runs the merge: a Word application object and a Word document object are created and used to open the mail merge document (*Newsletter.doc*):

```
Sub mail_merge( )
  Dim this_path As String
  Dim this_db As String
  this_path = Application.CurrentProject.Path & "\"
  this_db = this_path & Application.CurrentProject.Name
  Dim word_app As Word.Application
  Dim word_doc As Word.Document
  Set word_app = CreateObject("Word.Application")
  Set word_doc = word_app.Documents.Open(this_path & "Newsletter.doc")
  word_app.Visible = True

  If word_doc.MailMerge.State <> wdMainAndDataSource Then
    word_doc.MailMerge.OpenDataSource _
        Name:=this_db, _
        ReadOnly:=True, LinkToSource:=True, _
        SQLStatement:="SELECT * FROM [People] "
```

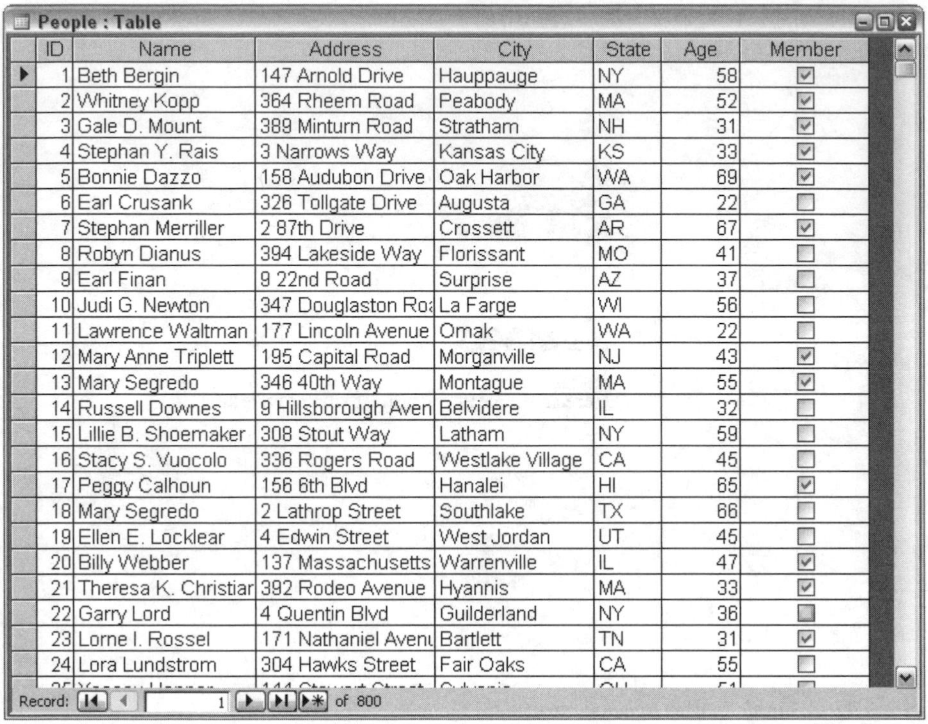
People : Table

ID	Name	Address	City	State	Age	Member
1	Beth Bergin	147 Arnold Drive	Hauppauge	NY	58	☑
2	Whitney Kopp	364 Rheem Road	Peabody	MA	52	☑
3	Gale D. Mount	389 Minturn Road	Stratham	NH	31	☑
4	Stephan Y. Rais	3 Narrows Way	Kansas City	KS	33	☑
5	Bonnie Dazzo	158 Audubon Drive	Oak Harbor	WA	69	☑
6	Earl Crusank	326 Tollgate Drive	Augusta	GA	22	☐
7	Stephan Merriller	2 87th Drive	Crossett	AR	67	☑
8	Robyn Dianus	394 Lakeside Way	Florissant	MO	41	☐
9	Earl Finan	9 22nd Road	Surprise	AZ	37	☐
10	Judi G. Newton	347 Douglaston Ro:	La Farge	WI	56	☐
11	Lawrence Waltman	177 Lincoln Avenue	Omak	WA	22	☐
12	Mary Anne Triplett	195 Capital Road	Morganville	NJ	43	☑
13	Mary Segredo	346 40th Way	Montague	MA	55	☑
14	Russell Downes	9 Hillsborough Aven	Belvidere	IL	32	☐
15	Lillie B. Shoemaker	308 Stout Way	Latham	NY	59	☐
16	Stacy S. Vuocolo	336 Rogers Road	Westlake Village	CA	45	☐
17	Peggy Calhoun	156 6th Blvd	Hanalei	HI	65	☑
18	Mary Segredo	2 Lathrop Street	Southlake	TX	66	☐
19	Ellen E. Locklear	4 Edwin Street	West Jordan	UT	45	☐
20	Billy Webber	137 Massachusetts	Warrenville	IL	47	☑
21	Theresa K. Christiar	392 Rodeo Avenue	Hyannis	MA	33	☑
22	Garry Lord	4 Quentin Blvd	Guilderland	NY	36	☐
23	Lorne I. Rossel	171 Nathaniel Avenu	Bartlett	TN	31	☑
24	Lora Lundstrom	304 Hawks Street	Fair Oaks	CA	55	☐

Record: 1 of 800

Figure 6-43. A table of data to be used in a mail merge

```
        word_doc.MailMerge.Destination = wdSendToNewDocument
        word_doc.MailMerge.Execute
    End If
End Sub
```

Within the code, the source is set as a select of all the records in the People table:

```
SQLStatement:="SELECT * FROM [People] "
```

The destination for the merge is set to a new document (instead of email or straight to a printer), and the Execute method runs the merge. The result is shown in Figure 6-44. The People table has 800 records, and the merge has created 800 letters.

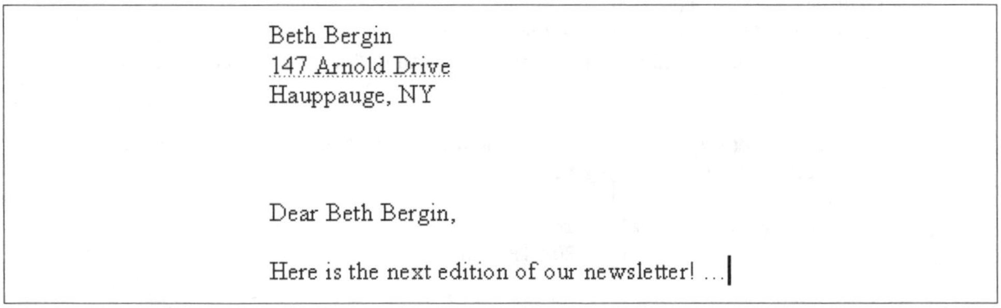

Figure 6-44. The merge is complete

Discussion

Altering the SQL statement will enable you to use a filtered set of records as the source of the merge. For example, to pull out only records for people who are members, and who live in NY as the source for the merge, you could use this SQL statement:

```
SQLStatement:="SELECT * FROM [People] Where State= 'NY' And Member=-1"
```

Using these criteria, just 45 letters are generated. To prove that this is the correct number, try running a query on the People table, setting State to NY and Members to True. Doing this returns the expected 45 records.

Being able to alter the SQL statement just prior to running a mail merge gives you an unusual degree of flexibility—you can change the results of the merge without changing the source from within the Word document.

6.16   Building a Multifaceted Query Selection Screen

Problem

What is the best way to build a form that allows a user to query data through a series of selections? In other words, how can you use a series of controls on a form to create a SQL statement without forcing the user to understand the nuts and bolts of the SQL language?

Solution

Query construction forms are a great way to let users build queries and select criteria in a paradigm they understand. Of course, the structure of such a form is dependent on the actual schema of the database in question. That is, the fields from which users will make selections are dependent on the database and the business case of the data.

Figure 6-45 shows two related tables. Each customer can have multiple purchases. A form, shown in Figure 6-46, has been designed that lets users filter records based on state, customer type, and total amount spent.

The custom query form has been designed to allow the user to select any mix of multiple states and multiple customer types, and to specify a minimum amount spent. All of the criteria are optional. If no selections are made, all records are returned. Each time the Go button is clicked, the query SQL is assembled, and the results are put in a new table. The user is required to enter the new table name on the form; if he does not provide a value, he will be prompted to do so.

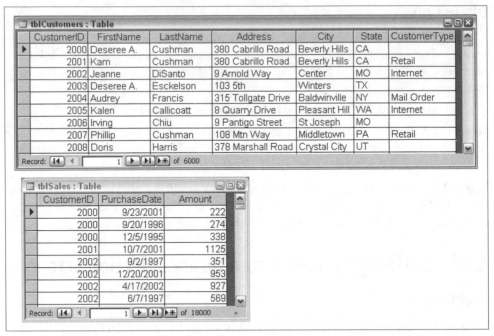

Figure 6-45. Related customer and sales tables

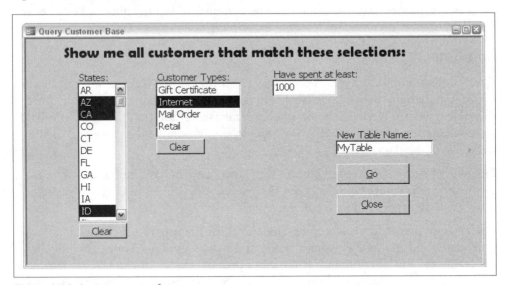

Figure 6-46. A custom query form

Discussion

The form is unbound—that is, it has no underlying table or query. The listboxes are filled by querying the actual values from the table fields themselves. For example, this query, which is the Row Source of the States listbox, fills the box:

```
SELECT tblCustomers.State
FROM tblCustomers
GROUP BY tblCustomers.State
ORDER BY tblCustomers.State;
```

The Click event of the Go button is where the workhorse code appears:

```
Private Sub cmdGo_Click( )
  On Error GoTo err_end
  Dim conn As ADODB.Connection
  Set conn = CurrentProject.Connection
  Dim ssql As String
  Dim z As Integer
  Dim state_criteria As Boolean
  Dim customer_type_criteria As Boolean
  Dim amount_criteria As Boolean
  Dim criteria_flag As Boolean

  criteria_flag = False

  'is a name provided for the new table?
  If IsNull(Me.txtTableName) Or Len(Me.txtTableName) < 1 Then
     MsgBox "Must provide a name for the new table"
     Exit Sub
  End If

  'delete table, if it exists
  On Error Resume Next
  DoCmd.DeleteObject acTable, Me.txtTableName
  On Error GoTo err_end

  'any amount entered?
  amount_criteria = False
  If IsNumeric(Me.txtAmount) Then
     amount_criteria = True
     criteria_flag = True
  End If

  'any customer types selected?
  customer_type_criteria = False
  For z = 0 To Me.lstCustomerTypes.ListCount - 1
    If Me.lstCustomerTypes.Selected(z) = True Then
       customer_type_criteria = True
       criteria_flag = True
    End If
  Next z

  'any states selected?
  state_criteria = False
  For z = 0 To Me.lstStates.ListCount - 1
    If Me.lstStates.Selected(z) = True Then
       state_criteria = True
       criteria_flag = True
    End If
  Next z
```

```
    ssql = "SELECT FirstName, LastName, Address, City, State, CustomerType, "
    ssql = ssql & "Sum(Amount) AS SumOfAmount INTO " & Me.txtTableName
    ssql = ssql & " FROM tblCustomers INNER JOIN tblSales ON "
    ssql = ssql & "tblCustomers.CustomerID = tblSales.CustomerID "
    ssql = ssql & "GROUP BY FirstName, LastName, Address, "
    ssql = ssql & "City, State, CustomerType "

    If criteria_flag = True Then
        ssql = ssql & " Having "
        If state_criteria = True Then
            ssql = ssql & "("
            For z = 0 To Me.lstStates.ListCount - 1
                If Me.lstStates.Selected(z) = True Then
                    ssql = ssql & " State='" & _
                        Me.lstStates.ItemData(z) & "' Or "
                End If
            Next z
            ssql = Left(ssql, Len(ssql) - 4)
            ssql = ssql & ") AND "
        End If

        If customer_type_criteria = True Then
            ssql = ssql & "("
            For z = 0 To Me.lstCustomerTypes.ListCount - 1
                If Me.lstCustomerTypes.Selected(z) = True Then
                    ssql = ssql & " CustomerType='" & _
                        Me.lstCustomerTypes.ItemData(z) & "' Or "
                End If
            Next z
            ssql = Left(ssql, Len(ssql) - 4)
            ssql = ssql & ") AND "
        End If

        If amount_criteria = True Then
            ssql = ssql & "(Sum(Amount)>=" & Me.txtAmount & ")"
        End If
        'remove trailing AND, if it is there
        If Right(ssql, 5) = " AND " Then
            ssql = Left(ssql, Len(ssql) - 5)
        End If
    End If

    conn.Execute ssql
    MsgBox "done"
    Exit Sub
err_end:
    MsgBox Err.Description
End Sub
```

The code assembles a SQL statement that is executed near the end of the routine.
Along the way, the existence of criteria is tested, and any supplied criteria are
included in the SQL assembly. An important point about the criteria is the consideration of AND and OR logic. Multiple states are treated with OR (for example, AZ or CA
or ID). Customer types are treated the same way. However, AND statements are used

to bring these individual criteria points together. Here is the SQL statement that is generated by the conditions shown in Figure 6-46:

```
SELECT FirstName, LastName, Address, City, State, CustomerType,
 Sum(Amount) AS SumOfAmount
INTO MyTable
FROM tblCustomers
INNER JOIN tblSales ON tblCustomers.CustomerID = tblSales.CustomerID
GROUP BY FirstName, LastName, Address, City, State, CustomerType
HAVING ( State='AZ' Or  State='CA' Or  State='ID')
 AND ( CustomerType='Internet') AND (Sum(Amount)>=1000)
```

OR statements separate the states, and AND statements separate the states, customer types, and amount.

 To learn more about the logic operators AND and OR, see Recipe 1.2.

Figure 6-47 shows the new table that is created to display the results when this query is run. Displaying the results in a new table is a subjective decision; other processing could be done with the results instead.

FirstName	LastName	Address	City	State	CustomerType	SumOfAmount
Woody	Benedict	129 Mchenry [	Mc Lean	CA	Internet	5736
Brother	Fields	8 4th	Matawan	CA	Internet	5098
Myles	Aceto	375 Northwes	Spanish Fort	CA	Internet	5062
Wolfgang	Theisen	122 Magnolia I	Tahlequah	ID	Internet	4988
Brother	Weimann	182 Hackberry	Mountlake Ter	CA	Internet	4552
Ju-Ellen	Cecil	168 Wurzbach	Palos Hills	CA	Internet	4457
Edward	Socia	140 Mills Blvd	Townshend	CA	Internet	4452
Molly	Deatrick	398 Castlewor	Orangevale	CA	Internet	4441
Mildred	Boye	121 Alamo Str	Haverhill	CA	Internet	4320
Clyde	Hendron	369 View Driv	Blacksburg	CA	Internet	3922
Abiie	Leshner	195 Haight	Lake Bluff	CA	Internet	3796
Ellen	Shute	4 Drakeside B	Benton City	CA	Internet	3700
Lillie	Rossel	1 Crossgate F	Mountain Hom	ID	Internet	3520
Thompkins	Clinton	139 Pontiac R	Lexington	CA	Internet	3337
Ronn	Bernier	334 Maxwellur	Auburn	CA	Internet	3303
Miles	Amizo	105 Ocean	East Meadow	CA	Internet	3272
Mildred	Cecil	350 Omega W	Bartonsville	CA	Internet	3225
Wendy	Tobin	7 Dolk Blvd	Rowley	CA	Internet	3130
Woody	Scholl	111 Devonshir	Waynesburg	CA	Internet	3009
Walt	Leishman	318 Plaza Stre	Pennsburg	CA	Internet	2999
Billy	Bates	351 Morristow	West Orange	CA	Internet	2961
Helena	Darnay	316 District Di	Liverpool	AZ	Internet	2895
Aloma	Julio	4 Evelyn Road	Virginia Beach	CA	Internet	2721

Record: 1 of 53

MyTable : Table

Figure 6-47. A table filled from a query

CHAPTER 7

Importing and Exporting Data

In many cases, the data you want to analyze isn't in the tool you want to use. This means that you'll frequently need to import data from other applications into Access so that you can use Access' tools, or, if you want to use a different tool to look at your Access data, you'll need to export your data. There are a number of possible approaches for doing this.

In this chapter, you'll learn how to import and export data using Access' tools, how to write Access code to save or load data, and how to process data using XML files. You'll also learn how to exchange data between Access and other Office tools (Excel, PowerPoint, and Outlook). Additional recipes detail sharing data with SQL Server, creating an RSS feed from Access, and more.

7.1   Creating an Import/Export Specification

Problem

I have to import the same information into my Access database on a regular basis. Having to specify all of the options each time I import the file can lead to mistakes, not to mention extra work. Is there a way to save the specifications I choose when I import or export a file?

Solution

You can store the information you specify while importing or exporting a file as an *import/export specification*. The specification becomes part of your Access database, which you can use each time you import or export a file.

To create an import/export specification, you simply use the appropriate Import or Export Wizard, and, after you've finished making all your choices, save the specification to the database. The next time you use the wizard, you can select the specification, and all of the settings will be restored, leaving you free to just press Finish to complete the import or export.

The instructions in this recipe apply to Access 2007. Creating import/export specifications in earlier versions of Access is quite similar.

Let's walk through an example. Choose the External Data command tab, then locate the Import gallery, and choose the Text File command. Access will display the window shown in Figure 7-1. Specify the name of the file to import by typing it or using the Browse button. Choose the way you want to store the data in the database, and then press OK to launch the Import Text Wizard.

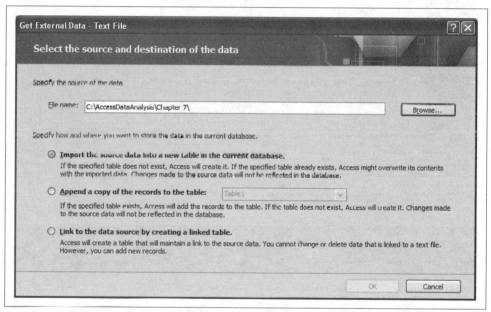

Figure 7-1. Starting the Import Text Wizard

The Import Text Wizard (see Figure 7-2) allows you to choose how you want to import the text file.

Once you've set all of the import options, press the Finish button to run the import. When the data has been imported, Access will prompt you to save the choices you've just made (Figure 7-3). Checking the "Save import steps" checkbox allows you to add the task to your list of Data Tasks. Enter a name and a description, then press the Save button.

Once the import steps have been saved, you can run them again by choosing the External Data command tab, and then by choosing the Saved Imports command from the Import gallery. This will end up displaying the Manage Data Tasks window (see Figure 7-4). Select the task you want to execute, and press the Run button.

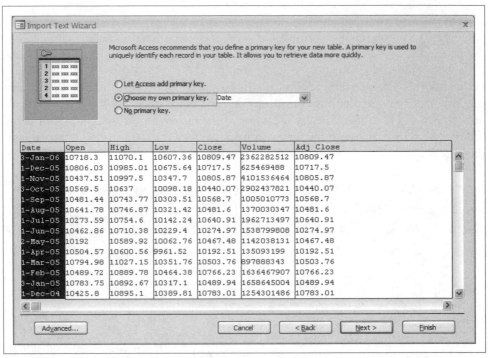

Figure 7-2. Running the Import Text Wizard

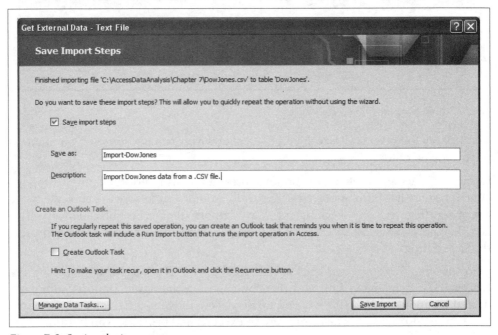

Figure 7-3. Saving the import steps

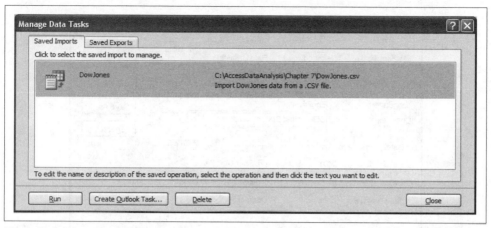

Figure 7-4. Selecting a saved import or export task

Discussion

Sometimes it's useful to save more detailed import/export information—for example, information about how individual fields should be treated. Information such as this can also be included in an import/export specification.

Let's step back through the previous example. Once you've set all of the import options through the wizard, instead of clicking Finish to run the import, press the Advanced button to display the Import Specification dialog box (see Figure 7-5). This dialog box allows you to tweak settings beyond those you can set in the wizard. For example, you can change the way date and time information is imported, along with other things, such as how text fields are qualified, and how numbers are formatted.

The Import/Export Specification dialog displays a summary of your settings. You can save these settings by pressing the Save As button. Then, you'll be prompted to give your specification a name (as shown in Figure 7-6). Press OK to save the specification to your database.

Once you've saved your import/export specification, you can select it the next time you import or export a file. To access your saved import/export specifications, press the Advanced button in the Import or Export Wizard.

> Using import/export specifications can simplify dealing with data that you import or export regularly, as you won't have to specify the detailed field information each time you import or export the file. However, bear in mind that while all of the field information is saved in the specification, some of the other information you specified in the wizard—such as the name of the primary key, and the name of the table to be created—may not be saved. So, if you're using an import/export specification, it's a good idea to specify these options in the wizard before selecting the specification.

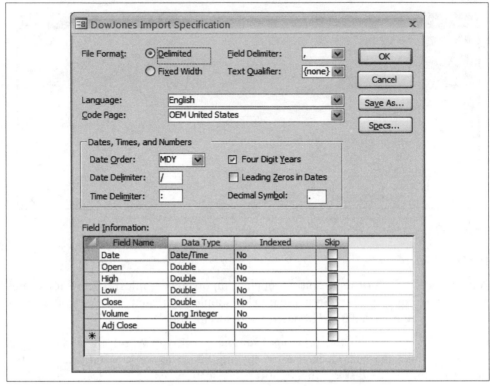

Figure 7-5. The Import Specification dialog box

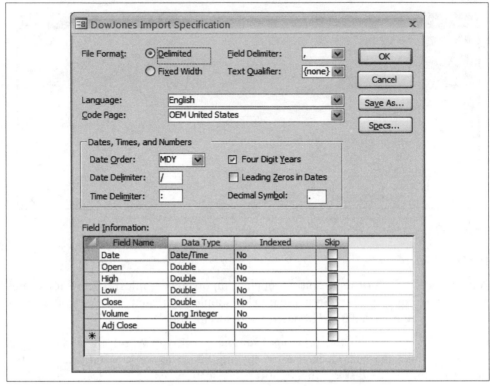

Figure 7-6. Choosing a name for your import/export specification

In the Import/Export Specification dialog box (shown in Figure 7-5), press the Specs button to display a list of import/export specifications in your database (see Figure 7-7).

Choose the specification you want to use and press Open. Then, press the Finish button to complete the import or export. You'll find that all of the settings you chose when you created the specification will be replicated.

Unfortunately, you can't browse the details of an import or export specification. The only way to see the results of the specification is to actually import or export a file. This can complicate matters if you wish to create a new database file. You can't drag and drop the specifications to the new database because you can't see them. However, you can import the specifications into your new database.

Figure 7-7. Selecting an import/export specification

First, create a new, blank database. Choose the External Data command tab, then locate the Import gallery, and choose the Access command. This will display the Import Objects dialog box. Press the Options button to see the hidden portion of the dialog box (see Figure 7-8).

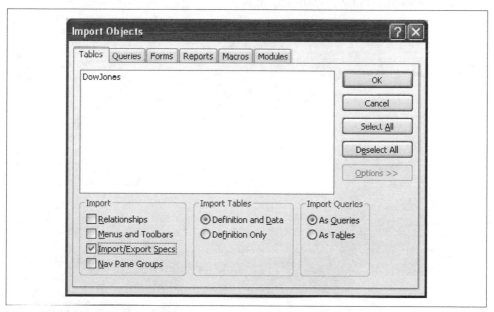

Figure 7-8. The Import Objects Wizard for an Access database file

At the bottom of the dialog box are three sections: Import, Import Tables, and Import Queries. Check the Import/Export Specs box in the Import frame. If you only want to import the specifications, uncheck the Relationships box and press OK. Otherwise, review the rest of the information in the dialog box, and choose those items you want to import before pressing OK.

When the import is complete, your import/export specification will be ready to use in your new database.

7.2   Automating Imports and Exports

Problem

Is there a way to automate import and export processes so that my users don't have to use the Import/Export Wizards?

Solution

Access provides a set of actions that you can use from a macro or a Visual Basic procedure to automate the transfer process. You can choose to transfer data to or from an Access database, a spreadsheet, a SQL Server database, or a text file.

Suppose you simply want to enable your users to transfer a table from one database to another. Create a macro, and select TransferDatabase as the action (see Figure 7-9). In the Action Arguments section, specify the transfer type, the database type, the database name, the type of object to be transferred, the source and destination, and whether you want to copy only the structure.

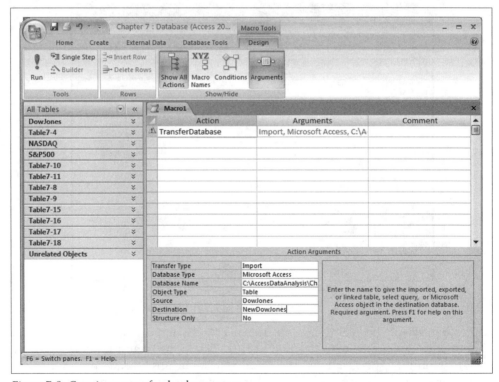

Figure 7-9. Creating a transfer database macro

Running this macro transfers the selected material from one database to another. While this example transfers only a single table, you can transfer multiple items by adding multiple actions to the macro.

> You can use the `TransferDatabase` action to transfer several different kinds of databases, including dBase, Paradox, and any OLE DB-compliant database. If you need to work with SQL Server, however, you should use the `TransferSQLDatabase` action.

Text files can be transferred using the `TransferText` action. Like the `TransferDatabase` action, the `TransferText` action relies on a set of arguments to control how it works (see Figure 7-10). You can import or export delimited data, fixed-width data, and HTML tables. You can also export data to Microsoft Word, or set up links to external data.

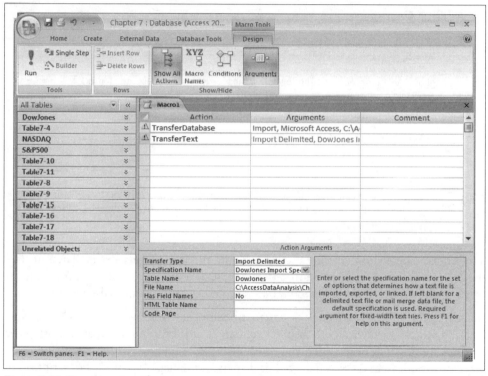

Figure 7-10. Creating a transfer text macro

The `TransferText` action relies on import/export specifications (see Recipe 7.1) to determine how the data is transformed. Beyond choosing the import/export specification, all you need to do is specify the table you want to use, and the name of the file containing the data. The Transfer Type argument determines whether the table is the source of the data, or the destination for the data.

Discussion

Macros are one option, but, as mentioned earlier, you can also invoke these transfer actions through the Visual Basic DoCmd object. The following routine uses this technique to export a database table:

```
Sub Example7_2( )

Dim fso As FileSystemObject

Set fso = New FileSystemObject

If fso.FileExists("C:\AccessData\Chapter7-2.csv") Then
    fso.DeleteFile "C:\AccessData\Chapter7-2.csv"

End If

On Error Resume Next

DoCmd.TransferText acExportDelim, "NASDAQ Import Specification", _
    "NASDAQ", "C:\AccessData\Chapter7-2.csv"
If Err.Number <> 0 Then
    MsgBox "An Error occured during the transfer (" & Err.Description & ")"

End If

On Error GoTo 0

End Sub
```

 To use this approach, you'll need to add a reference to the Microsoft Scripting Runtime library. See Recipe 7.3 for instructions on adding this reference.

This routine begins by deleting the output data file if it already exists. Then, it uses the DoCmd.TransferText method to export a table as a disk file. Note that the parameters are the same as those you would have entered as arguments to the macro.

Including the On Error Resume Next statement before starting the transfer forces Visual Basic to automatically execute the next statement, if it encounters an error during the transfer. Following the transfer, the routine checks the Err object to see whether an error occurred. If an error is detected, it displays a message box with a description of the error. Finally, On Error GoTo 0 is used to resume normal error handling.

One advantage of using VBA code to process an import or export is that you can do a lot of interesting things before and after the transfer. For instance, if you wanted to keep a history of the last three exports, you could use statements like these to rename the destination file before executing the transfer:

```
If fso.FileExists(BaseFile & "Backup2.csv") Then
    fso.DeleteFile BaseFile & "Backup2.csv"
```

```
End If

    fso.MoveFile BaseFile & "Backup1.csv", BaseFile & "Backup2.csv"
    fso.MoveFile BaseFile & ".csv", BaseFile & "Backup1.csv"
```

You can also modify any of the values passed to the `TransferText` method. For example, you can easily use different table names each time you import data.

7.3   Exporting Data with the FileSystemObject

Problem

Working with files (especially for text-oriented files) using normal VBA code can be challenging. The `FileSystemObject`—and its related objects—provide a simpler way to process external files.

Solution

By default, Access doesn't load the library containing the `FileSystemObject`. So, the first step is to choose Tools → References from the Visual Basic Editor's main menu to display the References dialog box. Scroll though the list of libraries until you find Microsoft Scripting Runtime (see Figure 7-11). Place a checkmark next to it, and press OK.

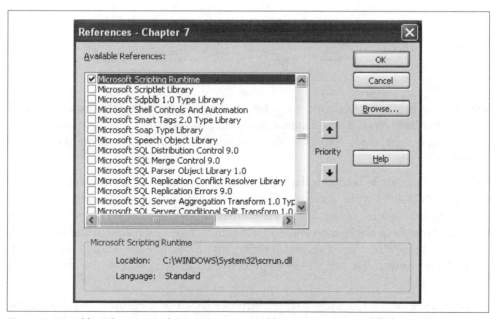

Figure 7-11. Adding the Microsoft Scripting Runtime library to your Access application

Despite its name, the Microsoft Scripting Runtime library contains only the FileSystemObject and its related objects. Once you've added a reference to this library, you can use the following routine to copy a series of rows from your database into a simple comma-separated values (CSV) text file:

```
Sub Example7_3( )

Dim fso As FileSystemObject
Dim txt As TextStream
Dim rs As ADODB.Recordset
Dim s As String

Set fso = New FileSystemObject
Set txt = fso.CreateTextFile("c:\AccessData\Chapter7-2.txt", True)

Set rs = New ADODB.Recordset
rs.ActiveConnection = CurrentProject.Connection
rs.Open "Select Date, Open, Close From NASDAQ", , adOpenForwardOnly, adLockReadOnly

txt.WriteLine "Date, Open, Close"
Do While Not rs.EOF
    s = """" & FormatDateTime(rs("Date"), vbShortDate) & """, "
    s = s & FormatNumber(rs("Open"), 2, vbFalse, vbFalse, vbFalse) & ", "
    s = s & FormatNumber(rs("Close"), 2, vbFalse, vbFalse, vbFalse)
    txt.WriteLine s

    rs.MoveNext

Loop

rs.Close
txt.Close

End Sub
```

The routine begins by declaring variables for the FileSystemObject, TextStream, and ADODB.Recordset. Next, a new instance of the FileSystemObject is created and used to create a new TextStream file. This object provides the method to write data to the external disk file.

With the external file ready for data, the routine opens a Recordset object that maps to one of the tables in the database. Then, before any data is processed, a single line of text containing the column headers is written out using the TextStream's WriteLine method. Next, a Do While loop is used to iterate through each row in the Recordset. Inside the loop, the routine creates a string that formats each field to output, followed by a comma. The WriteLine method is then used to output the string to the text file.

Finally, when all of the rows have been processed, the Recordset and TextStream objects are closed. The output generated by the routine is shown in Figure 7-12.

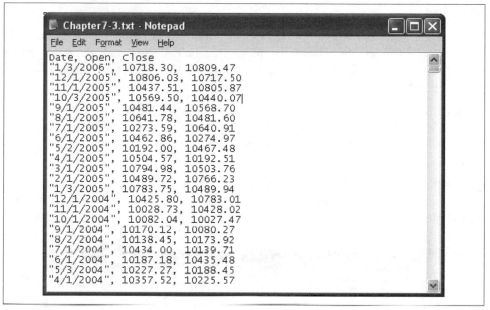

Figure 7-12. The text file generated by the routine

Discussion

The FileSystemObject family of objects provides an easy and powerful way for your Access application to interact with external files. While this example showed how to export data into a simple CSV text file, you can easily format the data any way you want.

In addition to a method for creating TextStream objects, the FileSystemObject contains a number of other methods that allow you to browse drives and folders on your computer, along with tools to copy and move files from one location to another.

The TextStream object includes methods to read and write character data. While you can choose to read your data by specifying the number of characters to be read, more than likely you'll choose to use the ReadLine method, which reads all of the characters from the file until the first newline character is found, or the ReadAll method, which loads the entire file into a single string variable.

7.4   Importing Data with the FileSystemObject

Problem

How can I import data using the FileSystemObject?

Solution

You learned how to export information using the FileSystemObject in Recipe 7.3, but the import process is a bit more challenging. When importing data, you don't just have to read the file, you have to disassemble the file into each piece that goes into the database.

To keep this example simple, I'll assume that the table into which the data will be imported exists and is empty. I'll also assume that the data is properly formatted, and that there's no need for error checking. You can easily add data-formatting and error-checking features if and when you need them.

Let's assume that the data is structured as shown in Figure 7-13. The first line of the data contains the name of the table to be used. In this case, we will import the data into Table7-4.

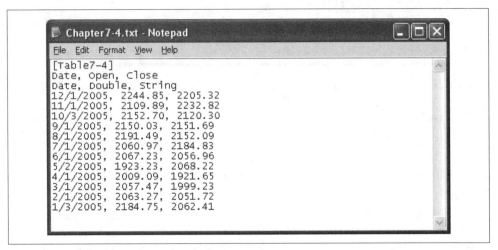

Figure 7-13. Some data to be imported into Access

The second line of the text file contains the names of the fields to be imported. The field names are separated by commas. Note that there is no comma following the last field name.

The data type for each field is found in the third line of the text file. These values don't have to match up with the data types available in Access, as only the import program uses this information.

Following these three lines of information is the data. Each line of data represents one row in the table. The values are separated by commas, just like the field names and data types.

Once you've constructed your data file, you can use the following routine to read the file, parse it, and load the information into the database:

```
Sub Example7_4()

Dim fso As FileSystemObject
Dim txt As TextStream

Dim rs As ADODB.Recordset
Dim Fields() As String
Dim Table As String
Dim Types() As String

Dim s As String
Dim x() As String

Dim i As Integer

Set fso = New FileSystemObject
Set txt = fso.OpenTextFile("c:\AccessData\Chapter7-4.txt", ForReading, False)

'get table name
Table = txt.ReadLine

Set rs = New ADODB.Recordset
rs.ActiveConnection = CurrentProject.Connection
rs.Open Table, , adOpenDynamic, adLockOptimistic

'get field names
s = txt.ReadLine
x = Split(s, ",")
ReDim Fields(UBound(x))
For i = 0 To UBound(x)
  Fields(i) = GetString(x(i))

Next i

'get field types
s = txt.ReadLine
x = Split(s, ",")
ReDim Types(UBound(x))

For i = 0 To UBound(x)
  Types(i) = GetString(x(i))

Next i

'load data
Do While Not txt.AtEndOfStream
  s = txt.ReadLine
  x = Split(s, ",")
  rs.AddNew
  For i = 0 To UBound(Fields)
    Select Case Types(i)

    Case "Date"
      rs.Fields(Fields(i)) = GetDate(x(i))
```

```
        Case "Double"
          rs.Fields(Fields(i)) = GetDouble(x(i))

        Case "String"
          rs.Fields(Fields(i)) = GetString(x(i))

      End Select

    Next i
    rs.Update

    Loop

  rs.Close
  txt.Close

  End Sub
```

While this routine is rather long, it's pretty straightforward. It begins by declaring some variables that will be used later. Then, it opens the text file using the OpenTextStream method, and, using the ReadLine method, reads the first line of the file to get the name of the table.

The table is then opened using optimistic locking and a dynamic cursor. This allows us to add the new records to the database as they're decoded.

The next block of code reads the second line of text from the file, and uses the Split function to break the single string into a string array whose elements represent the text between the commas (the first element contains the text before the first comma; the last element contains the text following the last comma).

Because the Split function returns all of the text apart from the commas, you may find that additional spaces that you may or may not want are included with the text. Rather than dealing with this issue here, I've created a separate function called GetString that cleans up the raw text (as described in the next section) and returns it; the result is saved in Fields.

The process used to get the names of the fields is then repeated to get the data types for each field, and the result is saved in the Types array.

We're now ready to load the data. The next line of data from the file is read in, and the Split function is used to break it apart into a string array. Then, a new row is added to the database, and a For loop is used to process each individual field.

Based on the type of the field, one of the string conversion routines (GetDate, GetDouble, and GetString) is called to get the string value into the proper format. The result is then saved into the corresponding database field.

Once all of the fields have been processed, the Update method is used to save the new row to the database. When all of the data has been processed, the Recordset and TextStream objects are closed, and the routine ends.

Discussion

The GetDate and GetDouble functions are nearly identical: they merely call the appropriate conversion functions to convert the string read from the text file to the desired data format. In the case of the GetDouble function, the CDbl function is used. In the case of the GetDate function (shown here), the CDate function is used to convert the supplied value into a Date value:

```
Function GetDate(val As String) As Date

GetDate = CDate(val)

End Function
```

While it would have been easy to call the CDate function directly in the appropriate Case clause in the Example7_4 routine, that probably isn't a good idea. In reality, you might want to do something like this, which returns the current date whenever it has to process an invalid date:

```
Function GetDate(val As String) As Date

If IsDate(val) Then
    GetDate = CDate(val)

Else
    GetDate = Now

End If

End Function
```

The GetString function, on the other hand, is slightly different. First, the Trim function is used to eliminate any extra spaces at the beginning and end of the string. Then, the routine examines the first character of the string, looking for a quotation mark. If it finds one, it looks at the last character in the string. If both are quotes, it throws them away, and returns the contents inside without any further processing. Otherwise, the value it returns is the trimmed string value. Here is the function:

```
Function GetString(val As String) As String

Dim r As String

r = Trim(val)

If Left(r, 1) = """" Then
    If Right(r, 1) = """" Then
        r = Mid(r, 2, Len(r) - 2)

    End If

End If
```

```
GetString = r

End Function
```

These conversion functions let you create data types that are processed differently by the import than normal data types. For instance, you may choose to create a `GetField` or `GetTable` function that automatically appends square brackets ([]) around field or table names to ensure that there is no confusion inside Access.

Likewise, you may wish to automatically convert some strings to all capital letters to simplify processing, or your data may contain Social Security numbers with dashes that need to be removed before you store them in your database.

Another obvious extension to this process would be to create a new table using the table name, field names, and data types. This is a relatively straightforward process using either DAO or ADOX (see Recipe 4.1), and it's something you may wish to consider if you choose to write your own import program.

7.5 Importing and Exporting Using XML

Problem

How do I save data from my database using an XML format? Also, how can I import XML-formatted data into my database?

Solution

To export an XML file, right-click on the name of the table or query you want to export, and choose Export from the context menu. Select the filename you want to use, and change the "Save as" type to XML. When you press the Export button, Access will display the Export XML dialog box (see Figure 7-14).

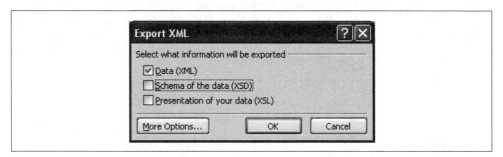

Figure 7-14. The Export XML dialog box

Make sure that only the Data (XML) checkbox is selected, and press OK to finish exporting your data. Access will generate a file similar to the one shown in Figure 7-15.

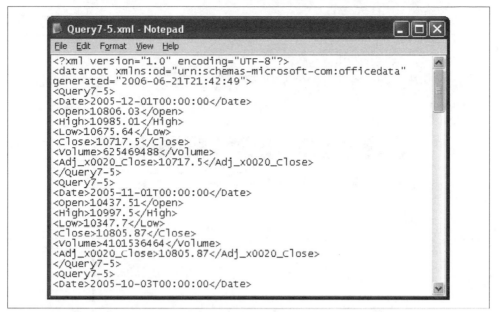

Figure 7-15. Data generated by the XML export process

> While Access normally saves only one table per file, if your Access database design includes Lookup fields, these tables will be exported as well.

To import an XML file, simply choose File → Get External Data → Import from Access' main menu, and then select the file containing your data. The Import XML dialog box will be displayed, containing the structure of your data (see Figure 7-16). Press OK to load the data into your database.

Discussion

When you export a table or query to XML, you'll see something like this (note that XML files can be opened and viewed with simple text editors such as Notepad):

```
<?xml version="1.0" encoding="UTF-8"?>
<dataroot xmlns:od="urn:schemas-microsoft-com:officedata"
generated="2006-01-29T17:09:13">
  <Query7-5>
    <Date>2005-12-01T00:00:00</Date>
    <Open>10806.03</Open>
    <High>10985.01</High>
    <Low>10675.64</Low>
    <Close>10717.5</Close>
    <Volume>625469488</Volume>
    <Adj_x0020_Close>10717.5</Adj_x0020_Close>
  </Query7-5>
  <Query7-5>
    <Date>2005-11-01T00:00:00</Date>
```

```
        <Open>10437.51</Open>
        <High>10997.5</High>
        <Low>10347.7</Low>
        <Close>10805.87</Close>
        <Volume>4101536464</Volume>
        <Adj_x0020_Close>10805.87</Adj_x0020_Close>
     </Query7-5>
  </dataroot>
```

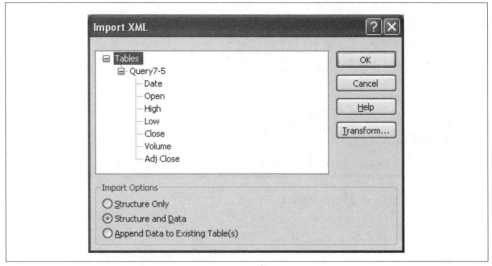

Figure 7-16. The Import XML dialog box

The first line indicates that this is an XML file. After this declaration, all XML data consists of pairs of *tags*, whose names are contained within less-than (<) and greater-than (>) signs. The opening tag differs from the closing tag, in that the closing tag includes a slash (/) character immediately following the less-than sign. For example, <Date> and </Date> represent a matching pair of XML tags.

 The characters inside the tags are case-sensitive, so <Date> can't be paired with </date>. An XML parser will treat them as two separate tags, and will probably generate an error message.

Each matching pair of tags is called a *node*. A node can contain other nodes, which makes for a very structured document. In the preceding example, the nodes are indented so that it's easy to determine which tags are paired. Unfortunately, Access doesn't bother with this indentation—but then again, you'll probably rarely need to look at the XML files it generates.

Take a look at the topmost node in the file (<dataroot>). You'll notice some additional information following the node's name. These pieces of information are known as *attributes*, and they contain values that are associated with the node itself. Working with attributes is discussed further in Recipe 7.9.

Inside the <dataroot> node is a pair of <Query7-5> nodes. These nodes represent a single row of data, exported from the Query7-5 table. Within the <Query7-5> node are a series of nodes representing the fields that make up the row. The tags are named after the fields, and the actual values for the fields are stored inside the nodes. For example, the <Date> node from the first row contains the date/time value 2005-12-01T00:00:00.

As long as you construct a file with the proper node names for your table and fields, you can easily import that data into Access, which will read the file and extract the table and field names directly from the nodes.

7.6 Generating XML Schemas

Problem

I like the idea of exporting data using XML, but I need to preserve more information about the structure of the data (such as the data types for each field and the primary key). Can Access supply this information?

Solution

If you need to include additional information in your exported data, begin the export of the table or query using the steps described in Recipe 7.5, but, when you reach the Export XML dialog box (look back to Figure 7-14), also check the box marked "Schema of the data (XSD)" before clicking OK. Access will automatically create a second file with the same filename as your XML file, but with .xsd as the file extension. This file contains the schema for the data you just exported.

If you wish to combine the exported data and the schema definition, press the More Options button on the Export XML dialog box to see all of the options available when exporting data in XML format (see Figure 7-17). To embed the schema in the same file, select the Schema tab, and choose "Embed schema in exported XML data document."

Note that Access will allow you to include information about any related tables when your table's definition is exported. These tables must have a defined relationship: choose Tools → Relationship from the Access main menu (Datasheet → Relationships in Access 2007) to verify whether the relationship exists, and define it, if necessary.

Discussion

Microsoft's tool for exporting XML is somewhat limited, in that it allows you to export only a single table at a time. However, you can easily write a little routine like this one that will export multiple pieces of information at once:

```
Sub Example7_6( )

Dim AddData As AdditionalData
```

```
Set AddData = CreateAdditionalData

AddData.Add "S&P500"
AddData.Add "DowJones"

ExportXML acExportTable, "NASDAQ", _
    "c:\accessdata\chapter7-6A.xml", , , , , acEmbedSchema, , AddData

End Sub
```

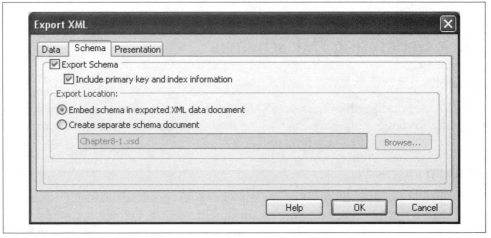

Figure 7-17. More options for exporting XML data

Rather than starting at the top, let's look first at the ExportXML statement toward the end of this routine. This statement does all the real work. acExportTable tells the statement to export the table. The next parameter is the DataSource, which contains the name of the table (in this case, NASDAQ).

I've omitted the SchemaTarget, PresentationTarget, and ImageTarget parameters, which would specify separate filenames for the XSD and XSLT information, and the path where any images would be stored. I've also omitted the Encoding argument, which would instruct Access to write the text in either UTF8 (the default) or UTF16.

The OtherFlags argument specifies acEmbedSchema in this example, but you can add other flags, such as acExcludePrimaryKeyAndIndexes, if you don't want to export primary key and index information when you export a schema, and acRunFromServer, if you want Access to generate XSLT for a web server rather than for a client computer.

The next-to-last parameter, FilterCriteria, allows you to specify a filter so that the contents of the entire table are not processed. The final parameter, AdditionalData, is a reference to an AdditionalData object containing a collection of other tables to be exported.

This object was created at the beginning of the routine: the variable `AddData` was defined as `AdditionalData`, and the `CreateAdditionalData` function was used to create a new instance of the `AdditionalData` object. The `Add` method was then used to add the names of the tables to export to the object.

7.7   Using XSLT on Import or Export

Problem

I'd like to transform my data using XSLT while I'm importing or exporting. Where do I begin?

Solution

XSLT (Extensible Stylesheet Language Transformations) is a powerful and complex language that you can use to transform your data, including both the values and the XML tags used. An XSLT transform (OK, I really mean "program," but an XSLT program is unlike anything you might create in any other programming language) is written in XML.

Let's assume that your XML data looks like this:

```
<?xml version="1.0" encoding="UTF-8"?>
<dataroot xmlns:od="urn:schemas-microsoft-com:officedata"
generated="2006-01-30T22:11:30">
  <Query7-7>
    <Date>2005-12-01T00:00:00</Date>
    <DowJonesClose>10717.5</DowJonesClose>
    <NASDAQClose>2205.32</NASDAQClose>
  </Query7-7>
  <Query7-7>
    <Date>2005-11-01T00:00:00</Date>
    <DowJonesClose>10805.87</DowJonesClose>
    <NASDAQClose>2232.82</NASDAQClose>
  </Query7-7>
</dataroot>
```

But, say the system to which you're sending your data doesn't like the format of the date. Instead, it wants dates to be formatted this way:

```
<Date>
   <Year2006</Year>
   <Month>01</Month>
   <Day>30</Day>
</Date>
```

You can easily accomplish this change using this XSLT transform:

```
<?xml version="1.0"?>
<xsl:stylesheet version="1.0" xmlns:xsl="http://www.w3.org/1999/XSL/Transform">

  <xsl:template match="/">
```

```
      <StockInfo>
        <xsl:apply-templates/>
      </StockInfo>
    </xsl:template>

    <xsl:template match="Query7-7">
      <Row>
        <Date>
          <Year><xsl:value-of select="substring(Date,1,4)"/></Year>
          <Month><xsl:value-of select="substring(Date,6,2)"/></Month>
          <Day><xsl:value-of select="substring(Date,9,2)"/></Day>
        </Date>
        <DowJones>
          <xsl:value-of select="DowJonesClose"/>
        </DowJones>
        <NASDAQ>
          <xsl:value-of select="NASDAQClose"/>
        </NASDAQ>
      </Row>
    </xsl:template>

  </xsl:stylesheet>
```

The transform begins by specifying that it's an XML file. The root node for this template declares that it's an xsl:stylesheet. All of the elements that transform the data are nested inside this node.

The first element is an xsl:template. The match attribute instructs the processor to match the root node and follow the instructions inside. This node contains <StockInfo> and </StockInfo> tags. These are called *literal result elements*, and will be copied exactly as shown to the output file.

In between the <StockInfo> tags is another XSL node that instructs the processor to apply templates. This means that the processor will examine the rest of the document, looking for other templates that may match a supplied value. Any data generated by these templates will be inserted before the </StockInfo> tag.

The only other template in the transform looks for nodes that match Query7-7. In our input XML file, the <Query7-7> tag indicates the start of a new row of data. So, when a match occurs, the processor will display a formatted result built around a set of literal result elements that maps into our new row of data.

Inside the <Date> tag enclosed within the <Row> tags, you'll see three separate tags that break out the date into year, month, and day. Because we can't simply copy over the value of the old <Date> tag, we need to do a little string processing. This means extracting the first four characters of the date value for <Year>, the two characters beginning at position 6 for <Month>, and the two characters beginning at position 9 for <Day>.

The two remaining tags are <DowJones> and <NASDAQ>. When the <DowJones> element is processed, the xsl:value-of element indicates that the value of the <DowJonesClose>

tag from the original XML document should be listed. The same is true for the
<NASDAQ> tag. Applying the XSLT transform results in a new file that looks like this:

```
<?xml version="1.0"?>
<StockInfo>
  <Row>
    <Date>
      <Year>2005</Year>
      <Month>12</Month>
      <Day>01</Day>
    </Date>
    <DowJones>10717.5</DowJones>
    <NASDAQ>2205.32</NASDAQ>
  </Row>
  <Row>
    <Date>
      <Year>2005</Year>
      <Month>11</Month>
      <Day>01</Day>
    </Date>
    <DowJones>10805.87</DowJones>
    <NASDAQ>2232.82</NASDAQ>
  </Row>
</StockInfo>
```

Discussion

While you can use a separate program to perform the transformation, Access
includes the necessary tools for you to embed it in your application. The following
routine will perform the export of the XML data and the transformation into its new
form:

```
Sub Example7_7( )

ExportXML acExportQuery, "Query7-7", "C:\AccessData\Chapter7-7.xml"
TransformXML "C:\AccessData\Chapter7-7.xml", "C:\AccessData\Chapter7-7.xslt", _
    "c:\AccessData\Chapter7-7Out.xml"

End Sub
```

This routine calls the ExportXML method to export the results of a query into a disk
file. Then the TransformXML method is called with three parameters: the names of the
input file, the XSLT file, and the output file.

This recipe barely scratches the surface of how to use XSLT with
Access. If you're looking for more information about XSLT, you may
want to refer to *XSLT Cookbook*, by Sal Mangano (O'Reilly).

One caution: Access 2003 is limited to version 1 of XSLT, meaning
that the new features found in version 2 can't be used with that version of Access. So, be careful if you are applying knowledge gained
from general-purpose XSLT books. They should make it clear which
features are available for version 1 and which require version 2.

7.8   Working with XML via the MSXML Parser

Problem

XML seems like a good solution for my problem, but none of Access' tools can handle the type of data I need to display. How can I build my own XML documents?

Solution

Included with Access 2003 is an external library that you can add to your VBA programs. It provides a complete set of objects that allow you to build a tree structure that will eventually form your XML file.

To use this library, you need to add it to your application. Choose Tools → References in the Visual Basic Editor to display the References dialog box (as shown in Figure 7-18), and select Microsoft XML, v5.0 from the list of references.

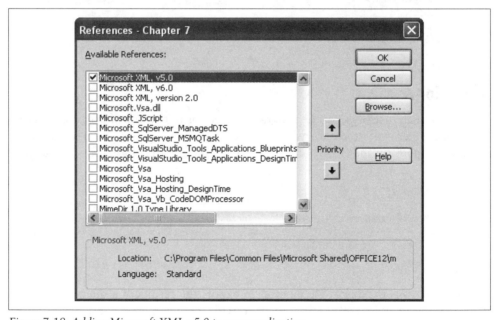

Figure 7-18. Adding Microsoft XML v5.0 to your application

> There are several versions of the Microsoft XML library. As long as you choose v3.0 or later, it really shouldn't matter which version you use. I chose v5.0 because it's installed along with Access 2003/2007.

The following routine uses two objects from the Microsoft XML library: the DOMDocument object, which provides the overall structure for the document, and the IXMLDOMElement object, which stores the information for a single node.

When working with the objects from this library, you use the New keyword to create an instance of the DOMDocument object, and then you use the appropriate Create method from the DOMDocument object to create any other objects you need. Once you've created an object, it's in a state of limbo until you append it to the appropriate parent object. The act of appending one object to another is the way you create the tree structure that characterizes an XML document.

The following example creates an XML document based on the results of a Select statement. Note that several IXMLDOMElement objects are needed, as we can't recycle one of the objects until it's appended to its parent object:

```
Sub Example7_8A()

Dim rs As ADODB.Recordset
Dim doc As MSXML2.DOMDocument
Dim root As MSXML2.IXMLDOMElement
Dim row As MSXML2.IXMLDOMElement
Dim fld As MSXML2.IXMLDOMElement
Dim procinst As MSXML2.IXMLDOMProcessingInstruction

Set doc = New MSXML2.DOMDocument
Set procinst = doc.createProcessingInstruction("xml", _
    "version=""1.0"" encoding='utf-8'")
doc.appendChild procinst

Set root = doc.createElement("Document")

Set rs = New ADODB.Recordset
rs.ActiveConnection = CurrentProject.Connection
rs.Open "Select Top 5 [Date], [Close] From NASDAQ Order By Date Desc", , _
    adOpenForwardOnly, adLockReadOnly

Do While Not rs.EOF
    Set row = doc.createElement("Row")

    Set fld = doc.createElement("Date")
    fld.Text = FormatDateTime(rs("Date"), vbShortDate)
    row.appendChild fld

    Set fld = doc.createElement("Close")
    fld.Text = FormatNumber(rs("Close"))
    row.appendChild fld

    root.appendChild row

    rs.MoveNext

Loop

rs.Close
```

```
doc.appendChild root
doc.Save "C:\AccessData\Chapter7-8.xml"

End Sub
```

This routine begins by creating a new DOMDocument object and a new object that will be the document's root. Then, it creates the XML header by using the createProcessingInstruction method and appending the results to the document.

Next, a Recordset object is created with the data to be converted to XML. In this case, a Select statement is used to retrieve the five most current rows from the table.

A new XML element that represents the first row is created, and within the Row element, a Date element is created. This element's Text property is set to a formatted date/time value. (Remember that XML is a character-oriented language, so you can't store binary information in XML unless you first convert it to a string.) The Date element is then appended to the Row element using the appendChild method. Next, this process is repeated for the Close element.

Once the Row element is complete, it's appended to the root element, and we move on to the next row in the Recordset.

When all the rows in the Recordset have been processed, the root element is appended to the XML document itself. Note that only one element can be appended to the document, as XML allows only one root element per document.

The final action is to save the document to disk. The Save method takes a single parameter, the name of the output file. If you open the resulting file with WordPad, you'll see something like Figure 7-19.

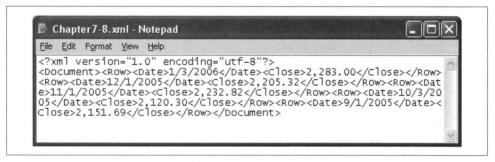

Figure 7-19. Your own custom XML document

Discussion

If you're having trouble reading Figure 7-19, you're obviously not a computer. By default, XML ignores spaces, carriage returns, and line feeds between nodes, so there's really no need to preserve this information if a human isn't going to be reading it. In fact, those extra characters can add up to quite a bit of space that you may not want when you're dealing with larger XML documents. The following listing shows the same material in a form that's much easier to read:

```xml
<?xml version="1.0" encoding="utf-8"?>
<Document>
  <Row>
    <Date>1/3/2006</Date>
    <Close>2,283.00</Close>
  </Row>
  <Row>
    <Date>12/1/2005</Date>
    <Close>2,205.32</Close>
  </Row>
  <Row>
    <Date>11/1/2005</Date>
    <Close>2,232.82</Close>
  </Row>
  <Row>
    <Date>10/3/2005</Date>
    <Close>2,120.30</Close>
  </Row>
  <Row>
    <Date>9/1/2005</Date>
    <Close>2,151.69</Close>
  </Row>
</Document>
```

Microsoft's XML library also includes facilities to load an XML document from a disk file, allowing you to parse your own XML documents. The following routine loads the XML file created earlier, parses it into its individual pieces, and loads them into a database table:

```
Sub Example7_8B()

Dim rs As ADODB.Recordset
Dim doc As MSXML2.DOMDocument
Dim root As MSXML2.IXMLDOMElement
Dim row As MSXML2.IXMLDOMElement
Dim fld As MSXML2.IXMLDOMElement

Set doc = New MSXML2.DOMDocument
doc.Load "C:\AccessData\Chapter7-8.xml"
Set root = doc.childNodes(0)

Set rs = New ADODB.Recordset
rs.ActiveConnection = CurrentProject.Connection
rs.Open "[Table7-8]", , adOpenDynamic, adLockOptimistic

For Each row In root.childNodes
  rs.AddNew

  For Each fld In row.childNodes
    Select Case fld.nodeName

    Case "Date"
      rs("Date").Value = CDate(fld.Text)
```

```
      Case "Close"
        rs("Close").Value = CDbl(fld.Text)

      End Select

    Next fld

    rs.Update

  Next row

  rs.Close

End Sub
```

This routine begins by declaring the same variables used in the previous example. It then creates a new DOMDocument object, and calls the Load method to load in an XML file. The XML nodes contained in each element are found in the childNodes collection. Since the DOMDocument object contains a single child, which is the root of the XML document, the root variable is set to point to doc's first child. The routine then opens a Recordset object to the table to be updated so it's ready to process the XML data.

Because the data in the document is nested root → rows → fields, a nested pair of For loops can be set up to process all of the rows in the root and all of the fields in a row. Inside the outer For loop, we add a new row to the Recordset, process the fields, and then call Update. In the inner loop, we determine the name of the field by examining the nodeName property, and then convert the node's Text value into the proper type and save it into the appropriate field in the Recordset object.

7.9   Reading and Writing XML Attributes

Problem

How do I store additional information in an XML node?

Solution

XML supports attributes, which are values that are stored inside the node's tag, like this:

```
<Row Date="1/3/2006" Close="2,283.00" />
```

As you might expect, Microsoft's XML library makes it easy to use attributes in your XML data. To illustrate their use, we'll use the framework of the Example7_8A routine from Recipe 7.8. Handling the nodes was discussed in that recipe, so here I'll simply focus on the differences in the routine, which appear inside the Do While loop.

The following code fragment begins by creating a new XML element that will hold the row's data. The setAttribute method is then used to create two attributes with the specified names and values. Once the attributes are set, the row is appended to the root object, and the loop moves on to the next row:

```
Do While Not rs.EOF
    Set row = doc.createElement("Row")

    row.setAttribute "Date", FormatDateTime(rs("Date"), vbShortDate)
    row.setAttribute "Close", FormatNumber(rs("Close"))

    root.appendChild row

    rs.MoveNext

Loop
```

Running the routine with this Do While loop in place of the original one creates an XML document that looks like this (I've added a little formatting to make it easier to read):

```
<?xml version="1.0" encoding="utf-8"?>
<Document>
  <Row Date="1/3/2006" Close="2,283.00"/>
  <Row Date="12/1/2005" Close="2,205.32"/>
  <Row Date="11/1/2005" Close="2,232.82"/>
  <Row Date="10/3/2005" Close="2,120.30"/>
  <Row Date="9/1/2005" Close="2,151.69"/>
</Document>
```

This document contains the same information as the one produced in the previous recipe, but it's much more compact.

The code to read the XML file likewise differs only in the main processing loop. (To see the code in its entirety, look back at the Example7_8B routine in Recipe 7.8.) In the new version of the For loop, the getAttribute method retrieves the value of the attribute as a string, so a simple conversion is all that's necessary to populate the value for the field:

```
For Each row In root.childNodes
    rs.AddNew

    rs("Date").Value = CDate(row.getAttribute("Date"))
    rs("Close").Value = CDbl(row.getAttribute("Close"))

    rs.Update

Next row
```

Discussion

Using attributes generally takes up less space in an XML file than using nested nodes, but you also lose flexibility in how you represent the data: you're limited to a flat arrangement, where there is a one-to-one correspondence between the node and the attributes in the node. If your data is hierarchal in nature, you need to stick with nested nodes. However, you're not limited to one approach or the other. You can use a mix of attributes and nested nodes to represent your data, which is what I frequently do when designing XML files for my own use.

7.10   Creating an RSS Feed

Problem

How can I create an RSS feed in Access?

Solution

Really Simple Syndication (RSS) RSS is an XML-based format aimed at content distribution. It's typically used to let people know about updates when content is added to a web site. RSS provides an easy way to package and distribute your most recent changes.

If you dig deep enough, you'll find that an RSS feed is nothing but an XML file structured according to a specific set of rules. Unfortunately, there are many different sets of rules, some of which are compatible and some of which are not. I won't debate the merits of one format over the other, but will simply use version 2, which is compatible with virtually all RSS tools.

In RSS, you typically create an XML document containing summary information about the blog or other Internet site for which you want to provide a content distribution feed. Here's a sample RSS file. This represents the minimum you really need to put in the file:

```
<?xml version="1.0" ?>
<rss version="2.0">
<channel>

  <title>Blog title</title>
  <link>Blog URL</link>
  <description>Description of the Blog</description>

  <item>
    <title>article title</title>
    <link>article link</link>
    <description>Description of the article</description>
    <pubDate>Thu, 2 Feb 2006 19:21:36 CST</pubDate>
  </item>
```

```
</channel>
</rss>
```

The file begins with the normal XML header, followed by an <rss> tag. The <rss> tag indicates the version of RSS used in this document. Inside the <rss> tag is a <channel> tag, which contains the actual feed. In the case of a blog, this represents the core information about the blog itself.

Inside the <channel> tag, you need to include three main pieces of information: the feed's title, which is contained inside the <title> tag; a description of the feed, which is stored inside the <description> tag; and a link to the blog, which is stored inside the <link> tag.

Following these tags are a set of one or more <item> tags. Each <item> tag represents a single article on the blog. Within each <item> tag are a <title> tag, a <link> tag, a <description> tag, and a <pubDate> (publication date) tag. (Yes, the D *is* capitalized inside the <pubDate> tag; recall that XML is case-sensitive.)

Generating the RSS feed document is merely a matter of using the techniques demonstrated in Recipe 7.8 and Recipe 7.9, as you can see in the following routine:

```
Sub Example7_10( )

Dim rs As ADODB.Recordset
Dim doc As MSXML2.DOMDocument
Dim rss As MSXML2.IXMLDOMElement
Dim channel As MSXML2.IXMLDOMElement
Dim item As MSXML2.IXMLDOMElement
Dim subitem As MSXML2.IXMLDOMElement
Dim procinst As MSXML2.IXMLDOMProcessingInstruction

Set doc = New MSXML2.DOMDocument
Set procinst = doc.createProcessingInstruction("xml", _
    "version=""1.0"" encoding='utf-8'")
doc.appendChild procinst

Set rss = doc.createElement("rss")
rss.setAttribute "version", "2.0"

Set channel = doc.createElement("channel")

Set item = doc.createElement("title")
item.Text = "Access World"
channel.appendChild item

Set item = doc.createElement("link")
item.Text = "www.JustPC.com/AccessWorld.htm"
channel.appendChild item

Set item = doc.createElement("description")
item.Text = "This is my blog about Microsoft Access."
channel.appendChild item
```

```
Set rs = New ADODB.Recordset
rs.ActiveConnection = CurrentProject.Connection
rs.Open "[Table7-10]", , adOpenForwardOnly, adLockReadOnly

Do While Not rs.EOF
    Set item = doc.createElement("item")

    Set subitem = doc.createElement("title")
    subitem.Text = rs("Title")
    item.appendChild subitem

    Set subitem = doc.createElement("link")
    subitem.Text = rs("Link")
    item.appendChild subitem

    Set subitem = doc.createElement("description")
    subitem.Text = rs("Description")
    item.appendChild subitem

    Set subitem = doc.createElement("pubDate")
    subitem.Text = MakeDate(rs("PubDate"))
    item.appendChild subitem

    channel.appendChild item

    rs.MoveNext

Loop

rs.Close

rss.appendChild channel
doc.appendChild rss
doc.Save "C:\AccessData\Chapter7-10.xml"

End Sub
```

This example begins by declaring a Recordset object, along with a group of XML objects (one for each major RSS node). Next, the routine creates a new DOMDocument object to hold the XML data, and an IXMLDOMElement object for the rss element. It sets the IXMLDOMElement object's version attribute to 2.0. Then, it creates a channel element, to which it appends elements for the site's title, link, and description nodes.

Once the header information is set up for the RSS feed, the individual items are added. These are extracted from the database using an ADODB Recordset. The current row for the Recordset contains the fields Title, Link, Description, and PubDate. Each field is stored in a new XML element object, which is then added to the item element object.

After all of the rows have been processed, the channel object is appended to the rss object, and the rss object is appended to the doc object. The results are then saved to a disk file for publication. The contents of the disk file look like this:

```
<?xml version="1.0" encoding="utf-8"?>
<rss version="2.0">
  <channel>

    <title>Access World</title>
    <link>www.JustPC.com/AccessWorld.htm</link>
    <description>This is my blog about Microsoft Access.</description>

    <item>
      <title>Archiving Access Automatically</title>
      <link>http://www.JustPC.com/aaa</link>
      <description>Archiving Access data.</description>
      <pubDate>Sat, 1 Jul 2006 0:0:0 CST</pubDate>
    </item>

    <item>
      <title>Building Better Building Blocks</title>
      <link>http://www.JustPC.com/bbb</link>
      <description>Creating reusable code.</description>
      <pubDate>Tue, 1 Aug 2006 0:0:0 CST</pubDate>
    </item>

    <item>
      <title>Creating Crafty Code</title>
      <link>http://www.JustPC.com/ccc</link>
      <description>Scripting with VBA.</description>
      <pubDate>Fri, 1 Sep 2006 0:0:0 CST</pubDate>
    </item>

  </channel>
</rss>
```

Discussion

There is a lot more to using RSS feeds than simply generating the XML file. For more information, check out *Developing Feeds with RSS and Atom*, by Ben Hammersley (O'Reilly). This book covers everything you need to know about creating and publishing your own feeds in much more depth than I can provide here. Just remember, you can create your own XML files from an Access database, and make your database a player in the RSS world.

7.11   Passing Parameters to SQL Server

Problem

Most of my data is stored in a SQL Server database. The DBA only allows me to access the database by using a stored procedure, but the stored procedures require parameters. How can I pass parameters to SQL Server to get the data I want?

Solution

Let's assume that the following stored procedure exists on the SQL Server database. The stored procedure takes two parameters, `@StartDate` and `@StopDate`, both of which have a type of datetime:

```
Select *
From DowJones
Where [Date] Between @StartDate And @StopDate
```

To call this procedure from an Access VBA script, you can use an ADO `Command` object to populate a `Recordset` object, like this:

```
Dim rs As ADODB.Recordset
Dim cmd As ADODB.Command

Set cmd = New ADODB.Command
cmd.ActiveConnection = "provider=sqloledb;Data Source=Athena;" & _
    "Database=Access;Uid=sa;pwd="

cmd.CommandText = "GetData"
cmd.CommandType = adCmdStoredProc

cmd.Parameters.Refresh

cmd.Parameters("@StartDate").Value = CDate("1/1/2005")
cmd.Parameters("@StopDate").Value = CDate("1/1/2006")

Set rs = cmd.Execute
```

After creating a new instance of the `Command` object, you need to specify how to connect to your database. This value is known as a *connection string*, and it can be assigned to the `Command` object's `ActiveConnection` property.

Next, specify the name of the stored procedure in `CommandText`, and indicate that this value refers to a stored procedure, not a table or a SQL statement. The `Parameters.Refresh` method instructs ADO to connect to the database to get the definitions of all the parameters. The results are saved in the `Parameters` collection.

Finally, you can specify the value for each parameter, and use the `Execute` method to create a new `Recordset` object populated with the results of the stored procedure.

Discussion

The `Refresh` method is a powerful tool because it is able to retrieve all the information you'd normally have to add manually in your program. Using the `Refresh` method forces your program to do extra work at runtime because it must communicate with the database server to retrieve each parameter's information. However, this information is easy to add using the `Command` object's `CreateParameter` method, as you can see in the following code fragment:

```
Dim p As ADODB.Parameter

Set p = cmd.CreateParameter("@StartDate", adDate, adParamInput, , _
    CDate("1/1/2005"))
cmd.Parameters.Append p
Set p = cmd.CreateParameter("@StopDate", adDate, adParamInput, , _
    CDate("1/1/2006"))
cmd.Parameters.Append p
```

To use CreateParameter, you need to declare a variable of type ADODB.Parameter. This method take five values: the name of the parameter; the SQL Server data type; whether the parameter is used as input to the stored procedure, an output from the stored procedure, or both; the size of the data type, which is used only for character data (i.e., char, varchar, etc.); and the parameter's value. Once the parameter is created, you then must add it to the Command object's Parameters collection by using the Parameter.Append method.

7.12   Handling Returned Values from SQL Server Stored Procedures

Problem

The stored procedures I want to use in my SQL Server database return values through their parameters rather than returning Recordsets. How can I retrieve this information?

Solution

This SQL Server stored procedure takes one parameter (@Date) as an input value, and uses it to select two other values from the database (@Open and @Close):

```
Select @Open=[Open], @Close=[Close]
From DowJones
Where [Date] = @Date
```

To use these values, you need to either define each parameter explicitly, as shown in the following code, or use the Refresh method discussed in Recipe 7.11. Note that both the @Open and @Close parameters are defined as output parameters, meaning that SQL Server will return values for them. Also, you need not assign them initial values when you create them, as these values will be discarded when the data is returned. The following routine implements this:

```
Sub Example7_12( )

Dim rs As ADODB.Recordset
Dim cmd As ADODB.Command
Dim p As ADODB.Parameter
```

```
Set cmd = New ADODB.Command
cmd.ActiveConnection = "provider=sqloledb;Data Source=Athena;" & _
    "Database=Access;Uid=sa;pwd="

cmd.CommandText = "FetchData"

cmd.CommandType = adCmdStoredProc

Set p = cmd.CreateParameter("@Date", adDate, adParamInput, , CDate("12/1/2005"))
cmd.Parameters.Append p

Set p = cmd.CreateParameter("@Open", adCurrency, adParamOutput)
cmd.Parameters.Append p

Set p = cmd.CreateParameter("@Close", adCurrency, adParamOutput)
cmd.Parameters.Append p

cmd.Execute

MsgBox cmd.Parameters("@Open").Value

End Sub
```

Because this stored procedure doesn't return a Recordset object, you can simply use the Execute method, as shown. When the call completes, you can access the returned values through the Parameters collection, as was done here when using MsgBox to display the value for @Open.

Discussion

When you're using stored procedures, the order of the parameters doesn't matter. However, you do have to have the right number of parameters, and each parameter must have the correct data type; otherwise, SQL Server will return an error when you attempt to call it. This is a big advantage of the Command.Refresh method. Because the Refresh method returns all of the parameters with their correct types, you'll always have the proper definitions.

 Like Access' underlying Jet database engine, SQL Server supports Null values. Therefore, it's a good idea to verify that the data returned is not Null before attempting to use it.

7.13   Working with SQL Server Data Types

Problem

SQL Server and Access use different data types. How do I know which data types to use in Access?

Solution

Table 7-1 contains a list of normal Jet data types, the corresponding SQL Server data types, and the types of variables you would use in your VBA program.

Table 7-1. Access (Jet), SQL Server, and Visual Basic data types

Access (Jet) data type	SQL Server data type	Visual Basic data type	Storage size
Currency	money	Currency	8 bytes
Date/Time	datetime, shortdatetime	Date	8 bytes
Image	image	Byte Array	1 byte per character
Memo	text	String	1 byte per character
Number (Byte)	tinyint	Byte	1 byte
Number (Decimal)	decimal	Currency	8 bytes
Number (Double)	double	Double	8 bytes
Number (Integer)	smallint	Integer	2 bytes
Number (Long Integer)	int	Long	4 bytes
Number (Single)	single	Single	4 bytes
Text	char, varchar, nchar, nvchar	String	1 byte per character
Uniqueidentifier	GUID	String	16 bytes
Yes/No	bit	Boolean	1 byte

Discussion

SQL Server supports every data type available in Jet, and quite a few more. So, if you need to move data from a Jet database to a SQL Server database, you shouldn't run into any problems.

Moving data from SQL Server to Jet is a little more complex, but it isn't difficult if you keep a few things in mind:

- Text fields in Jet are limited to 255 characters, while SQL Server can store strings of up to 8,192 characters. If you have a large SQL Server string, simply use a Mcmo field instead of a Text field to hold it.

- SQL Server can store more precise time values in a datetime value than Jet can store in a Date/Time value. However, you'll run into very few situations where you need to store Date/Time values with an accuracy down to a few milliseconds. If you do need that level of accuracy, you can easily create a SQL Server query to extract the detailed time information into a separate field and download both fields.

- When dealing with data types supported by SQL Server, but not by Jet, such as decimal or bigint, first check to see whether the data stored in SQL Server actually requires the higher precision used in SQL Server. If not, use the equivalent

Jet data type referenced in Table 7-1. If the extra precision is necessary, split the data value into two pieces as part of a SQL Server query, and store both pieces in your Jet database. If that isn't practical, simply store the data as a string in Jet until you find an alternate way to handle the accuracy problem.

In practice, you'll rarely run into situations where there are data type compatibly problems between SQL Server and Jet.

7.14 Handling Embedded Quotation Marks

Problem

What's the best way to handle embedded quotation marks in my application?

Solution

One way to handle embedded quotation marks is to convert them to some other format. For example, the following routines convert all quotation marks into the string " and back again (a commonly used approach in web development), using the Replace function to handle the conversions:

```
Function RemoveQuotes(s As String) As String

RemoveQuotes = Replace(s, """", "&quot;")

End Function

Function RestoreQuotes(s As String) As String

RestoreQuotes = Replace(s, "&quot;", """")

End Function
```

These routines can be used to process data that you store in and retrieve from a database. For example, the following SELECT statement will retrieve a string of text from the database and restore the quotes:

```
SELECT [Table7-14].Id, RestoreQuotes([Value]) AS NewValue
FROM [Table7-14];
```

Discussion

The real issue is why you should care about embedded quotation marks in the first place. The answer is to protect yourself from SQL injection attacks. This type of attack occurs when someone enters data into an input field that is designed to allow that person to execute a SQL statement.

For example, consider the following statement:

```
SQLText = "Select * From MyData Where MyData = """ & UserField & """"
```

This query statement uses the data stored in the UserField field (or parameter). Now assume that this query ends up using this data for UserField:

```
123"; Delete From MyData;
```

This gives you the following query:

```
Select * From MyData Where MyData = "123"; Delete From MyData;"
```

You now have two legal SQL statements in a row, followed by a double quote. Executing this statement as part of an ADO Command object against a SQL Server database would delete all of the data from the table MyData. Obviously, this is a serious security concern.

If you had used the RemoveQuote function in the original statement, the query produced would look like this:

```
Select * From MyData Where MyData = "123&quot;; Delete From MyData;"
```

This new statement would probably cause some sort of error, but because all of the quotes have been removed from the user's input data, the attack would fail, and your database would remain safe.

 Another way to avoid injection attacks is to use parameterized queries. In such queries, any user-supplied data is handled independently of the SQL statement, meaning that users can't add their own SQL statements to yours.

7.15   Importing Appointments from the Outlook Calendar

Problem

Is there a way that I can import information from my Outlook calendar into an Access table?

Solution

To import your data, you'll first need to build a table to hold the information. Table 7-2 lists the fields associated with Outlook's calendar appointments that you'll need to include in your table.

Table 7-2. Fields in the Outlook calendar table

Field	Data type
Id	AutoNumber
Start	Date/Time
End	Date/Time

Table 7-2. Fields in the Outlook calendar table (continued)

Field	Data type
Subject	Text(255)
Location	Text(255)
Body	Memo
Duration	Number(Long Integer)
RequiredAttendees	Text(255)
OptionalAttendees	Text(255)
Resources	Text(255)

Next, you'll need to add a reference to the Outlook Object Library (see Figure 7-20). To display the References dialog, choose Tools → References from the Visual Basic Editor's main menu.

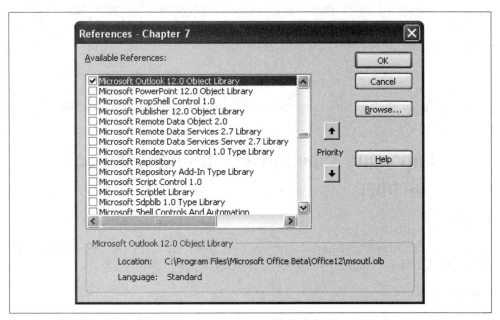

Figure 7-20. Adding the Outlook Object Library to your application

Finally, here is a routine that will do the work. It begins by declaring a bunch of variables needed to access Outlook's data, plus an ADO Recordset object that will be used to save the information into Access:

```
Sub Example7_15( )

Dim Outlook As Outlook.Application
Dim namespace As Outlook.namespace
Dim root As Outlook.MAPIFolder
Dim cal As Outlook.MAPIFolder
```

```
Dim item As Object
Dim appt As Outlook.AppointmentItem

Dim rs As ADODB.Recordset

Set Outlook = New Outlook.Application
Set namespace = Outlook.GetNamespace("MAPI")
Set root = namespace.Folders("Mailbox - Wayne S. Freeze")
Set cal = root.Folders("Calendar")

Set rs = New ADODB.Recordset
rs.ActiveConnection = CurrentProject.Connection
rs.Open "[Table7-15]", , adOpenDynamic, adLockOptimistic

For Each item In cal.Items
  If item.Class = olAppointment Then
    Set appt = item

    rs.AddNew
    rs("Start") = appt.Start
    rs("End") = appt.End
    rs("Subject") = appt.Subject
    rs("Location") = appt.Location
    rs("Body") = appt.Body
    rs("Duration") = appt.Duration
    rs("RequiredAttendees") = appt.RequiredAttendees
    rs("OptionalAttendees") = appt.OptionalAttendees
    rs("Resources") = appt.Resources

    rs.Update

  End If

Next item

rs.Close

End Sub
```

To get to Outlook's data, you must create an instance of Outlook.Application. This essentially loads the Outlook program without showing its user interface, which gives you complete access to all of the data and functions available in Outlook.

Once Outlook is running, you use the GetNamespace method to return a Namespace object, which contains the data specific to your system. Using Namespace makes it possible to open the mailbox folder associated with your local user. In my case, it's Mailbox - Wayne S. Freeze; check your system to make sure you have the right folder name. Once you have the root folder for your mailbox, you can use it to open the folder containing the calendar items.

The next three lines of code create a new instance of the ADO Recordset object and use it to open the table that will hold the imported data.

The data from the calendar folder can be accessed through the Items collection, so you can use a For Each statement to iterate through the entire collection. But because there is no guarantee that the items will be the correct data type, you'll need to verify that each item contains the data you want before using it. The routine does this by verifying that the item's Class property has a value of olAppointment.

Once you're sure you have an appointment item, you can point the appt object variable to the same instance of the item object, and rely on Visual Basic's IntelliSense to help you pick the appropriate property. Then, it's merely a matter of copying the properties you want into the appropriate database fields, and saving the row to the database.

Discussion

One of the downsides of using Outlook's object model is that Outlook displays a dialog box (see Figure 7-21) whenever someone tries to access its data. This mechanism exists primarily to protect email data from viruses and trojans, but it also makes it more difficult for users to use their own data in other places.

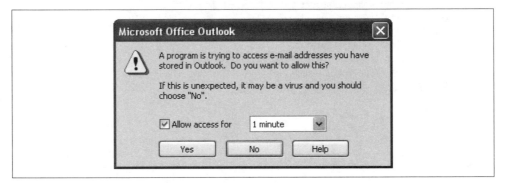

Figure 7-21. Asking for permission to access Outlook's data

7.16   Importing Emails from Outlook

Problem

I want to import selected messages from my Outlook inbox into an Access database.

Solution

The first step in the import process is to create a table in your Access database to hold the imported messages. Table 7-3 contains the list of fields associated with each message in Outlook.

Table 7-3. Fields in the Outlook inbox table

Field	Data type
Id	AutoNumber
Importance	Number(Long Integer)
Message Class	Text(255)
Priority	Number(Long Integer)
Subject	Text(255)
From	Text(255)
Message To Me	Yes/No
Message CC To Me	Yes/No
Sender Name	Text(255)
CC	Text(255)
To	Text(255)
Received	Date/Time
Message Size	Number(Long Integer)
Body	Memo
Creation Time	Date/Time
Subject Prefix	Text(255)
Has Attachments	Yes/No
Normalized Subject	Text(255)
Object Type	Number(Long Integer)
Content Unread	Number(Long Integer)

After you've constructed your table, running this routine will load all of the messages from the specified inbox into your database. The routine begins by declaring two ADO Recordset objects and an ADO Field object:

```
Sub LoadInbox(inboxName As String)

Dim InTable As ADODB.Recordset
Dim OutTable As ADODB.Recordset
Dim fld As ADODB.Field

Set InTable = New ADODB.Recordset
InTable.ActiveConnection = "Provider=Microsoft.Jet.OLEDB.4.0;" & _
    "Exchange 4.0;MAPILEVEL=Mailbox - " & inboxName & "|;Database=c:\temp;"

InTable.Open "Select * From inbox", , adOpenDynamic, adLockReadOnly

Set OutTable = New ADODB.Recordset
OutTable.ActiveConnection = CurrentProject.Connection
```

```
OutTable.Open "inbox", , adOpenDynamic, adLockOptimistic

Do While Not InTable.EOF
   OutTable.AddNew

   For Each fld In InTable.Fields
      OutTable.Fields(fld.Name) = fld.Value

   Next fld

   OutTable.Update
   InTable.MoveNext

Loop

InTable.Close
OutTable.Close

End Sub
```

The InTable variable holds the data from Outlook. It uses a special connection string that specifies the name of the mailbox, along with some other parameters that are needed to talk to Outlook. Then, it opens the OutTable Recordset object, which points to a local table containing the fields listed in Table 7-3.

The remaining logic simply steps through the input table one row at a time, and, for each input row, adds a new output row. Then, it copies each field from the input table to the output table before calling Update to save the new output row. Finally, both tables are closed when all of the data has been processed.

Discussion

This routine simply copies every row and every field from the input table to the output table. This probably isn't desirable in most situations, as it's unlikely that you'll want to copy every message in your inbox into the database.

However, once you have a complete copy of the data loaded into your program, you can use functions such as InStr or Mid to search the subject line or message body for particular words that mean the data is interesting. You can also discard any fields that aren't important. You might even want to extract just the important content from certain messages, and throw away all of the other data.

7.17   Working with Outlook Contacts

Problem

I want to import my Outlook contact list into Access.

Solution

The technique demonstrated in Recipe 7.16 can also be used to import your contact list. First, you'll need to create an Access table to hold the imported data. Table 7-4 lists the fields to include.

Table 7-4. Fields in the Outlook contacts table

Field	Data type
Id	AutoNumber
First	Text(255)
Last	Text(255)
Title	Text(255)
Company	Text(255)
Department	Text(255)
Office	Text(255)
Post Office Box	Text(255)
Address	Text(255)
City	Text(255)
State	Text(255)
Zip code	Text(255)
Country	Text(255)
Phone	Text(255)
Mobile Phone	Text(255)
Pager Phone	Text(255)
Home2 Phone	Text(255)
Assistant Phone Number	Text(255)
Fax Number	Text(255)
Telex Number	Text(255)
Display name	Text(255)
E-mail type	Text(255)
E-mail address	Text(255)
Alias	Text(255)
Assistant	Text(255)
Send Rich Text	Yes/no
Primary	Text(255)

Then you need some code to open an ADO Recordset object that can read the Outlook contacts table. Substitute the following code fragment into the routine found in Recipe 7.16:

```
Set InTable = New ADODB.Recordset
InTable.ActiveConnection = "Provider=Microsoft.JET.OLEDB.4.0;" & _
    "Exchange 4.0;MAPILEVEL=Outlook Address Book\;PROFILE=Outlook;" & _
    "TABLETYPE=1;DATABASE=c:\temp"
InTable.Open "SELECT * FROM [Contacts]", , adOpenStatic, adLockReadOnly
```

The resulting routine will copy all of your contact information into your newly created table.

Discussion

Using ADO to access your Outlook folders avoids a lot of the problems encountered when using the normal Outlook objects. Because the process is read-only, you don't run into the issue of the user being prompted each time the data is accessed; also, you have an easy way to extract the data you want through the use of Where clauses and programmed code.

On the other hand, navigating an Outlook folder can be a challenge. Many of the fields are dynamic, and while I've included sample table structures in these recipes, it's probably a good idea to use some code like this to verify the table's structure before you get started:

```
Sub Example7_17B( )

Dim rs As ADODB.Recordset
Dim fld As ADODB.Field

Set rs = New ADODB.Recordset
rs.ActiveConnection = "Provider=Microsoft.Jet.OLEDB.4.0;" & _
    "Exchange 4.0;MAPILEVEL=Mailbox - Wayne S# Freeze|;Database=c:\temp;"

rs.Open "Select * From inbox", , adOpenDynamic, adLockReadOnly

Do While Not rs.EOF
    For Each fld In rs.Fields
        Debug.Print fld.Name & ": " & fld.Value

    Next fld

    rs.MoveNext

Loop

rs.Close

End Sub
```

Data aside, the real trick to processing data via a database connection is the connection string. The connection string includes a few parameters specific to Outlook. The Exchange 4.0 parameter allows ADO to connect to Outlook/Exchange via a MAPI interface. The MAPILEVEL parameter indicates the name of the folder containing the Outlook folders you want to search. Not specifying a value (MAPILEVEL=;) means that the top-level folders will be made available. If you don't know the name of your main folder, you can use code like this to get a list of all the folders:

```
Sub Example7_17C( )

Dim cat As ADOX.Catalog
Dim tbl As ADOX.Table

Set cat = New ADOX.Catalog
cat.ActiveConnection = "Provider=Microsoft.Jet.OLEDB.4.0;" & _
   "Exchange 4.0;MAPILEVEL=;Database=c:\temp;"

For Each tbl In cat.Tables
   Debug.Print "FOLDERS:" & tbl.Name

Next tbl

End Sub
```

Finally, the Database parameter points to a temporary directory where the ADO drivers build a temporary file containing the available fields from the collection of folders. You can safely ignore this file, as the drivers will create a new version each time you open your Outlook folders.

7.18   Importing Data from Excel

Problem

Importing data from Excel is a straightforward task using the standard Office tools, but I want to process the information before storing it in my database.

Solution

One way you can import data from Excel is to use ADO and treat the Excel workbook as a database. Within the workbook, each worksheet is a table, and the first row can contain the field names. Data types are a little tricky, but, realistically, your VBA program can treat the data as strings. Excel will recognize the data according to its usual rules. Values that contain valid numbers will be treated as numbers, and the same goes for valid dates. All other values will be treated as strings.

The key to the import process is the ADO connection string. The following connection string uses the workbook C:\AccessData\Chapter7-18.xls. Setting the HDR field to Yes indicates that the first row of the worksheet contains the column headings. Setting the IMEX field to 1 specifies that values in columns containing a mixture of text and numbers should be treated as text:

```
InTable.ActiveConnection = "Provider=Microsoft.Jet.OLEDB.4.0;" & _
    "Data Source=C:\AccessData\Chapter7-18.xls;" & _
    "Extended Properties=""Excel 8.0;HDR=Yes;IMEX=1"""
```

While this connection string grants you access to the workbook, you have to address the individual worksheets by their names, as you would if they were tables. However, you need to format the names properly in order for the database driver to locate the right worksheets. This means appending a dollar sign ($) to the end of the worksheet name and enclosing the entire string in brackets ([]). In other words, you would access Sheet1 as [Sheet1$].

You can then use the following code (based on the example in Recipe 7.16) to copy data from Excel to Access:

```
Sub Example7_18A( )

Dim InTable As ADODB.Recordset
Dim OutTable As ADODB.Recordset
Dim fld As ADODB.Field

Set InTable = New ADODB.Recordset
InTable.ActiveConnection = "Provider=Microsoft.Jet.OLEDB.4.0;" & _
    "Data Source=C:\AccessData\Chapter7-18.xls;" & _
    "Extended Properties=""Excel 8.0;HDR=Yes;"""
InTable.Open "SELECT * FROM [Sheet1$]", , adOpenStatic, adLockReadOnly

Set OutTable = New ADODB.Recordset
OutTable.ActiveConnection = CurrentProject.Connection
OutTable.Open "[Table7-18]", , adOpenDynamic, adLockOptimistic

Do While Not InTable.EOF
   OutTable.AddNew

   For Each fld In InTable.Fields
      OutTable.Fields(fld.Name).Value = fld.Value

   Next fld

   OutTable.Update
   InTable.MoveNext

Loop

Set InTable = Nothing
Set OutTable = Nothing

End Sub
```

Discussion

You don't have to use ADO to read data from Excel. However, ADO has the advantage of being faster than using Excel objects. Excel objects force the Excel application to be loaded in the background, consuming both memory and processor cycles. Also, each time you reference a piece of information inside Excel, you're forced to make an expensive out-of-process call. On the other hand, ADO runs in the same process as Access, which saves a lot of resources when retrieving pieces of data.

However, from a practical viewpoint, unless you're dealing with a lot of data, or you're running this as part of a real-time application, there won't be much of a performance difference. The logic to process the data isn't that different either, as you can see in the following routine:

```
Sub Example7_18B()

Dim OutTable As ADODB.Recordset
Dim i As Long

Dim ex As Excel.Application
Dim wb As Excel.WorkBook
Dim ws As Excel.WorkSheet

Set ex = New Excel.Application
Set wb = ex.Workbooks.Open("C:\AccessData\Chapter7-18.xls")
Set ws = wb.Sheets("Sheet1")

Set OutTable = New ADODB.Recordset
OutTable.ActiveConnection = CurrentProject.Connection
OutTable.Open "[Table7-18]", , adOpenDynamic, adLockOptimistic

i = 2
Do While ws.Cells(i, 1) <> ""
    OutTable.AddNew

    OutTable.Fields("Date") = ws.Cells(i, 1)
    OutTable.Fields("Open") = ws.Cells(i, 2)
    OutTable.Fields("High") = ws.Cells(i, 3)
    OutTable.Fields("Low") = ws.Cells(i, 4)
    OutTable.Fields("Close") = ws.Cells(i, 5)
    OutTable.Fields("Volume") = ws.Cells(i, 6)
    OutTable.Fields("Adj Close") = ws.Cells(i, 7)

    OutTable.Update
    i = i + 1

Loop

OutTable.Close
Set OutTable = Nothing

Set ws = Nothing
wb.Close
Set wb = Nothing
Set ex = Nothing

End Sub
```

The primary difference between this routine and the previous one is that it uses Excel objects explicitly. You can add the Excel Object Library to your application by choosing Tools → References in the Visual Basic Editor, and checking the box next to

Microsoft Excel 11.0 Object Library, as shown in Figure 7-22. (Your version number may differ; don't worry.)

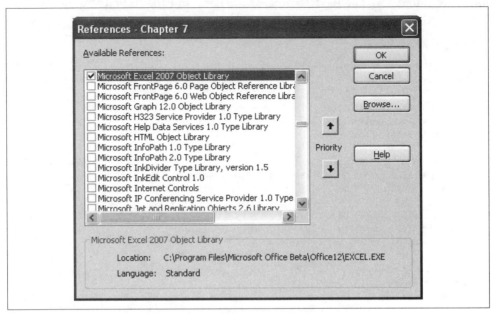

Figure 7-22. Adding the Excel Object Library to your application

The `Excel.Application` object is created to grant access to Excel's functions. This object allows you to open the workbook where your data is stored, and to gain access to the particular worksheet containing your data.

Once you have the `Worksheet` object, the rest of the application revolves around using the `Cell` object to retrieve the particular piece of data you want, using the specified row and column values. Both the row and column numbers start with 1, so the normal Excel cell address of `A1` is translated into `Cell(1, 1)`, while cell `A5` is `Cell(5, 1)`, and cell `C7` becomes `Cell(7, 3)`. Note that since row 1 contains column headers, the data begins in row 2.

Access is smart enough to perform the proper type conversions between the `Cell` object and the `Field` object, so you don't need to worry about handling type conversions explicitly.

7.19 Exporting Data to Excel

Problem

I want to process my data in Access and use ADO to store the results in an Excel workbook.

Solution

You can't.

Because of a legal judgment, Microsoft was forced to disable the ability to interactively update data in an Excel workbook from Access.

The only supported option is to save your data in Access, start Excel, load your data, make your changes, and save it again. Finally, you can load your data in Access and resume working.

 This applies to Microsoft Access 2007, Access 2003 with SP2, and Access 2002 with the update KB904018 applied. For more information on this subject, refer to Knowledge Base article KB904953 on Microsoft's web site.

Discussion

While the judgment prevents the use of ADO to store data into Excel, you can use the Excel Object Library to store your data. Here's an example that is similar to the one found in Recipe 7.18, but that has been modified to save the data instead:

```
Sub Example7_19( )

Dim InTable As ADODB.Recordset
Dim i As Long

Dim ex As Excel.Application
Dim wb As Excel.WorkBook
Dim ws As Excel.WorkSheet

Set ex = New Excel.Application
Set wb = ex.Workbooks.Add
Set ws = wb.Sheets("Sheet1")

Set InTable = New ADODB.Recordset
InTable.ActiveConnection = CurrentProject.Connection
InTable.Open "DowJones", , adOpenDynamic, adLockOptimistic

ws.Cells(1, 1) = "Date"
ws.Cells(1, 2) = "Open"
ws.Cells(1, 3) = "High"
ws.Cells(1, 4) = "Low"
ws.Cells(1, 5) = "Close"
ws.Cells(1, 6) = "Volume"
ws.Cells(1, 7) = "Adj Close"

i = 2
Do While Not InTable.EOF

    ws.Cells(i, 1) = FormatDateTime(InTable.Fields("Date"), vbShortDate)
```

```
      ws.Cells(i, 2) = FormatNumber(InTable.Fields("Open"), 2)
      ws.Cells(i, 3) = FormatNumber(InTable.Fields("High"), 2)
      ws.Cells(i, 4) = FormatNumber(InTable.Fields("Low"), 2)
      ws.Cells(i, 5) = FormatNumber(InTable.Fields("Close"), 2)
      ws.Cells(i, 6) = FormatNumber(InTable.Fields("Volume"), 2)
      ws.Cells(i, 7) = FormatNumber(InTable.Fields("Adj Close"), 2)

      InTable.MoveNext
      i = i + 1

  Loop

  InTable.Close
  Set InTable = Nothing

  Set ws = Nothing
  wb.Close True, "C:\AccessData\Chapter7-19.xls"
  Set wb = Nothing
  Set ex = Nothing

  End Sub
```

The routine first creates a new instance of the Excel application, then adds a new workbook to the Workbooks collection. The Worksheet object, ws, is then set to point to the worksheet labeled Sheet1 inside the new workbook.

Next, the column names for the data are saved in the first row of the worksheet. Then, inside the main loop, each field is copied from the database to the worksheet. The data is formatted as a string so that Excel can interpret it.

Once all of the data has been processed, the workbook is closed and saved using the specified filename. At this point, you're ready to start Excel and begin using your data.

7.20 Talking to PowerPoint

Problem

I want to create a small table in PowerPoint using my Access data.

Solution

While you can't use ADO to access a table in PowerPoint, you can use the Power-Point Object Library. Choose Tools → References from the main menu in Visual Basic Editor, and select the latest version of the PowerPoint Object Library (see Figure 7-23).

The following routine uses the object library to extract data from Access and create a PowerPoint presentation:

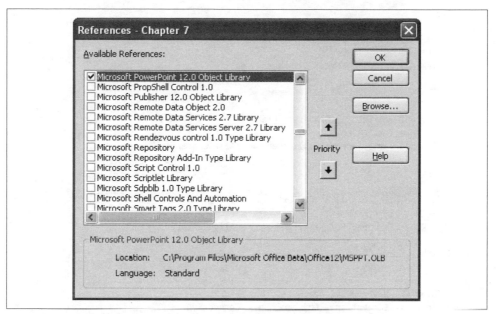

Figure 7-23. Adding the PowerPoint Object Library to your application

```
Sub Example_20( )

Dim InTable As ADODB.Recordset

Dim pp As PowerPoint.Application
Dim p As PowerPoint.Presentation
Dim sl As PowerPoint.slide
Dim sh As PowerPoint.Shape
Dim i As Long

Set pp = New PowerPoint.Application
Set p = pp.Presentations.Add

Set sl = p.Slides.Add(1, ppLayoutBlank)
sl.Name = "Dow Top 5 Days by Volume"

Set sh = sl.Shapes.AddLabel(msoTextOrientationHorizontal, 1, 10, 750, 75)
sh.TextFrame.TextRange.Text = "Dow Top 5 Days by Volume"
sh.TextFrame.TextRange.Font.Size = 48
sh.TextFrame.TextRange.ParagraphFormat.Alignment = ppAlignCenter

Set sh = sl.Shapes.AddTable(6, 4)

With sh.Table.Cell(1, 1).Shape.TextFrame
  .TextRange.Text = "Date"
  .TextRange.ParagraphFormat.Alignment = ppAlignCenter
```

```
End With

With sh.Table.Cell(1, 2).Shape.TextFrame
  .TextRange.Text = "High"
  .TextRange.ParagraphFormat.Alignment = ppAlignCenter

End With

With sh.Table.Cell(1, 3).Shape.TextFrame
  .TextRange.Text = "Low"
  .TextRange.ParagraphFormat.Alignment = ppAlignCenter

End With

With sh.Table.Cell(1, 4).Shape.TextFrame
  .TextRange.Text = "Volume"
  .TextRange.ParagraphFormat.Alignment = ppAlignCenter

End With


Set InTable = New ADODB.Recordset
InTable.ActiveConnection = CurrentProject.Connection
InTable.Open "Select Top 5 Date, High, Low, Volume From DowJones Order " & _
    "By Volume Desc", , adOpenDynamic, adLockOptimistic

i = 2
Do While Not InTable.EOF

    With sh.Table.Cell(i, 1).Shape.TextFrame
      .TextRange.Text = FormatDateTime(InTable.Fields("Date"), vbShortDate)
      .TextRange.Font.Size = 18
      .TextRange.ParagraphFormat.Alignment = ppAlignLeft

    End With

    With sh.Table.Cell(i, 2).Shape.TextFrame
      .TextRange.Text = FormatNumber(InTable.Fields("High"), 2, _
        vbFalse, vbFalse, vbTrue)
      .TextRange.Font.Size = 18
      .TextRange.ParagraphFormat.Alignment = ppAlignLeft

    End With

    With sh.Table.Cell(i, 3).Shape.TextFrame
      .TextRange.Text = FormatNumber(InTable.Fields("Low"), 2, _
        vbFalse, vbFalse, vbTrue)
      .TextRange.Font.Size = 18
      .TextRange.ParagraphFormat.Alignment = ppAlignLeft

    End With


    With sh.Table.Cell(i, 4).Shape.TextFrame
```

```
    .TextRange.Text = FormatNumber(InTable.Fields("Volume") / 1000000, _
        2, vbFalse, vbFalse, vbTrue)
    .TextRange.Font.Size = 18
    .TextRange.ParagraphFormat.Alignment = ppAlignLeft

End With

InTable.MoveNext
i = i + 1

Loop

p.SaveAs "c:\AccessData\Chapter7-20.ppt"

pp.Quit

End Sub
```

The routine begins by creating a new PowerPoint presentation, and then it adds the
first slide and gives it a name in a label at the top. Next, it adds a table to the slide
and sets the values for the column headers. It then runs a query that returns the data
for the table. For each row returned, the data is formatted and stored in the appropriate cells in the table. Once all of the data has been processed, the table is saved.
The final results can be seen in Figure 7-24.

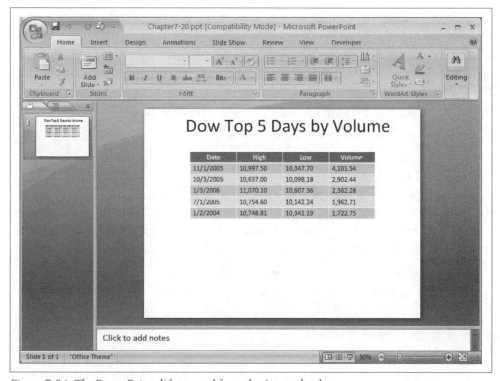

Figure 7-24. The PowerPoint slide created from the Access database

Note in the code that the Volume value in Access is divided by 1,000,000 when placed in the PowerPoint table. This provides a cleaner presentation of the Volume data in the slide. A thoughtful further step would be to go into PowerPoint and highlight that the Volume values are in millions.

Discussion

Using this technique to store your data in a PowerPoint slide may be overkill, as you can simply run a query in Access and paste the results directly into PowerPoint with a lot less effort. However, if you have a lot of tables in your presentation that need to be updated on a regular basis, you may want to employ this technique to minimize cutting-and-pasting errors.

7.21   Selecting Random Data

Problem

I want to create a new table consisting of randomly selected rows of data from my database.

Solution

Sometimes you have too much data to analyze in detail. To make the data more manageable, you may want to choose a random sample.

One trick you can use is to make a copy of the table and assign a randomly generated number to each row. Then, you can pull out a random subset of your data based on those random values.

In theory, you can accomplish this with a SELECT statement like this:

```
SELECT DowJones.Date, DowJones.Close, DowJones.Volume
INTO [Table7-21]
FROM DowJones
WHERE Rnd( ) < .1;
```

However, this statement won't work. Access is too smart—it assumes that the Rnd function generates the same value for each row, so it only evaluates the function once and assigns that value to every row. If the value happens to be below .1, it returns all records; if it's above .1, it returns no records.

Instead, you need to use a statement like this one:

```
SELECT DowJones.Date, DowJones.Close, DowJones.Volume
INTO [Table7-21]
FROM DowJones
WHERE Rnd(DowJones.Volume) < .1;
```

In this statement, the value of Rnd changes for each row because it is evaluated once per row. This statement will select a random sample consisting of approximately 10 percent of your total data elements.

Discussion

When choosing a random subset of data using the random key concept, it's very important that the random number be totally independent of any of the data in the row. If the random number is affected by the data in any way, it isn't really random, so your selected data won't be truly random either.

The Rnd function returns a random value greater than or equal to 0.0, but always less than 1.0. You can use this number as-is, or you can scale it by multiplying it by a constant and/or adding a constant to it. For instance, you can return a set of random integers between 1 and 100 inclusive by multiplying Rnd by 100, truncating the values beyond the decimal point, and adding 1. This can be accomplished using an expression like this:

```
Int(Rnd( ) * 100) + 1
```

The Rnd function takes an optional parameter. If its value is less than zero, the same random number will be returned each time. When you omit the parameter or supply a value greater than zero, the next random number in the sequence will be returned.

Passing a value of zero returns the most recently generated random number. Passing a negative value for the first call, and then omitting this parameter, or passing a positive number for the remaining calls, will generate a repeatable sequence of random numbers. The negative value you send is also called the *seed value*. Having a repeatable sequence of random numbers can be useful, especially when you want to run a program multiple times and get the exact same set of answers.

Another approach you might use to generate a random selection of data is to add a new field called RandomKey to your table, and then use an UPDATE statement like this one to populate the new field with random values:

```
UPDATE [Table7-21A]
SET NewTable.RandomKey = Rnd(NewTable.Volume);
```

Then you can create multiple Select statements like this one:

```
Select *
From [Table7-21A]
Where RandomKey < .1
```

Using this approach, you can create multiple subsets of data of varying sizes, depending on the value you use to compare with the RandomKey field. Just make sure that RandomKey is either a Number(Single) or Number(Double) type, so that you don't lose any accuracy when saving your random numbers.

Date and Time Calculations

Nearly every database that has ever existed has contained some sort of date and time data. Yet date and time data is often the most challenging type of data to analyze. While you can analyze date/time values mathematically, the results you get may not be what you expect. Sometimes, you need to do a little programming to get the information you want from your date/time data.

In this chapter, you'll learn how to correctly perform mathematical operations using date/time values—for example, you'll see how to compute the time elapsed between two date/time values, and how to compensate for holidays and weekends. You'll also learn how to work with date/time values recorded in different time zones, and how to extract the components of a date/time value (such as the month, day, and year).

8.1   Counting Elapsed Time

Problem

I record the start and end times for tasks I perform at work, and I need to compute how much time I've spent on each task. How can I do this without getting out my calculator?

Solution

Access allows you to include VBA functions in calculated fields. The DateDiff function provides an easy way to subtract one date/time value from another and return the difference as a number measured in the units of your choice.

Suppose you have a table containing task identifiers along with start times and stop times for each task (see Figure 8-1), and you want to compute the number of minutes between the two date/time values.

As Figure 8-2 illustrates, you can use the Expression Builder tool to create an expression using the DateDiff function that will compute the values for you.

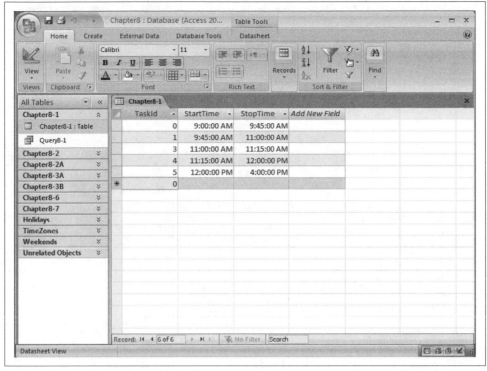

Figure 8-1. A table containing date/time values

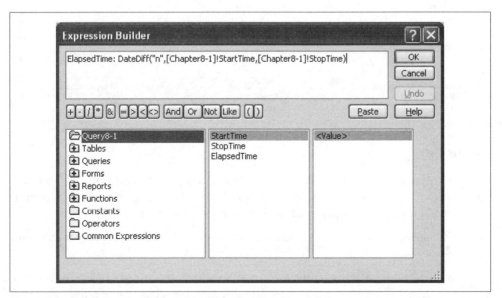

Figure 8-2. Computing the difference between the start time and the stop time

Or, if you're more comfortable writing out the SQL by hand, you can create an expression that looks like this:

```
SELECT [Chapter8-1].StartTime, [Chapter8-1].StopTime,
    DateDiff("n",[Chapter8-1]![StartTime],[Chapter8-1]![StopTime]) AS ElapsedTime
FROM [Chapter8-1];
```

Running this query will generate a new column, ElapsedTime, containing the number of minutes between StartTime and StopTime (see Figure 8-3).

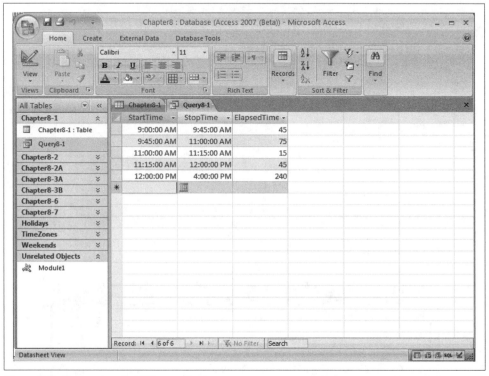

Figure 8-3. Computing the difference in time

Discussion

The ability to use functions like DateDiff in a query means that you don't always have to resort to writing a program to analyze your data. But, as with all programming tools, you need to understand how the function works to use it properly.

DateDiff takes a total of five arguments: interval, date1, date2, firstdayofweek, and firstweekofyear.

date1 and date2 are the two values to compare. If date1 occurs before date2, the value returned will be positive, while if date1 occurs after date2, a negative value will be returned.

interval determines the units of the return value (see Table 8-1). Note that the values d and y will produce identical results if you want to count the number of days between date1 and date2, and w and ww will return the number of weeks between date1 and date2. However, there's a subtle difference in how the number of elapsed weeks is determined. When interval is w (weekday), DateDiff returns the number of weeks starting from that day of the week (i.e., if date1 falls on a Monday, DateDiff counts the number of Mondays until date2; date2 is counted if it also falls on a Monday, but date1 is not counted). If interval is ww (week), however, the DateDiff function returns the number of calendar weeks between the two dates—that is, it counts the number of Sundays between date1 and date2. DateDiff counts date2 if it falls on a Sunday, but not date1. Also, note that minutes are represented with n, since m is used for months.

Table 8-1. Possible values for interval

Value	Description
yyyy	Returns the number of years between the date/time values
q	Returns the number of quarters (three-month intervals) between the date/time values
m	Returns the number of months between the date/time values
y	Returns the number of days between the date/time values
d	Returns the number of days between the date/time values
w	Returns the number of weeks between the date/time values
ww	Returns the number of weeks between the date/time values
h	Returns the number of hours between the date/time values
n	Returns the number of minutes between the date/time values
s	Returns the number of seconds between the date/time values

firstdayofweek and firstweekofyear are both optional parameters, and are important only if you use a nonstandard calendar. By default, firstdayofweek is Sunday. However, you can choose to use the system value based on the National Language Support (NLS) setting or any other day of the week you choose.

firstweekofyear defaults to the week containing 1 January, meaning that the first week will be numbered 1, and the following week will be numbered 2. However, you can override this setting by choosing to use the NLS setting, the first week that contains at least four days, or the first full week of the year.

8.2 Counting Elapsed Time with Exceptions

Problem

Can I use the DateDiff function to count intervals that aren't contiguous? Specifically, I need to compute the number of working days between two dates, taking into account weekends and holidays.

Solution

With a little creativity, you can easily compute the number of days between two date/time values, skipping any weekends and holidays that fall between them. First, you need to create a table containing the holidays you wish to subtract (like the one shown in Figure 8-4). Next, you'll need to create a similar table containing weekend dates.

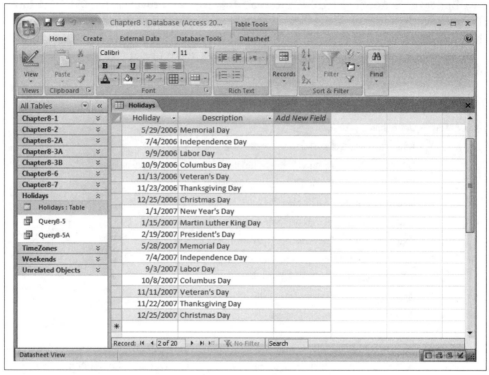

Figure 8-4. A list of holidays

You can then compute the number of working days between any two dates by finding the total number of days between the dates and subtracting the number of holidays and weekend days. If you use this SQL statement, your results should look like the datasheet view shown in Figure 8-5:

```
SELECT [Chapter8-2A].TaskId, [Chapter8-2A].StartDate, [Chapter8-2A].StopDate,
DateDiff("d",[StartDate],[StopDate]) AS Days,
DateDiff("d",[StartDate],[StopDate])
-(Select count(*) From Holidays Where Holiday Between StartDate And StopDate)
AS NoHolidays,
DateDiff("d",[StartDate],[StopDate])
```

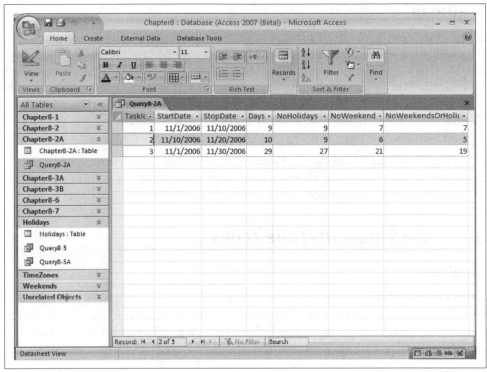

Figure 8-5. Counting days, excluding weekends and holidays

```
-(Select count(*) From Weekends Where Weekend Between StartDate And StopDate)
AS NoWeekends,
DateDiff("d",[StartDate],[StopDate])
-(Select count(*) From Weekends Where Weekend Between StartDate And StopDate)
-(Select count(*) From Holidays Where Holiday Between StartDate And StopDate)
AS NoWeekendsOrHolidays
FROM [Chapter8-2A];
```

You can verify these results using the calendar shown in Table 8-2.

Table 8-2. Calendar

Sunday	Monday	Tuesday	Wednesday	Thursday	Friday	Saturday
			1	2	3	4
5	6	7	8	9	10	11
12	*13*	14	15	16	17	18
19	20	21	22	*23*	24	25
26	27	28	29	30		

Discussion

This technique relies on SQL's ability to execute a Select statement within a Select statement. The first nested Select statement uses the values in the StartDate and StopDate fields to identify the number of holidays that occur within the specified time period. Simply subtracting this value from the number of days between the two dates computed by the DateDiff function returns the number of nonholiday days. The same approach is used with the Weekends table to determine the number of weekend days to subtract.

If you prefer, you can combine the Holidays and Weekends tables into one table listing all of the days to ignore when performing the calculation. If you do this, you'll only need to execute one nested Select statement to get the desired value.

8.3   Working with Time Zones

Problem

Date/time values depend on two things: the location of the computer, and the location of the person changing the data on the computer. If both happen to be in the same place, there's no problem. But if they aren't, you may end up with values that can't be compared with each other.

Solution

There are two solutions to this problem—both affect the overall design of the database. The first approach is to store all date/time values using a single time zone, and then to convert them to local time as necessary. The second approach is to capture the local time zone whenever a date/time value is entered into the database; then, when you need to compare values, you can convert them to a common time zone.

Regardless of which approach you choose, the first thing you'll need is a table containing the information that will allow you to convert one time zone to another (see Figure 8-6). The important elements in this table are TimeZone, Location, and Offset.

The TimeZone field contains the standard abbreviations for the time zones. The values in this field are not unique, but the people that originally defined time zones did so in a way that would allow everyone to understand the appropriate time zone given their geographical location. Offset contains the number of hours that need to be added to Coordinated Universal Time, or UTC, to get the local time (for further details, see the Discussion section).

Assuming that all of the time values in your database are stored in UTC, the following SQL statement will convert these time values into Central Standard Time (CST):

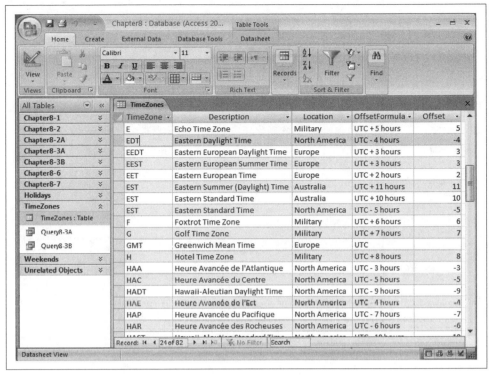

Figure 8-6. A table of time zones

```
SELECT [Chapter8-3A].TaskId, [Chapter8-3A].StartTime, [Chapter8-3A].StopTime,
StartTime+[Offset]/24 AS CSTStartTime,
StopTime+[Offset]/24 AS CSTStopTime, [Offset]
FROM [Chapter8-3A], TimeZones
WHERE TimeZones.TimeZone="CST" And TimeZones.Location="North America";
```

The results are shown in Figure 8-7.

To compare time values, you must convert them all into a single time zone (usually
UTC). You can accomplish this by merely reversing the offset formula and subtracting
the Offset value from the local time, as illustrated in this SELECT statement:

```
SELECT [Chapter8-3B].StartTime, [Chapter8-3B].StartTimeZone, TimeZones.Offset,
StartTime-Offset/24 AS UTCTime
FROM [Chapter8-3B], TimeZones
WHERE TimeZone=StartTimeZone and Location="North America";
```

The results are shown in Figure 8-8.

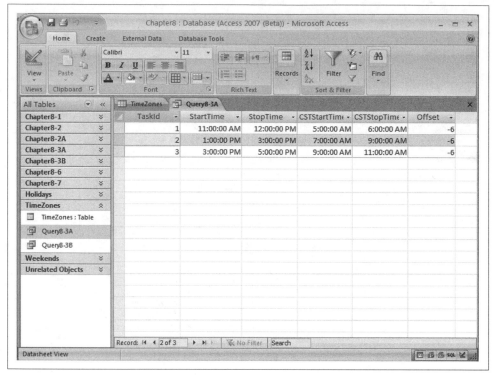

Figure 8-7. Converting UTC into CST

Discussion

There is a town in England known as Greenwich, whose longitude is zero degrees, zero minutes, and zero seconds. The time at this location is known as Greenwich Mean Time (GMT). It is also known as Zulu time, but most people now refer to this time as Coordinated Universal Time (UTC). This is the base time for all time zones in the world. In other words, all other time zones are measured relative to this zone. This relative measurement is known as the *time offset*.

The time offset can range from +12 to –12 hours, depending on the location of the time zone. To convert from UTC to your local time zone, merely add the offset value to the UTC time value. To convert your local time zone to UTC, subtract the offset value.

 While the preceding discussion applies to UTC, you can pick any time zone as the "zero" time zone for your database and convert all values to or from that zone. This may seem like a poor solution, but remember that even big web sites like eBay that are based on Pacific Time don't attempt to convert to your local time zone.

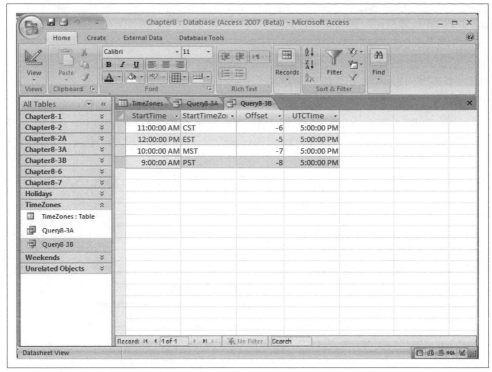

Figure 8-8. Converting local time into UTC

8.4 Working Around Leap Years

Problem

On some computer systems, doing calculations involving leap years can cause big problems. This is because some years include 29 February, while others do not.

Solution

This isn't a problem in Access.

Discussion

The extra day is added to the month of February when the year is divisible by 4, except when the year ends in 00, in which case it isn't added, except when the century is divisible by 4, in which case it is added. Confused? The year 2008 will have a 29 February, but the year 2100 will not; however, the year 2000 did have a 29 February.

The reason leap years are not a problem in Access is that all date/time values are stored using two parts. The first part is a positive or negative integer, where 0 means 30 December 1899, 1 means 31 December 1899, –1 means 29 December 1899, and so on.

Time values are stored as decimal values, where midnight = 0 and noon = 0.5. This means that 6 A.M. = .25 and 6 P.M. = .75. Another way to think of this value is the number of hours past midnight divided by 24.

This approach also applies to minutes and seconds. For instance, 12:01 A.M. would be stored internally as 0.0006944. To arrive at this value, just convert the minutes and seconds into fractional hours, and then divide by 24.

One nice thing about this technique for storing date and time information is that you can easily add a value containing a specified number of days, hours, etc., to this field to arrive at a new value.

Key to making this work is the ability to convert normal date and time expressions to and from this internal format. Fortunately, Microsoft includes a number of VBA functions that you can use (see Table 8-3).

Table 8-3. Selected VBA date and time functions

Function	Description
DateAdd	Adds the specified number of date/time units to the specified date
DateDiff	Returns the difference between two date/time values using the requested units
DateSerial	Constructs a date/time value using the specified day, month, and year values
DatePart	Returns the requested date value from the specified date/time value
DateValue	Converts the specified string with a formatted date value into a date/time value
Now	Returns the current date and time
TimeSerial	Constructs a date/time value using the specified hours, minutes, and seconds values
TimeValue	Converts the specified string with a formatted time value into a date/time variable

8.5   Isolating the Day, Month, or Year

Problem

I need to be able to collect statistics on my data by day, month, or year. In other words, I need a way to extract only that part of a date/time value.

Solution

Access provides a number of VBA functions that allow you to extract various parts of a date, including Year, Month, Day, and Weekday. These functions can be incorporated into a SQL SELECT statement like this:

```
SELECT Holidays.Holiday, Holidays.Description,
Year([holiday]) AS [Year],
Month([holiday]) AS [Month],
Day([Holiday]) AS [Day],
Weekday([holiday]) AS Weekday,
MonthName(Month([holiday])) AS MonthName,
```

```
WeekdayName(Weekday([holiday])) AS WeekdayName
FROM Holidays;
```

You can see the results of this query in Figure 8-9.

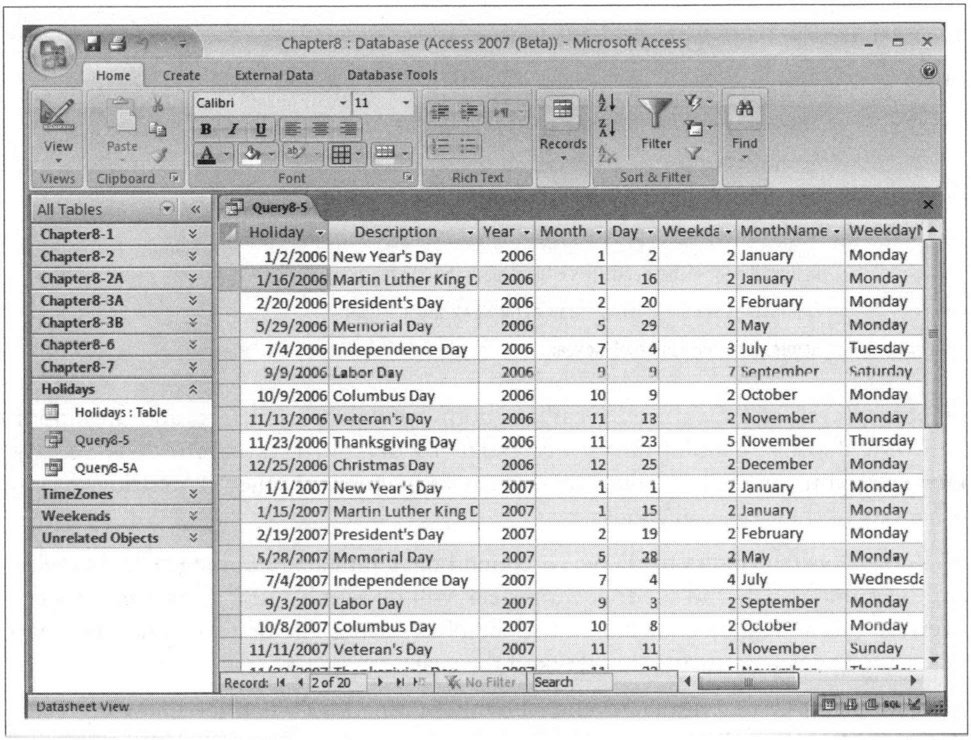

Figure 8-9. Extracting information from a date/time value

Discussion

The Year, Month, Day, and Weekday functions each return an integer value with the requested information. These values in turn can be used as part of a more complex query that sorts and/or summarizes the data by these values.

> To make your reports easier to understand, you may want to convert the numbers returned by the Month and Weekday functions into text values. You can do this with the MonthName and WeekdayName functions.

Another way to extract more detailed date information from a date/time value is to use the DatePart function. The DatePart function returns the same values that you can get from the Year, Month, Day, and Weekday functions, but it can also return the quarter, the day of the year, and the week of the year.

DatePart takes four arguments: interval, date, firstdayofweek, and firstweekofyear.

interval determines the units of the return value (see Table 8-4). date is the date/time value from which the value determined by interval will be extracted.

Table 8-4. Possible values for interval

Value	Description
yyyy	Returns the year (this is the same as the Year function)
q	Returns the quarter
m	Returns the month (this is the same as the Month function)
y	Returns the day of the year
d	Returns the day of the month (this is the same as the Day function)
w	Returns the weekday (this is the same as the Weekday function)
ww	Returns the week number of the year

firstdayofweek and firstweekofyear are both optional parameters, and are important only if you use a nonstandard calendar. By default, firstdayofweek is Sunday. However, you can choose to use the system value based on the NLS setting, or any other day of the week you choose.

firstweekofyear defaults to the week containing 1 January, meaning that this week will be numbered 1, and the following week will be numbered 2. However, you can override this setting by choosing to use the NLS setting, the first week that contains at least four days, or the first full week of the year.

Figure 8-10 shows the results produced by these functions when the following query is run:

```
SELECT Holiday, Description,
DatePart("q", Holiday) as Quarter,
DatePart("y", Holiday) as DayOfYear,
DatePart("ww", Holiday) as WeekOfYear
FROM Holidays;
```

8.6   Isolating the Hour, Minute, or Second

Problem

What functions can I use to extract the hour, minute, or second value from a time field?

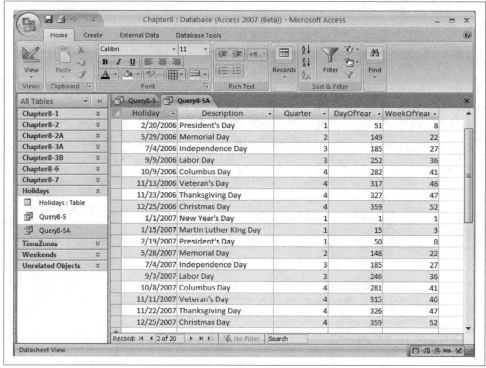

Figure 8-10. Extracting the quarter, day of year, and week of year values from a date/time value

Solution

Like the Year, Month, Day, and Weekday functions described in Recipe 8.5, you can use the Hour, Minute, and Second VBA functions to extract those values from a date/time field. For example, the following SQL statement will generate the results in Figure 8-11:

```
SELECT [Chapter8-6].TaskId, [Chapter8-6].Time,
Hour([time]) AS [Hour],
Minute([time]) AS [Minute],
Second([time]) AS [Second]
FROM [Chapter8-6];
```

Discussion

The Minute and Second functions return integer values in the range of 0 to 59. The Hour function returns an integer value in the range of 0 to 23 because there isn't a practical way to return an A.M. or P.M. indicator along with the hour value.

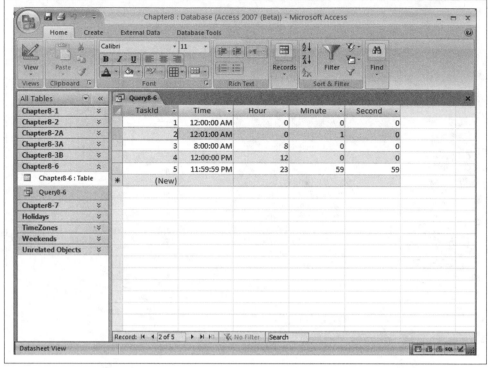

Figure 8-11. Extracting the hour, minute, and second values from a date/time value

8.7   Adding Time

Problem

Occasionally I want to analyze my data by selecting records around a particular date. For example, given a specific date, I might want to select all of the records in the range of seven days before that date to seven days after that date.

Solution

The DateAdd VBA function allows you to add date or time values to a specified date/time value. Thus, you can generate new date/time values relative to that value.

Let's assume that you have the data shown in Figure 8-12.

Running the following query prompts the user for two values (DateArg, which is the date around which the rows will be selected, and DateInterval, which is the offset from DateArg that determines the range of dates to be selected):

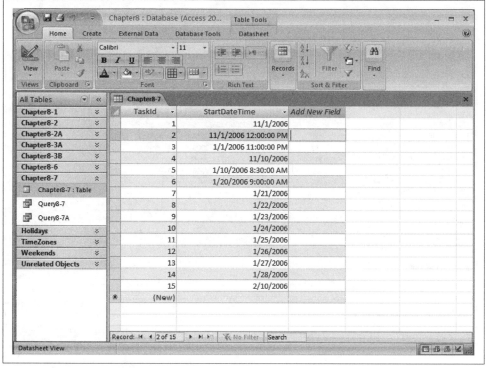

Figure 8-12. A list of date/time values

```
SELECT [Chapter8-7].TaskId, [Chapter8-7].StartDateTime, DateArg, DateInterval
FROM [Chapter8-7]
WHERE [Chapter8-7].StartDateTime Between DateAdd("d",-DateInterval,DateArg)
And DateAdd("d",DateInterval,DateArg);
```

If the user supplies values of 24 Jan 06 and 2 for DateArg and DateInterval, respectively, you should see the results shown in Figure 8-13.

Discussion

The DateAdd function gives you the ability to add many different types of offset values to compute a new date. In addition to days, you can add years, quarters, months, weeks, hours, minutes, and seconds to a date/time value.

The DateAdd function takes three arguments: interval, number, and date.

The interval argument determines the units of the number (an integer value) to be added to date (a date/time value). Possible values for interval are listed in Table 8-5. Negative values for number will result in a new value that is earlier than date, while positive values will result in a new value that is later than date.

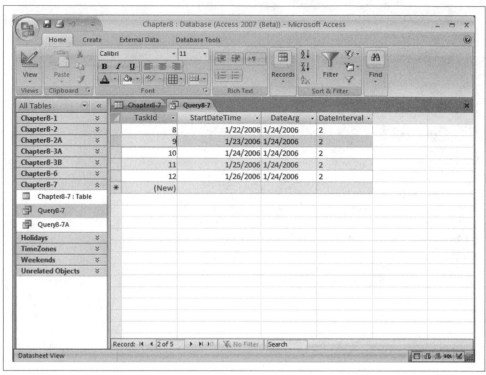

Figure 8-13. Selecting dates around 24 Jan 06

Table 8-5. Possible values for interval

Value	Description
yyyy	Adds the specified number of years to the date/time value
q	Adds the specified number of quarters to the date/time value
m	Adds the specified number of months to the date/time value
y	Adds the specified number of days to the date/time value (same as d and w)
d	Adds the specified number of days to the date/time value (same as y and w)
w	Adds the specified number of days to the date/time value (same as d and y)
ww	Adds the specified number of weeks to the date/time value
h	Adds the specified number of hours to the date/time value
n	Adds the specified number of minutes to the date/time value
s	Adds the specified number of seconds to the date/time value

Business and Finance Problems

The need to solve business and finance problems is common to many Access users. While you can always export your data to Excel for analysis, it might be easier for you to find ways to solve these problems inside Access. Fortunately, using the capabilities found in the Access database engine and the VBA scripting language, you can tackle nearly any business or finance task.

In this chapter, you'll learn how to solve a number of common problems, such as computing return on investment, straight-line depreciation, accelerated depreciation, interest, and moving averages. You'll also learn how to use Access' PivotTables and PivotCharts, which will help you decode some of the hidden information in your data.

9.1   Calculating Weighted Averages

Problem

I want to calculate a weighted average for a series of values.

Solution

You can use a SELECT statement like this to compute a weighted average:

```
SELECT Sum(Value * Weight) / Sum(Weight) AS WeightedAverage
FROM [Table9-1];
```

This statement will return the value in Figure 9-1 for the data found in Figure 9-2.

Discussion

To compute a weighted average, take the sum of the products of the values and the weights, and then divide the result by the sum of the weights. That is:

$$\text{Weighted Average} = \frac{\Sigma\ V_i * W_i}{\Sigma\ W_i}$$

where V_i represents the ith value and W_i represents the ith weight.

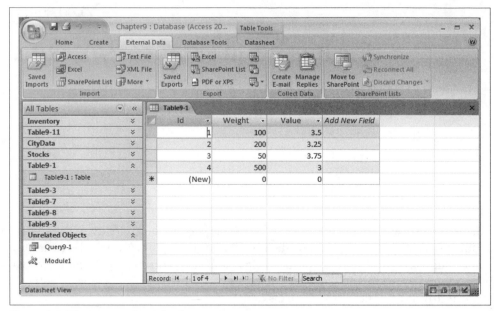

Figure 9-1. The computed weighted average

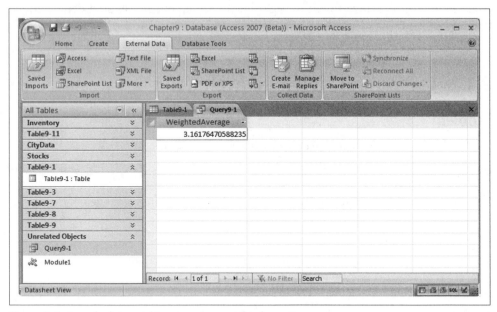

Figure 9-2. Sample data used to compute a weighted average

The key to understanding when to use weighted averages rather than simple averages is to look at how the items are related to each other. If all items have the same impact, you can use a simple average. But if the relative impacts of the items are different, you should use a weighted average.

For instance, when you are trying to compute the average price paid for a set of items, you should use a weighted average if the prices of the items vary. In this case, the price is the value, and the number of items is the weight. Computing the weighted average will give you an average price that is biased toward the price you paid for the most items.

9.2 Calculating a Moving Average

Problem

I want to compute a moving average for my data.

Solution

You can use a SELECT statement like the following to compute a moving average:

```
SELECT A.Date, DisneyClose,
  (Select Avg(DisneyClose)
  From Stocks B
  Where B.Date Between A.Date And DateAdd("d", -7, A.Date)) AS MovingAverage
FROM Stocks AS A
WHERE A.Date Between #1-1-2000# And #12-31-05#
ORDER BY Date DESC;
```

This statement scans a table containing daily values, and uses a nested query to compute the average across the previous seven days.

You can easily adjust this range to change how the moving average is computed. For example, you could use a Where clause like this to compute the moving average over a 14-day window, with the current date in the middle:

```
Where B.Date Between DateAdd("d", 7, A.Date) And DateAdd("d", -7, A.Date)
```

Discussion

A moving average is used to smooth time-series data that contains noticeable jumps between observations. The time scale for the observations can be days (as in the preceding example), months, or even years. Alternatively, you can use a simple AutoNumber column in place of a date field, since the values in that column will also increase over time.

The larger the range used to compute the moving average is, the smoother the resulting curve will be. In Figure 9-3, you can see how a moving average smoothes the individual observations of a stock price.

See Also

- Recipe 9.10

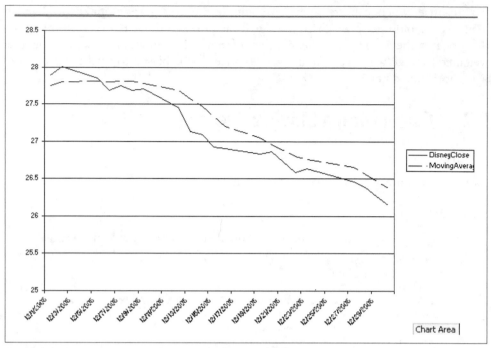

Figure 9-3. Using a moving average to smooth a set of values

9.3   Calculating Payback Period

Problem

I want to know how long it will take to recover my original investment.

Solution

You can use the following routine to compute the payback period:

```
Function PaybackPeriod(rs As ADODB.Recordset, Time As String, _
    Interest As String, CashFlow As String, InitialInvestment As Currency) _
    As Double

Dim OldNPV As Currency
Dim OldTime As Long
Dim NPV As Currency
Dim Temp As Currency

NPV = 0
OldTime = 0
Do While Not rs.EOF
    OldNPV = NPV
    Temp = (1 + rs.Fields(Interest)) ^ rs.Fields(Time)
    NPV = NPV + rs.Fields(CashFlow) / Temp
```

```
    If NPV > InitialInvestment Then
        PaybackPeriod = OldTime + _
            (NPV - InitialInvestment) / (NPV - OldNPV) * (rs.Fields(Time) - OldTime)
        Exit Function

    End If

    Debug.Print NPV, OldNPV, rs.Fields(Time), OldTime
    OldTime = rs.Fields("Time")
    rs.MoveNext

Loop

PaybackPeriod = -1

End Function
```

To use this routine, you need to pass a Recordset object containing the information used to compute the net present value, along with the value of the initial investment. The result will be returned as a Double, representing the number of time periods needed to recover the initial investment. If the initial investment is not recovered within the series of data in the table, a value of -1 will be returned.

The following code shows how to call PaybackPeriod:

```
Sub Example9_5()

Dim rs As ADODB.Recordset
Dim pp As Currency

Set rs = New ADODB.Recordset
Set rs.ActiveConnection = CurrentProject.Connection

rs.Open "Select Time, InterestRate, CashFlow From [Table9-3]", , _
    adOpenStatic, adLockReadOnly

pp = PaybackPeriod(rs, "Time", "InterestRate", "CashFlow", 300)

rs.Close

Debug.Print "Payback period = ", pp

End Sub
```

Discussion

Calculating the payback period is a way to determine the amount of time required to break even on an initial investment. Essentially, the PaybackPeriod routine computes the net present value for the supplied data on a time period-by-time period basis. When the current net present value exceeds the value of the initial investment, the initial investment is considered "paid back."

Rather than simply returning the time period during which the investment was recovered, however, this routine also attempts to approximate the actual point at which it was recovered. Assuming a linear cash flow during each time period, the routine determines the percentage of the current time period's cash flow that was needed to pay back the initial investment. This value is then multiplied by the difference in time between the current time period and the previous time period to give the approximate point during the current time period at which the investment was recovered.

9.4 Calculating Return on Investment

Problem

I need to know what the return on investment (ROI) will be for a particular set of cash flows.

Solution

This routine computes the ROI:

```
Function ReturnOnInvestment(rs As ADODB.Recordset, Time As String, _
    Interest As String, CashFlow As String, InitialInvestment As Currency) _
    As Double

Dim ROI As Currency
Dim NPV As Currency

NPV = NetPresentValue(rs, Time, Interest, CashFlow)

ROI = (NPV - InitialInvestment) / InitialInvestment

End Function


Function NetPresentValue(rs As ADODB.Recordset, Time As String, _
    Interest As String, CashFlow As String) As Currency

Dim NPV As Currency
Dim temp As Currency

NPV = 0

Do While Not rs.EOF
    temp = (1 + rs.Fields(InterestRate)) ^ rs.Fields(Time)
    NPV = NPV + rs.Fields(CashFlow) / temp

    rs.MoveNext

Loop
```

```
    rs.Close

    NetPresentValue = NPV

    End Function
```

The routine first calls the NetPresentValue function, using values returned in a recordset. It then computes the ROI by dividing the difference between the net present value and the initial investment by the initial investment.

Discussion

ROI gives you an indication of potential gain or loss on a particular investment. It is calculated using the following simple formula:

```
                            Net Present Value - Initial Investment
    Return on Investment =  --------------------------------------
                                     Initial Investment
```

Subtracting the initial investment from the net present value gives you the amount of money that the investment would yield; dividing this value by the initial investment gives you the percentage of change relative to the initial investment.

9.5   Calculating Straight-Line Depreciation

Problem

How do I calculate straight-line depreciation for a series of items?

Solution

You can use the following function to compute straight-line depreciation:

```
Function StraightLineDepreciation(Purchase As Currency, Salvage As Currency, _
    UsefulLife As Long, Year As Long)

StraightLineDepreciation = (Purchase - Salvage) / UsefulLife

End Function
```

The StraightLineDepreciation function takes four parameters, but only three are used here. Purchase contains the initial purchase price of the item, while Salvage represents the salvage value of the item at the end of its useful life. UsefulLife contains the useful life of the item, in years. Year contains the year for which you wish to compute the depreciation; it's ignored in this function, but was included to maintain the same set of parameters used in other depreciation functions.

The following routine shows how to use this function. It begins by opening an input table containing the items to be depreciated (see Figure 9-4). Then, it opens an empty table, which will hold the calculated depreciation for each year of each item's useful life:

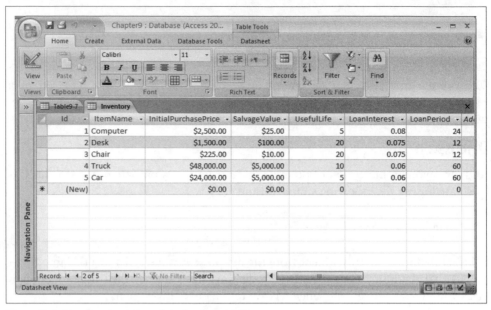

Figure 9-4. Creating inventory data for depreciation

```
Sub Example9_7( )

Dim intable As ADODB.Recordset
Dim outtable As ADODB.Recordset

Dim Year As Long
Dim Purchase As Currency
Dim Salvage As Currency
Dim UsefulLife As Long

Set intable = New ADODB.Recordset
Set intable.ActiveConnection = CurrentProject.Connection
intable.Open "Select Id, InitialPurchasePrice, SalvageValue, UsefulLife " & _
    "From Inventory", , adOpenStatic, adLockReadOnly

Set outtable = New ADODB.Recordset
Set outtable.ActiveConnection = CurrentProject.Connection
outtable.Open "[Table9-7]", , adOpenDynamic, adLockOptimistic

Do While Not intable.EOF

    Purchase = intable.Fields("InitialPurchasePrice")
    Salvage = intable.Fields("SalvageValue")
    UsefulLife = intable.Fields("UsefulLife")

    For Year = 1 To UsefulLife
        outtable.AddNew
        outtable.Fields("Id") = intable.Fields("Id")
        outtable.Fields("Year") = Year
```

```
    outtable.Fields("StraightLine") = StraightLineDepreciation(Purchase, _
        Salvage, UsefulLife, Year)
    outtable.Update

Next Year

intable.MoveNext

Loop

intable.Close
outtable.Close

End Sub
```

For each item in the Inventory table, the data values used to compute depreciation are stored in a set of local variables. Then, a For loop is executed for each year of the item's useful life. Inside the loop, a new row is added to the output table. This row contains Id, Year, and the newly computed depreciation value (see Figure 9-5). After all of the data has been processed, both tables are closed.

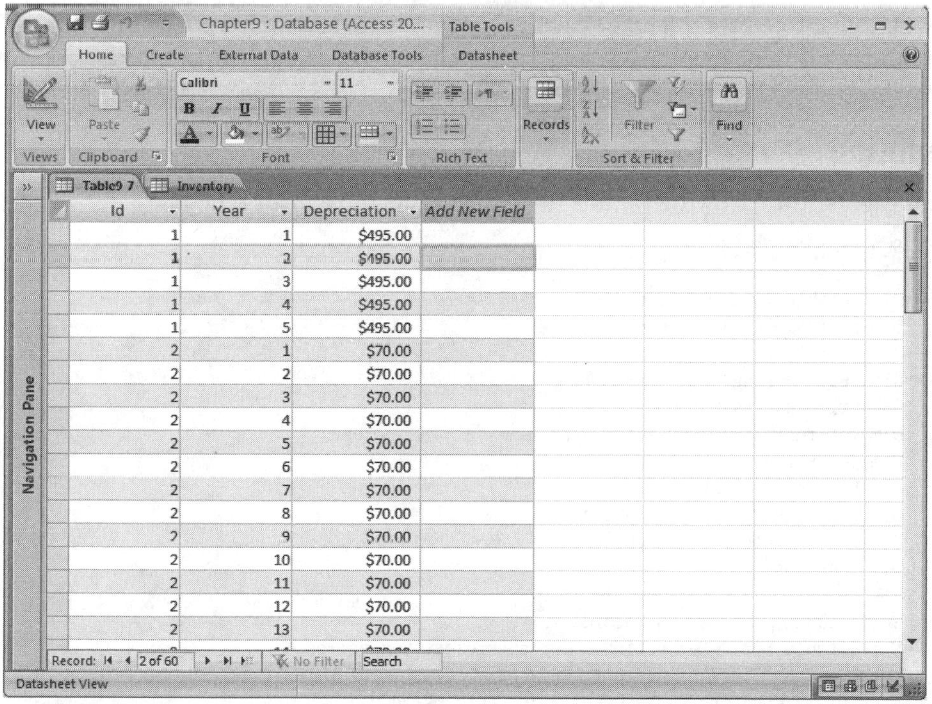

Figure 9-5. Calculating depreciation

Discussion

Depreciation is a way to account for the fact that most items used in business lose value from the beginning of their lives until the end. Straight-line depreciation spreads the loss equally over each year of the item's useful life:

```
                              Initial Purchase Price - Salvage Value
Straight-Line Depreciation = --------------------------------------
                                          Useful Life
```

Of course, most items lose more of their value in earlier years than in later years. For example, consider a new car. Just driving it off the showroom floor decreases its value significantly, but the decrease in value between, say, years 10 and 11 is minimal. A more sophisticated version of this routine might attempt to calculate depreciation on a sliding scale. This is known as declining-balance depreciation.

9.6   Creating a Loan Payment Schedule

Problem

I would like to create a loan payment schedule that identifies the monthly payment amounts and the percentages of those amounts that are applied to interest and the principal, respectively.

Solution

You can use the following routine to calculate a loan payment schedule:

```
Sub Example9_11( )

Dim intable As ADODB.Recordset
Dim outtable As ADODB.Recordset

Dim Year As Long
Dim Principal As Currency
Dim Interest As Double
Dim LoanPeriod As Long
Dim Payment As Currency
Dim CurrentPrincipal As Currency
Dim CurrentInterest As Double
Dim i As Long

Set intable = New ADODB.Recordset
Set intable.ActiveConnection = CurrentProject.Connection
intable.Open "Select Id, InitialPurchasePrice, LoanInterest, LoanPeriod " & _
    "From Inventory", , adOpenStatic, adLockReadOnly

Set outtable = New ADODB.Recordset
```

```
Set outtable.ActiveConnection = CurrentProject.Connection
outtable.Open "[Table9-11]", , adOpenDynamic, adLockOptimistic

Do While Not intable.EOF

    Principal = intable.Fields("InitialPurchasePrice")
    Interest = intable.Fields("LoanInterest") / 12
    LoanPeriod = intable.Fields("LoanPeriod")
    Payment = LoanPayment(Principal, Interest, LoanPeriod)

    For i = 1 To LoanPeriod
        CurrentInterest = Principal * Interest
        CurrentPrincipal = Payment - CurrentInterest
        Principal = Principal - CurrentPrincipal

        outtable.AddNew
        outtable.Fields("Id") = intable.Fields("Id")
        outtable.Fields("Period") = i
        outtable.Fields("Payment") = Payment
        outtable.Fields("Principal") = CurrentPrincipal
        outtable.Fields("Interest") = CurrentInterest
        outtable.Update

    Next i

    intable.MoveNext

Loop

intable.Close
outtable.Close

End Sub
```

This routine begins by defining two Recordset objects, intable and outtable. The intable Recordset reads an item from the Inventory table and extracts the information necessary to calculate the interest on a loan. The outtable Recordset maps to an empty table that will hold the loan payment schedules.

Next, the routine loops through the rows in the input table. Inside the loop it extracts the key fields into variables, taking care to ensure that the interest rate is converted from an annual rate to a monthly rate.

Once the variables are set, a For loop is used to process each month of the loan. The current principal and interest are calculated. Once the calculations are complete, the information for the month is written to the output table; once all of the months have been processed, the next row is read from intable.

Discussion

Storing the routine's result in a table enables you to create reports to present the data. Figure 9-6 shows a simple report that lists key information about an item, including the repayment schedule for the loan taken out to purchase it.

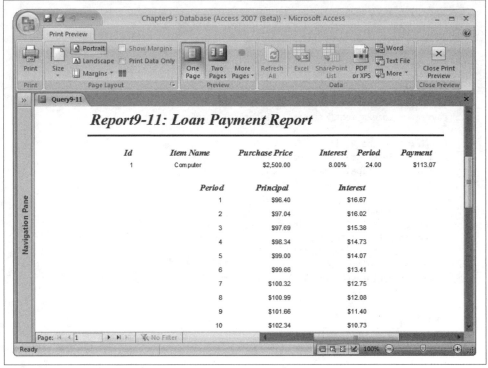

Figure 9-6. A loan repayment report

9.7 Using PivotTables and PivotCharts

Problem

Tables and reports are nice, but are there any other tools that can help me analyze my data?

Solution

Access includes two data analysis tools that are similar to those found in Excel. A *PivotTable* (see Figure 9-7) is a way to summarize your data into a compact report while including the ability to expand particular sets of values to show the underlying detail. A *PivotChart* (see Figure 9-8) has the same basic features as a PivotTable, but the results are displayed graphically instead of as a tabular report.

Discussion

PivotTables and PivotCharts are ideal tools to use when you're trying to understand your data, but don't know where to begin. Because of their dynamic nature, you can

CityData : Table

State ▼ (Multiple Items)

City		Level ▼						
		10-15	15-20	20-25	25-30	30-35	35-40	40-45
		Income ▼	Income ▼	Income ▼	Income ▼	Income ▼	Income ▼	Income ▼
Abilene	±	3753	3763	4116	3651	3723	3189	3197
Alexandria	±	4580	3843	4023	3598	2985	2897	2289
Amarillo	±	6227	6016	6801	6304	5724	5181	4847
Austin--San Marcos	±	22137	22613	27338	27209	29211	26737	25867
Baton Rouge	±	15754	15422	14926	14753	13879	12971	12099
Beaumont--Port Arthur	±	11478	10078	10523	9679	9514	8314	7614
Biloxi--Gulfport--Pascagoula	±	9441	9167	10214	10269	10328	9477	8475
Brownsville--Harlingen--San Benito	±	10419	9048	8790	7400	6453	5715	4668
Bryan--College Station	±	5171	4538	4065	3203	2997	2627	2437
Corpus Christi	±	10450	9892	9887	9305	8761	7852	7754
Dallas--Fort Worth	±	90033	98041	114465	119119	122165	115023	107591
El Paso	±	19130	18820	17965	16527	14900	12857	11861
Hattiesburg	±	3826	3767	3182	2979	2933	2487	2288
Houma	±	5802	4939	4835	4441	4696	4547	3958
Houston--Galveston--Brazoria	±							

Figure 9-7. A sample PivotTable

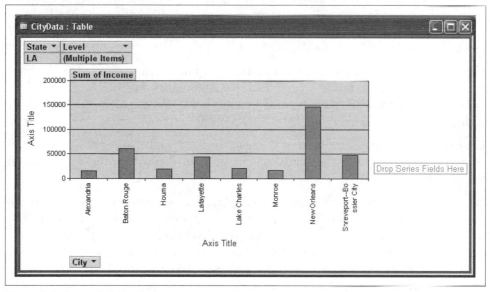

Figure 9-8. A sample PivotChart

quickly change the way the data is organized. This allows you to identify the information you want to present.

Excel also has PivotTables and PivotCharts, and Excel's implementations are much more powerful than Access'. If you prefer, you can export your data to Excel and use

Excel's tools to analyze it. However, using PivotTables in Access has the advantage that you can quickly change the underlying query to retrieve different data and/or compute different values. One useful option is to use Access to tune your query and test your PivotTables and PivotCharts, and then export the data into Excel and use Excel's capabilities to fine-tune the presentation of your data.

See Also

- Recipe 9.8
- Recipe 9.9

9.8   Creating PivotTables

Problem

How do I create a PivotTable?

Solution

You can create a PivotTable from a table or a query. First, open the table or query by double-clicking on its name. Then, in datasheet view, right-click on the window and choose PivotTable from the context menu. This will display an empty PivotTable similar to that shown in Figure 9-9.

There are four main areas in the PivotTable: the column area, the row area, the filter area, and the detail area. The column and row areas contain the fields whose values form the basic grid, while the filter area contains fields that can be used to include or exclude rows from the query.

The detail area occupies the bulk of the space in the PivotTable window, and represents the individual cells that make up the grid. In Figure 9-9, the detail section contains only the entry No Totals.

In addition to the PivotTable window itself, there are two other windows that you'll use to create the table. The Field List window (the top-right window in Figure 9-9) contains the fields that you can use with your PivotTable. The Properties window (the lower-right window in Figure 9-9) contains properties of the PivotTable. These windows float above the other windows, and can easily be moved elsewhere on the screen, including outside the main Access window.

To populate your PivotTable, simply drag fields from the Field List window to the desired area in the PivotTable window. You can drag more than one field into each area. When you drag multiple fields into the row or column area, these fields are combined to form a nested index (see Figure 9-10).

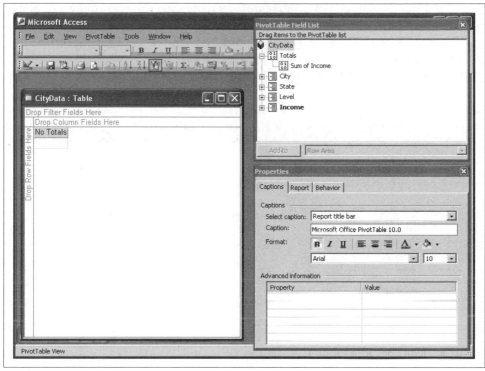

Figure 9-9. An empty PivotTable

State	City		Level ▾				Grand Total
			10-15	15-20	20-25	25-30	
			+/-	+/-	+/-	+/-	+/-
			Sum of Income	Sum of Income	Sum of Income	Sum of Income	Sum of Income
⊟ LA	Alexandria	±	4580	3843	4023	3598	16044
	Baton Rouge	±	15754	15422	14926	14753	60855
	Houma	±	5602	4939	4835	4441	19817
	Lafayette	±	13623	10788	10454	9914	44779
	Lake Charles	±	5746	5242	4744	4638	20370
	Monroe	±	4573	4305	3819	4235	16932
	New Orleans	±	39225	36206	35866	35186	146483
	Shreveport--Bossier City	±	12720	12223	11827	10934	47704
	Total	±	101823	92968	90494	87699	372984
⊟ TX	Abilene	±	3753	3763	4116	3651	15283
	Amarillo	±	6227	6016	6801	6304	25348
	Austin--San Marcos	±	22137	22613	27338	27209	99297
	Beaumont--Port Arthur	±	11478	10078	10523	9679	41758
	Brownsville--Harlingen--San Benito	±	10419	9048	8790	7400	35657
	Bryan--College Station	±	5171	4538	4065	3203	16977
	Corpus Christi	±	10450	9892	9887	9305	39534
	Dallas--Fort Worth	±	90033	98041	114465	119119	421658
	El Paso	±					

Figure 9-10. A PivotTable with two fields in the row area and one field in the column area

The Grand Total column shown in Figure 9-10 represents the sum of the values displayed in each row. Hidden values are not included in this calculation, though there is an option you can choose that will perform calculations on all data, rather than just the visible data. You can choose which values are displayed by clicking on the arrows next to the field names and choosing values from the drop-down lists (see Figure 9-11).

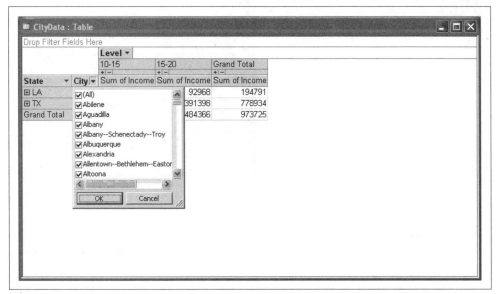

Figure 9-11. Choosing information for your PivotTable

Discussion

By default, Access computes the sum of the values you select. However, this isn't appropriate in all circumstances. For example, if you were dealing with stock prices rather than populations, computing averages would be more appropriate. To see a list of the options that you can use to summarize the data in the PivotTable, either right-click on the value you wish to change and choose AutoCalc from the pop-up menu, or choose AutoCalc from the toolbar (see Figure 9-12).

If your data includes date values, Access will automatically generate a set of fields that you can use as columns or rows, which represent aggregations of date values. You can choose from three basic sets of fields: Date, Date By Week, and Date By Month (see Figure 9-13). These three fields also include automatically summarized fields that span years, quarters, months, weeks, days, hours, minutes, and seconds.

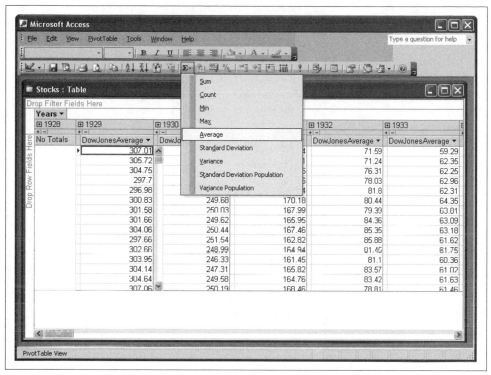

Figure 9-12. Choosing alternate calculation methods

Setting properties in an Access PivotTable is a little different than it is in most applications. You can display the Properties window (shown in Figure 9-14) by right-clicking on the PivotTable window and choosing Properties from the context menu. While this appears to be a normal properties window, it behaves somewhat differently. Under "General commands" is a drop-down list. Choosing a different option from this list will display a different set of tabs, which contain properties specific to the selected item.

If you click on a field, you'll be able to change the way the field is displayed in the PivotTable, along with its behavior. Clicking elsewhere on the PivotTable allows you to change the way information is displayed in the drag-and-drop areas (e.g., rows, columns, and filters), along with other general properties related to the PivotTable.

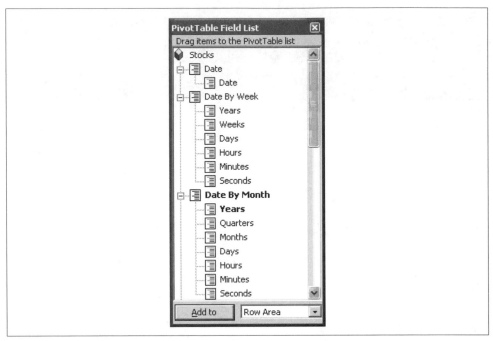

Figure 9-13. Automatically generated date fields

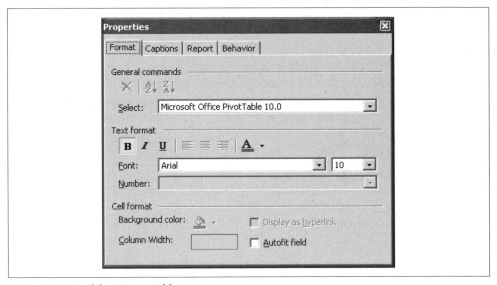

Figure 9-14. Modifying PivotTable properties

9.9 Charting Data

Problem

I want to analyze my data for trends, but looking at numbers is difficult for me. Is there a better alternative?

Solution

You can easily create a PivotChart using the result from any query. Simply run the query, right-click on the result, and choose PivotChart. Alternatively, you can work out which data you want to display in a PivotTable before switching the view to PivotChart (creating and working with PivotTables is covered in Recipe 9.8). Much of the structure will be carried over, including fields in the row, column, filter, and detail areas. If you've defined how the information is summarized in the PivotTable, those specifications will also be carried over. For example, the PivotTable shown in Figure 9-15 could be converted into the PivotChart shown in Figure 9-16 simply by right-clicking on the PivotTable and selecting PivotChart from the context menu.

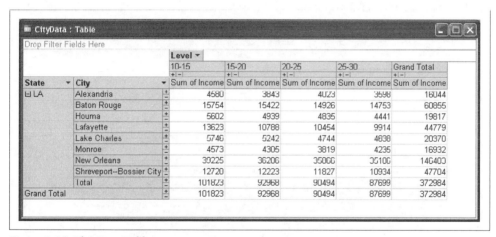

Figure 9-15. This PivotTable...

Discussion

When dealing with PivotCharts, you need to consider the amount of data you want to display. As with any chart, it's very easy to try to include too much data. Figure 9-17 shows what this can look like.

Of course, the amount of data you can comfortably include depends partly on the type of chart you're displaying. Access supports most, but not all, of the chart types

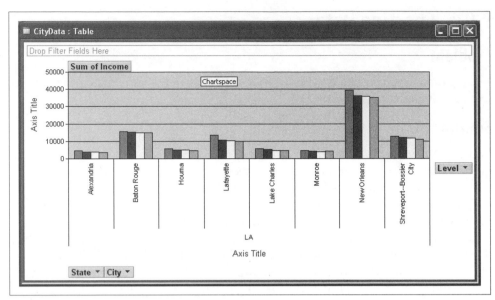

Figure 9-16. …becomes this PivotChart

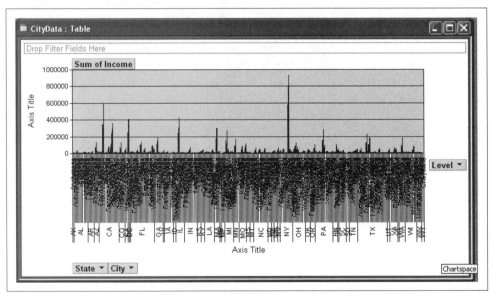

Figure 9-17. Way too much data in a chart

offered by Excel (see Figure 9-18). You can change the chart type by right-clicking a blank area in the chart and choosing Chart Type from the context menu.

As with a PivotTable, you can easily modify the way the data is displayed on a PivotChart. The interface for working with PivotCharts is the same as that for PivotTables; for more information, see Recipe 9.8.

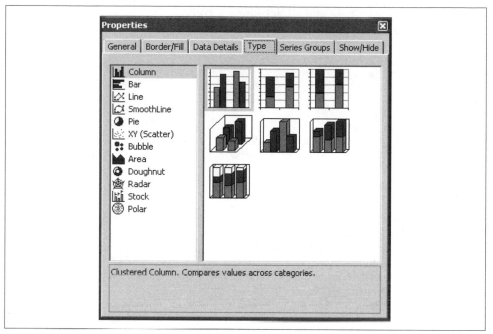

Figure 9-18. Types of PivotCharts supported by Access

9.10 Finding Trends

Problem

I have financial data that spans several months. At times, an upward or downward trend is apparent, but in some ranges of dates, the data is volatile and it's hard to discern a trend.

What are some techniques to apply to large data sets to determine the overall trend?

Solution

The moving average (discussed in Recipe 9.2) is the de facto standard for pulling a trend out of seemingly random data. The approach used in Recipe 9.2 computed an average based on calendar days, with all seven days of the week counted in the calculation. In this example, however, we'll need to use actual data points without regard to the calendar.

Say you want to calculate 20- and 50-day moving averages for your data. Twenty data points are needed to get a 20-day moving average. But in financial markets, data is based on days the market is open (which excludes weekends and holidays). Thus, while the 20-day average will be based on 20 days of activity, the calendar spread will cover more than 20 days.

This routine calculates a 20- and 50-day moving average:

```
Sub compute_moving_averages()
Dim db As DAO.Database
Dim rs As DAO.Recordset
Dim ssql As String
Dim sumit As Integer
Dim avg20 As Single
Dim avg50 As Single
Set db = CurrentDb
ssql = "Select * From Yahoo Order By Date"
Set rs = db.OpenRecordset(ssql, dbOpenDynaset)
'move down to the 20th row to start
rs.Move 19
Do While Not rs.EOF
    avg20 = 0
    rs.Move -19
    For sumit = 1 To 20
        avg20 = avg20 + rs.Fields("Close")
        rs.MoveNext
    Next sumit
    If rs.EOF Then GoTo do_50
    rs.Move -1 'put avg with correct ending date
    rs.Edit
    rs.Fields("20 day moving average") = avg20 / 20
    rs.Update
    rs.Move 1
Loop
do_50:
rs.MoveFirst
'move down to the 50th row to start
rs.Move 49
Do While Not rs.EOF
    avg50 = 0
    rs.Move -49
    For sumit = 1 To 50
        avg50 = avg50 + rs.Fields("Close")
        rs.MoveNext
    Next sumit
    If rs.EOF Then GoTo endd
    rs.Move -1 'put avg with correct ending date
    rs.Edit
    rs.Fields("50 day moving average") = avg50 / 50
    rs.Update
    rs.Move 1
Loop
endd:
rs.Close
Set rs = Nothing
db.Close
Set db = Nothing
MsgBox "done"
End Sub
```

In this case, the 20-day moving average starts on the 20th day in the data, and the 50-day moving average starts on the 50th day. Figure 9-19 shows the data points of the closing values for Yahoo! stock for July through December 2005. Between October and December, the data points are more erratic. The 20-day and 50-day moving averages provide a clearer picture of the stock's direction.

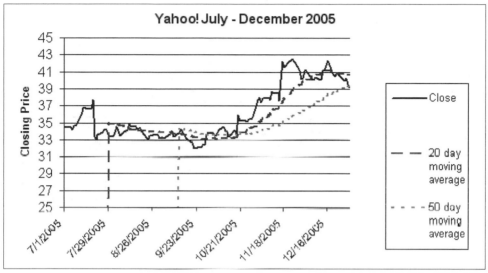

Figure 9-19. Moving averages

There are other trend lines besides the moving average. Each follows a mathematical pattern, as illustrated in Table 9-1.

Table 9-1. A sample of trend line formulas

Type of trend line	Formula
Linear	$y = mx + b$ (m is the slope and b is the intercept)
Logarithmic	$y = c \ln x + b$
Polynomial	$y = b + c1x + c2x2 + c3x3 \ldots$
Power	$y = cxb$
Exponential	$y = cebx$

In all the formulas in Table 9-1, y represents the positioning on the vertical (value) axis, and x represents the positioning on the horizontal (category) axis. While the formulas may look a bit complex if you are not math-savvy, an easy way to think of them is that y changes as x changes. On a chart, there is always a place where x and y intersect. Of course, other variables influence the value of y in each of these formulas.

Detailed explanations of the different types of trends are more in the realm of a good algebra or finance book, but let's look briefly at a few examples. Figure 9-20 and Figure 9-21 show the Yahoo! data coupled with a linear trend line and a polynomial trend line, respectively. The trend lines appear different, but still clearly show the direction of the trend.

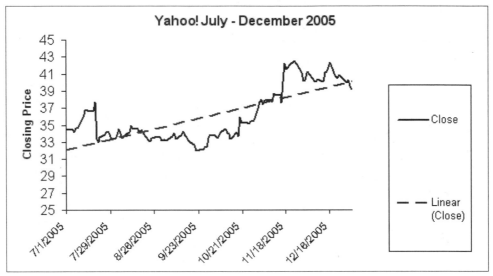

Figure 9-20. Yahoo! linear trend

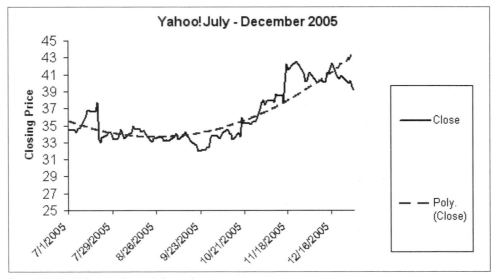

Figure 9-21. Yahoo! polynomial trend

Discussion

Finding trends in data can help you intelligently guesstimate the direction the data may take within some future period (this is known as *forecasting*).

However, it's important to consider that trends may be cyclical. *Cyclical trends* are trends that are expected to move in certain directions at different times, usually over the course of a year. This is a common phenomenon in some commodity markets. For example, the price of heating oil generally increases during cold months and decreases in warmer months. This is a standard case of prices being determined by supply and demand. More heating oil is needed in the winter than in the summer, and, all other things being equal, an increase in demand will raise prices, while a decrease in demand will lower prices.

A related but nearly opposite example is the cost of electricity. In summertime, the demand for electricity goes up (because all of the air conditioners are turned on); conversely, demand decreases in winter. Prices, to the extent of any market regulations, will go up along with the higher demand. Anyone care to guess the trend of air conditioner sales as the summer ends and autumn heads toward winter?

9.11   Finding Head and Shoulders Patterns

Problem

I've been studying the technical analysis of stocks, and I've read a lot about the so-called "Head and Shoulders" pattern. This is reasonably easy to identify when viewing a chart, but what's a good routine that will look for the pattern just by testing data?

Solution

Head and Shoulders patterns found in sequential security prices serve as an investment tool to predict future price moves. The Head and Shoulders pattern does indeed resemble the general look of a head with a shoulder on each side. The pattern has these attributes:

- A left shoulder, determined by ensuring that it is a pinnacle—that is, that the data point before and the data point after are both less than the shoulder data point.

- A dip, or a point that is lower than the left shoulder, and is a nadir—that is, the data points before and after must be higher than the dip data point.

- The head, which is a point higher than both shoulders. The head is a pinnacle.

- A second dip, after the head, that is lower than the head and is a nadir.

- The right shoulder, a pinnacle that comes after the second dip. This shoulder must be of a value that is between the head and the second dip.

That being said, there are variations on how to measure these data points. For example, must the second dip be lower than the first shoulder? Must the head be a certain percentage higher than the shoulders? Must all the data points lie within a given range of points? Clearly, identifying Head and Shoulders patterns involves a bit of art as well as financial acumen.

Figure 9-22 shows a chart in which the five key data points are enhanced with markers.

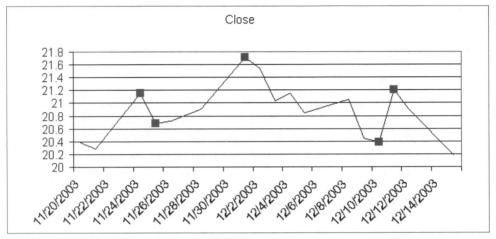

Figure 9-22. A Head and Shoulders top formation

These points were identified via a code routine written in Access VBA. Working with a table of financial data containing the closing prices for Apple Computer stock, the shoulder, dip, and head points were determined with a couple of parameters used in the routine. In this case, a user enters the parameter values on an Access form. The first parameter is the range, which indicates how many sequential data points should be tested to see if a particular key data point (shoulder, dip, or head) has been found.

The second parameter is a percentage. This percentage is used in the routine as a guide for the minimum required difference between the vital data points. For example, the first dip must be at least the percentage amount lower than the first shoulder, the head must be at least the percentage amount above the first shoulder, and so on. Figure 9-23 shows the form and the results of running the procedure with the entered parameters. The listbox on the form displays the results of dates and data points that met the criteria. A complete set of points—shoulder1, dip1, head, dip2, shoulder2—is always returned. (By the way, the purported line running from dip1 to dip2 is called the "neckline.")

Here is the code that locates the key values:

```
Private Sub cmdFindPattern_Click( )
Dim head_flag As Boolean
Dim shoulder1_flag As Boolean
```

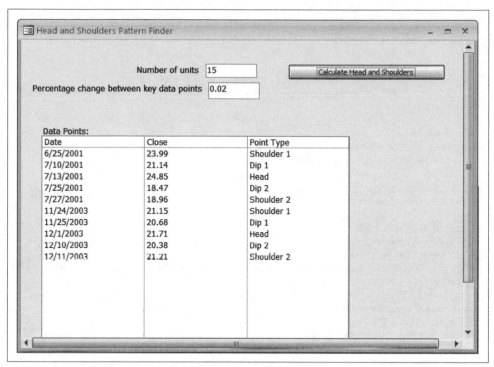

Figure 9-23. Finding key Head and Shoulders data points

```
Dim shoulder2_flag As Boolean
Dim dip1_flag As Boolean
Dim dip2_flag As Boolean
Dim head_date As Date
Dim shoulder1_date As Date
Dim shoulder2_date As Date
Dim dip1_date As Date
Dim dip2_date As Date
Dim head_value As Single
Dim shoulder1_value As Single
Dim shoulder2_value As Single
Dim dip1_value As Single
Dim dip2_value As Single
Dim rec_count As Integer
Dim check_point As Single
Dim last_close As Single
Dim loop_1 As Integer
Dim loop_2 As Integer
Dim loop_3 As Integer
Dim loop_4 As Integer
Dim loop_5 As Integer
Dim loop_6 As Integer
Dim period_count As Integer
Dim total_periods As Integer
```

```
Dim percentage As Single
Dim current_row As Integer
Dim item_count As Integer

'clear listbox
For item_count = Me.listDataPoints.ListCount - 1 To 0 Step -1
  Me.listDataPoints.RemoveItem (item_count)
Next item_count

'add headers to listbox
With Me.listDataPoints
  .AddItem "Date;Close;Point Type", 0
End With

percentage = CSng(Me.txtPercent)

Dim db As DAO.Database
Set db = CurrentDb
Dim rs As DAO.Recordset
Set rs = db.OpenRecordset("Select * from Apple order by Date")
rs.MoveLast
rs.MoveFirst
rec_count = rs.RecordCount
period_count = 0
total_periods = Me.txtPeriods
head_flag = False
shoulder1_flag = False
shoulder2_flag = False
dip1_flag = False
dip2_flag = False
'make sure that the number of units to analyze is not
'bigger than the entire data set!
If CInt(Me.txtPeriods) > rec_count Then
    MsgBox "# of units bigger than recset"
    Exit Sub
End If

On Error GoTo err_end
start_row = 0
current_row = 0
For loop_1 = start_row To rec_count - 1
  shoulder1_flag = False
  shoulder1_date = Date
  shoulder1_value = 0
  dip1_flag = False
  dip1_date = Date
  dip1_value = 0
  head_flag = False
  head_date = Date
  head_value = 0
  dip2_flag = False
  dip2_date = Date
  dip2_value = 0
  shoulder2_flag = False
```

```
shoulder2_date = Date
shoulder2_value = 0
total_datapoints = 0
period_count = 0
last_close = rs.Fields("Close")
rs.MoveNext
For loop_2 = current_row To rec_count - 1
  If rs.Fields("Close") > (last_close * _
       (1 + percentage)) Then
      'shoulder must be a pinnacle - higher than the
      'value before it and the value after it
      rs.MovePrevious
      check_point = rs.Fields("Close")
      rs.MoveNext 'back to current position
      If rs.Fields("Close") > check_point Then
          rs.MoveNext
          check_point = rs.Fields("Close")
          rs.MovePrevious 'back to current position
          If rs.Fields("Close") > check_point Then
              shoulder1_flag = True
              shoulder1_date = rs.Fields("Date")
              shoulder1_value = rs.Fields("Close")
              current_row = rs.AbsolutePosition
              period_count = 0
              Exit For
          End If
      End If
  Else
      period_count = period_count + 1
      If period_count = total_periods Then Exit For
      rs.MoveNext
  End If
Next loop_2
Select Case shoulder1_flag
  Case True
    last_close = rs.Fields("Close")
    rs.MoveNext
    For loop_3 = current_row To rec_count - 1
      If rs.Fields("Close") > shoulder1_value And shoulder1_flag = True Then
          shoulder1_date = rs.Fields("Date")
          shoulder1_value = rs.Fields("Close")
      End If

      If rs.Fields("Close") <= shoulder1_value * (1 - percentage) Then
          'dip must be a nadir - lower than the value before it
          'and the value after it
          rs.MovePrevious
          check_point = rs.Fields("Close")
          rs.MoveNext 'back to current position
          If rs.Fields("Close") < check_point Then
              rs.MoveNext
              check_point = rs.Fields("Close")
              rs.MovePrevious 'back to current position
              If rs.Fields("Close") < check_point Then
```

```
                    dip1_flag = True
                    dip1_date = rs.Fields("Date")
                    dip1_value = rs.Fields("Close")
                    current_row = rs.AbsolutePosition
                    period_count = 0
                    Exit For
               End If
          End If
     Else
          period_count = period_count + 1
          If period_count = total_periods Then Exit For
          rs.MoveNext
     End If
Next loop_3
Select Case dip1_flag
   Case True
     last_close = rs.Fields("Close")
     rs.MoveNext
     For loop_4 = current_row To rec_count - 1
        If rs.Fields("Close") < dip1_value And dip1_flag = True Then
           dip1_date = rs.Fields("Date")
           dip1_value = rs.Fields("Close")
        End If
        If (rs.Fields("Close") >= (shoulder1_value * (1 + percentage))) Then
           'head must be a pinnacle - higher than the
           'value before it and the value after it
           rs.MovePrevious
           check_point = rs.Fields("Close")
           rs.MoveNext 'back to current position
           If rs.Fields("Close") > check_point Then
               rs.MoveNext
               check_point = rs.Fields("Close")
               rs.MovePrevious 'back to current position
               If rs.Fields("Close") > check_point Then
                  head_flag = True
                  head_date = rs.Fields("Date")
                  head_value = rs.Fields("Close")
                  current_row = rs.AbsolutePosition
                  period_count = 0
                  Exit For
               End If
           End If
        Else
           period_count = period_count + 1
           If period_count = total_periods Then Exit For
           rs.MoveNext
        End If
     Next loop_4
     Select Case head_flag
       Case True
         last_close = rs.Fields("Close")
         rs.MoveNext
         For loop_5 = current_row To rec_count - 1
            If rs.Fields("Close") > head_value And head_flag = True Then
```

```
                    head_date = rs.Fields("Date")
                    head_value = rs.Fields("Close")
                End If
                If rs.Fields("Close") < shoulder1_value Then
                    'dip must be a nadir - lower than the value before it
                    'and the value after it
                    rs.MovePrevious
                    check_point = rs.Fields("Close")
                    rs.MoveNext 'back to current position
                    If rs.Fields("Close") < check_point Then
                        rs.MoveNext
                        check_point = rs.Fields("Close")
                        rs.MovePrevious 'back to current position
                        If rs.Fields("Close") < check_point Then
                            dip2_flag = True
                            dip2_date = rs.Fields("Date")
                            dip2_value = rs.Fields("Close")
                            current_row = rs.AbsolutePosition
                            period_count = 0
                            Exit For
                        End If
                    End If
                Else
                    period_count = period_count + 1
                    If period_count = total_periods Then Exit For
                    rs.MoveNext
                End If
            Next loop_5
            Select Case dip2_flag
                Case True
                    last_close = rs.Fields("Close")
                    rs.MoveNext
                    For loop_6 = current_row To rec_count - 1
                        If rs.Fields("Close") < dip2_value And dip2_flag = True Then
                            dip2_date = rs.Fields("Date")
                            dip2_value = rs.Fields("Close")
                        End If
                        If (rs.Fields("Close") >= (dip2_value * _
                                (1 + (percentage)))) And rs.Fields("Close") _
                                < head_value Then
                            'shoulder must be a pinnacle - higher than the
                            'value before it and the value after it
                            rs.MovePrevious
                            check_point = rs.Fields("Close")
                            rs.MoveNext 'back to current position
                            If rs.Fields("Close") > check_point Then
                                rs.MoveNext
                                check_point = rs.Fields("Close")
                                rs.MovePrevious 'back to current position
                                If rs.Fields("Close") > check_point Then
                                    shoulder2_flag = True
                                    shoulder2_date = rs.Fields("Date")
                                    shoulder2_value = rs.Fields("Close")
                                    current_row = rs.AbsolutePosition
```

```
                    period_count = 0
                    Exit For
                End If
            End If
        Else
            rs.MoveNext
            period_count = period_count + 1
            If period_count = total_periods Then Exit For
        End If
    Next loop_6
    Select Case shoulder2_flag
      Case True
        'success!
        With Me.listDataPoints
          .AddItem "" & shoulder1_date & ";" & shoulder1_value & _
              ";Shoulder 1"
          .AddItem "" & dip1_date & ";" & dip1_value & ";Dip 1"
          .AddItem "" & head_date & ";" & head_value & ";Head"
          .AddItem "" & dip2_date & ";" & dip2_value & ";Dip 2"
          .AddItem "" & shoulder2_date & ";" & shoulder2_value & _
              ";Shoulder 2"
        End With
      Case False 'shoulder2_flag
      End Select 'shoulder2
    Case False 'dip2
    End Select 'dip2
  Case False 'head
  End Select 'head
Case False 'dip1
End Select 'dip1
Case False 'shoulder1
End Select 'shoulder1
Next loop_1
If Me.listDataPoints.ListCount = 0 Then
    MsgBox "no patterns found"
End If
Exit Sub
err_end:
MsgBox "ran out of data - pattern not found"
Err.Clear
End Sub
```

This routine is a comprehensive shot at finding occurrences of the pattern in a data set. You might consider it as a springboard to a more intricate solution—for example, you might prefer to input a separate percentage for each leg of the pattern. Also, as it is, the routine uses the range input to control how many data points can exist between any two successive key data points. An additional input could control the overall range within which the five key data points must fall.

Discussion

Figure 9-22 showed the typical Head and Shoulders pattern generally used to find a reversal from an uptrend to a downtrend. This is also known as a "top" Head and Shoulders pattern.

The opposite and equally valid pattern is the "bottom" Head and Shoulders pattern, which resembles an upside-down head and shoulders. The dips are the two highest points, and the head is lower than the shoulders. This structure is used to find a reversal of a downtrend to an uptrend. Figure 9-24 shows what a bottom Head and Shoulders plot looks like.

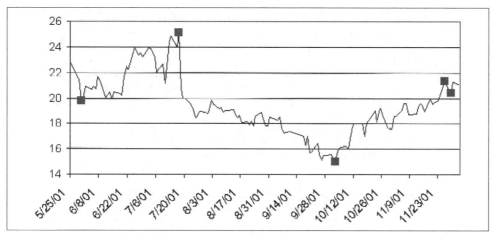

Figure 9-24. A Head and Shoulders bottom formation

The code to locate the key values in a bottom Head and Shoulders pattern is an alteration of the preceding routine. Only the portion of the routine that changes is shown here. The variables, Dim statements, and such are the same in both routines. Here is the rewritten section:

```
For loop_2 = current_row To rec_count - 1
  If (last_close - rs.Fields("Close")) / last_close > percentage Then
      'shoulder must be a nadir - lower than the
      'value before it and the value after it
      rs.MovePrevious
      check_point = rs.Fields("Close")
      rs.MoveNext 'back to current position
      If rs.Fields("Close") < check_point Then
        rs.MoveNext
        check_point = rs.Fields("Close")
        rs.MovePrevious 'back to current position
        If rs.Fields("Close") < check_point Then
          shoulder1_flag = True
          shoulder1_date = rs.Fields("Date")
          shoulder1_value = rs.Fields("Close")
          current_row = rs.AbsolutePosition
          period_count = 0
```

```
            Exit For
         End If
      End If
   Else
      period_count = period_count + 1
      If period_count = total_periods Then Exit For
      rs.MoveNext
   End If
Next loop_2
Select Case shoulder1_flag
   Case True
      last_close = rs.Fields("Close")
      rs.MoveNext
      For loop_3 = current_row To rec_count - 1
         If rs.Fields("Close") < shoulder1_value And shoulder1_flag = True Then
            shoulder1_date = rs.Fields("Date")
            shoulder1_value = rs.Fields("Close")
         End If
         If rs.Fields("Close") > shoulder1_value * (1 + percentage) Then
            'dip must be a pinnacle - higher than the value before it
            'and the value after it
            rs.MovePrevious
            check_point = rs.Fields("Close")
            rs.MoveNext 'back to current position
            If rs.Fields("Close") > check_point Then
               rs.MoveNext
               check_point = rs.Fields("Close")
               rs.MovePrevious 'back to current position
               If rs.Fields("Close") > check_point Then
                  dip1_flag = True
                  dip1_date = rs.Fields("Date")
                  dip1_value = rs.Fields("Close")
                  current_row = rs.AbsolutePosition
                  period_count = 0
                  Exit For
               End If
            End If
         Else
            period_count = period_count + 1
            If period_count = total_periods Then Exit For
            rs.MoveNext
         End If
      Next loop_3
      Select Case dip1_flag
         Case True
            last_close = rs.Fields("Close")
            rs.MoveNext
            For loop_4 = current_row To rec_count - 1
               If rs.Fields("Close") > dip1_value And dip1_flag = True Then
                  dip1_date = rs.Fields("Date")
                  dip1_value = rs.Fields("Close")
               End If
               If (shoulder1_value - rs.Fields("Close")) / _
                     shoulder1_value > percentage Then
```

```
      'head must be a nadir - lower than the value before it
      'and the value after it
      rs.MovePrevious
      check_point = rs.Fields("Close")
      rs.MoveNext 'back to current position
      If rs.Fields("Close") < check_point Then
          rs.MoveNext
          check_point = rs.Fields("Close")
          rs.MovePrevious 'back to current position
          If rs.Fields("Close") < check_point Then
              head_flag = True
              head_date = rs.Fields("Date")
              head_value = rs.Fields("Close")
              current_row = rs.AbsolutePosition
              period_count = 0
              Exit For
          End If
      End If
  Else
      period_count = period_count + 1
      If period_count = total_periods Then Exit For
      rs.MoveNext
  End If
Next loop_4
Select Case head_flag
  Case True
      last_close = rs.Fields("Close")
      rs.MoveNext
      For loop_5 = current_row To rec_count - 1
          If rs.Fields("Close") < head_value And head_flag = True Then
              head_date = rs.Fields("Date")
              head_value = rs.Fields("Close")
          End If
          If rs.Fields("Close") > shoulder1_value * (1 + percentage) Then
              'dip must be a pinnacle - higher than the value before it
              'and the value after it
              rs.MovePrevious
              check_point = rs.Fields("Close")
              rs.MoveNext 'back to current position
              If rs.Fields("Close") > check_point Then
                  rs.MoveNext
                  check_point = rs.Fields("Close")
                  rs.MovePrevious 'back to current position
                  If rs.Fields("Close") > check_point Then
                      dip2_flag = True
                      dip2_date = rs.Fields("Date")
                      dip2_value = rs.Fields("Close")
                      current_row = rs.AbsolutePosition
                      period_count = 0
                      Exit For
                  End If
              End If
          Else
              period_count = period_count + 1
```

```
                If period_count = total_periods Then Exit For
                rs.MoveNext
            End If
        Next loop_5
        Select Case dip2_flag
            Case True
                last_close = rs.Fields("Close")
                rs.MoveNext
                For loop_6 = current_row To rec_count - 1
                    If rs.Fields("Close") > dip2_value And dip2_flag = True Then
                        dip2_date = rs.Fields("Date")
                        dip2_value = rs.Fields("Close")
                    End If
                    If (dip2_value - rs.Fields("Close")) / dip2_value > _
                            percentage And rs.Fields("Close") > head_value Then
                        'shoulder must be a nadir - lower than the
                        'value before it and the value after it
                        rs.MovePrevious
                        check_point = rs.Fields("Close")
                        rs.MoveNext 'back to current position
                        If rs.Fields("Close") < check_point Then
                            rs.MoveNext
                            check_point = rs.Fields("Close")
                            rs.MovePrevious 'back to current position
                            If rs.Fields("Close") < check_point Then
                                shoulder2_flag = True
                                shoulder2_date = rs.Fields("Date")
                                shoulder2_value = rs.Fields("Close")
                                current_row = rs.AbsolutePosition
                                period_count = 0
                                Exit For
                            End If
                        End If
                    Else
                        rs.MoveNext
                        period_count = period_count + 1
                        If period_count = total_periods Then Exit For
                    End If
                Next loop_6
                Select Case shoulder2_flag
                    Case True
                        'success!
                        With Me.listDataPoints
                            .AddItem "" & shoulder1_date & ";" & shoulder1_value & _
                                ";Shoulder 1"
                            .AddItem "" & dip1_date & ";" & dip1_value & ";Dip 1"
                            .AddItem "" & head_date & ";" & head_value & ";Head"
                            .AddItem "" & dip2_date & ";" & dip2_value & ";Dip 2"
                            .AddItem "" & shoulder2_date & ";" & shoulder2_value & _
                                ";Shoulder 2"
                        End With
```

9.12   Working with Bollinger Bands

Problem

How can I create Bollinger Bands? What are they used for?

Solution

Bollinger Bands are a financial indicator that relates volatility with price over time. Given a set of sequential prices, to create Bollinger Bands, a moving average is created, and then the bands themselves are created on each side of the moving average. The bands are positioned two standard deviations away from each side of the moving average line. In other words, one band is created above the moving average line by adding the doubled standard deviation value to the moving average line. The other band sits under the moving average and is calculated by subtracting the doubled standard deviation from the moving average line.

Assuming you have a table filled with dates and prices, this query will return the moving average, the standard deviation, the doubled standard deviation value, the upper band, and the lower band. Price data from closing prices of McDonald's stock is used in this statement. Substitute the table name with your table, and field names with yours, if required:

```
SELECT A.Date, A.Close, (Select Avg(Close)
From McDonalds B
Where B.Date Between A.Date And DateAdd("d", -20, A.Date)) AS
[20 Day Moving Average], (Select StDevP(Close)
From McDonalds B
Where B.Date Between A.Date And DateAdd("d", -20, A.Date)) AS
[Standard Deviation], (Select StDevP(Close)  * 2
From McDonalds B
Where B.Date Between A.Date And DateAdd("d", -20, A.Date)) AS
[2 Standard Deviations],
[20 Day Moving Average]+[2 Standard Deviations] AS [Upper Band],
[20 Day Moving Average]-[2 Standard Deviations] AS [Lower Band]
FROM McDonalds AS A
ORDER BY A.Date;
```

Figure 9-25 shows the result of running the query, and Figure 9-26 shows a plot of the data. Three series are in the chart: the moving average, the upper band, and the lower band. The standard deviation and doubled standard deviation values are included in the query for reference, but are not plotted.

Discussion

Bollinger Bands contract and expand around the moving average. This is an indicator of the volatility of the underlying price. Viewing the chart in Figure 9-26, it is apparent that the upper and lower bands are widest apart in the September–October period, and closer together in the rest of the plot. The wider the difference in the bands, the higher the volatility of the underlying data points. In fact, you could

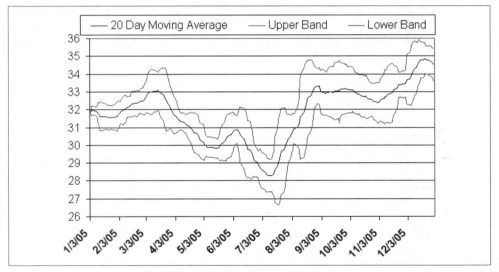

Date	Close	20 Day Moving Average	Standard Deviation	2 Standard Deviations	Upper Band	Lower Band
4/3/2006	34.73	34.664	0.24066020305189	0.48132040610378	35.1453204061	34.1826795939
4/4/2006	34.66	34.6906666666667	0.215235271789016	0.430470543578031	35.1211372102	34.2601961231
4/5/2006	34.81	34.6933333333333	0.216446041517255	0.432892083034511	35.1262254164	34.2604412503
4/6/2006	34.6	34.6626666666667	0.193716860964438	0.387433721928877	35.0501003886	34.2752329447
4/7/2006	34.88	34.648	0.166461206690712	0.332922413381425	34.9809224134	34.3150775866
4/10/2006	35.35	34.6893333333333	0.241673792997511	0.483347585995022	35.1726809193	34.2059857473
4/11/2006	35.55	34.7326666666667	0.320862725926412	0.641725451852824	35.3743921185	34.0909412148
4/12/2006	35.19	34.7586666666667	0.340467652240437	0.680935304480874	35.4396019711	34.0777313622
4/13/2006	34.85	34.7793333333333	0.335945762817515	0.67189152563503	35.451224859	34.1074418077
4/17/2006	34.32	34.7685714285714	0.36286276711059	0.725725534221179	35.4942969628	34.0428458944
4/18/2006	34.48	34.7807142857143	0.34992783512575	0.6998556702515	35.480569956	34.0808586155
4/19/2006	34.55	34.7771428571429	0.352003014828989	0.704006029657978	35.4811488868	34.0731368275
4/20/2006	35.08	34.815	0.354032887898526	0.708065775797052	35.5230657758	34.1069342242
4/21/2006	34.6	34.8321428571429	0.336986192413264	0.673972384826529	35.506115242	34.1581704723
4/24/2006	34.26	34.7985714285714	0.367517874061445	0.73503574812289	35.5336071767	34.0635356804
4/25/2006	33.85	34.7407142857143	0.441158609081665	0.88231721816333	35.6230315039	33.8583970676
4/26/2006	34.11	34.6907142857143	0.469246573709798	0.938493147419595	35.6292074331	33.7522211383
4/27/2006	34.62	34.6921428571429	0.468998607542972	0.937997215085943	35.6301400722	33.7541456421
4/28/2006	34.57	34.67	0.466919999265175	0.933839998530349	35.6038399985	33.7361600015

Record: I◄ ◄ 1 of 261 ► ►I ►☆ | ☜ No Filter | Search

Figure 9-25. Using a query to calculate Bollinger Bands

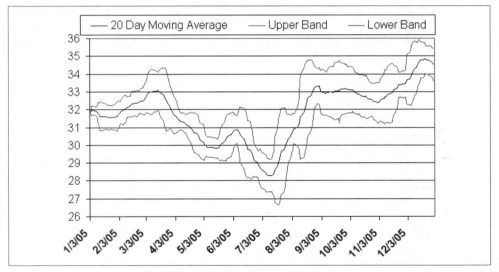

Figure 9-26. Chart with Bollinger Bands

subtract the lower band from the upper band, over the time frame of the chart, to glean a clear picture of the deviation between the bands.

The chart shown in Figure 9-26 does not include the actual prices as a chart series, but you could include these in the chart. When price is included in the plot, it is the least smooth line, and it can actually cross the upper or lower band (providing buy or sell guidance).

For further information about Bollinger Bands, visit *http://www.bollingerbands.com*, or check out any comprehensive financial web site, such as Yahoo! Finance, or *http://www.stockcharts.com*.

9.13   Calculating Distance Between Zip Codes

Problem

I've seen several web sites where one can enter a zip code and a mileage amount, and then a list of stores, doctors, and other information within the defined region is returned. How is this done?

Solution

The trick is to use longitude and latitude settings. Each zip code is centered around a particular longitude and latitude intersection, and you'll need a table containing these values. Lists are available on the Web. Some cost a bit, but others are free—run a search with "zip," "longitude," and "latitude" as keywords, and you're bound to find many choices.

Figure 9-27 shows a section of a table that contains the necessary information.

Zip	State	City	Latitude	Longitude	Add New Field
60007	IL	ELK GROVE VILLAGE	42.013178	-87.990068	
60008	IL	ROLLING MEADOWS	42.067808	-88.018485	
60010	IL	BARRINGTON	42.15837	-88.159174	
60012	IL	CRYSTAL LAKE	42.276721	-88.307805	
60013	IL	CARY	42.220273	-88.23379	
60014	IL	CRYSTAL LAKE	42.234266	-88.30677	
60015	II	DEERFIELD	42.174325	-87.880962	
60016	IL	DES PLAINES	42.052478	-87.890617	
60018	IL	DES PLAINES	41.998597	-87.902842	
60020	IL	FOX LAKE	42.395852	88.17493	
60021	IL	FOX RIVER GROVE	42.194698	-88.219942	
60022	II	GLENCOE	42.130626	-87.767813	
60025	IL	GLENVIEW	42.085477	-87.824664	
60029	IL	GOLF	42.057027	-87.792008	
60030	IL	GRAYSLAKE	42.331556	-88.054523	
60031	IL	GURNEE	42.373751	-87.944	
60033	IL	HARVARD	42.404061	-88.602296	
60034	IL	HEBRON	42.455151	-88.430666	
60035	IL	HIGHLAND PARK	42.188961	-87.806265	
60037	IL	FORT SHERIDAN	42.211092	-87.80904	
60040	IL	HIGHWOOD	42.203474	-87.813166	
60041	IL	INGLESIDE	42.367671	-88.149683	
60042	IL	ISLAND LAKE	42.280446	-88.201938	

Record: 1 of 33331   No Filter   Search

Figure 9-27. Table of zip codes

Now, let's consider the process. When a user enters a zip code on the web page, it has to be found in the zip code table to access its longitude and latitude values. A second scan of the zip table is then run to identify zip codes near the entered zip code. How near is "near" depends on the selected mileage setting. There is a formula to calculate what other zips are within the mileage parameter.

Longitude and latitude are measured in degrees, minutes, and seconds. Roughly, a degree is 69 miles, a minute is one-sixtieth of a degree (or 1.15 miles), and a second is about 100 feet.

These are approximations—nautical miles are measured differently than land miles, and there are other factors that affect longitude and latitude calculations.

A 1-mile variance of a longitude and latitude setting is a factor of approximately .008. A 10-mile variance is about .08.

This routine calculates a range around the entered zip code, in parameters of 10, 20, and 30 miles:

```
Private Sub cmdFindZips_Click()
Dim this_lat As Double
Dim this_long As Double
Dim conn As ADODB.Connection
Dim rs As New ADODB.Recordset
Dim drop_it As Integer
'validation
If Len(Me.txtZip) <> 5 Then
   MsgBox "Enter a 5 digit zip code"
   Exit Sub
End If
If IsNull(Me.lstMiles.Value) Then
   MsgBox "Select a mileage range"
   Exit Sub
End If
'setup
For drop_it = Me.lstResults.ListCount - 1 To 0 Step -1
   Me.lstResults.RemoveItem (drop_it)
Next
lblMatches.Caption = "Matches=0"
'processing
Set conn = CurrentProject.Connection
ssql = "Select * from tblUSZipData  Where Zip='" & Me.txtZip & "'"
rs.Open ssql, conn, adOpenKeyset, adLockOptimistic
If rs.RecordCount = 0 Then
   rs.Close
   Set rs = Nothing
   Set conn = Nothing
   MsgBox "Zip Not Found"
   Exit Sub
Else
   this_lat = rs.Fields("Latitude")
   this_long = rs.Fields("Longitude")
   rs.Close
   Select Case Me.lstMiles.Value
     Case 10
       ssql = "Select Zip, State, City from tblUSZipData  Where " & _
           "(Latitude Between " & this_lat + 0.08 & " and " _
           & this_lat - 0.08 & ") And " & _
```

```
                "(Longitude Between " & this_long + 0.05 & " and " _
                & this_long - 0.05 & ")"
        Case 20
          ssql = "Select Zip, State, City from tblUSZipData  Where " & _
                "(Latitude Between " & this_lat + 0.17 & " and " _
                & this_lat - 0.17 & ") And " & _
                "(Longitude Between " & this_long + 0.17 & " and " _
                & this_long - 0.17 & ")"
        Case 30
          ssql = "Select Zip, State, City from tblUSZipData  Where " & _
                "(Latitude Between " & this_lat + 0.26 & " and " _
                & this_lat - 0.26 & ") And " & _
                "(Longitude Between " & this_long + 0.26 & " and " _
                & this_long - 0.26 & ")"
    End Select
    rs.Open ssql, conn, adOpenKeyset, adLockOptimistic
    If rs.RecordCount = 0 Then
        rs.Close
        Set rs = Nothing
        Set conn = Nothing
        MsgBox "No Zips in Radius"
        Exit Sub
    Else
        match = 0
        Do Until rs.EOF
            Me.lstResults.AddItem rs.Fields("Zip") & ";" & _
                rs.Fields("City") & ";" & rs.Fields("State")
            match = match + 1
            rs.MoveNext
        Loop
        lblMatches.Caption = "Matches=" & match
    End If 'If rs.RecordCount = 0 Then
End If 'If rs.RecordCount = 0 Then
rs.Close
Set rs = Nothing
Set conn = Nothing
MsgBox "Done"
End Sub
```

Figure 9-28 shows the entry form with a zip code entered and a mileage factor selected. The zip codes found within the designated range of the entered zip code are returned in a listbox.

 The calculation in this routine looks for longitude and latitude settings that fit in a geographical box. Searching within a given radius requires a more complex calculation—check the Web for details. There is a lot more to know about how longitude and latitude work; with a little online research, you'll be able to fine-tune your calculations to get more accurate results than those produced by the general solutions shown here.

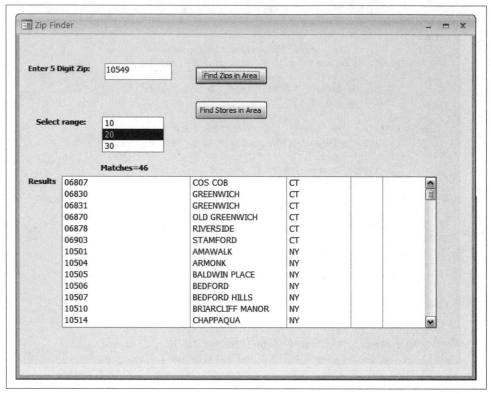

Figure 9-28. Finding zip codes in a given area

Discussion

Finding zip codes in a certain area is useful if all you need are the zip codes. However, a more realistic application is to return a list of stores that are in the area surrounding the entered zip code.

The following code is a variation of the preceding routine. This time, a second table containing store names and addresses is involved. The tblCustomers table also contains the longitude and latitude for each store. In this variation, the tblCustomers table is queried, and the stores found within the area defined by the entered zip code and mileage range are returned in the listbox:

```
Private Sub cmdFindStores_Click()
Dim this_lat As Double
Dim this_long As Double
Dim conn As ADODB.Connection
Dim rs As New ADODB.Recordset
Dim drop_it As Integer
'validation
If Len(Me.txtZip) <> 5 Then
    MsgBox "Enter a 5 digit zip code"
```

```
      Exit Sub
End If
If IsNull(Me.lstMiles.Value) Then
    MsgBox "Select a mileage range"
    Exit Sub
End If
'setup
For drop_it = Me.lstResults.ListCount - 1 To 0 Step -1
    Me.lstResults.RemoveItem (drop_it)
Next
lblMatches.Caption = "Matches=0"
'processing
Set conn = CurrentProject.Connection
ssql = "Select * from tblUSZipData  Where Zip='" & Me.txtZip & "'"
rs.Open ssql, conn, adOpenKeyset, adLockOptimistic
If rs.RecordCount = 0 Then
    rs.Close
    Set rs = Nothing
    Set conn = Nothing
    MsgBox "Zip Not Found"
    Exit Sub
Else
    this_lat = rs.Fields("Latitude")
    this_long = rs.Fields("Longitude")
    rs.Close
    Select Case Me.lstMiles.Value
      Case 10
        ssql = "Select Store, Address, City, State, Zip from tblCustomers " & _
            "Where (Latitude Between " & this_lat + 0.08 & " and " _
            & this_lat - 0.08 & ") And " & _
            "(Longitude Between " & this_long + 0.05 & " and " _
            & this_long - 0.05 & ")"
      Case 20
        ssql = "Select Store, Address, City, State, Zip from tblCustomers " & _
            "Where (Latitude Between " & this_lat + 0.17 & " and " _
            & this_lat - 0.17 & ") And " & _
            "(Longitude Between " & this_long + 0.17 & " and " _
            & this_long - 0.17 & ")"
      Case 30
        ssql = "Select Store, Address, City, State, Zip from tblCustomers " & _
            "Where (Latitude Between " & this_lat + 0.26 & " and " _
            & this_lat - 0.26 & ") And " & _
            "(Longitude Between " & this_long + 0.26 & " and " _
            & this_long - 0.26 & ")"
    End Select
    rs.Open ssql, conn, adOpenKeyset, adLockOptimistic
    If rs.RecordCount = 0 Then
        rs.Close
        Set rs = Nothing
        Set conn = Nothing
        MsgBox "No Zips in Radius"
        Exit Sub
    Else
        match = 0
```

```
    Do Until rs.EOF
        Me.lstResults.AddItem rs.Fields("Store") & ";" & _
            rs.Fields("Address") & ";" & rs.Fields("City") & ";" & _
            rs.Fields("State") & ";" & rs.Fields("Zip")
        match = match + 1
        rs.MoveNext
    Loop
    lblMatches.Caption = "Matches=" & match
End If 'If rs.RecordCount = 0 Then
End If 'If rs.RecordCount = 0 Then
rs.Close
Set rs = Nothing
Set conn = Nothing
MsgBox "Done"
End Sub
```

Figure 9-29 shows a returned list of stores found within the specified number of miles from the entered zip code.

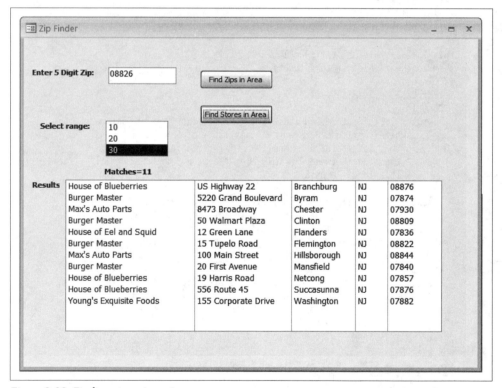

Figure 9-29. Finding stores in a given area

Statistics

You can't write a book about data analysis and not talk about statistics. *Statistics* is the science of collecting and analyzing data. When combined with probability theory, you can use statistics to make guesses about the future.

Access is a good tool for collecting data, and it offers a number of features that can help you analyze that data. In this chapter, you'll learn how to compute statistics using aggregate functions and how to build custom tools to analyze your data. You'll also learn how to display useful types of charts that will give you new insights into your data.

10.1 Creating a Histogram

Problem

I'd like to understand how the values of a data element I'm collecting are distributed.

Solution

You can use a frequency table and a histogram to identify how the data values are distributed.

A frequency table begins by defining a set of "buckets," and associating a range of data values with each bucket. Each row is then read from the database, and each element is placed in the appropriate bucket based on its value. Once all of the rows have been processed, the frequency table can be constructed by counting the number of data elements in each bucket.

For example, consider the following list of values:

    43, 45, 17, 38, 88, 22, 55, 105, 48, 24, 11, 18, 20, 91, 9, 19

Table 10-1 contains the number of data elements for each given set of ranges.

Table 10-1. A simple frequency table

Below 25	25 to 50	50 to 75	75 to 100	Above 100
8	4	1	2	1

While you may think that this process sounds complicated enough that you'd have to write a VBA program to do the counting, it turns out that it's fairly easy to build a SQL SELECT statement that does the job without a single line of code. Consider the following statement:

```
SELECT Sum(IIf([DisneyClose]<25,1,0)) AS Below25,
    Sum(IIf([DisneyClose]>=25 And [DisneyClose]<30,1,0)) AS 25to29,
    Sum(IIf([DisneyClose]>=30 And [DisneyClose]<34,1,0)) AS 30to34,
    Sum(IIf([DisneyClose]>=35 And [DisneyClose]<39,1,0)) AS 35to39,
    Sum(IIf([DisneyClose]>=40,1,0)) AS Above40
FROM Stocks
WHERE (((Stocks.Date)>#1/1/2000# And (Stocks.Date)<#1/1/2006#));
```

This statement returns a single row of data representing the frequency table and a total of five columns, where each column represents a particular range, and the value of the column represents the number of values that fall into that range.

The statement uses the Sum and IIf functions. The Sum function is an aggregate function that returns the sum of all the values generated by the expression inside. The IIf function takes three parameters: the first is a Boolean expression, the second is the value returned if the Boolean expression is true, and the third is the value returned if the Boolean expression is false.

The real trick to this statement is the way the IIf function returns 1 if the value is in the column's range, and 0 if it isn't. This means that for any particular row, one column will have a 1, while the rest of the columns will have 0s. The Sum function thus returns the number of rows that contain values in each given range. Running the query will return a result table similar to Figure 10-1.

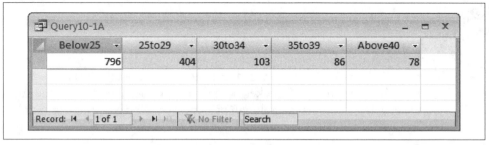

Figure 10-1. Running the query results in this simple frequency table

You can convert a frequency table into a histogram in one of two ways: by exporting the data to Excel and using its charting tools to create a bar or column chart, or you by viewing the result table in Access as a PivotChart (see Figure 10-2).

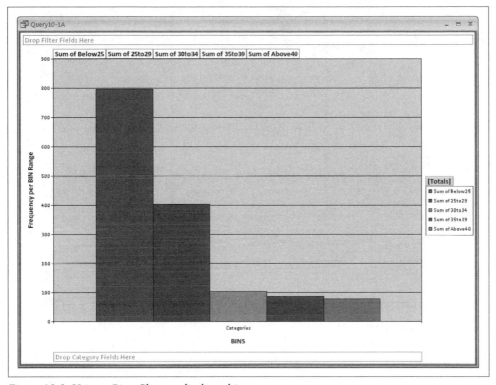

Figure 10-2. Using a PivotChart to display a histogram

To create the PivotChart, right-click on the datasheet view of the query result, and choose PivotChart from the context menu. Then, drag the fields from the Chart Field List (see Figure 10-3) onto the plot area to create your histogram.

Discussion

If you need a neatly formatted chart, you should export your data into Excel, where you'll have more control over the chart's formatting. On the other hand, using Access' PivotCharts makes it easy to determine the right level of granularity.

If you don't like how the chart looks, you can easily change the ranges in the query and see the results much faster than you would in Excel.

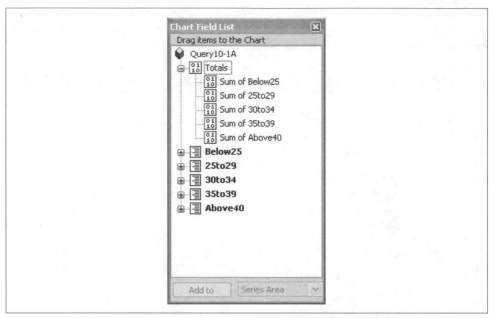

Figure 10-3. The list of fields that can be displayed in the PivotChart

10.2 Finding and Comparing the Mean, Mode, and Median

Problem

I want to compute the mean, mode, and median of a particular column.

Solution

To compute the mean of a column, you can simply use the Avg aggregate function, like this:

```
SELECT Avg(Stocks.DisneyClose) AS Average
FROM Stocks
```

The result of this query is shown in Figure 10-4.

Computing the mode of a column is a little more complex, but the following SELECT statement should give you an idea of how to do it:

```
SELECT Top 1 Stocks.DisneyClose, Count(*) AS [Count]
FROM Stocks
GROUP BY Stocks.DisneyClose
ORDER BY Count(*) DESC;
```

You can see the result in Figure 10-5.

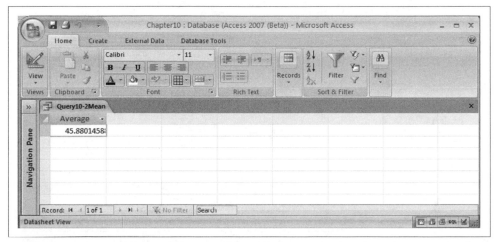

Figure 10-4. Computing the mean for a set of data

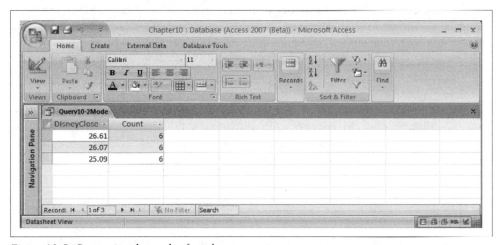

Figure 10-5. Computing the mode of a column

Computing the median of a column is more complicated still. The following SELECT statement will generate the result shown in Figure 10-6:

```
SELECT A.DisneyClose
FROM Stocks AS A, Stocks AS B
GROUP BY a.DisneyClose
HAVING (((Sum(IIf(a.DisneyClose<=b.DisneyClose,1,0)))>=(Count(*)/2))
    And ((Sum(IIf(a.DisneyClose>=b.DisneyClose,1,0)))>=(Count(*)/2)));
```

Discussion

The *mean* is really just the average of the numbers. In other words, to get the mean, you need to compute the sum of the values and divide the result by the number of values, which is what the Avg function does for you.

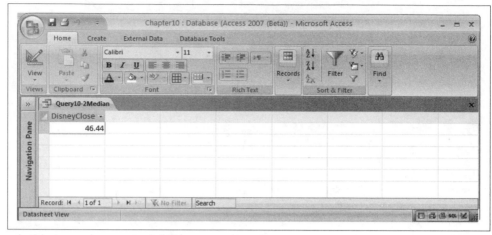

Figure 10-6. Computing the median of a column

On the other hand, to find the *mode*, you must create a list of all of your numbers, order them, and find the most common value. Note that this value is not necessarily the same as the average. Consider the following set of numbers:

    1, 1, 1, 1, 496

The average of these numbers is 100, while the mode is 1.

The SELECT statement that returns the mode works by using the GROUP BY clause to count the number of occurrences of each individual value, then orders them from the value with the highest count to the one with the lowest count. Finally, it returns the number or numbers that have the largest count:

```
SELECT Top 1 Stocks.DisneyClose, Count(*) AS [Count]
FROM Stocks
GROUP BY Stocks.DisneyClose
ORDER BY Count(*) DESC;
```

The *median* is the most complicated value to compute. To find the median, you arrange the numbers in order, and then select either the middle value (if there is an odd number of values) or the average of the two values in the middle (if there is an even number of values). Thus, in this set of numbers, 3 is the median:

    1, 2, 3, 4, 5

while in this set of numbers, the median is 3.5:

    1, 2, 3, 4, 5, 6

The following SQL statement may look tricky at first, but it's really easy to follow. It begins by using the GROUP BY clause to reduce the number of individual data values to process. Then, it uses the IIf function to determine how many numbers appear before and after the current value in the sequence. When the number of data values before and after are the same, you've found the median value:

```
SELECT A.DisneyClose
FROM Stocks AS A, Stocks AS B
GROUP BY a.DisneyClose
HAVING (((Sum(IIf(a.DisneyClose<=b.DisneyClose,1,0)))>=(Count(*)/2))
    And ((Sum(IIf(a.DisneyClose>=b.DisneyClose,1,0)))>=(Count(*)/2)));
```

The downside to using a SELECT statement to compute the median is the amount of processing that's required. Basically, this approach reads the entire table for each value it processes. For small tables this is fine, but if your table contains a thousand or more rows, you'll find that running the query takes a long time. However, the following VBA routine is very quick, no matter what the size of your table is:

```
Sub Example10_2Median( )

Dim rs As ADODB.Recordset
Dim d As Double

Set rs = New ADODB.Recordset
rs.ActiveConnection = CurrentProject.Connection

rs.Open "Select DisneyClose From Stocks Order By DisneyClose", , _
    adOpenStatic, adLockReadOnly

If rs.RecordCount Mod 2 = 1 Then
    rs.Move rs.RecordCount / 2 + 1
    d = rs.Fields("DisneyClose")

Else
    rs.Move rs.RecordCount / 2
    d = rs.Fields("DisneyClose")

    rs.MoveNext
    d = (d + rs.Fields("DisneyClose")) / 2

End If

rs.Close

Debug.Print "Median = ", d

End Sub
```

The routine begins by opening a static, read-only Recordset. Once the Recordset is open, the code determines whether the RecordCount property is even or odd. If the value of RecordCount is odd, it uses the Move method to skip to the exact center of the table, and retrieves the middle value. To find the center row, the routine divides the value of RecordCount by 2, rounds down the result to the nearest integer value, and then adds 1. The value in this row is then returned as the median.

If the value of RecordCount is even, the same process is followed, but after retrieving the value in the "center" row, the routine moves to the next row and retrieves its value as well. Then, it computes the average of the two values and returns this as the median.

10.3   Calculating the Variance in a Set of Data

Problem

I'd like to understand how much my data varies by using standard statistical functions like standard deviation and variance.

Solution

Given a column of data, the following SELECT statement returns a Recordset containing the average, minimum, maximum, variance, and standard deviation values, using the Avg, Min, Max, Var, and StDev functions:

```
SELECT Avg([DisneyClose]) AS Average,
    Min([DisneyClose]) AS Minimum,
    Max([DisneyClose]) AS Maximum,
    Var([DisneyClose]) AS Variance,
    StDev([DisneyClose]) AS StdDeviation
FROM Stocks
```

The results are shown in Figure 10-7.

Discussion

The *variance* is a measure of the spread of a list of numbers. It's computed by first determining the average value, and then, for each individual number, calculating the square of the difference between that number and the average. Finally, these values are summed and divided by the total number of values.

Here is the formula to calculate variance:

$$\text{Variance} = \frac{\Sigma\ (x - X)^2}{N}$$

where N is the number of values, x is the current value, and X is the average value.

Consider the following set of numbers:

```
1, 2, 3, 4, 5
```

The average is 3, and the sum of the difference of the squares is 10. There are five values, so the variance is 2.

If you replace the 5 with a 10, the average becomes 4, but the variance becomes 10. This indicates that this list of numbers is more spread out than the original list.

One of the issues with using variance is that the number returned as the variance isn't measured in the same units as the original numbers. Instead, the variance is measured in units squared. If the original numbers were in dollars, for example, the variance would be measured in dollars squared.

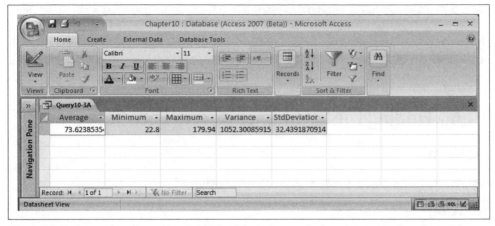

Figure 10-7. Computing the variance, standard deviation, and other summary values for a column

Because this isn't always useful, you can compute the *standard deviation* by taking the square root of the variance. Standard deviation is measured in terms of the original units. For the set of numbers 1 through 5 (whose variance was 2), the standard deviation is 1.41; for the numbers 1 through 4 and 10, the standard deviation is 3.16.

One way to use variance and standard deviation is to compare two lists of numbers. Consider the following query, which computes the standard deviation for four different stock prices over a five-year period:

```
Select StDev(DisneyClose) As Disney,
    StDev(TimeWarnerClose) As TimeWarner,
    StDev(GeneralMotorsClose) As GeneralMotors,
    StDev(FordClose) As Ford
From Stocks
Where Date Between #1-1-2000# and #12-31-2005#;
```

The results are shown in Figure 10-8.

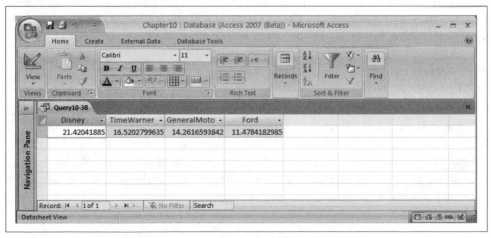

Figure 10-8. Using standard deviation to understand stock prices

Notice that Disney has a standard deviation of 21.42, while Ford has a standard deviation of 11.47. This means that the stock prices for Disney varied much more than the stock prices for Ford during the same period of time. This doesn't necessarily tell you which stock to buy, but it does help you understand how volatile stock prices are when compared with each other.

10.4 Finding the Covariance of Two Data Sets

Problem

I want to compute the covariance of two sets of data.

Solution

You can use a SELECT statement like the following to compute the covariance for two columns of data:

```
SELECT
    Sum(
        (DisneyClose -
            (Select Avg(DisneyClose)
                From Stocks
                Where Date Between #1-1-2000# And #12-31-2005#))
        * (TimeWarnerClose -
            (select Avg(TimeWarnerClose)
                From Stocks
                Where Date Between #1-1-2000# And #12-31-2005#))
        )
    / Count(*) AS Covariance
FROM Stocks
WHERE Date Between #1/1/2000# And #12/31/2005#;
```

The result is shown in Figure 10-9.

The SELECT statement begins by computing the sum of the products of the differences between each of the values and their average. Then, the covariance is computed by dividing the sum by the number of values processed.

Discussion

Here is the formula to calculate covariance:

$$\text{Covariance} = \frac{(x - X)(y - Y)}{N}$$

where N is the number of values, x is the current value for the first column, X is the average value for the first column, y is the current value for the second column, and Y is the average value for the second column.

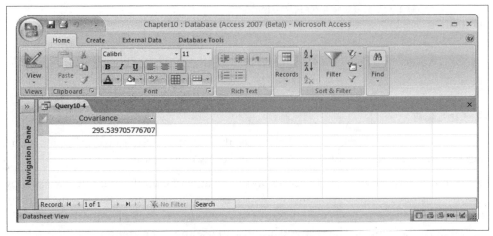

Figure 10-9. Computing the covariance between two columns of data

Variance, discussed in Recipe 10.3, provides an indication of how much the values for a single variable vary. *Covariance*, by contrast, measures how much the values for two separate variables vary *together*. A positive value for covariance means that as the value of one variable increases, so does the value of the other. A negative value for covariance means that as one variable increases, the other one decreases. A value of 0 implies that the two variables are linearly independent—that is, there is no linear relationship between one variable and the other.

10.5   Finding the Correlation of Two Sets of Data

Problem

I want to compute the correlation of two columns of data.

Solution

To compute the *correlation*, which is an indication of the strength and direction of the linear relationship between two variables, you merely divide the covariance by the product of the two standard deviations. The SELECT statement from Recipe 10.4 can easily be modified for this purpose. All we have to do is divide the result by the standard deviation aggregate functions described in Recipe 10.3. The resulting SELECT statement looks like this:

```
SELECT
    Sum(
        (DisneyClose -
            (Select Avg(DisneyClose)
                From Stocks
                Where Date Between #1-1-2000# And #12-31-2005#))
        * (TimeWarnerClose -
```

```
        (select Avg(TimeWarnerClose)
            From Stocks
            Where Date Between #1-1-2000# And #12-31-2005#))
        )
    / Count(*) AS Covariance / StDev(DisneyClose) / StDev(TimeWarnerClose)
FROM Stocks
WHERE Date Between #1/1/2000# And #12/31/2005#;
```

Discussion

Unlike covariance, correlation returns a result within a strict range. This makes it possible to compare multiple correlations and draw conclusions.

Correlations return a value between -1 and 1. A value of 0 implies that the two sets of data do not have a linear relationship. A positive value indicates that the two sets of data are linearly related (i.e., as one set of values rises, so does the other). The larger the value is, the stronger the relationship. If you use the same column for both sets of data, you should get a value of 1.

A negative value, on the other hand, means that the data values move in opposite directions from each other. As the correlation coefficient becomes closer to -1, the relationship becomes stronger, with the strongest possible relationship being -1. This would happen if the data values in the second set of data were identical to those in the first (except for their signs).

10.6   Returning All Permutations in a Set of Data

Problem

I'd like to create a table containing all possible permutations of the data that could be returned from a table of values for the specified number of output columns.

Solution

The following routine selects all of the values from a table and generates all possible permutations for a given number of slots. It begins by loading the entire source table into an array. While this might seem to waste a lot of memory, it isn't nearly as bad as you might think. An array of 10,000 names that are 100 characters long occupies a single megabyte of memory. This will save a huge amount of I/O over processing the set of data multiple times.

The sample table we'll use in this recipe contains 12 values, and we'll aim to calculate all the possible permutations when 3 of those values are selected at random. Here's the routine:

```
Sub Example10_6()

Dim rs As ADODB.Recordset
Dim StockNames() As String
```

```
Dim i As Long
Dim j As Long
Dim k As Long

Set rs = New ADODB.Recordset
rs.ActiveConnection = CurrentProject.Connection

rs.Open "SELECT StockName From StockNames Order By StockName", , _
    adOpenForwardOnly, adLockReadOnly

i = 0
ReDim StockNames(0)

Do While Not rs.EOF
    ReDim Preserve StockNames(i)
    StockNames(i) = rs.Fields("StockName")
    i = i + 1
    rs.MoveNext

Loop

rs.Close

rs.Open "StockPermutations", , adOpenDynamic, adLockOptimistic

For i = 0 To UBound(StockNames)
    For j = 0 To UBound(StockNames)
        For k = 0 To UBound(StockNames)

            If i <> j And j <> k And i <> k Then
                rs.AddNew
                rs.Fields("First") = StockNames(i)
                rs.Fields("Second") = StockNames(j)
                rs.Fields("Third") = StockNames(k)
                rs.Update

            End If

        Next k

    Next j

Next i

rs.Close

End Sub
```

After the data has been loaded, the output table is opened. Note that the output table has already been created and has three columns: First, Second, and Third.

Because we want to fill all three fields, a three-deep nested loop is set up to process the array. If the loop variables are all different (meaning that they point to three unique names), the routine adds a new row to the output table and saves the three selected values to their respective fields. It then updates the row and loops around to process the next set of names.

You can easily modify this routine to accommodate the number of choices you want by adding or subtracting nested For loops. One For loop is required for each choice you wish to generate. You'll also have to modify the If statement to ensure that you never have two subscripts with the same value.

Discussion

Permutations describe the possible ways that a group of items can be ordered. Assume that you have three different items: A, B, and C. Here is a list of all possible permutations:

```
A B C
A C B
B A C
B C A
C A B
C B A.
```

Mathematically, you can compute the number of permutations using the factorial method. To compute the factorial of a number, simply multiply it by all of the numbers smaller than it. Thus, three items have 3! (i.e., 6) permutations:

```
3 x 2 x 1
```

The problem with generating permutations is that the number of permutations grows incredibly quickly. Four items have 24 permutations, five items have 120, six items have 720, seven items have 5,040, and eight items have 40,320. By the time you reach 14 items, there are already more than 87 billion possible permutations.

Now, let's return to the task of choosing a subset of items at random from a larger group of items. The number of possible permutations can be computed by the following formula, where n represents the total number of items, and r represents the number of items to return:

```
n!/(n-r)!
```

If, for example, you wanted to choose three items out of a set of five, the equation would look like this:

```
5!/(5-3)! = 5!/2! = 60
```

Thus, when choosing three items out of five, there are a total of 60 possible permutations. When choosing 3 items out of a set of 12, as was done in the code routine presented earlier, there are a total of 1,320 possible permutations; consequently, 1,320 rows will be generated when the routine is executed.

10.7   Returning All Combinations in a Set of Data

Problem

I'd like to create a table containing all possible combinations from another table of data values for the specified number of output columns.

Solution

You can use the following routine to compute the number of possible combinations:

```
Sub Example10_7( )

Dim rs As ADODB.Recordset
Dim StockNames( ) As String
Dim i As Long
Dim j As Long
Dim k As Long

Set rs = New ADODB.Recordset
rs.ActiveConnection = CurrentProject.Connection

rs.Open "SELECT StockName From StockNames Order By StockName", , adOpenForwardOnly,
adLockReadOnly

i = 0
ReDim StockNames(0)

Do While Not rs.EOF
    ReDim Preserve StockNames(i)
    StockNames(i) = rs.Fields("StockName")
    i = i + 1
    rs.MoveNext

Loop

rs.Close

rs.Open "StockCombinations", , adOpenDynamic, adLockOptimistic

For i = 0 To UBound(StockNames) - 2
    For j = i + 1 To UBound(StockNames) - 1
        For k = j + 1 To UBound(StockNames)

            rs.AddNew
            rs.Fields("First") = StockNames(i)
            rs.Fields("Second") = StockNames(j)
            rs.Fields("Third") = StockNames(k)
            rs.Update

        Next k
```

```
        Next j

    Next i

    rs.Close

    End Sub
```

The routine begins by loading the source table into memory, and then it opens a new Recordset object referencing the output table. Note that the output table has already been created and has three columns: First, Second, and Third.

The actual combinations are generated by a set of three nested For loops. The loops are structured such that the ranges of index variables never overlap, which guarantees that each set of names will be unique.

Assume that the UBound of the array is 11. When i is 0, j will start at 1 and go to 10, and k will start at 2 and go to 11. When j is 2, k will start at 3, and so forth, until j reaches 10. At that point, k can only take on the value of 11. The last combination of data is generated when i reaches 9, at which point j is 10 and k is 11.

If you need a different number of choices, be sure to include one loop for each choice. The key is to ensure that the loop variables never overlap.

Discussion

Combinations represent unordered groups of data. This differs from permutations (see Recipe 10.6), in which the order of the items is important. Just like with permutations, each item can appear in the list only once. But since the order isn't important, the number of combinations will always be less than the number of permutations.

For example, suppose you have a list of five items: A, B, C, D, and E. If you look for every possible combination of three items from the list, you'll get these 10 combinations:

```
A B C
A B D
A B E
A C D
A C E
A D E
B C D
B C E
B D E
C D E
```

If you take a look back at Recipe 10.6, however, you will see that there are 60 possible *permutations*.

You can compute the number of possible combinations using the following formula, where n represents the total number of items, and r represents the number of items to include:

```
n!/r!(n-r)!
```

So, for the preceding example of choosing three items out of five, you'll have the following equation:

```
5!/3!(5-3)! = 5!/3!(2!) = 10
```

And, in the earlier code example, choosing 3 items out of 12 results in 220 possible combinations.

10.8 Calculating the Frequency of a Value in a Set of Data

Problem

I'd like to know how many times a particular value appears in a table.

Solution

The following Select statement will determine the number of times the specified value appears in the table. Simply modify the Where clause to select the desired value:

```
Select Count(*) As Frequency
From Stocks
Where DisneyClose = 24.76;
```

Discussion

Suppose you want to identify the frequency of each unique value in the table. For this, you can use a SELECT statement like the following:

```
SELECT DisneyClose, Count(*) AS Frequency
FROM Stocks
WHERE DisneyClose Is Not Null
GROUP BY DisneyClose
ORDER BY Count(*) DESC, DisneyClose;
```

The results for the sample table are displayed in Figure 10-10.

If you break down the SELECT statement, you'll see that the WHERE clause eliminates any Null values from the result. The GROUP BY statement collapses all of the rows with the same value into a single row and returns the selected items (in this case, the value they have in common and a count of the number of rows in that particular group). Finally, the ORDER BY clause sorts the grouped rows by their frequency so that the values that occur most frequently are displayed first.

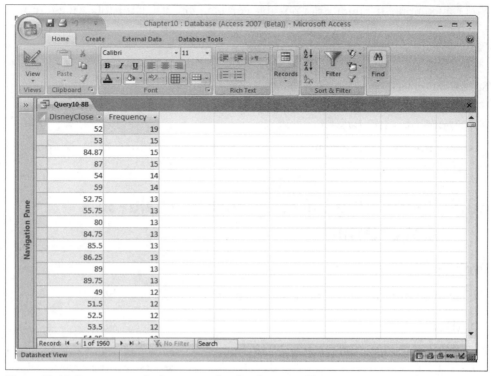

Figure 10-10. Determining the frequency of each value in a table

10.9   Generating Growth Rates

Problem

How do you calculate a growth rate?

Solution

You can use a SELECT statement like this to compute annual growth rate:

```
SELECT Year(Date) As Year, Avg(DisneyClose) As Average,
    (Select Avg(DisneyClose) From Stocks b Where Year(b.date) = Year(a.Date) -1)
        As LastYear,
    (Average - LastYear) / LastYear * 100 As Growth
FROM Stocks A
Where DisneyClose Is Not Null
Group By Year(Date)
Order By Year(Date) Desc
```

The result is displayed in Figure 10-11.

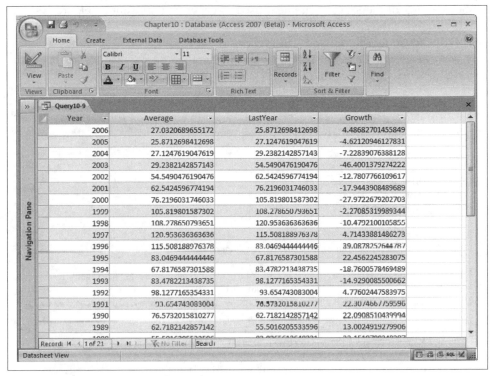

Figure 10-11. Computing annual growth rate

Discussion

The formula for calculating the growth rate looks like this:

```
GrowthRate = (ThisYear - LastYear) / LastYear * 100
```

where ThisYear represents an average or sum of the values for the current year, and LastYear represents the same value computed for the previous year. GrowthRate represents the percentage increase or decrease over the previous year.

Note that you aren't restricted to computing annual growth rates. As long as you're consistent, you can use any time period (months, quarters, etc.). The key is that the growth rate is calculated by comparing values for the current time period with values for the previous time period and examining the percentage difference.

In addition, you don't have to use averages to compute your statistics. In this case, they're appropriate, as we're looking at the average value of a stock price. However, if you're looking at a different value, such as sales, it may be appropriate to compare the total sales rather than average sales figures.

A shortcoming of the SELECT statement used to generate the result in Figure 10-11 is that it computes the LastYear value by physically retrieving the rows for the previous year and calculating the average. This slows down the process considerably. You can compute the growth factor faster if you precalculate the average values for each year and store them in another table so you can access those values directly.

The following routine does exactly that. It opens two tables: one for input and the other for output. The input table uses a SELECT statement to get the averages by year, and orders the results in increasing order by year:

```
Sub Example10_9( )

Dim InTable As ADODB.Recordset
Dim OutTable As ADODB.Recordset
Dim LagAverage As Double

Set InTable = New ADODB.Recordset
InTable.ActiveConnection = CurrentProject.Connection

InTable.Open "SELECT Year(Date) As ThisYear, Avg(DisneyClose) As Average " & _
    "From Stocks Where DisneyClose Is Not Null " & _
    "Group By Year(Date) Order By Year(Date)", , adOpenForwardOnly, adLockReadOnly

Set OutTable = New ADODB.Recordset
OutTable.ActiveConnection = CurrentProject.Connection

OutTable.Open "Growth", , adOpenDynamic, adLockOptimistic

LagAverage = InTable.Fields("Average")
OutTable.AddNew
OutTable.Fields("Year") = InTable.Fields("ThisYear")
OutTable.Fields("Growth") = Null
OutTable.Update

InTable.MoveNext

Do While Not InTable.EOF
    OutTable.AddNew
    OutTable.Fields("Year") = InTable.Fields("ThisYear")
    OutTable.Fields("Growth") = (InTable.Fields("Average") - LagAverage) _
        / LagAverage * 100#
    OutTable.Update

    LagAverage = InTable.Fields("Average")
    InTable.MoveNext

Loop

InTable.Close
OutTable.Close

End Sub
```

The average value for the first year is written to the output table. Growth is set to Null, as there isn't a previous year's data to use to perform the growth calculation. The average value for this year is saved into LagAverage.

Then, for each of the rest of the input rows, the corresponding output row is constructed by copying in the current year's average value and computing the growth factor, using the average for this year and the previous year (stored in LagAverage). After the output row is saved, the current year's average is saved into LagAverage before moving to the next row.

10.10 Determining the Probability Mass Function for a Set of Data

Problem

I'd like to compute a probability for each item in a table.

Solution

You can use a SELECT statement like this to determine the probability of each data item:

```
SELECT Round(DisneyClose,0) AS StockValue, Count(*) AS Days,
    (Select Count(*) From Stocks Where Date Between #1-1-2000# And #12-31-2005#)
    AS Total, Days/Total AS Probability
FROM Stocks
WHERE Date Between #1/1/2000# And #12/31/2005#
GROUP BY Round(DisneyClose,0)
ORDER BY Round(DisneyClose,0);
```

The result of this query is displayed in Figure 10-12.

In this statement, each data item is rounded to the nearest dollar using the Round function. You can instead round to one or more decimal places by changing the 0 in the function to the number of decimal places you want to keep.

While the nested Select statement may seem expensive, it really isn't. Jet only computes the value once because it doesn't depend on anything from the current row. It can then return the value for each row it returns.

Discussion

Figure 10-13 shows the probability distribution curve for the probability mass function. This was created by viewing the query results as a PivotChart, using StockValue as a category field and Sum of Probability as a series field, and dropping Probability onto the chart.

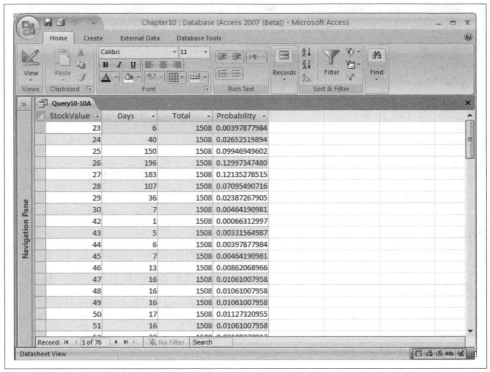

Figure 10-12. Computing the probability mass function for a set of data

While this doesn't fit the traditional normal distribution, often called the "bell curve," you can see that most of the stock prices fall within a narrow range of values. However, since the data spans five years, and the stock price varies over time, you may want to break it out by year.

If you rewrite the query to include a new column, Year(Date), and include this field in the GROUP BY clause, you can construct a new PivotChart in which you can select data from one or more years:

```
SELECT Round(DisneyClose,0) AS StockValue, Year(Date) As Year, Count(*) AS Days,
    (Select Count(*) From Stocks Where Date Between #1-1-2000# And #12-31-2005#) AS
        Total,
    Days/Total AS Probability
FROM Stocks
WHERE Date Between #1/1/2000# And #12/31/2005#
GROUP BY Round(DisneyClose,0), Year(Date)
ORDER BY Round(DisneyClose,0), Year(Date)
```

You can then easily compare the distribution of the data for different years. The distribution for 2000, for example (shown in Figure 10-14), is significantly different from the distribution for 2005 (shown in Figure 10-15).

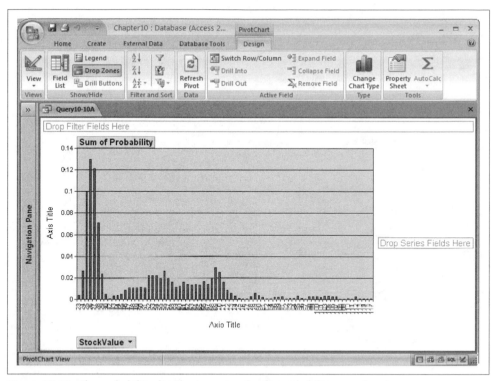

Figure 10-13. The probability distribution curve for the probability mass function

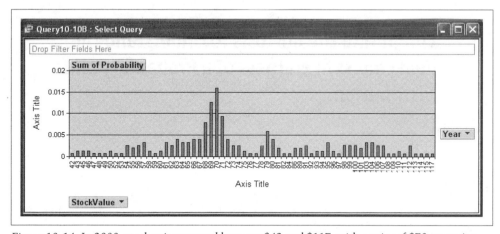

Figure 10-14. In 2000, stock prices ranged between $42 and $117, with a price of $70 occurring most often

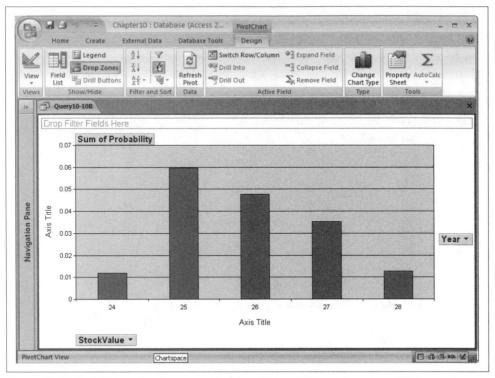

Figure 10-15. In 2005, stock prices ranged between $24 and $28, with a price of $25 occurring most often

10.11 Computing the Kurtosis to Understand the Peakedness or Flatness of a Probability Mass Distribution

Problem

I'd like to learn more about my data's distribution by computing the kurtosis.

Solution

You can use the following routine to compute the kurtosis (i.e., the "peakedness" of the distribution of values) of a data set:

```
Sub Example10_11( )

Dim rs As ADODB.Recordset
Dim DisneyAvg As Double
Dim DisneyVal As Double
Dim Sum2 As Double
Dim Sum4 As Double
Dim TotalRows As Double
```

```
Dim temp As Double
Dim Kurtosis As Double
Dim StdError As Double

Set rs = New ADODB.Recordset
rs.ActiveConnection = CurrentProject.Connection

rs.Open "SELECT Avg(DisneyClose) AS AvgDisney, " & _
    "Count(*) As TotalRows FROM Stocks " & _
    "WHERE Date Between #1/1/2000# And #12/31/2005#", , _
    adOpenForwardOnly, adLockReadOnly

DisneyAvg = rs.Fields("AvgDisney")
TotalRows = rs.Fields("TotalRows")

rs.Close

rs.Open "Select DisneyClose From Stocks " & _
    "Where Date Between #1-1-2000# And #12-31 2005#", , _
    adOpenStatic, adLockReadOnly

Sum2 = 0
Sum4 = 0

Do While Not rs.EOF
    DisneyVal = rs.Fields("DisneyClose")

    temp = (DisneyVal - DisneyAvg) * (DisneyVal - DisneyAvg)

    Sum2 = Sum2 + temp
    Sum4 = Sum4 + temp * temp

    rs.MoveNext

Loop

rs.Close

Kurtosis = (TotalRows * Sum4 / (Sum2 * Sum2)) - 3
StdError = Sqr(24 / TotalRows)

Debug.Print "Kurtosis = ", Kurtosis
Debug.Print "Standard error = ", StdError

If Kurtosis > 2 * StdError Then
    Debug.Print "Peaked distribution"

ElseIf Kurtosis < -2 * StdError Then
    Debug.Print "Flat distribution"

Else
    Debug.Print "Normal distribution"

End If

End Sub
```

The routine begins by executing a SELECT statement to return the number of rows in the sample along with the average value for the specified column. It then retrieves each of the individual values from the table, and sums the differences between the values and the average squared, and the differences between the values and the average raised to the fourth power.

 When customizing this routine for your own use, you'll need to modify the first SELECT statement to compute the average of the column. Then, you'll need to modify the second Select statement to return the same column.

Once all of the rows in the table have been processed, kurtosis can be computed by multiplying the number of rows times the sum of the difference between the current value and the average value raised to the fourth power. This value is then divided by the square of the sum of the differences between the current value and the average value squared. Finally, subtracting from the previous result completes the calculation for kurtosis.

Discussion

Here is the formula to compute kurtosis:

$$\text{Kurtosis} = \frac{N * \Sigma (x - X)^4}{(\Sigma (x - X)2)^2} - 3$$

N is the number of values, x is the current value, and X is the average value.

A perfect normal distribution will return a kurtosis of 0. A negative value indicates the distribution is relatively flat, while a positive value means the distribution is relatively peaked.

Looking at the kurtosis can reveal what has caused the variance in a distribution. A higher value for kurtosis indicates the variance was caused by infrequent extreme deviations, while a lower value indicates it was caused by more frequent, modestly sized deviations.

To determine if the kurtosis value is significantly different from zero, you can use the following formula to compute the *standard error*:

```
sqrt(24/number of items)
```

One advantage of computing kurtosis is that you can use the result to determine whether the data is outside the range of a normal distribution. If so, you won't be able to trust the results from any statistical tests that assume a normal distribution.

10.12 Determining the Skew of a Set of Data

Problem

How can I determine if my data has asymmetric "tails" when compared to the tails associated with a normal distribution?

Solution

The following code computes the skew (i.e., the asymmetry of the distribution of values) for a given column of data:

```
Sub Example10_12()

Dim rs As ADODB.Recordset
Dim DisneyAvg As Double
Dim DisneyVal As Double
Dim Sum2 As Double
Dim Sum3 As Double
Dim TotalRows As Double
Dim Skewness As Double
Dim StdError As Double

Set rs = New ADODB.Recordset
rs.ActiveConnection = CurrentProject.Connection

rs.Open "SELECT Avg(DisneyClose) AS AvgDisney, " & _
    "Count(*) As TotalRows FROM Stocks " & _
    "WHERE Date Between #1/1/2000# And #12/31/2005#", , _
    adOpenForwardOnly, adLockReadOnly

DisneyAvg = rs.Fields("AvgDisney")
TotalRows = rs.Fields("TotalRows")

rs.Close

rs.Open "Select DisneyClose From Stocks " & _
    "Where Date Between #1-1-2000# And #12-31-2005#", , _
    adOpenStatic, adLockReadOnly

Sum2 = 0
Sum3 = 0

Do While Not rs.EOF
    DisneyVal = rs.Fields("DisneyClose")

    Sum2 = Sum2 + (DisneyVal - DisneyAvg) * (DisneyVal - DisneyAvg)
    Sum3 = Sum3 + (DisneyVal - DisneyAvg) * (DisneyVal - DisneyAvg) * _
        (DisneyVal - DisneyAvg)
```

```
        rs.MoveNext

    Loop

    rs.Close

    Skewness = Sqr(TotalRows) * Sum3 / (Sum2 ^ 1.5)
    StdError = Sqr(6 / TotalRows)

    Debug.Print "Skewness = ", Skewness
    Debug.Print "Standard error = ", StdError

    If Skewness > 2 * StdError Then
        Debug.Print "Skewed to the right"

    ElseIf Skewness < -2 * StdError Then
        Debug.Print "Skewed to the left"

    Else
        Debug.Print "Normal distribution"

    End If

    End Sub
```

The code used to compute skew is similar to the one used to compute kurtosis (see Recipe 10.11).

The total number of values and the average value are computed for the entire set of data. Then, each row of data is processed, and the square and the cube of the difference between each item's value—and the average for all values—are summed over the selected rows. Finally, the square root of the number of rows is multiplied by the sum of cubes, and then the total is divided by the sum of squares raised to the 1.5 power.

Discussion

Here is the formula to compute skew:

$$\text{Skew} = \frac{N^{1/2} * \Sigma \, (x - X)^3}{(\, \Sigma \, (x - X)^2 \,)^{3/2}}$$

where N is the number of values, x is the current value, and X is the average value.

In a perfect normal distribution, both tails of the distribution will mirror each other, and the skew will have a value of 0. However, in real life, the tails are likely to be asymmetric. Testing for skewness determines whether the distribution is skewed to one side. A positive value means the distribution is skewed to the right, while a negative value means the data is skewed to the left.

Because most data can have a random component, however, you may compute a nonzero value for skew and still have a normal distribution. The standard error for skew can be computed with the following formula:

```
sqrt(6/number of items)
```

Generally, skew values that are greater than twice the standard error are considered outside the range of a normal distribution.

10.13 Returning a Range of Data by Percentile

Problem

I want to extract a range of data from my database by percentile.

Solution

Suppose you want to choose the top 10 percent of values in a particular column. You can do this with a SELECT statement that retrieves all possible values for the column, sorts them in descending order so that the highest values are listed first, and then returns the top 10 percent of the values:

```
SELECT Top 10 Percent DisneyClose
FROM Stocks
ORDER BY DisneyClose Desc
```

If you want the bottom 10 percent, simply change the ORDER BY clause to sort the data in ascending order, like this:

```
SELECT Top 10 Percent DisneyClose
FROM Stocks
ORDER BY DisneyClose Asc
```

What if you want to choose a range of values from the middle? You might be tempted to use a SELECT statement like this:

```
SELECT Top 10 Percent DisneyClose
FROM Stocks
WHERE Not DisneyClose In
    (Select Top 10 Percent DisneyClose
    From Stocks
    Order By DisneyClose Desc)
ORDER BY DisneyClose Desc
```

This statement retrieves the top 10 percent of the rows from the table, but only if they're not already in the top 10 percent. In other words, it effectively returns the second 10 percent.

The big problem with this approach is that the query is very inefficient because it runs the nested Select statement each time it processes a new row. A better approach would be to select the top 20 percent of the rows, place them into a separate table, and then select the bottom half of the new table. This would give you the same result, but with a lot less processing (although it does require you to run two queries and use a temporary table to get your result).

Discussion

If you frequently select rows this way, you'd be better off using the following routine to precalculate the percentile value for each row and storing the results in a separate table:

```
Sub Example10_13( )

Dim intable As ADODB.Recordset
Dim outtable As ADODB.Recordset
Dim Count As Long

Set intable = New ADODB.Recordset
intable.ActiveConnection = CurrentProject.Connection

intable.Open "SELECT Date, DisneyClose As [Value], " & _
    "(Select Count(*) From Stocks " & _
    " Where DisneyClose Is Not Null) As Total " & _
    "From Stocks " & _
    "Where DisneyClose Is Not Null " & _
    "Order By DisneyClose", , adOpenStatic, adLockReadOnly

Set outtable = New ADODB.Recordset
outtable.ActiveConnection = CurrentProject.Connection
outtable.Open "Percentage", , adOpenDynamic, adLockOptimistic

Count = 0

Do While Not intable.EOF
    outtable.AddNew
    outtable.Fields("Date") = intable.Fields("Date")
    outtable.Fields("Value") = intable.Fields("Value")
    outtable.Fields("Percentage") = Count / intable.Fields("Total") * 100#
    outtable.Update
    intable.MoveNext

    Count = Count + 1

Loop

intable.Close
outtable.Close

End Sub
```

This routine begins by selecting all of the data you may wish to use and sorting it in the proper order. It also computes the total number of rows that will be returned to avoid querying the database twice. Next, it opens a second Recordset that will hold the processed data.

The routine then loops through each row of the input table and copies the Date and Value fields to the output table. It also computes the row's relative percentile, and stores that value in the output table. Finally, it closes both tables before returning.

Once this work table has been generated, you can construct statements to retrieve data between any two percentiles. For example, this Select statement retrieves all rows between the 80th and 90th percentiles:

```
Select Date, Value
From Percentage
Where Percentage Is Between 80 and 90
```

10.14 Determining the Rank of a Data Item

Problem

I'd like to know the rank of a particular data value in my database.

Solution

One way to compute the rank of a particular data value is to create an append query like this one:

```
INSERT INTO Rank
SELECT Date AS [Date], DisneyClose AS [Value]
FROM Stocks
WHERE DisneyClose Is Not Null
ORDER BY DisneyClose DESC;
```

You'll also need to create an empty table with matching fields and an AutoNumber field. When you run the query, the AutoNumber field will automatically assign a sequential number to each new row. Because the rows are stored in the table from highest to lowest, the highest value will have a rank of 1, while the lowest will have a rank equal to the number of rows in the table.

Discussion

Using this approach to automatically generate ranks has the advantage of requiring no programming. However, each time you run the append query, you'll need to delete and re-create the output table to ensure that the AutoNumber field starts numbering from 1. Alternatively, you could create a generic Rank table and create a new copy of the table each time you want to run the query.

However, a better approach would be to modify the routine used in Recipe 10.13 to regenerate the data each time, thus avoiding the problems with the AutoNumber field.

Here's the updated routine:

```
Sub Example10_14( )

Dim intable As ADODB.Recordset
```

```
Dim outtable As ADODB.Recordset
Dim Count As Long

Set intable = New ADODB.Recordset
intable.ActiveConnection = CurrentProject.Connection

intable.Open "SELECT Date, DisneyClose As [Value] " & _
    "From Stocks " & _
    "Where DisneyClose Is Not Null " & _
    "Order By DisneyClose Desc", , adOpenStatic, adLockReadOnly

Set outtable = New ADODB.Recordset
outtable.ActiveConnection = CurrentProject.Connection
outtable.Open "[Table10-14]", , adOpenDynamic, adLockOptimistic

Count = 1

Do While Not intable.EOF
    outtable.AddNew
    outtable.Fields("Date") = intable.Fields("Date")
    outtable.Fields("Value") = intable.Fields("Value")
    outtable.Fields("Rank") = Count
    outtable.Update
    intable.MoveNext

    Count = Count + 1

Loop

intable.Close
outtable.Close

End Sub
```

The routine begins by creating an input Recordset containing the desired data items in the proper order. Next, it opens the output Recordset. After that, each row is copied from the input Recordset to the output Recordset, and a sequential counter is assigned to each new row's Rank field. Finally, the routine finishes the process by closing the input and output Recordsets.

10.15 Determining the Slope and the Intercept of a Linear Regression

Problem

I'd like to use linear regression to determine the slope and intercept point for two columns of data.

Solution

The following routine computes the slope and *y* intercept point for two sets of values. It's based on the code originally used in Recipe 10.11:

```
Sub Example10_15()

Dim rs As ADODB.Recordset
Dim DisneyAvg As Double
Dim TimeWarnerAvg As Double
Dim DisneyVal As Double
Dim TimeWarnerVal As Double
Dim Sum1 As Double
Dim Sum2 As Double
Dim TotalRows As Double
Dim Slope As Double
Dim YIntercept As Double

Set rs = New ADODB.Recordset
rs.ActiveConnection = CurrentProject.Connection

rs.Open "SELECT Avg(DisneyClose) AS AvgDisney, " & _
    "Avg(TimeWarnerClose) As AvgTimeWarner " & _
    "FROM Stocks WHERE Date Between #1/1/2000# And #12/31/2005#", , _
    adOpenForwardOnly, adLockReadOnly

DisneyAvg = rs.Fields("AvgDisney")
TimeWarnerAvg = rs.Fields("AvgTimeWarner")

rs.Close

rs.Open "Select DisneyClose, TimeWarnerClose " & _
    "From Stocks Where Date Between #1-1-2000# And #12-31-2005#", , _
    adOpenStatic, adLockReadOnly

Sum1 = 0
Sum2 = 0

Do While Not rs.EOF
    DisneyVal = rs.Fields("DisneyClose")
    TimeWarnerVal = rs.Fields("TimeWarnerClose")

    Sum1 = Sum1 + (DisneyVal - DisneyAvg) * (TimeWarnerVal - TimeWarnerAvg)
    Sum2 = Sum2 + (DisneyVal - DisneyAvg) * (DisneyVal - DisneyAvg)

    rs.MoveNext

Loop

rs.Close

Slope = Sum1 / Sum2
YIntercept = TimeWarnerAvg - Slope * DisneyAvg
```

```
Debug.Print "Slope= ", Slope
Debug.Print "Y intercept= ", YIntercept

End Sub
```

The routine begins by getting the average values for the two different columns. It then opens a Recordset that retrieves each individual pair of values. Next, it processes the data. Two sums are kept. The first sum is computed by subtracting each value from its column average and then multiplying the two resulting values together. The second sum is the square of the difference between the first value and its column average.

Once all the data has been processed, the routine computes the slope by dividing the first sum by the second. The y intercept point is then computed by plugging the average values for each column into the basic equation for a line using the newly computed value for slope.

Discussion

Linear regression attempts to find the best possible straight line that matches a given set of pairs of data. The line is represented by slope and y intercept, where:

$$Slope = \frac{\Sigma \ (\ x - X\ )\ (\ y - Y\ )}{\Sigma\ (\ x - X\ )^2}$$

and:

```
y intercept = Y - Slope X
```

x and y are individual data points, and X and Y represent the averages for of all of the x and y values, respectively.

10.16 Measuring Volatility

Problem

I'd like to measure the volatility of my data to know how much values move around.

Solution

Volatility is a measure of uncertainty (risk) in the price movement of a stock, option, or other financial instrument. An alternate definition is that volatility is the dispersion of individual values around the mean of a set of data.

There are various approaches to calculating volatility, and, in a nutshell, there are two basic types of volatility: historical and implied. *Historical* volatility is easier to measure because the calculation is based on known values. *Implied* volatility is trickier because the purpose here is to guesstimate the level of volatility that will occur in the future (be that tomorrow, next month, or next year). In other words, implied volatility is calculated for forecasting purposes.

One reasonable approach to calculating volatility is to simply use the standard deviation as the measure. A standard deviation measurement requires >1 data points to provide a value. Figure 10-16 shows a table of values on the left, and the result of running a query against this data using the StDev aggregate function.

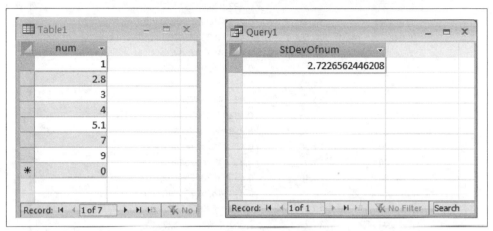

Figure 10-16. Calculating the standard deviation of a set of numbers

The volatility (as interpreted in this approach) is 2.7226562446208. But what does this tell us about the data? As a rule:

- The higher the standard deviation, the higher the volatility.

- The closer together the source data points are, the lower the volatility is. A wide variance of data points results in a high volatility. A set of identical values produces a standard deviation of 0—i.e., there is no dispersion among the values.

A standard deviation of 2.722656 is relatively small; therefore, the risk is also small. Standard deviation values can run from 0 to very large numbers—in the thousands or more. The standard deviation is a representation of the variance of the datum around the mean.

The SQL of the query in Figure 10-16 is:

```
SELECT StDev(Table1.num) AS StDevOfnum FROM Table1
```

As you can see, it's quite simple. A snapshot like the one this query provides can be useful, but in numerical analysis, trends are worth their weight in gold (or at least in silver). A series of volatility values may enable better analysis of the data. To determine the trend, a moving volatility line (similar to a moving average) is needed. Decision one is how many data points to base each standard deviation on. In the following example, we'll use 20-day intervals.

Figure 10-17 shows a table listing a year's worth of closing prices for Ford Motor Company stock (not all data is visible in the figure). The third column contains computations of volatility based on the given range (that is, from the closing price 20 days ago through the current date's closing price).

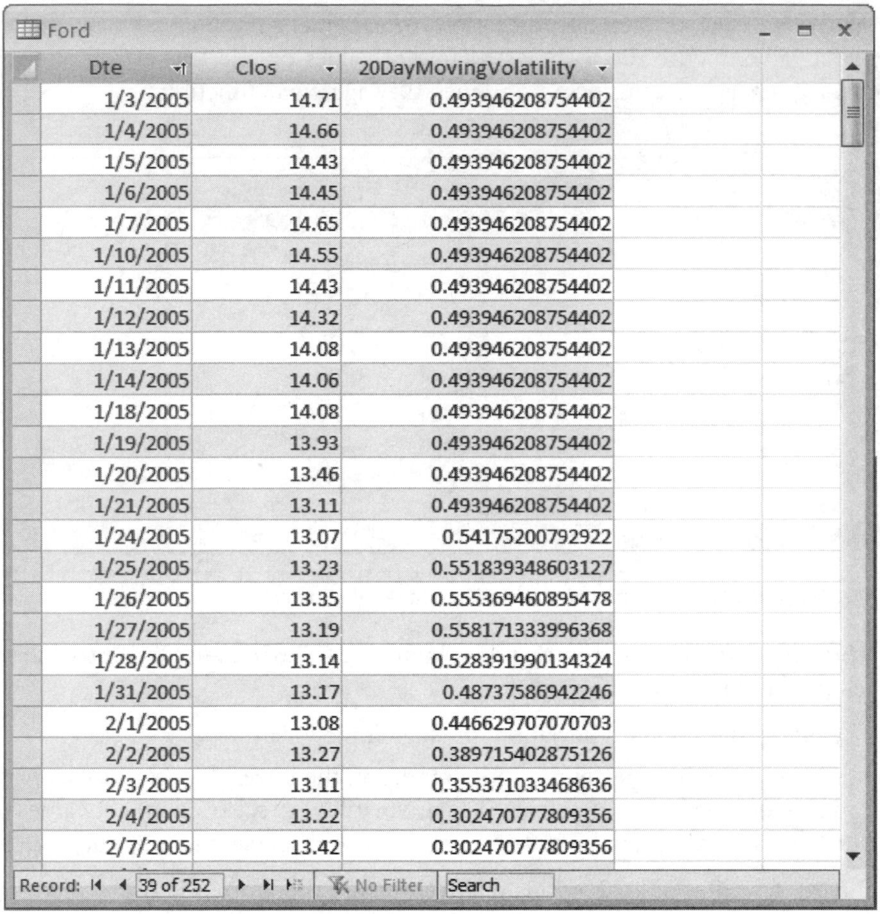

Ford

Dte	Clos	20DayMovingVolatility
1/3/2005	14.71	0.493946208754402
1/4/2005	14.66	0.493946208754402
1/5/2005	14.43	0.493946208754402
1/6/2005	14.45	0.493946208754402
1/7/2005	14.65	0.493946208754402
1/10/2005	14.55	0.493946208754402
1/11/2005	14.43	0.493946208754402
1/12/2005	14.32	0.493946208754402
1/13/2005	14.08	0.493946208754402
1/14/2005	14.06	0.493946208754402
1/18/2005	14.08	0.493946208754402
1/19/2005	13.93	0.493946208754402
1/20/2005	13.46	0.493946208754402
1/21/2005	13.11	0.493946208754402
1/24/2005	13.07	0.54175200792922
1/25/2005	13.23	0.551839348603127
1/26/2005	13.35	0.555369460895478
1/27/2005	13.19	0.558171333996368
1/28/2005	13.14	0.528391990134324
1/31/2005	13.17	0.48737586942246
2/1/2005	13.08	0.446629707070703
2/2/2005	13.27	0.389715402875126
2/3/2005	13.11	0.355371033468636
2/4/2005	13.22	0.302470777809356
2/7/2005	13.42	0.302470777809356

Record: 39 of 252 No Filter Search

Figure 10-17. Ford dates, prices, and volatility

As shown in Figure 10-18, we can use this data to plot a moving volatility line along with the prices. The figure contains two charts, one on top of the other. The bottom chart is a plot of the second column from Figure 10-17, and the top chart is a plot of the third column.

In Figure 10-17, you'll notice that the first 14 rows show the same value in the third column. This is because a change in the volatility calculation's result will not appear until 20 days into the data. The 14 rows actually comprise 20 calendar days because the column of dates does not include weekends or holidays (when the markets are closed). Considering this factor alone, it is obvious that there are numerous ways to calculate the volatility. For example, a similar but more developed process might include only trading days in the 20-day ranges.

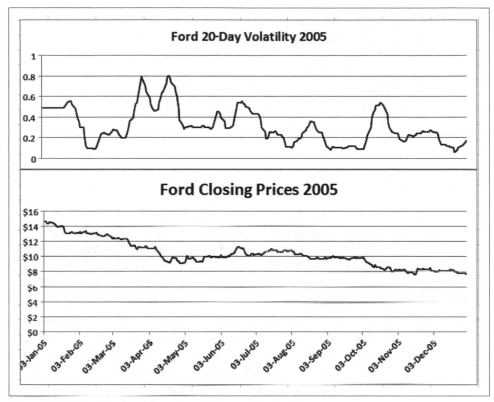

Figure 10-18. Ford closing prices charted along with volatility

Because the values for the first 20 days do not vary (as there is no preceding data), the first bit of the volatility line in Figure 10-18 is flat. Only after 20 days does the line vary.

Here is the VBA code routine that produced the results in the third column in Figure 10-17:

```
Sub fill_volatility()
Dim conn As ADODB.Connection
Set conn = CurrentProject.Connection
Dim rs As New ADODB.Recordset
rs.Open "Select * From Ford", conn, adOpenDynamic, adLockOptimistic
Dim rs2 As New ADODB.Recordset
Dim arr(20)
Dim arr_count As Integer

Do Until rs.EOF
    ssql = "Select Clos from Ford Where" & _
        "(Dle Between #" & rs.Fields("Dte") - 20 & _
        "# And #" & rs.Fields("Dte") & "#) Order By Dte "
    rs2.Open ssql, conn, adOpenKeyset, adLockOptimistic
    arr_count = 0
```

```
        Do Until rs2.EOF
            arr(arr_count) = rs2.Fields("Clos")
            arr_count = arr_count + 1
            rs2.MoveNext
        Loop

        rs.Fields("Volatility") = Excel.WorksheetFunction.StDev(arr())
        rs2.Close

    rs.MoveNext
    Loop
    rs.Close
    Set rs = Nothing
    Set conn = Nothing
    MsgBox "done"
    End Sub
```

The standard deviation is returned using Excel's version of the StDev function. A reference to the Excel library is therefore required to run this routine. You can set the reference in the VB Editor, under Tools → References.

Discussion

Those who attempt to make profits on fast price changes, such as day or swing traders, view high volatility as a positive thing. Conversely, investors who are in for the long haul tend to prefer securities with low volatility. Volatility has a positive correlation with risk, which means an investment with high volatility is, well, risky—not something that's typically seen as desirable in long-term investments.

There are many formulas for calculating risk, and people tend to select methods that suit their particular circumstances (often having to do with the type of investment vehicle—stock, option, etc.). Unlike other formulas, volatility is broadly used to determine the variance among a set of values. However, as you've seen, many different approaches can be taken to determine the volatility.

A major consideration is whether you're attempting to calculate historical volatility (which provides answers based on existing data and is useful for *backtesting*, or seeing whether a given investing approach would have been successful) or implied volatility (which provides a guess as to the level of volatility in the future). Clearly, the latter is more involved because "assumptions" must be included within the calculations. This leads to complex formulas. Perhaps the best-known implied volatility method is the Black-Scholes model. This model is a standard for determining the future volatility of options. Options have more data points to consider than vanilla stock investments; calculations must involve the price of the option, the length of the option until expiration, and the expected value at the end of the option's life.

Index

Symbols

% (percent sign), 17
& (ampersand character), 121–122
+ operator, 121
: (colon), 35, 47
[ ] (brackets) and parameterized queries, 12

A

action queries, 73–91
  appending data, 79–83
    from record set, 82–83
    to table that has different field
      names, 79
  creating programmatically, 107
  delete query, 84–88
    cascading deletes, 88
  make-table query, 88–91
  update queries, 73–79
ADO (ActiveX Data Objects), 94
  indexes, 104
  using to export data to Excel, 238–240
  using to import Excel data, 235–238
ADOX, 92, 94
aggregate functions, 46–48
aliases, 37–39
All keyword, 34
Alter Column construct, 101
amount function, 54
ampersand character (&), 121–122
AND operator, 4–7
append queries, 73, 79–83
  appending from record set, 82–83

appending to table that has different field
  names, 79
rank of a particular data value, 337
appending data, 79–83
  from record set, 82–83
  to table that has different field names, 79
appointments, importing, 227–230
arrays, 136–139
  multidimensional, 140–143
  sorting, 144–147
  three-dimensional, 142
Asc function, 129
ASCII codes, categorizing characters
  with, 127–130
asterisk wildcard, 14
attributes, 206
AutoCalc, 278
automating data imports and
  exports, 194–197
AutoNumber field, 18, 100
averages
  moving, 265
  weighted, 263
averaging records, 26–31
AVG function, 26–31
Avg function, 46–48, 314

B

Between/And SQL construct, 13
Black-Scholes model, 344
Bollinger Bands, 299–300
brackets and parameterized queries, 12
bubble sort, 144
business and finance problems, 263–306

We'd like to hear your suggestions for improving our indexes. Send email to *index@oreilly.com*.

C

Cartesian join, 61–65
Cartesian product, 62
Central Standard Time (CST), 252
character codes, 128
charting data, 281–282
charts, 165–169
Chr function, 129
CInt function, 125
code routines, 131–187
collections, 139
colon (:), 35, 47
column areas, 276
connection strings, 222
Coordinated Universal Time (UTC), 254
Count function, 50–51
covariance, calculating, 316–317
Create View SQL statement, 107
criterion (see parameters)
crosstab query, 65–72
    sophisticated crosstabs, 69
custom functions, 54–57
cyclical trends, 287

D

DAO (Data Access Objects), 92, 93
    creating action queries, 107
    creating stored queries, 106
    Database object, 107
    indexes, 104
    QueryDef object, 107
data
    appending, 79–83
        from record set, 82–83
        to table that has different field
            names, 79
    charting, 281–282
    charts, creating, 165–169
    correlation of two sets of, 317–318
    deleting, 84–88
        cascading deletes, 88
    encrypting, 153–156
        key phrases, 155
        XOR, 155
    exporting, 188–245
        automating, 194–197
        creating import/export
            specification, 188–193
        DoCmd object, 196
        Excel, 238–240
        Export Wizard, 188

FileSystemObject, 197–199
Visual Basic and, 196
XML, using, 204–207
XSLT, 209–211
frequency of a value in, 323
Head and Shoulders pattern, 287–299
importing, 188–245
    automating, 194–197
    creating import/export
        specification, 188–193
    embedded quotation marks,
        handling, 226
    Excel, 235–238
    FileSystemObject, 200–204
    Import Wizard, 188
    Outlook calendar
        appointments, 227–230
    Outlook contact lists, 232–235
    Outlook emails, 230–232
    PowerPoint, 240–244
    randomly selected data, creating a new
        table from, 244
    RSS feed, 218–221
    SQL Server, passing parameters, 221
    TransferText action, 195
    XML, using, 204–207
    XSLT, 209–211
optimizing, 149
peakness of distribution of values
    in, 330–332
permutations, 318–320
programming to manipulate, 131–187
    arrays, 136–139
    Excel functions, 131–135
    expanding to a set of parent and child
        tables, 151–153
    flattening, 147–150
    mail merges, 180–183
    multidimensional arrays, 140–143
    query selection screen, 183–187
    removing redundancy, 152
    report formatting, custom, 173–177
    rounding values, 177–180
    scraping Web HTML, 170–173
    sorting arrays, 144–147
proximate matching, 157–160
rank of a particular data value, 337–338
returning all combinations in, 321–323
returning range of data by
    percentile, 335–337
skew of, 333–335
transaction processing, 160–162

probability, 327–328
programming data, 131–187
    arrays, 136–139
    collections, 139
    Excel functions, 131–135
    expanding to a set of parent and child
        tables, 151–153
    flattening, 147–150
    in-memory data, 136–139
    multidimensional arrays, 140–143
    removing redundancy, 152
    sorting arrays, 144–147
    three-dimensional data, 142
proximate matching, 157–160

Q

queries
    action (see action queries)
    append (see append queries)
    creating programmatically, 106–108
    make-table (see make-table queries)
    nested, 29–31
    passive (see passive queries)
    update, 73–79
queries, calculating with, 46–72
    Avg function, 46–48
    Cartesian join, 61–65
    crosstab query, 65–72
        sophisticated crosstabs, 69
    custom functions, 54–57
    expressions, 52–53
    number of items per group, 50–51
    regular expressions, 57–61
    returning all combinations of data, 61–65
    Sum function, 46–48
query construction, 1–44
    aliases, 37–39
    AND operator, 4–7
    combining data, 31–34
    data filtering with subqueries, 26–31
    DistinctRow predicate, 21
    excluding records, 10–11
    finding unmatched records, 1–4
    IN operator, 7–10
    LEFT JOIN, 39–41
    left join, 1–4
    NOT operator, 10–11
    on-the-fly fields, 35–37
    OR operator, 4–7
    OUTER JOIN, 43–44
    parameters, 11–15
        brackets, 12
        Like operator, 14
        multiple, 13
        specifying data type, 14
    returning distinct records, 19–23
    returning random records, 24–26
    returning top or bottom number of
        records, 16–18
    RIGHT JOIN, 41
    UNION clause, 31–34
query grid, 6
Query Parameters dialog, 15
query selection screen, building, 183–187
QueryDef object, 107
quotation marks, embedded, handling, 226

R

random data, importing, 244
rank of a particular data value, 337–338
ReadAll method, 199
ReadLine method, 199
RecordCount property, 313
records
    averaging, 26–31
    excluding, 10–11
    finding unmatched, 1–4
    returning distinct, 19–23
    returning random, 24–26
    returning top or bottom number
        of, 16–18
Recordset object, 267
Recordset, opening, 313
redundancy in data, removing, 152
regular expressions, 57–61
    pattern matching, 59
remove_first_space function, 118
Replace function, 117, 119–120
Replace method (regexp object), 61
report formatting, 173–177
return on investment (ROI), calculating, 268
Right function, 109–110
Rnd function, 24, 245
Round function, 71, 327
rounding values, 177–180
row areas, 276
RSS, creating a feed, 218–221
RTrim function, 115–116

S

schemas, XML, 207–209
scraping Web HTML, 170–173

creating queries
        programmatically, 106–108
creating with make-table query, 88–91
deleting programmatically, 104–105
indexes, 102–104
overwriting, 91
primary key, 102
testing for existence, 98
tags, XML and, 206
temporary fields, 91
Test method (regexp object), 61
test_function sub, 118
text-based data (see string data)
three-dimensional data, 142
time
    adding, 260–262
    counting elapsed, 246–249
    counting elapsed time with
        exceptions, 249–252
    isolating hour, minute, or
        second, 258–259
    offset, 254
    zones, 252–254
TimeSerial function, 256
TimeValue function, 256
TOP predicate, 16–18
Totals menu option, 46
transaction processing, 160–162
TransferDatabase action, 194
TransferText action, 195
TRANSFORM keyword, 69
trends in data, finding, 283–287
trends, charting data for, 281–282
trends, cyclical, 287
Trim function, 115–116, 121, 122

U

UBound, 322
UNION clause, 31–34
UPDATE keyword, 78, 79
update queries, 73–79

V

Values keyword, 81
Var function, 314

variance, calculating, 314–316
VBScript Regular Expressions library, 58
Visual Basic
    data exporting and, 196
    MSXML parser and, 212
volatility of data, 340–344
    historical, 340
    implied, 340

W

Weekday function, 256–258
weighted averages, calculating, 263
WHERE clause
    paramerterized queries, 13
wildcard, 14
Windows Registry, 162–165
Word mail merges, 180

X

XML
    attributes, reading and writing, 216–218
    importing and exporting, using, 204–207
    MSXML parser, 212–216
    RSS feed, 218–221
    schemas, 207–209
XML/XSD, 92
XOR encryption, 155
XSD schema, 95–96
XSLT
    importing or exporting data, 209–211
    literal result elements, 210
    transforms, 209

Y

Year function, 256–258
year, isolating, 256–258
years, leap, 255–256

Z

zip codes, calculating distance
        between, 301–306
Zoom box, 53

About the Authors

Ken Bluttman has written many articles and computer books, including *Excel Charts for Dummies* and O'Reilly's *Access Hacks*. His technical chops include Microsoft Office, XML, VBA, VB.NET, SQL Server, and assorted web technologies.

Wayne S. Freeze is head of software development for Electrical Controls, Inc., where he builds software 3D graphics applications. He has also written several books and articles on Visual Basic, SQL Server, DirectX, ASP.NET, Microsoft Office, and many other Microsoft technologies.

Colophon

The animal on the cover of *Access Data Analysis Cookbook* is a crab-eating mongoose (*Herpestes urva*), an endangered, essentially nocturnal mammal that is also an expert swimmer.

Comparable in size to the stripe-necked mongoose, the four-foot crab-eating mongoose is grayish-brown in color, with a white, contoured stripe running from a corner of its mouth to its shoulder. It has a long, tapered head with a protruding snout, a somewhat rotund body, short, lean legs, and five claws on each paw. An elongated tail normally accounts for two-thirds of its body length.

More aquatic by nature than others of its species, the crab-eating mongoose not only hunts freshwater crabs, it also preys on reptiles, fish, snails, rodents, frogs, insects, birds, and whatever else it can snatch from underneath stones and pull from rock crevices along stream banks and other damp parcels of land.

Though native to Southeast Asia, sightings of the creature in the wild have been relatively rare—in India, the last sighting occurred more than 75 years ago; in Hong Kong, one sighting occurred more than 50 years ago, but, by luck, a healthy population was apparently discovered in 1988. Other countries that have reported sightings of the crab-eating mongoose include Nepal, Vietnam, Thailand, Myanmar, China, Laos, and Malaysia.

The cover image is from *Lydekker's Royal History*. The cover font is Adobe ITC Garamond. The text font is Linotype Birka; the heading font is Adobe Myriad Condensed; and the code font is LucasFont's TheSans Mono Condensed.

Better than e-books

Buy *Access Data Analysis Cookbook* and access
the digital edition FREE on Safari for 45 days.

Go to www.oreilly.com/go/safarienabled
and type in coupon code MIPZSAA

Search
thousands of
top tech books

Download
whole chapters

Cut and Paste
code examples

Find
answers fast

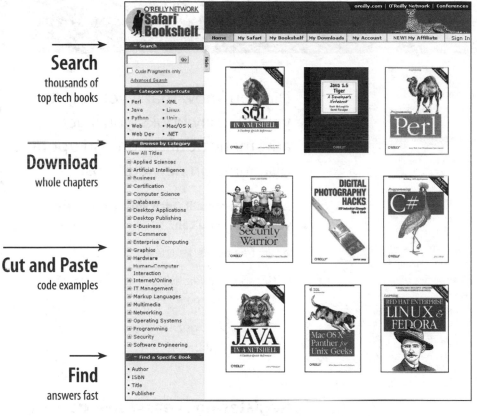

Search Safari! The premier electronic reference
library for programmers and IT professionals.